HEART   CRIES

♥

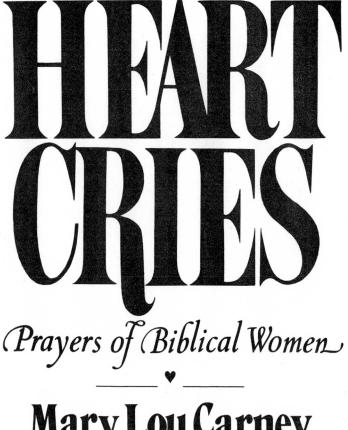

HEART CRIES

Prayers of Biblical Women

♥

Mary Lou Carney

Illustrations by Bruce Preheim

ABINGDON PRESS
Nashville

HEART CRIES

Copyright © 1986 by Abingdon Press

This book is printed on acid-free paper.

Library of Congress Cataloging-in-Publication Data

Carney, Mary Lou, 1949—
Heart Cries.
1. Women in the Bible. 2. Women—Prayer books and
devotions—English. I Title.
BS575.C29   1986   242'.5   85-23033

ISBN 0-687-16762-0

The poems of Leah, Jochebed, and Mary of Nazareth
originally appeared in the January 1985 issue of TIME OF
SINGING: A Magazine of Christian Poetry. Used by
permission.

Manufactured by the Parthenon Press at
Nashville, Tennessee, United States of America

To Rachel
my forever friend

_____ ♥ _____

with love,
and one free copy

CONTENTS

INTRODUCTION

The last several years have heralded the awakening of the women's movement. Women have been struggling to evaluate their contributions, to redefine their roles. And with the spotlight on the female of the species, a new surge of interest in women of the Bible has also occurred. A great deal of material has been written on this subject—everything from detailed reference books to serial study books to fictionalized romances.

Like most Christian women, I met this barrage of printed matter enthusiastically. Some of it is quite good. But frequently I am left disappointed. Too often the women of the Bible are portrayed as flawless paragons of virtue, as a group of females whose faith and acceptance hint of sainthood. And I am left asking—while I fold diapers, scour sinks, or wait for a break in freeway traffic—"What does this have to do with *me?*" Somewhere among the research and the well-worded phrases, the relevance has been lost.

In *Heart Cries*, I have attempted to present the women of the Bible in a new light—one that shows not only their strengths but also their *humanness*. In the following pages you will meet each of these women at her own particular point of crisis: Sarah when Abraham takes Isaac to Moriah to be offered as a human sacrifice; Jochebed as she weaves the ark that will float her baby on the treacherous Nile; Rahab while the cries of battle ring outside her house, and the city of Jericho tumbles into rubble; Mary as she realizes how hard it will be to convince her carpenter husband that she is a virgin still, but with child! You will see that, like us, these women often made mistakes, sometimes struggled with accepting God's will, worried about their children, fought feelings of inadequacy, and sought new ways to serve God.

So read these heart cries of Bible women—prayers prayed in fear, in desperation, in suffering, but most of all, prayers prayed in faith. For while they did not know the outcome of their crises, they did know One who did. And to him they presented their fears and their futures, even as we do today.

It is my hope that *Heart Cries* will draw you closer to the women of the Bible, will move their experiences thousands of years ago nearer to your daily duties, frustrations, and concerns. To assist you in this, I have included thought-provoking questions on each of the women. Whether used in your personal devotion or as discussion starters for your women's group, these questions will increase both your awareness of the women of the Bible and your ability to identify with them. Your faith will grow by seeing their prayers answered, their needs met at the most basic levels.

Come now and share these timeless prayers.

1.

Eve

Adam lay with his wife Eve, and she became pregnant and gave birth to Cain. She said, "With the help of the Lord I have brought forth a man." Later she gave birth to his brother Abel. Now

Cain said to his brother Abel, "Let's go out to the field." And while they were in the field, Cain attacked his brother Abel and killed him. (Genesis 4:1-2a, 8)

O God! Why?
Why did you let this happen?

You control the rising of the sun
    and the greening of the earth.
  Could you not also control
    the anger of my firstborn?

Is this what knowing
  good and evil means?
Is this the knowledge
  I craved in the garden?

Oh for the simplicity
  of innocence!
Oh to be ignorant
  of evil!

But it is too late for that now.
  Even in my motherhood
  I have been a failure.

O Lord!
  How long will you
    stay angry with me?
  Must my remembered sin
    weight every waking hour?

Eden was a lifetime ago!

I only wanted to be like you—
  knowing good and evil.
And the serpent was so subtle,

so subtle and
   so very clever.

Did you hear my screams of pain
   as I gave birth to sons—
      first, ruddy Cain
      and later my delicate Abel?

I looked to you in my travail,
   trusting my maternity
   might merit your redemption.

But I see it is not so,
   and this final blow
   is more than I can bear!

Both my sons are lost to me!
   Cain's hands are red
      with the blood of his brother.
   Abel's eyes are closed
      in the confines of an early grave.

Great God,
      who even in anger
      spared me and clothed me,
   care for my wayward Cain;
and let Earth receive to her bosom
   the body of my beloved Abel.

Forgive me, God—
   for I am your last creation
   and would claim again
      your closeness,
      your friendship.

I know you care about completeness:
   every flower has

the right amount of petals,
every tree has
    just enough roots,
every night sky has
    the perfect number of stars.

Make me complete, too—
    for I feel so alone.
Adam's days are filled with work,
    his nights with long, sound sleep.

I have no mother
            no sister
                no neighbor—
no father
    but you, God.

And now I have no children—
    no warmth of a suckling infant
    no music of childish laughter
    no tiny fingers wrapped around mine.

Take pity on me,
    O Great Creator.
Fill my womb again
    and let my heart sing—

like the twilight cooing
    of turtledoves
    in my lovely,
            lost
            Eden.

*Adam lay with his wife again, and she gave birth to a
son and named him Seth, saying, "God has granted me
another child in place of Abel, since Cain killed him."*
(Genesis 4:25)

2.

Noah's Wife

*A*nd rain fell on the earth *forty days and forty nights. On that very day Noah and his sons, Shem, Ham and Japheth, together with his wife and the wives of his three sons, entered the ark.*

They had with them every wild animal according to its kind, all livestock according to their kinds, every creature that moves along the ground according to its kind and every bird according to its kind, everything with wings. The animals going in were male and female of every living thing, as God had commanded Noah. Then the Lord shut him in. (Genesis 7:12-14, 16)

God of power,
  hear my prayer
  above the drumming
    of endless rain.

Remember this remnant of creation,
  waiting beneath a sheet of water
  for the fury of your justice
    to abate.

For days on end
  I have been
  in the belly
    of this boat.

The sides of my compartment
  crowd in on me.
I close my eyes,
  hold my breath,
    and try to imagine

space   silence   solitude

but soon a gasp of stale air
  and the sigh of wooden walls
restores me to this
  watery reality.

My head pounds
  with the deafening
  thunder of the rain.
My stomach lurches
  with the lap of water
  rising, rising,
    always rising . . .

My nostrils wince
  with the stench of
animals confined
  in stalls and booths and pens:

lions and foxes
jackals, goats
oxen, donkey
  antelope
leopard, camel
wolf and hog
serpent, eagle
  dove and dog . . .

Almighty One,
  who in your mercy
    warned us
      spared us
        shut us in—
  when will all this end?

My heart is hungry
  for our earth!
I miss the rough beauty of tree bark
    the pungent perfume of wild flowers.

My eyes tingle
    to remember color—
not the shades of feathers and fur—
      but the tints of
        purple sunsets
        scarlet dawns.

It's not that I'm ungrateful, Lord!

I can still hear the screams
    of those left outside our ark—
      their pleas and poundings
      as the relentless rain
      made the rivers begin to rise—
until their voices were lost
    in the slosh of waves.

But what is to become of us?

What will we find left of
    earth when finally the
    fountains of the deep
      desist?

You opened the
    windows of heaven and
    poured forth this Flood;

now open those windows
    to pour out your
    mercy and love.

Great Creator,
    we are only dust.
Who can stand against
    your righteousness?

Grant that we may
  soon see the day
when our prayers are
  offered on dry gound.

But for now,
flood my being with
  the patience of the spider
    courage of the lion
and the song of the canary.

Noah then removed the covering from the ark and saw that the surface of the ground was dry. So Noah came out, together with his sons and his wife and his sons' wives. And God said, "This is the sign of the covenant I am making between me and you and every living creature with you, a covenant for all generations to come: I have set my rainbow in the clouds, and it will be the sign of the covenant between me and the earth. Never again will the waters become a flood to destroy all life." (Genesis 8:13b, 18; 9:12-13, 15b)

3.

Hagar

*B*ut Sarah saw that the son
whom Hagar the Egyptian had borne to Abraham was
mocking, and she said to Abraham, "Get rid of that
slave woman and her son, for that slave woman's son

will never share in the inheritance with my son Isaac."
Early the next morning Abraham took some food and a
skin of water and gave them to Hagar. He set them on
her shoulders and then sent her off with the boy. She
went on her way and wandered in the desert of
Beersheba. When the water in the skin was gone, she
put the boy under one of the bushes. Then she went off
and sat down nearby . . . for she thought, "I cannot
watch the boy die." (Genesis 21:9-10, 14-16)

God of Abraham,
> with my heart I cry out to you—
>> for my tongue is but
>> a swollen hunk of sour flesh
>>> that cannot part my parched lips.

Help us!

Each day the sun grows bigger,
> casting its glare on rocks and sand—
>> turning bushes into caravans
>> and rippled dunes into lakes.

My Ishmael and I
> have chased these mirages
>> till now our strength
>> is as drained as
>>> our waterskins.

We are dying of thirst, God!

We lick dew from bitter rocks,
> but it is not enough!

Sand and sky swirl before my eyes,
   while my head pounds
      like the sound of tent pegs
      driven into dry ground.

I crawl on all fours,
   fighting—not for *my* life—
but for Ishmael's!

He must not die, God!

Where is your justice
   Abraham spoke of so often?
Would a righteous God
   torture a child
   with a slow, desert death?

Ishmael is but a boy—
   what evil has he done?
Yet each day I've watched him waste away,
   until he could no longer sweat
         no longer spit
         no longer speak.
And now he is too weak to move;
   his life evaporates
   like our pursued mirages.

I hear the rattle in his throat
   as the desert chokes
      my babe.

No, God!
   No!

This is Sarah's fault.

She is the one who sent us here—
   that pale wisp of a woman
   who hates me because
     I gave Abraham
     what she could not.

How her eyes would burn with jealousy
   each time I nursed my tiny son!
And I would sneer at her,
   at her and her barren belly,
     until she turned away.

But now Isaac has been born,
   their long-awaited child of promise.
And Ishmael and I
   have been cast aside
   like maggoty meat!

I am no longer considered
   the mother of Abraham's son;
I am again simply
   Sarah's slave.

And yet—
in my heart I know
   I am the one
   who has done wrong.

Memories of
   my arrogance,
   my insolence toward Sarah
     haunt me in the noonday heat,
         the midnight chill.

But my son, O Lord—
   spare him!

Reach out your arm
    and help him—
    for I cannot.

Spots burn before my eyes—
    then burst into flames
    when I try to rise.
I am surrounded by
    endless, endless sand.

Beersheba is as hostile to me
    as I have been to Sarah.
I cannot outwit this beast
    whose hot breath
    scorches my skin.

I was never one for tears, God—
    and now the desert has stolen
    the few I want to shed.

Life has given me
    little to boast about:
        the bed of a concubine
        the life of a servant.
I am a piece of property,
    owned and ordered about
    by both master and mistress.

I thought a son by Abraham
    would change all that.

Yet now I find my Ishmael
    not only dispossessed—
        but dying beneath
        a desert scrub bush!

And I can do nothing for him!

My useless tongue
    cannot call his name.
My arm refuses to brush
    the flies from his face.

Once I worried about riches,
    but what is the wealth
      of all Abraham's herds and flocks
    when compared to the treasure
      of one cup of water?

Great Jehovah,
    who blessed barren Sarah,
is your hand big enough
so that *some* blessing remains
    for my son and me?

Even now my Ishmael groans—
    a raspy cough sputters
    from his closing throat.

Please, God!

I have never begged before;
    submission is hard for me.

I have always boasted in
    my subtle scheming
    my fierce independence.
But now I am helpless—
    wandering in the heat of flight
    watching my son consumed
      by the sun's fierce might.

Save him, God!

Both you and I know
    it is *I* who have sinned.
My sin of self-reliance
    has brought us to this end.
Forgive me.
    Do with *me* as you wish—

but save my son!

Take the reins of my life,
    offered with open hand.
I will not want them
    back again—

even if you
    answer my prayers
      with mercy
      and pardon
        and water.

*God heard the boy crying, and the angel of God called
to Hagar from heaven and said to her, "What is the
matter, Hagar? Do not be afraid; God has heard the
boy crying as he lies there. Lift the boy up and take him
by the hand, for I will make him into a great nation."
Then God opened her eyes and she saw a well of water.
So she went and filled the skin with water and gave the
boy a drink. God was with the boy as he grew up. He
lived in the desert and became an archer. While he was
living in the Desert of Paran, his mother got a wife for
him from Egypt.* (Genesis 21:17-21)

4.

Sarah

Some time later God tested
Abraham. He said to him, "Abraham!" "Here I am," he
replied. Then God said, "Take your son, your only son,
Isaac, whom you love, and go to the region of Moriah.

Sacrifice him there as a burnt offering on one of the mountains I will tell you about." (Genesis 22:1-2)

My heart is heavy
  with the horror
    of my fears!

This morning
  I watched the two of them
    set out for Moriah—
Isaac striving to match
    the long strides of his father.

Carefully Abraham cut wood
    for the burnt offering,
but he took neither lamb nor ram
    as sacrifice to you, O God.
And in the depths of his eyes
        the set of his chin
    I saw my fear affirmed.

Isaac! To be sacrificed!
    The blood of my firstborn
      to be spilled in secret
        on the crags of some
          distant mountain?

No! No!

Not my curly-headed Isaac—
    who fills my tent with childish antics
        my heart with aching love.

My only baby, God!
    My son!

But the mountains
    soak up my screams.
Abraham and Isaac
    are gone,
and I sit alone—
    an old woman
    foolish enough to believe
        in miracles and
            laughter.

O God,
    against whom no man can stand,
    who pours out
        justice like rainfall
        wisdom like moonlight—
spare the life of Isaac!

Give me back
    the blessing of my old age
    the flower of my barren womb.
Don't demand the blood
    of Abraham's seed.
Don't snatch from us
    the souce of our hope.

God of great power,
    hear my prayer
as I bow now before you,
    placing my son
    where he always has been—

in the care
    of Him who has promised
        of Him who is faithful.

"Do not lay a hand on the boy," [God] said. "Do not do anything to him. Now I know that you fear God, because you have not withheld from me your son, your only son." Abraham looked up and there in a thicket he saw a ram caught by its horns. He went over and took the ram and sacrificed it as a burnt offering instead of his son. (Genesis 22:12-13)

5.

Leah

Now ow Laban had two daughters; the name of the older was Leah, and the name of the younger was Rachel. Leah had weak eyes, but Rachel was lovely in form, and beautiful. Jacob was in love with Rachel. (Genesis 29:16-18)

God of Abraham,
  hear my case!

Notice my suffering!

My belly grows large
  with the fourth son
  of my husband Jacob.

Husband! I spit at the word!

For even when he does
  relent and lie with me,
the presence of my sister Rachel
  haunts my happiness.
I know it is
  her hair
    he dreams he touches,
  her breasts
    he wishes to caress.

And yet I love him, Lord—
  I have loved Jacob
  from that moment years ago
  when he stepped
  into my father's tent,
    his eyes dark as dates
    his hair wind-blown, boyish.

Am I so ugly
  that I must live forever
    on the fringes?
Must I always be reminded
  that through trickery

I became his bride—
while my peevish sister,
    barren as a stone,
basks in the love of Jacob?

Sometimes I want to
    claw out Rachel's dancing eyes
    from beneath her
    flirtatious lashes!

I am a good wife, God—
    and I have given birth to sons:
        Reuben
        Simeon
        Levi.

But I am tired of being
    second best to my sister
    second choice to my husband.
Avenge me through
    my children, Lord.

And let me live
    well enough, long enough
    to be Jacob's beloved.

When the Lord saw that Leah was not loved, he opened her womb. She conceived again, and when she gave birth to a son she said, "This time I will praise the Lord." So she named him Judah. (Genesis 29:31, 35)

So Rachel died and was buried. (Genesis 35:19)

A record of the genealogy of Jesus Christ the son of David, the son of Abraham: Abraham was the father of Isaac, Isaac the father of Jacob, Jacob the father of Judah and his brothers. (Matthew 1:1-2)

6.

Jochebed

(mother of Moses)

W*hen Pharaoh gave this order to all his people: "Every boy that is born to the Hebrews you must throw into the Nile." Now a man of the house of Levi married a Levite and she became*

*pregnant and gave birth to a son. When she saw that he
was a fine child, she hid him for three months. But
when she could hide him no longer, she got a papyrus
basket for him and coated it with tar and pitch. Then
she placed the child in it and put it among the reeds
along the bank of the Nile.* (Exodus 1:22; 2:1-3)

Mighty God,
    calm the beating of my anxious heart
    still the trembling of my busy hands.

In my mission,
    make me as firm and stubborn
    as these papyrus stems
      I use to weave
      an ark for my son.

Only three months
    since his birth, Lord—
and already he is such
    a beautiful child!

While he sucks my milk
    he stares up at me
    with wise, round eyes.

Yet I have had to hide him—
    this source of my pride and joy—
in the storeroom among clay jars
    filled with peppercorns and onions
in the donkey stable loft
    pungent with odors of fodder and fresh straw.

But he grows bigger each day,
   his cry more lusty than before.
I cannot keep him quiet!

And that cursed Pharaoh's men
   are everywhere,
searching for our babies
   eager to throw yet another Hebrew boy
   to the crocodiles lurking along the Nile.

But these things are not news to you;
   surely our mourning
      has reached your throne
         battered on your heart.
Certainly you know my plan,
   conceived in desperation
      filled with peril
         laced with prayer and love.

O Great One,
   secure this tiny ark
      bound by bulrushes
      plastered with pitch
      lined with clay as smooth
         as my baby's forehead.

Be my accomplice
   in this daring sheme.

Rule every current;
   subdue every crocodile;
      banish every snake.
Let my precious one slumber soundly,
   soothed by the scent of
      flowering flags.

God of compassion,
   you have been my confidant
   while I snuggled my babe
      through countless nights,
      shushing his cries with kisses.

Hear my prayer
   as I place my boy
   in this fragile,
      floating ark.

Protect him from harm;
   accept your obligation
      for his destiny.
And forgive these foolish tears . . .

for I have known from the beginning
   that he was to be
      yours—
not mine.

Then Pharaoh's daughter went down to the Nile to bathe. . . . She saw the basket among the reeds and sent her slave girl to get it. She opened it and saw the baby. He was crying, and she felt sorry for him. "This is one of the Hebrew babies," she said. Then his sister asked Pharaoh's daughter, "Shall I go and get one of the Hebrew women to nurse the baby for you?" "Yes, go," she answered. And the girl went and got the baby's mother. Pharaoh's daughter said to her, "Take this baby and nurse him for me, and I will pay you." So the woman took the baby and nursed him. When the child grew older, she took him to Pharaoh's daughter and he became her son. She named him Moses, saying, "I drew him out of the water." (Exodus 2:5-10)

7.

Rahab

"*Now then, please swear to me by the Lord that you will show kindness to my family, because I have shown kindness to you. Give me a sure sign that you will spare the lives of my father*

and mother, my brothers and sisters, and all who belong to them, and that you will save us from death." "Our lives for your lives!" the men assured her. "This oath you made us swear will not be binding on us unless, when we enter the land, you have tied this scarlet cord in the window through which you let us down, and unless you have brought your father and mother, your brothers and all your family into your house." (Joshua 2:12-14a, 17)

> Righteous God of the Israelites,
>   will you listen to the
>   stuttering plea of a
>   poor prostitute?
>
> Even now my house rattles
>   with the roar of battle
>   that rages around me.
>
> Squeals of goats and asses
>   mingle with the screams of women.
>
> O God of all power,
>   who rolls back the sea as papyrus
>   who treads our land with a heavy foot,
> have mercy on my family
>   and me!
>
> For even in my sin
>   I saw your glory,
> the glory of one who asserts his will
>   in heavenly realms
>   and earthly affairs.

The shouts of Joshua's men
   ring out your name
   as they ransack Jericho.

Please, O Great One,
    give them eyes like eagles'
    so they can see the scarlet cord
      dangling in my window.

Remember my covenant
   with your spies:
   their lives I spared.

Now I beg you
   do the same
   for me and mine.

O God!

A tremor tears
   at the foundations of my house!
Cracks creep across my floor;
   fissures shatter my walls!

Be quick to act,
   O God of justice—
or I shall be doomed,
   buried beneath the rubble
     of my past.

Don't let me die
   before I know you!

Please, O Holy One,
   let the pounding I hear
   be the sound of my deliverers—

and not simply the beating
of my terrified heart!

*Joshua said to the two men who had spied out the land,
"Go into the prostitute's house and bring her out and
all who belong to her, in accordance with your oath to
her."* (Joshua 6:22)

*By faith the prostitute Rahab, because she welcomed
the spies, was not killed with those who were
dishonest.* (Hebrews 11:31)

*The genealogy of Jesus Christ the Son of David
. . . Salmon [was] the father of Boaz [by Rahab],
Boaz . . . of Obed, . . . Obed . . . of Jesse, and Jesse
the father of King David."* (Matthew 1:1-6)

8.

Deborah

*After Ehud died, the Israel-
ites once again did evil in the eyes of the Lord. So the
Lord sold them into the hands of Jabin, a king of
Canaan. . . . The commander of his army was Sisera. . . . Because he had nine hundred iron chariots*

*and had cruelly oppressed the Israelites for twenty
years, they cried to the Lord for help. Deborah . . . was
leading Israel at that time. She held court under the
Palm of Deborah . . . and the Israelites came to her to
have their disputes decided.* (Judges 4:1-5)

O Jehovah,
   my ears grow weary
   with repeated wrongdoings—

neighbor against neighbor
   kinsman against kinsman.

The parade of petitioners
   stretches snakelike
   toward the setting sun.

Is there no end to evil?

Must injustice in Israel
   be as common as the
     bleating of sheep?

I used to spend my days
   in womanly ways:
     baking bread, weaving cloth
     caring for tabernacle lamps.

But now I spend my time
   sitting underneath
   this out-stretched palm—
     judging Israel.

While other women hear
   the light laughter of children or
   idle chatter at the well,

I hear
   heated complaints
   shouted accusations.

I know that you
   have chosen me for this,
yet at times I feel so alone, God—
   so different.

It's true I'm not like the other women:
   meek
     submissive
       sometimes even silly,

But what am I then?

A mutant, perhaps—
   some strange strain of human
     bearing a woman's heart,
       a man's responsibility.

And my woman's heart is broken
   by continual reports of
   Jabin and his evil Sisera,
those heathen scum who
   destroy our vineyards
     dishonor our women
       mutilate our children.

How dare Jabin toy with the God of Israel,
   who covered Egypt with lice and frogs
   who flattened Pharaoh with a wink of the eye!

I am sick of these
   spineless whimperings!

I am tired of cowardly rumors
    praising Sisera's chariots of iron!

Jehovah is on *our* side;
    let Sisera's heart pale with fear!

O Lord,
    arouse your people!

Awake them to the folly of
    placing their faith in
        weapons and warriors.
Scatter their fears;
    stir them up to fight.

Great God,
    who made me what I am,
    allow me to lead
    Israel to victory—
your victory.

Make even the stars in their courses
    fight against Sisera!

Be with me as I judge
    beneath this Palm of Deborah.

Let my roots reach deep
    into your wisdom and courage
the way this stately tree
    reaches deep
    beneath the earth
      for strength.

And may we both,
    this ancient palm and I,

live to be fruitful
  in a land filled with
    justice
      rest
        peace.

[Deborah] sent for Barak and said to him, "The Lord, the God of Israel, commands you: 'Go, take with you ten thousand men of Naphtali and Zebulun and lead the way to Mount Tabor. I will lure Sisera, the commander of Jabin's army, with his chariots and his troops to the Kishon River and give him into your hands.' " Barak said to her, "If you go with me, I will go; but if you don't go with me, I won't go." "Very well," Deborah said, "I will go with you." So Barak went down Mount Tabor, followed by ten thousand men. At Barak's advance the Lord routed Sisera and all his chariots and army by the sword, and Sisera abandoned his chariot and fled on foot. On that day God subdued Jabin, the Canaanite king, before the Israelites. And the hand of the Israelites grew stronger and stronger against Jabin, the Canaanite king, until they destroyed him. Then the land had peace forty years. (Judges 4:6-9a, 14c-15, 23-24; 5:31c)

9.

Ruth

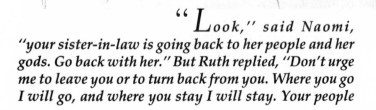

"*Look*," *said Naomi,*
"*your sister-in-law is going back to her people and her*
gods. Go back with her." *But Ruth replied,* "*Don't urge*
me to leave you or to turn back from you. Where you go
I will go, and where you stay I will stay. Your people

will be my people and your God my God." So Naomi returned from Moab accompanied by Ruth the Moabitess, her daughter-in-law, arriving in Bethlehem as the barley harvest was beginning. (Ruth 1:15-16, 22)

O God,
 every bone in my body aches!

Since early light
I have followed the reapers,
 gleaning bits of barley
 stuffing stalks of grain
  into my sagging sack.

Now my back pains each time I bend;
 my feet stumble forward.
I will myself to keep working,
 but something inside me keeps screaming:
 Stop this hard work! Go rest in the
  shade of the olive grove!

I squint into ripe rows,
 where reapers thrashing the grain
are rhythmic silhouettes
 against the noonday sun.

Lord, give me strength,
 both of will
 and of limb.

Wrap me in your might;
 don't let me disappoint
  or disgrace
 good Naomi.

See the sweat that
   runs down my sunburned nose,
   then settles on my chapped lips
     with a salty, hot taste.
Honor my hard work;
   give me grain
   for Naomi and me.

I am only a Moabite maiden,
   raised by my father
   to worship wooden idols—
   but the coming of
     my husband Mahlon and his
     family to our land
       changed all that!
They taught me that you
   are the only true God.

And I know it is so!
   None of my father's idols
   could ever compare to you!

So I have chosen to be a stranger
   among *your* people
   rather than be at home
     with mine.

Let your servant Naomi find joy
   in this, her homeland.

And as for me,
   give me courage to face
     life

the way I face
 this barley field—

with your hand in mine,
 one
  step
   at a
    time.

Now Naomi had a relative on her husband's side . . . a man of standing, whose name was Boaz. So Boaz said to Ruth, "My daughter, listen to me. Don't go and glean in another field and don't go away from here." (Ruth 2:1, 8)

So Boaz took Ruth and she became his wife. And the Lord enabled her to conceive, and she gave birth to a son. The women said to Naomi: "Praise be to the Lord, who this day has not left you." (Ruth 4:13-14)

10.

Rizpah

During the reign of David, there was famine for three successive years; so David sought the face of the Lord. The Lord said, "It is on account of Saul and his blood-stained house; it is because he put the Gibeonites to death." The king took

*Armoni and Mephibosheth, the two sons of . . . Riz-
pah, whom she had borne to Saul. He handed them over
to the Gibeonites, who killed and exposed them on a
hill before the Lord. Rizpah . . . took sackcloth and
spread it out for herself on a rock. . . . She did not let
the birds of the air touch [the bodies] by day or the wild
animals by night.* (II Samuel 21:1, 8, 9a-10)

O God—
    where are you?

I cannot see your face
  in the parched land's
    withered crops.

I cannot hear your voice
  in the night wind's
    swirling dust.

Awake, O Mighty One,
  to the misery that
  envelopes Israel
    like desert whirlwinds.

Look! Can't you see them?
Here are the bodies of my sons,
  hung between heaven and earth—
    dead—
  but denied the rites of death.

For weeks now I have guarded them—
  while red-eyed vultures swooped near,
    their open beaks poised
    for a piece of flesh.

Only the tremor of my screams,
the terror of my club
have kept these demons from
gorging themselves on my children!

And at night
wild dogs creep in,
their padded feet
soundless
against the rock.

But *I* hear them!
I hear *everything*!

Sometimes,
when the wind is from the south,
I even hear their voices calling,
"Mother! Mother! Help us!"

How long, O Lord?
How long!

Help me,
and help these
who hang—
not for their own sins,
but for sins of their father.

My sackcloth is wet
with tears of
frustration,
exhaustion.

Grief has made me
reckless, bold

in defending each
   blackening
      blood-covered
         corpse.

O Holy One,
   forgive the sins of Saul;
   visit your land with
      sounds of falling rain.

Wake me, God,
   from this nightmare vigil!

And may you never see
   the untold agony
of *your* son left to die
   on a stark, dark tree.

When David was told what Aigh's daughter Rizpah, Saul's concubine, had done, he went and . . . the bones of those who had been killed and exposed were gathered up. . . . After that, God answered prayer in behalf of the land. (II Samuel 21:11, 13-14)

11.

The Widow at Zarephath

[E_lijah] went to Zare-
phath. When he came to the town gate, a widow was
there gathering sticks. He called to her and asked,
"Would you bring me a little water in a jar so I may
have a drink?" As she was going to get it, he called,

"and bring me, please, a piece of bread." "As surely as the Lord your God lives," she replied, "I don't have any bread—only a handful of flour in a jar and a little oil in a jug. I am gathering a few sticks to take home and make a meal for myself and my son, that we may eat it—and die." Elijah said to her, "Don't be afraid. Go home and do as you have said. But first make a small cake of bread for me from what you have and bring it to me, and then make something for yourself and your son. For this is what the Lord, the God of Israel, says: 'The jar of flour will not be used up and the jug of oil will not run dry until the day the Lord gives rain on the land.' " (I Kings 17:10-14)

O God of Israel,
    I am only a poor widow,
    and I am confronted by calamity!

The wrath of your hand
    is heavy upon all the land:
        barley withers in the scorched fields
        no dew refreshes the parched leaves
            of olive trees.

Food has become as scarce
    as the scent of midnight rain.

And so,
    finally,
my son and I are about to die—
    for nothing remains to us but
        a handful of meal in the barrel
        a few drops of oil in the cruise.

And now a strange prophet
  has asked for these!

In the sultry silence of early morning
  I stumbled toward the city gate,
    my head spinning as I bent to gather
    a few stray sticks for our fire.

One more meager meal and then
  sleep, surrender, death—
    and the end of this
    constant fire in our empty bellies.

When suddenly
  he appeared from nowhere—
    his rough garment of camel's hair
      drawn loosely around his thin frame
    his sandals covered with
    desert dust.
The mantle of a prophet
  was thrown across his broad shoulders.
I would have passed on in silence,
  for what have I to do
    with a holy man?

But he called to me,
  asking for water.

Water! Indeed!
He may as well have asked for
  mountains of silver
  bushels of rubies.

Still—a dying woman
  has no need to hoard.

Yet as I turned to go for water,
  he commanded me to bring him bread, also.

Where did he think I,
  a poor widow,
would get bread for him,
  a dusty traveler?

I told him I had only
  a handful of meal
  a few drops of oil,
    and a son whose eyes
    were glazed with hunger.

And yet, God, this man persisted!
He insisted I make him a little cake—
  and that I serve him
first . . .

promising all the while
  that my supplies
would not cease,
  would not run dry.

Is he mad with heat and hunger, Lord?
Has the sun played havoc
  with his head?

Or does he speak the truth—
  this bearer of riddles
  and perhaps, also, miracles?

Great Jehovah,
  I cannot comprehend this puzzle;
    I am too tired to reason.

But my heart tells me that
   another's needs
     must now come before
   my son's and mine.

So as I mix this hoecake
   for the hungry stranger,
remember our hunger as well.

Great Giver of rain,
             grain and
              miracles,
feed my faith—
   even as I now feed your prophet.

She went away and did as Elijah had told her. So there was food every day for Elijah and for the woman and her family. For the jar of flour was not used up and the jug of oil did not run dry, in keeping with the word of the Lord spoken by Elijah. (I Kings 17:15-16)

12.

Esther

When the turn came for Esther (the girl Mordecai had adopted, the daughter of his uncle Abihail) to go to the king, she asked for nothing other than what Hegai, the king's eunuch who *was in charge of the harem, suggested. And Esther won the favor of everyone who saw her. Now the king was attracted to Esther more than to any of the other women, and she won his favor and approval more than any of the other virgins. So he set a royal crown on her head and made her queen instead of Vashti.* (Esther 2:15, 17)

When Haman saw that Mordecai would not kneel down or pay him honor, he was enraged. Yet having learned who Mordecai's people were, he scorned the idea of killing only Mordecai. Instead Haman looked for a way to destroy all Mordecai's people, the Jews, throughout the whole kingdom of Xerxes. So the king took the signet ring from his finger and gave it to Haman, . . . the enemy of the Jews . . . . The king said to Haman, "Do with the people as you please." (Esther 3:5-6, 10)

God of Abraham and Isaac and Jacob—
    hear my prayer!

Do you still hear the pleas
    of your chosen people?
Do my cries for justice
    reach further than
    this palace ceiling?

Help us!
    For wicked Haman
    would see the blood
        of all Jews
    licked from the streets
        by dogs.

Great God,
    I know of your power—
for you sent bitter plagues on Pharaoh
        felled the walls of Jericho
        slaughtered Sennacherib's soldiers—

and now you have taken
    a poor Jewish orphan like me
    and made her queen of all Persia!

But what good are royal robes
    when my heart is wrapped
        in sackcloth?

My people, God—
    spare them!

I know that I must act
        in their behalf,
    but what am I to do?

King Xerxes is
    as moody as
    he is powerful—
and for more than a month
    he has not asked to see me.

Perhaps some saucy concubine
    has caught his eye,
and he is looking for an excuse
    to rip me from the throne
    as he did Vashti before me!

Yet the words of my cousin Mordecai
    echo in my ears

like the clatter of soldiers' feet
  on marble hallways:

"Who knows but perhaps
  you have come to the kingdom
  for just such a time as this."

Great Jehovah,
  you who gave me this exalted position,
  show me now how to use
    my power for *your* good.

Honor the prayers and the fasts
  on my behalf. . . .

for I go now—
  uninvited—
  to the king.

O Lord, let him
  look on me and see
    not some interloper
    who rudely intrudes
    on his royal presence—
but rather the queen he loves,
      the star of his choosing.

Answer this prayer, Jehovah,
  or it will be my last—
    for no one can stand
    against the king's wrath.

O powerful God
  of my ancestors,
    be *my* God, too!

On the third day Esther put on her royal robes and stood in the inner court of the palace, in front of the king's hall. The king was sitting on his royal throne in the hall, facing the entrance. When he saw Queen Esther standing in the court, he was pleased with her and held out to her the gold scepter that was in his hand. So Esther approached and touched the tip of the scepter. Then the king asked, "What is it, Queen Esther? What is your request? Even up to half the kingdom, it will be given you." (Esther 5:1-3)

King Xerxes replied to Queen Esther and to Mordecai the Jew, "Because Haman attacked the Jews, I have given his estate to Esther, and they have hanged him on the gallows." For the Jews it was a time of happiness and joy, gladness and honor. In every province and in every city, wherever the edict of the king went, there was joy and gladness among the Jews, with feasting and celebrating. And many people of other nationalities became Jews because fear of the Jews had seized them. (Esther 8:7, 16-17)

13.

Mary

(of Nazareth)

*B*ut the angel said to her, "Do not be afraid, Mary, you have found favor with God. You will be with child and give birth to a son, and you are to give him the name Jesus. He will be great and will be called the Son of the Most High." (Luke 1:30-32)

Tonight the skies are filled with
   stars, stars, stars!
O God! I have never seen beauty
   in such abundance!

And my heart has never beat
   with such a load of praise.
If only I had the talent
   of King David, then
     what a psalm I would
     sing for you this night!

But my thoughts tumble over themselves
   as I try to understand today's news—
   the news that I, a lowly maiden,
     have found favor with you—
with you, who formed dry land
       with a sweep of your hand,
     who hurled fire from heaven
      on the heads of Sodomites,
     who held back the Red Sea
      with the breath of your nostrils.

And yet I know the truth
   of all the angel spoke.

Miracle of miracles—
   that I shall be mother
   of the Messiah!
But a twinge of sadness
   tugs at my heart
when I think of my
   own dear Joseph.

He will not understand
  this wonder, Lord.

He is too used to dealing with reality:
  the smell of shavings and sawdust
  the rhythm of tireless planing
  the strength of his own strong arms,
    reshaping the cedars from Lebanon.

Angels and visions and impossibilities
  are foreign stuff
    to my carpenter.

And how shall I make him understand
  that I am virgin still—

but with child!

O Loving Lord,
  do me this one favor:

let my beloved Joseph
    believe—

let this miracle
  be as real to him
    as oxen yokes and
    ax handles.

Let him know that
  it is your hand—
that you, O Lord, have done it.

Almighty God,
  add to this miraculous news

just one miracle more—

let Joseph believe!

Because Joseph her husband was a righteous man and did not want to expose her to public disgrace, he had in mind to divorce her quietly. But after he had considered this, an angel of the Lord appeared to him in a dream and said, "Joseph son of David, do not be afraid to take Mary home as your wife, because what is conceived in her is from the Holy Spirit. She will give birth to a son, and you are to give him the name Jesus, because he will save his people from their sins." When Joseph woke up, he did what the angel of the Lord had commanded him and took Mary home as his wife. (Matthew 1:19-21, 24)

14.

Anna

When the time of their
purification according to the Law of Moses had been
completed, Joseph and Mary took him [Jesus] to
Jerusalem to present him to the Lord . . . and to offer a
sacrifice. . . . Now there was a man in Jerusalem called

*Simeon, who was righteous and devout. There was
also a prophetess, Anna. . . . She was very old; she had
lived with her husband seven years after her marriage,
and then was a widow until she was eighty-four. She
never left the temple but worshiped night and day,
fasting and praying.* (Luke 2:22, 24-25a, 36-37)

It's me again, Lord—
   the old woman
   who prays her days away.

I have grown old
here in your Temple,
   stirred by the readings from the scrolls
   calmed by the sounds of sacred psalms.

I have no husband
      no children
         no grandchildren . . .
  only you,
and it is enough—
   it is abundance!

But I mustn't ramble this way.
   Not today.
I have something important
  to say to you—
  something that concerns
  both you and me.

Since I first came to stay
  in your temple—
    a wide-eyed young widow
     seeking to make some

sense of life—
I have asked for nothing
    but the peace of your presence,
        the coming of your promise.

My life has been rich
    with the former.
        And today, as every day,
        I thank you for that.
But now, O God,
    attend swiftly
    to the latter—
        the coming of your promise—
        for my eyes are dim and
            my steps grow slow.

I know that soon
    I shall be gathered to you,
like the reaping of sheaves
    in due season.

And I'll go
    willingly, eagerly.
Death holds no fear
    for such as me.
But first I would see
    your promise come to pass—
        your Messiah!

The One who will teach
    Jew and Gentile
    Roman and Greek
        the ways of peace.

The One who will
    slay the wicked with the
      breath of his lips
  and plead the cause of
    Israel's poor.

I am very old
  in years.
    Sometimes I cannot recall
    the number of Passovers I
    have celebrated!

But my heart—
  my heart is
  young in hope!

I know the prophecies
  long foretold are
  soon to be fulfilled.

Grant me just a glimpse
  of the One who will be called
    Wonderful Counselor,
    Prince of Peace!

This is my last request;
  I shall not clutter my prayers
    with other pleas.

Your prophet Isaiah promised that
  from the roots of Jesse
  a branch would come forth,
    a Messiah would be born.

I believe this, Great Jehovah.
  I know the time is near.

And I am an old woman
   who does not ask to behold
the Branch blossom and
   bear fruit.

But, before I die,
   allow me only to see
     the Sprout
spring from the stump—
   the start of things to come!

When the parents brought in the child Jesus to do for him what the custom of the Law required, Simeon took him in his arms and praised God, saying: "Sovereign Lord, as you have promised, you now dismiss your servant in peace. For my eyes have seen your salvation, which you have prepared in the sight of all people, a light for revelation to the Gentiles and for glory to your people Israel." Coming up to them at that very moment, she [Anna] gave thanks to God and spoke about the child to all who were looking forward to the redemption of Jerusalem. (Luke 2:27-32, 38)

15.

Bride

(at the marriage in Cana)

On the third day a wedding took place at Cana in Galilee. Jesus' mother was there, and Jesus and his disciples had also been invited to the wedding. (John 2:1-2)

Such a beautiful day, Lord!

Shafts of sun
   pattern the floor
   with slats of light.
Smiles of guests
   line long tables.
Sounds of music
   warm the room.

My whole life has been spent
     preparing for,
     waiting for
   this day—

but even in my dreams
   my wedding feast
   was never this grand!

And when the tiresome duties
   of being a wife
fill all my waking hours,
   I will remember again and again
   the giddy, girlish way
     I feel today.

While drawing water or
     baking bread
   I will remember the
   feasting and laughing and loving
     that ushered me
     to the marriage bed.

Great God,
   accept the happy

beating of my heart
   as praise.

And now the stewards come again,
   bearing wine for the cups
     of our friends.

But why do they hesitate?
Where is their eagerness to serve?
Why do they seem embarrassed?

What! They offer the
   master of our feast
   a half-filled cup!
How dare they insult him so!

My husband's eyes
   meet the steward's,
and in that instant
   I realize—

We have no more wine!

No, God, no! How awful!

Our guests must think us
   stingy or
     foolish or
       both!

And Mary has come
   all the way from Nazareth,
   with her son Jesus
     and his friends.
How rude we must seem

to scrimp so
at our wedding feast!

What can I do?

I have no hidden skins of wine
to fetch and serve our guests.
I have no money in reserve
to send and buy again.

Help me, God!
You are my only hope.

How can I ever again
face my friends
if my wedding feast ends
in such an awful way?

There must be some way
we can still be good hosts!

O God—
give me a miracle,
so I can begin my marriage
without shame or regret.

Somehow, let the end
of this feast be
as bountiful as
its beginning—

somehow . . .

When the wine was gone, Jesus' mother said to him,
"They have no more wine." Nearby stood six stone

water jars, the kind used by the Jews for ceremonial washing, each holding from twenty to thirty gallons. Jesus said to the servants, "Fill the jars with water"; so they filled them to the brim. Then he told them, "Now draw some out and take it to the master of the banquet." They did so, and the master of the banquet tasted the water that had been turned into wine. He did not realize where it had come from, though the servants who had drawn the water knew. Then he called the bridegroom aside and said, "Everyone brings out the choice wine first and then the cheaper wine after the guests have had too much to drink; but you have saved the best till now." This, the first of his miraculous signs, Jesus performed in Cana of Galilee. He thus revealed his glory, and his disciples put their faith in him. (John 2:3, 6-11)

16.

Woman Taken in Adultery

The teachers of the law and the Pharisees brought in a woman caught in adultery. They made her stand before the group and said to Jesus, "Teacher, this woman was caught in the act of

**adultery. *In the Law Moses commanded us to stone
such women. Now what do you say?"*** (John 8:3-5)

O God! Help me!
I confess that I have sinned—
   but help me!

Everything is happening so quickly.
An hour ago I was just another woman
   in the marketplace . . .

I meant no harm to anyone,
   yet now I am on my way
   to be stoned for my mistake!

I shiver with fear
   as from every doorway
   people stare and point and smirk
      while the Scribes scream,
         "Adultery! Adultery!
         We caught her in the very act!"

My vision blurs and I stumble—
   but this Pharisee
   drags me through the streets,
      bruises already darkening my arm
      beneath his brutal grasp.

Adultery.

Such a cold term, God,
   such a dirty word—

nothing like the promises
   my lover whispered

while passion swept away
   my will.

Now my virginity is lost—
   and I must lose my life, as well!

Oh, why was I so foolish,
   so impetuous?

O, God, no!
The temple court!

They have brought me to the Temple
   to satisfy the morbid curiosity
      of their pious peers
   to parade my public disgrace
      like a spoil of war.

Everyone gazes—
   amazed, amused
   at my plight.

Their hatred gouges me,
   a prelude to the
   stones that soon will
      rip my flesh
      shatter my bones
      crush my spirit.

O Lord!
  Help me!

Remember your love
   for the children of Israel,
whose sins of backsliding

caused you to show
both your omnipotence
and your patience.

Extend, I pray,
that love
that patience
to me . . .

not because of *my* worth,
but because of *your* wonder.

Great Builder
of earth and sky and stars—
is there nothing left
from which you can
rebuild my life?

O God of might,
become my God of mercy.

Don't cut me off
in your righteous anger;
instead,
the tangled knots
of my life
untie.

Great Giver of
second chances—
give me just
one
more
try!

When they kept on questioning him, he straightened up and said to them, "If any one of you is without sin, let him be the first to throw a stone at her." At this, those who heard began to go away one at a time, until only Jesus was left, with the woman still standing there. Jesus straightened up and asked her, "Woman, where are they? Has no one condemned you?" "No one, sir," she said. "Then neither do I condemn you," Jesus declared. "Go now and leave your life of sin." (John 8:7, 9-11)

17.

The Widow with Two Mites

*J*esus *sat down opposite the place where the offerings were put and watched the crowd putting their money into the temple treasury. Many rich people threw in large amounts.* (Mark 12:41)

Jerusalem's streets overflow
  with streams of visitors,
    strangers come to celebrate
    the yearly Passover.

Gold bracelets
  flash on passing wrists.
Swirls of purple garments
  brush against my skirt,
    making its plain cloth
    seem even more shabby.

And with every step I take,
  the coins tied to my girdle
  tinkle with a tinny, hollow sound.

Great Giver of all good things,
  how can I bear to bring
    a meager two mites
    into your holy Temple?

Two mites—
  hardly enough to buy
  even one loaf of bread!

Surely others in the Temple
  will scoff at my gift:
the Pharisees will call it
    "paltry,"
and the Scribes will turn
  their proud heads
    in disgust.

Yet it is not the opinion of others

that concerns me, God.

Would that I could please you
  with an offering so large
  the Temple chest itself
  could not hold the whole!

And the sounds of coins falling
  noisily into your treasury
  would fill the Court of Women
    with music!

But it cannot be so.

I am only a poor widow
  who works daily for her bread
and forgoes a morsel here and there
  to save an offering—
    a small one, true—
  but one wrapped in
    layers and
    layers of
      prayer.

Great Creator,
  who makes lilies bloom in abundance and
    grass grow on unseen hills,

accept my all from me:
  two mites,
  and joyful adoration!

But a poor widow came and put in two very small copper coins, worth only a fraction of a penny. Calling his disciples to him, Jesus said, "I tell you the truth, this poor widow has put more into the treasury than all the others. They all gave out of their wealth; but she, out of her poverty, put in everything—all she had to live on." (Mark 12:42-44)

18.

Mary Magdalene

Early on the first day of the week, while it was still dark, Mary of Magdala went to the tomb and saw that the stone had been removed from the entrance. So she came running to Simon Peter

and the other disciple, the one Jesus loved, and said,
"They have taken the Lord out of the tomb, and we
don't know where they have put him!" (John 20:1-2)

O God—
　　when will this nightmare end!

Is there no limit to
　　the cruelty of the Romans
　　the treachery of the Sanhedrin?

Now they have taken his body!

The spices I have brought
　　to anoint him
　　lie at my feet
　　　　in mocking silence.

Isn't it enough
　　they scourged him
　　　　　　humiliated him
　　　　　　　crucified him?

Did they then have to steal
　　his mangled body
　　from Joseph's tomb,
　　　　denying him even the
　　　　rites of burial?

But what do they hope to gain?
　　This makes no sense,
　　　　no sense at all . . .

but then nothing in Jerusalem
　　has made sense these last few days.

Only a week ago
  Jesus rode into the city
while the people waved palm branches
  and pledged their allegiance, shouting
    "Blessed is the King who comes
      in the name of the Lord!"

Such allegiance!

Those are the same people
  who only a few days later
clamored for the release
  of that scum Barabbas—

and demanded that
  Jesus be crucified.

I cannot bear to think
  my Master will not have
  the simple rituals of death!

God, I hate them!
  I hate them all—
    those pious, scheming priests
    that self-centered Sanhedrin.
They are all hypocrites
  whose mouths mumbled scripture
  while their hearts planned his murder!

Oh, to be a man—
  a man with the
  courage and strength of Samson!

Then I would rip out the hearts
  of those cowardly dogs

who cluster in the Temple
licking their chops
savoring their victory.

And my laughter
would drown the sounds
of their death groans.

How my mouth waters
for the taste of vengeance!

But even as my anger burns, O God,
I hear the voice of my gentle Jesus
saying, "Love your enemies."

Love! How is that possible?

Standing here in the garden,
I feel the flush of rage
on my face,
the rush of blood
that leaves my hands
tingling for revenge.

I can't do it.
I can't love *those* enemies—
the very ones who nailed
my Rabboni to the cross!

O God,
you whom Jesus called Father,
free me from this consuming hatred
as once your son freed me
from Satan's evil spirits.

God of all power,
   allow me—somehow—
      to complete this
      last act of devotion.

Teach me anew
   to trust you—
or my hopes and dreams
      will remain as dead as
      the crucified Christ.

Mary stood outside the tomb crying. As she wept, she bent over to look into the tomb and saw two angels in white, seated where Jesus' body had been, one at the head and the other at the foot. They asked her, "Woman, why are you crying?" "They have taken my Lord away," she said, "and I don't know where they have put him." At this, she turned around and saw Jesus standing there, but she did not realize that it was Jesus. "Woman," he said, "Why are you crying? Who is it you are looking for?" Thinking he was the gardener, she said, "Sir, if you have carried him away, tell me where you have put him, and I will get him." Jesus said to her, "Mary." She turned toward him and cried out in Aramaic, "Rabboni!" (which means Teacher). Mary of Magdala went to the disciples with the news: "I have seen the Lord!" (John 20:11-16, 18a)

19.

Peter's Wife

After a little while, those standing there went up to Peter and said, "Surely you are one of them, for your accent gives you away." Then he began to call down curses on himself and he swore

to them, "I don't know the man!" Immediately a rooster crowed. Then Peter remembered the word Jesus had spoken: "Before the rooster crows, you will disown me three times." And he went outside and wept bitterly. (Matthew 26:73-75)

Resurrected Jesus,
  to you I pray.

Once you walked among us as a man,
  making our sicknesses your own.
And now you have thrown back
  death's black cloak
  with the thrust of
    your mighty arm.

All powerful Christ,
  hear this prayer
  for my beloved Peter.

Remember, Master
  when you were with us,
  when all Capernaum buzzed with
    the blessed news of
      your miracles?

Remember the Peter
  who stood by your side—
    controlling the crowds
    piloting your vessel
      across choppy Galilee
    proclaiming you to be
      the Son of God?

Remember *that* Peter, Lord—
  and not the one who now
  sits idly in his boat,
    staring at the horizon
    cursing himself for denying you—
repeatedly.

Visit us again.

Fill our house once more
  with the joy of your presence.

Don't cast my husband aside
  like a rotten net
  ripped beyond repair.

Your gentleness was difficult
  for impulsive Peter to understand;
but his own failure has taught him
  the hard lesson of humility.

O Jesus!

Come to my Peter again
  and find in him
    a fisherman fit
    for the task of
      catching men.

Use him to build your kingdom;
  use us both.

For I, too, would have a part in
  "fishing for men"—

if only
  to wash the net.

Then Peter stood up, raised his voice and addressed the crowd. "Repent and be baptized, every one of you, in the name of Jesus Christ for the forgiveness of your sins. And you will receive the gift of the Holy Spirit." With many other words he warned them; and he pleaded with them, "Save yourselves from this corrupt generation." Those who accepted his message were baptized, and about three thousand were added to their number that day. (Acts 2:14, 38, 40-41)

20.

Dorcas

In Joppa there was a disciple named Tabitha (which, when translated, is Dorcas), who was always doing good and helping the poor. (Acts 9:36)

O Father—
  how often can my heart break,
    yet continue to beat?

From my roof I see the
  homeless of Joppa,
    wandering the beach
    searching for rags and scraps
      washed in by the sea.

Too often
  bloated bodies of dead seamen
    wash ashore—
and the sound of their widows' wailing
  haunts me for
  nights without end.

O compassionate Jesus!
  You would have gathered Jerusalem to you
    like a hen gathers her chicks.
  I feel the same way
    about the needy of Joppa.

I am only a simple woman.
  But use me somehow, Lord.

All I have in my hand
  is a needle—
    no rod to part seas
      or break springs from desert rocks
    no lyre to soothe tired spirits
      with psalms of praise.

Only a needle—
  and the desire to help clothe

these poor people who
hover in hopelessness
on Joppa's street corners.

Bless my efforts, Lord—
meager though they be.

I know I am no leader;
I have no eloquent words
to win hearts to you.

But I do know that
being good means *doing* good.

And I have this needle, Lord,
and a little talent
and a lot of love.

Let my needle be swift and sure,
like the gulls who
dive for fish in the
choppy bay.
Increase my talent the
way you once multiplied
five loaves and two small fishes—

that I may show to Joppa
the love you show to me.

*About that time she [Dorcas] became sick and died,
and her body was washed and placed in an upstairs
room. Lydda was near Joppa; so when the disciples
heard that Peter was in Lydda, they sent two men to
him and urged him, "Please come at once!" Peter went
with them, and when he arrived he was taken upstairs*

to the room. All the widows stood around him, crying and showing him the robes and other clothing that Dorcas had made while she was still with them. Peter sent them all out of the room; then he got down on his knees and prayed. Turning toward the dead woman, he said, "Tabitha, get up." She opened her eyes, and seeing Peter she sat up. He took her by the hand and helped her to her feet. Then he called the believers and the widows and presented her to them alive. This became known all over Joppa, and many people believed in the Lord. (Acts 9:37-42)

21.

Lydia

*F*rom there we [Paul, Silas, and Timothy] traveled to Philippi, a Roman colony and the leading city of that district of Macedonia. . . . On the Sabbath we went outside the city gate to *the river where we expected to find a place of prayer. We sat down and began to speak to the women who had gathered there. One of those listening was a woman named Lydia, a dealer in purple cloth . . . who was a worshiper of God.* (Acts 16:12-14)

O God,
    my sandals seem weighted
    as I make my way to
      Sabbath prayer.

A hollow space
    inside me
    smolders.

Why do I feel this void?

My life is complete—
    my business successful
      my servants well fed
        my purse heavy with silver.

And yet that yearning is there,
    like the gnawing of an empty belly.

This morning I pass
    many of my customers
    adorned with cloth of my creation:
      crimson, indigo, purple.

And I am proud of
    my talent,
    my hard work.

It is no small thing

to be the most successful
businesswoman in all Philippi!
But my success
    is not enough—

life is more
    than dyeing cloth
        counting coins.

And so I have joined this group of women,
        mostly Jewish,
    who meet and pray together
        at the river's edge.

Attend our Sabbath keeping, God.
Fill this nagging void I feel
    with new meaning for my life
        new spring for my step.

Let me know you better.

For I am like the timid shellfish
        of my trade,
    whose colorless juice
    changes to purple
        only when exposed to sun.

My life—
        for all its success—
    is colorless, too.

Shine on me, O God,
    with the renewing rays
    of your Truth—

and transform my hueless heart
    into a rainbow of
    power and praise.

The Lord opened her [Lydia's] heart to respond to Paul's message. When she and the members of her household were baptized, she invited us to her home. "If you consider me a believer in the Lord," she said, "come and stay at my house." And she persuaded us. (Acts 16:14-15)

22.

Priscilla

*A*fter this, Paul left Athens
and went to Corinth. There he met a Jew named Aquila,
a native of Pontus, who had recently come from Italy
with his wife Priscilla, because Claudius had ordered

*all the Jews to leave Rome. Paul went to see them, and
because he was a tentmaker as they were, he stayed
and worked with them.*

*Paul stayed on in Corinth for some time. Then he left
the brothers and sailed for Syria, accompanied by
Priscilla and Aquila.* (Acts 18:1-3, 18)

Again, God!
  We're moving again!

Paul and Aquila
  have gone down to book passage
  on a grain freighter
  so the three of us
    can sail to Ephesus.

And I stand here in the midst of
  pots and plates and rugs and cloaks
    trying to decide what to pack
    in the few hampers we can take.

But it's hard to see
  through the tears, Lord.
Ephesus! That's across the Aegean!
  In Asia, God!

Some women spend their whole lives
  in one country,
      one town,
        one house.
But not me!
  First Italy, then Greece, and now—
        Asia!

I like it here in Corinth!
   The bustle, the diversity,
   the challenge of sharing
     my Savior.

When we first came here from Rome,
     exiled by that tyrant Claudius,
   I thought my heart would break
     from loneliness!
Every eye in the marketplace
   seemed unfriendly.
Every face in the street
   was that of a stranger.

But now I have *friends*
   here in Corinth—
Christian friends
   who have become my family.

We laugh together and cry together
   and worship together in my home
     every Sabbath.

Must I move, God?

There is still much work here;
   our tentmaking has never before
     prospered like this.
And there's still *your* work
   to do, too—
     for in spite of its
     beauty and wealth,
       Corinth is a wicked city.

But I am my husband's wife—

and Aquila and Paul have talked
of nothing else for weeks now
but taking the news of salvation
  to Ephesus,
    that city so bound
    to the worship of
    the goddess Diana.

And I agree—
  Ephesus needs to be told!

But why me?

Help me, Lord,
  for my heart is not
  in this move.
My future seems as dark
  as the goats' hair cloth
  I weave for the tents.

Give us fair wind, God
  as we cross the Aegean Sea.

Roll back the clouds
  that obscure the heavens
  so the sailors can chart
    a true course.

And roll back this
  black, billowy doubt
  that blocks my view of you—

of both you and the course
  you would have
    me travel.

They arrived at Ephesus, where Paul left Priscilla and Aquila. Meanwhile a Jew named Apollos came to Ephesus. He was a learned man, with a thorough knowledge of the Scriptures. He had been instructed in the way of the Lord, and he spoke with great fervor and taught about Jesus accurately, though he knew only the baptism of John. He began to speak boldly in the synagogue. When Priscilla and Aquila heard him, they invited him to their home and explained to him the way of God more adequately. (Acts 18:19a, 24-26)

The churches in the province of Asia send you greetings. Aquila and Priscilla greet you warmly in the Lord, and so does the church that meets at their house. (I Corinthians 16:19)

QUESTIONS FOR
DISCUSSION / MEDITATION

<u>EVE</u>

1. Think of times when you feel that, as a mother, you have failed. What prompted these feelings? How did you overcome them?

2. Have you ever wanted to go back "home," to an earlier time that seems now more innocent, more loving, more idyllic than your present state? Is that ever possible? What can you do to make your present situation more satisfying?

3. Have you ever felt as though God were punishing you for some shortcoming or sin? Does God do this? Read Jeremiah 3:12 and I John 1:9.

4. Why are we as Christian women often reluctant to forgive ourselves even after God has forgiven us?

5. Do past sin or mistakes still haunt you? On a separate piece of paper write out what burdens you. Then as you read I John 1:9, tear the paper into little pieces and throw them away—claiming God's forgiving and forgetting grace. Read Isaiah 43:25; 44:22-23.

6. Does being alone mean we cannot be complete?

NOAH'S WIFE

1. Do you ever have days when—although you believe you are in God's will—you feel trapped by circumstances? How do you handle these feelings? What does Philippians 4:4-7 say to you? How can you put these verses into practice?

2. Discuss your own need for solitude and renewal. How can you achieve it in the midst of a demanding schedule?

3. How does meditating on God's past mercies strengthen us for times of stress?

4. Share with a friend or your study group a time when God brought you through a "flood" time and gave you a sign of his love and promise—like the rainbow given to Noah's family.

HAGAR

1. Can you think of a time in your own life when you blamed your troubles on someone else? Why do we do this?

2. How would you define jealousy? Why is it such a dangerous emotion?

3. Often our circumstances determine the things we desire, our "treasures." Discuss how, as you have matured, the things you want have changed.

4. Are the material/physical desires of Christians different from those of non-Christians? If so, in what way? Read Matthew 6:19-21.

5. How does a Christian address the problem of self-determination and independence?

6. What does God's answer to Hagar's prayer tell you about God?

SARAH

1. Do you think that today God still "tests" people? What purposes do "tests" serve?

2. What do you do when you find yourself confronted with situations you cannot alter—a sick loved one, an abused friend, a dying neighbor? Read II Corinthians 12:9.

3. Does God ever ask us, as contemporary Christians, to "sacrifice" things that are dear to us? Read John 10:10.

4. Does a Christian mother have to give up her children?

LEAH

1. Have you ever felt that God was unaware of or unconcerned about your troubles? Share any such feelings with a friend or your study group. Read Matthew 10:29-31.

2. How can we handle our anger when it is directed toward our spouses? Is anger an unChristian emotion? Is anger ever constructive? Read Ephesians 4:26-27 and James 1:19-20.

3. Do we as Christian women put too much emphasis on external beauty? Read I Peter 3:3-4.

4. What do the concluding scriptures say to you in the light of what Judah's name means ("praise")?

JOCHEBED

1. Many of the biblical heroines were women of *action*. What can we as Christian women *do* in our own communities to advance God's cause?

2. Jochebed disobeyed the orders of the ruling authority. Are we ever justified in refusing to obey the government? Discuss.

3. Unlike Jochebed, we modern-day mothers do not worry about our babies being kidnapped by armed

soldiers or eaten by hungry crocodiles. But our concerns are often just as immediate and as frightening.

On a separate piece of paper, write three "worries" you have for your children. Turn to Job 42:2. Read the verse silently first. Now read it aloud, making it a statement of faith to the Lord.

Look once more at your "worries." Now, one by one, commit them to God's power and purpose. Turn to Isaiah 30:31. Copy the verse on the same piece of paper, substituting your children's names for the "you" pronouns.

Finally, pray a prayer of thanksgiving, praising God both for what he *has* done and *will* do for your children.

RAHAB

1. After we become adults, what are our responsibilities to our parents? Do these responsibilities change when we marry?

2. Does God hear and answer the prayers of a (unrepentant) sinner?

3. Does God ever use non-Christians to execute his will? Cite examples to support your answer.

4. What does Rahab's name in the genealogy of Jesus say to you?

DEBORAH

1. What makes a person who has known the fullness and goodness of God return to evil ways, like the Israelites of long ago?

2. Have you known a woman who pursued an unusual or male-dominated career? What special problems did she face? How did she overcome them?

3. Does being a good Christian wife and mother mean you cannot have career goals? Read Proverbs 31:10-31.

4. Do we as Christian women sometimes compromise our individuality because of pressure from our peers?

5. Are our talents given to us by God and therefore meant to be used?

RUTH

1. How would you describe your relationship with your mother-in-law? Can you isolate certain events, comments, or attitudes that molded that relationship? What can *you* do to improve the relationship between your mother-in-law and yourself?

2. Ruth's allegiance attests to Naomi's goodness. What are some of the things that may have attracted Ruth to Naomi and her life-style? How did Ruth demonstrate her loyalty? Read Ruth 2:1-7.

3. What about your Christian life will the world find attractive and inviting?

4. In what ways are we called to be missionaries?

5. What is an idol? What "idols" do people in the United States worship today?

RIZPAH

1. This was a cruel time, and justice often was very rough, as this story shows. Rizpah's action calls attention to the grief that accompanies every civil war, every attempt to create justice by retaliatory execution. What does Rizpah's "foolish" action in watching over rotting corpses say to you? Would you say the "foolishness" worked?

2. When we suffer, why does God often seem so far away?

3. Read Psalm 27:14. What does it mean to "wait upon the Lord"? Read Isaiah 40:31 (in the King James Version of the Bible) for the benefits of waiting on the Lord.

4. Are God's answers to our prayers sometimes *conditional*? Explain.

THE WIDOW AT ZAREPHATH

1. Someone once told me: "When two priorities conflict, one of them isn't a priority. Find out which one." How can we as Christian wives, mothers, and laywomen know what our true priorities are?

2. In what ways can we minister to God's chosen messengers today?

3. What made the widow a candidate for the miraculous? What can we as Christian women in the twentieth century do to make ourselves better avenues for God's miracles?

4. Read John 6:1-13. What parallels can you draw between the widow of Zarephath and the boy whom Andrew brought to Jesus? Between the miracle of flour and oil and the miracle of loaves and fishes?

5. Spend the next several minutes in prayer. Fill the first few minutes with praise to God, not only for *what he has done* but also for *who he is*. Spend the last minutes praying that God will use *you* to answer the prayer of someone else.

ESTHER

1. What spiritual qualities does Esther demonstrate during her time of crisis?

2. Describe a time of crisis in your own life. What enabled you to come through this difficult time?

3. Consider the role Mordecai played in Esther's life. Share instances where your life has been influenced by a godly relative.

4. How can we today make the "God of our ancestors" *our* God, too? What is the danger in dwelling on God's *past* victories?

MARY
(of Nazareth)

1. Read Luke 1:26-28. What particular attributes do you suppose Mary possessed that caused her to "find favor with God"? How can we cultivate those same qualities?

2. Why do some people have more difficulty accepting the realities of miracles than do others?

3. Can you share a time in your own life when God has performed a miracle?

ANNA

1. Why is it important to dedicate our children to the Lord? Does this mean they will never sin?

2. Is fasting an option or a requirement for Christian living? Read Matthew 6:16-18. Now read (in the King James Version of the Bible) the story of the demon-possessed child found in Matthew 17:14-21.

3. What are some of the benefits of old age? How can young Christians profit from the experiences of their senior sisters in Christ?

4. Does God ever allow us to see only the initial stages of the answer to our prayers? If so, why?

BRIDE
(at the Marriage in Cana)

1. Recall a time when you were embarrassed in front of your friends. How did you feel?

2. It has been said that one of the things that distinguishes human beings from the lower animals is our ability to remember large blocks of information. Zero in now on some happy moment in your past. Share its details. What purposes do happy memories serve?

3. Do our prayers have to be specific to be effective? Discuss.

WOMAN TAKEN IN ADULTERY

1. Do you think of God as a God of mercy or justice? Are the two incompatible?

2. What is our Christian responsibility to sinners? Are we to rebuke them? Read James 5:20.

3. Jesus put a new application on the Mosaic law against adultery when he said, "Whoever lusts after a woman [man] has already committed adultery with her [him] in his [her] heart." With this "heart principle" as our example, what other extensions can we apply to the Ten Commandments? (See Exodus 20:1-17.)

4. When I taught school, one of the posters I kept on my wall featured a mass of brightly colored ribbons and

these words: NEVER CUT WHAT YOU CAN UNTIE. How can you apply that idea to your own relationships? How can we "untie" resentments, hurt feelings, or prejudices?

5. My grandma used to speak of "bad blood"— meaning that a person's character was based on one's heredity. Is there any truth to that idea? What role does environment play in forming character and determining destiny? How can we "change" our life-styles? Read II Corinthians 5:17.

THE WIDOW WITH TWO MITES

1. Why do you think Jesus watched the people putting in their offerings? Throughout his earthly ministry, what was Christ's attitude toward wealth?

2. As Christians, how concerned should we be with the opinions of others? What do we mean when we speak of our "Christian witness"? Read I Corinthians 10:32-33.

3. What parallels can you draw between the widow at Zarephath and the widow with two mites?

4. Speculate on what happened to the widow after she left the Temple.

MARY MAGDALENE

1. Why was it so important to Mary that she anoint the body of Jesus?

2. Why do you suppose that Mary immediately assumed his body had been stolen and not that Christ had risen?

3. It has been said that "mob psychology" accounts for much of the behavior of the Jerusalem crowd—both on Palm Sunday and Good Friday. Have you ever been in a situation—whether a ballgame or a department store sale or a church service—where you let your behavior be determined by the crowd around you? How did you feel later about your actions? How can we preserve our integrity in the midst of such pressure?

4. Have you ever wanted to take revenge on someone for something he did to you or to one of your family members? How was the situation resolved? Read Romans 12:19-21.

5. Is it really possible to differentiate a person's actions from the person him or herself—so that we "love the sinner but hate the sin"? Give examples.

PETER'S WIFE

1. How do you define humility? Read John 13:2-5. How is it different from self-negation or self-castigation? Give other instances when Christ demonstrated this trait. Have you known someone in your life you would describe as being "humble"? Why, in the world today, is humility an unsought virtue? Was it different in Christ's time?

2. Why do we find it easier to forgive others their faults than we do to forgive our own personal

shortcomings? Would you say pride might be involved?

3. What one word would you choose to describe Peter in these opening verses? In the closing scripture passage? What accounts for the change? See John 21 and Acts 2:1-4.

4. What does the story of Peter's failure and ultimate success say to us today?

5. What do you think Peter's wife means when she says, "For I, too, would have a part in 'fishing for men'—if only to wash the net"?

DORCAS

1. Charitable acts are not limited to the Christian community. How do the "good deeds" we as Christian women do differ from the world's philanthropy? What is our motivation?

2. Sometimes God chooses to use us in ways we would not expect. Has this ever happened to you? If so, share the experience with your group.

3. Name several overlooked or "low-profile" areas of service where Christian women are ministering today. How can we let such people know they are appreciated?

4. How can we share Christ's love with others? Read Matthew 25:31-46.

LYDIA

1. How would you describe "success"? Characterize for the group someone you consider successful.

2. Is pride always a sinful emotion? Should Christians be proud of their work, their accomplishments, their talents?

3. Notice that Lydia's conversion was followed by an offer of hospitality to Paul and his friends. How can we as women extend Christian hospitality today?

4. Both Lydia and her entire household were baptized. How can we influence non-Christians within our own homes to accept Christ?

PRISCILLA

1. Priscilla has been described as a "team worker," working with both her husband Aquila and with the apostle Paul. What is the first image that pops into your mind when you hear the word "team"? With what kinds of teams have you been directly involved? Is the "team approach" the best way to spread the gospel? Defend your answer.

2. Have you ever had to relocate, leaving family and friends? Share with the group your experiences. Were your worries about your new location justified?

3. There is a belief that Priscilla wrote the book of Hebrews. Note that twice in Acts 18 she is mentioned before Aquila. List the characteristics Priscilla possessed that made her both a good wife and a good lay teacher. How can you apply these to your own life?

PRAISE FOR SUSANNA KEARSLEY

"Spellbinding! I've loved every one of Susanna's books!"
—Diana Gabaldon, #1 *New York Times*
bestselling author, for *Bellewether*

"Kearsley weaves a richly told contemporary story with an imaginative, authentically detailed tale from the past, throwing in just the right elements of romance and the paranormal."
—*Booklist*, Starred Review, for *Bellewether*

"Kearsley makes the impossible seem real as she weaves a tale full of genuine characters and a strong sense of place and makes history come alive."
—*Booklist* for *The Rose Garden*

"Kearsley brilliantly brings together past and present as her heroine slips back and forth through time... Realistic characters and wondrous descriptions turn this into a magical, not to be missed read."
—*RT Book Reviews* for *The Rose Garden*,
4½ Stars, Top Pick

"Kearsley blends history, romance, and a bit of the supernatural into a glittering, bewitching tale."
—*Kirkus Reviews* for *The Firebird*

"Authentic historic detail, a touch of the paranormal, and romance come together with a synergistic effect in versatile Kearsley's lovely and memorable novel."
—*Booklist* Starred Review for *The Firebird*

bellewether

SUSANNA KEARSLEY

sourcebooks
landmark

Published by Sourcebooks Landmark, an imprint of Sourcebooks, Inc.
P.O. Box 4410, Naperville, Illinois 60567-4410
(630) 961-3900
Fax: (630) 961-2168
sourcebooks.com

Originally published in 2018 in Canada by Simon & Schuster.

Library of Congress Cataloging-in-Publication Data

Names: Kearsley, Susanna.
Title: Bellewether / Susanna Kearsley.
Description: Naperville, Illinois : Sourcebooks Landmark, [2018]
Identifiers: LCCN 2017061404 | (softcover : acid-free
    paper)
Subjects: | GSAFD: Romantic suspense fiction. | Love stories.
Classification: LCC PR9199.3.K4112 B45 2018 | DDC 813/.54--dc23 LC
record available at https://lccn.loc.gov/2017061404

Printed and bound in the United States of America.
VP 10 9 8 7 6 5 4 3 2 1

This is for Violet, Newport, Cesar, Crown, Dinah, Boston, Dick, and Jack; and all the other women, men, and children—held in slavery by my ancestors—whose names I've not yet learned. I can't repair the damage done, nor wipe the ledger clean, but with my whole heart I apologize, and honor you in memory.

Wilde House Museum

Ground Floor

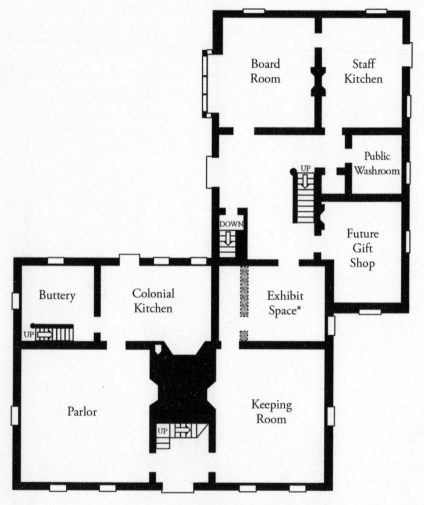

Board Room

Staff Kitchen

Public Washroom

UP

DOWN

Future Gift Shop

Buttery

Colonial Kitchen

Exhibit Space*

UP

Parlor

UP

Keeping Room

*was French officers' chamber & part of Colonial kitchen—gray line shows original wall, since removed

Wilde House Museum

Upper Floor

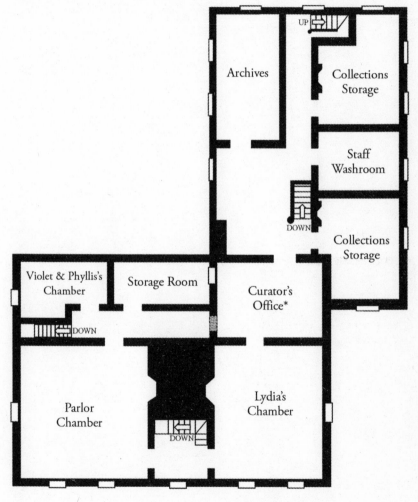

Archives

UP

Collections Storage

Staff Washroom

DOWN

Collections Storage

Violet & Phyllis's Chamber

Storage Room

Curator's Office*

DOWN

Parlor Chamber

Lydia's Chamber

DOWN

*was Joseph's chamber

All houses wherein men have lived and died
Are haunted houses. Through the open doors
The harmless phantoms on their errands glide,
With feet that make no sound upon the floors.

We meet them at the door-way, on the stair,
Along the passages they come and go,
Impalpable impressions on the air,
A sense of something moving to and fro.

There are more guests at table than the hosts
Invited; the illuminated hall
Is thronged with quiet, inoffensive ghosts,
As silent as the pictures on the wall.

The stranger at my fireside cannot see
The forms I see, nor hear the sounds I hear;
He but perceives what is; while unto me
All that has been is visible and clear.

—Henry Wadsworth Longfellow,
"Haunted Houses"

THRESHOLD

S OME HOUSES SEEM TO want to hold their secrets.

The Wilde House, standing silent in its clearing in the woodlands on the eastern shore of Messaquamik Bay, Long Island, holds more secrets than most houses.

From the start, in 1682, when Jacob Wilde came across from England and first chose the rise of land above a small cove of the bay to build his house on, it was rumored he was fleeing a dark scandal in his family. There were whispers he had killed his only brother in a rage, and so had fled to the Americas by way of doing penance. What the truth was, Jacob never said, and if the hands that laid the first square timbers of the Wilde House had indeed been stained by blood, the house stood stoic in that knowledge and concealed it.

Like most houses of its time and place, it started as a basic square with two large rooms—a ground-floor hall or "keeping room" and one great chamber on the floor above—and a stone fireplace on the eastern wall. Beneath the rafters was a garret used for storage, and below the hall, reached by a trapdoor, was a cellar lined with dry-laid fieldstone.

In defiance of the rumors, or perhaps to show his soul was blameless, Jacob painted his house white. A pure and blinding white.

And yet the whispers held, and grew.

They grew when Jacob's firstborn son, a boy he had named Samuel—for his brother, it was said—breathed only one brief hour and then no more, becoming the first Wilde to be buried in the private family graveyard at the forest's edge, above the cove.

They grew still more when Jacob's barn was struck by lightning in a storm and burned until it scorched the ground. He built another in its place. And when the living children started coming—first two daughters, then a son he christened Reuben—Jacob took his tools in hand again and made his small house larger in the customary way, doubling its size with the addition of a second downstairs room and upstairs chamber on the east side of the great stone chimney stack, which now became the central warming heart of this expanded dwelling.

The house, for those few years, appeared content.

Until his younger daughter died of ague and his wife fell ill, and Jacob shuttered up the white house on the cove and moved his family west along the island to the settled farms at Newtown, where he deemed the air more healthful. Another son, named Zebulon, was born there. And in time, when Jacob died, the house at Newtown passing to the elder of his sons, it was this Zebulon who brought his wife, Patience, and their own two small boys back to Messaquamik Bay, and to the little wooded cove, and to the solid four-roomed house that had, for all those years between, stood silently amid the trees and waited.

It was not an easy homecoming. His first two children grew and thrived but three more sons were born and lost and buried in the private family graveyard, and through these years of tribulation Zebulon, a carpenter by trade, enlarged the house yet further, stubbornly improving it by building a lean-to along the back wall, thus creating a kitchen and pantry and one more small chamber downstairs, with a steeply sloped garret above.

At last another son was born, and lived. And then another. And a daughter, Lydia.

It seemed for a time that the Wilde House, at last, would know happiness. But there were locals who still nodded sagely and said there'd been blood on the hands of the man who had built it, and blood would have blood, they warned. Blood would have blood.

In truth there were few who were truly surprised by what

happened next; for in the mid-eighteenth century, with one war winding its way to a close and another about to begin, it was not such an uncommon thing to find families dividing and splintering under the strain. And if one of the bodies that found its way into the Wilde family graveyard was that of an outsider...well, there was violence that happened, sometimes.

It was then, in those years, that the light in the forest first started to shine.

Sailors on the ships that came to anchor off the cove in Messaquamik Bay would often claim they saw the light within the trees, much like a lantern swinging from an unseen hand. The British officers who occupied the Wilde House in the Revolution swore they'd seen it also, and a young spy for the Patriots had written in his journal of the light that seemed to guide him safely round the posted sentries and which, having seen it first at dusk, he'd fancied had been carried by a soldier in French uniform.

The British officers told other tales, of steps that trod the stairs by night, and doors that opened by themselves when no breeze blew to move them, but those tales were told with ale in hand, to test each other's courage, and when they were gone the old house closed again upon its secrets.

As the years passed, its remote location and lack of amenities reduced it to a summer home for Zebulon's descendants, who by then had relocated to the city of New York. In due time, one of these descendants—Lawrence Wilde, a poet of some reputation— chose to take the money he had earned through publication and invest it in what he desired to be a grand retreat, away from civilized distractions, so in 1854 he had the Wilde House enlarged a final time with a new Victorian addition that amounted to a second complete house, overlapping the footprint of the original and indeed attached to the first by means of opening up a part of the lean-to wall.

The house, in this condition, carried down the generations, and the light within the trees still beckoned to the ships offshore.

Who held the light, and why, and what that spirit's purpose might be in the forest, no one knew, though locals often fell to speculating, nodding just as sagely as their forebears had when telling stories of the secrets held within the Wilde House.

The house, when I first saw it, seemed intent on guarding what it knew within its walls as long as it stayed standing; but we all learned, by the end of it, that secrets aren't such easy things to keep.

CHARLEY

ROUTINES, MY MOTHER CLAIMED, could help you get through almost anything.

No matter what calamity occurred, she rose and made the bed and made my father's coffee and her tea and read the morning paper, in that order. Life, she'd taught me, ran more smoothly when you tamed it with these rituals and kept it in control.

I tried; I really did. But even though I was, in many ways, my mother's daughter, I'd lived almost thirty years now without settling on a pattern that would keep my own life organized.

And that was why, although I had been working for a week now at the Wilde House, in this little upstairs room that was assigned to be my office in the new museum, and although I'd known for all that time the local paper would be sending a reporter out on Saturday to interview me, I had waited until Saturday to start to clean.

I'd brought my breakfast with me and had made a bit of progress. When I'd started, it had looked as though a paper bomb had detonated on my desk, but now its sturdy dark oak breadth was almost tidy, with the papers split between the stacks of those I'd dealt with and the ones still needing my attention. My computer, which had started off half-buried by those papers, had a small desk of its own now in the corner just behind me, by the window.

But that left me with a pile of things that didn't have a place to go.

I tried to fit a few of them on shelves, to fill the bare spots, but they cluttered. In the end I simply opened the big empty bottom file drawer of my desk and swept the spare things into there, and slid it shut.

That, too, was something I'd been taught at home: whatever parts of life you couldn't organize, you hid.

And that I *could* do.

⤸

I'd been waiting for the question, so it came as no surprise. The elephant, as some might say, had been there in the room since the beginning of the interview and both of us could see it, but it still took the reporter from the local paper several minutes before she acknowledged it.

"Your last name's kind of famous in this area." Her smile was bright. "I take it you're a relative?"

I found a smile—not quite as bright, but nearly natural—to answer with. "Yes, I am. Werner Van Hoek was my grandfather."

From there it was a simple thing to work out the connection. Of my grandparents' two children, both conveniently born boys to carry down the family name, only one had survived long enough to marry and have children. But she asked me, all the same, "So then your father would be…?"

"Theo. Theo Van Hoek." I waited to see if she'd take it a step further, and if so, which term she'd use. My father called himself a draft resister, though most other people, I had learned, preferred the more alliterative "draft dodger."

The reporter was younger than me. Not by much, though, and people of our generation weren't all that concerned with the Vietnam War or the draft or the men who had dodged it, but even so, I'd heard my father called other names, too: Coward. Traitor.

I could see her take a moment to consider, then she simply asked, "And he lives up in Canada?"

"In Toronto, yes."

"That's where you were born?"

I'd actually been born in Montreal, as had my brother, but my parents had moved to Toronto just a few months afterward, so in the interest of simplicity I just said, "Yes."

"So you're a Canadian?"

I didn't see the point of getting into the complexities of what I was on each side of the border. There were many who believed my father should have lost his right to be American when he tore up his draft card and refused to fight in Vietnam, but immigration laws relied on facts and dates and, in the case of both my brother and myself, they'd made it possible for us to claim our citizenship in the States and cross that border back again. I said, "I'm an American, too. At least, that's what the IRS thinks. They keep taking my taxes."

The young reporter smiled. She clearly felt that we were back on safer ground now, and it showed in how she settled much more comfortably within her chair, the tricky question over.

I was starting to get used to people asking it. Even when I'd lived upstate the name Van Hoek had opened doors, spurring some of the higher-society types to ask whether my brother Niels and I were "of the Long Island Van Hoeks"—a question we'd never known quite how to answer, in honesty, because we were, and we weren't. But down here, in this part of Long Island's north shore, with my grandparents' mansion set off in its own gated park looking over the bay, a short drive from where I was now sitting, I couldn't just walk around town with a name like Van Hoek and expect people not to remark on it.

Usually, after the "Are you a relative?" question, came the inevitable ones about my father, and then a final one aimed more directly, with a pointed barb: "And what does your grandmother think about you coming back here to live?"

I could have answered that I wasn't "coming back," since I had never lived here to begin with. But I didn't. I could have answered simply it was none of their damn business. But I didn't do that, either. I had learned to simply shrug and smile and tell them they would have to ask my grandmother.

Truth was, I didn't know. I'd never met her. Never seen her, save in photographs. She'd never taken notice of my brother,

Niels, the whole time he had lived here, and she hadn't bothered coming to his funeral in the spring.

To be fair, my father hadn't been there either, but that hadn't been his fault. He'd been stuck in the hospital, recovering from surgery to fix his stubborn heart. The doctors hadn't told him about Niels for several days—not out of fear the shock would do him in, but out of fear he'd rip his tubes out, rise up from his bed, and take the next flight to LaGuardia. He would have, too, but by the time he'd learned his only son had died, my mother had arranged a second service in memoriam, at their church in Toronto.

I had gone to that one, also, even though I never found much comfort in the ritual of eulogizing. Niels, I knew, had hated it. I hadn't told my parents that. I'd stood there and supported them as I'd supported Niels's daughter, Rachel, who had looked so lost. And when they'd asked a favor of me, I had told them yes, of course. *Of course I will.* No hesitation.

The reporter asked me, "How long were you with the…Hall-McPhail Museum, was it?"

I regrouped my thoughts and did the math and told her, "Almost seven years." The Hall-McPhail was not a large museum and a lot of people didn't recognize the name, so she wasn't alone. "It's a historic house, a lot like this one, only our focus was all on the Seven Years' War. The French and Indian War," I explained, when she looked at me blankly.

"Oh," she said. "Like *The Last of the Mohicans.*"

"Yes."

"And what did you do there?"

The board of trustees who had hired me here as curator two weeks ago had asked me that same question. I'd sat at the end of the table downstairs and I'd faced them and dutifully detailed the various titles I'd held at the museum—a succession of positions that had seen me doing everything from being a museum guide to managing the interns and the volunteers; from dealing with the paperwork to helping manage budgets. I'd assisted with the conservation of historic texts and then translated those same texts from French. I'd helped to handle documents and weaponry and textiles. I'd created exhibitions and installed them. I had—

"Well, a bit of everything," I said. "But for the past two years I've been assistant to the curator."

"They must," she offered, friendly, "have been sad to see you go."

They'd wished me well, in fact. I told her that, and showed her what they'd given me my last day as a parting gift—a reproduction powder horn designed to look like many of the ones I'd catalogued for the collection, and engraved: CHARLOTTE VAN HOEK HER POWDER HORNE, and during the whole time that I was doing this I tried to keep in mind the cheerful voices of the party on that last day, and not dwell on Tyler's more reproachful comments as he'd watched me packing up my car.

"I can't believe," he'd said, "that you would say yes without talking to me first."

"They're my family."

"Yes, but—"

"What? You would have told me to say no?"

"No. No, I—" He had broken off again to rake a hand through his endearingly unruly hair. "I just don't think you're thinking about *us*."

And he was right. I hadn't been. But in reply I'd only told him, "Ty, I have to go."

"But two years? Really? That's a hell of a long time."

"I'll still be in New York, and you can drive there in five hours. We can make it work."

He'd looked at me with open irritation. "Do you *want* to make it work?"

"Of course I do." My face had probably displayed some irritation too, because I'd thought it crazy he would even ask. "Of course I want to make it work."

I hated arguing. We'd almost never argued, from the time six months before when we'd been introduced by friends at a reception. Our relationship so far had been a relatively calm one, free of drama, so this recent patch of turbulence had left us both off balance.

I restored my balance now by briefly fixing on the broader world that showed beyond my window, which looked out across the mossy shingles of the older section of the house and gave a peaceful green view of the branches of the nearer trees.

Their shade was welcome. Even with the window-mounted air conditioner along the hall, it was still August, and the morning sun would otherwise have made this room an oven.

As it was, the young reporter had begun to use her notepad as a fan.

I sent her a small smile as I acknowledged this, apologizing for the heat. "We can finish this downstairs, if you'd like? And there's no air-conditioning in the colonial part of the house, so if you still want that tour we should probably go while the sun's where it is."

She still wanted the tour. She had gathered her notebook and pen and recorder and stood in the time that it took me to push back my chair, and by the time I'd crossed to join her she had flipped the stapled pages I had given her when we'd begun our interview, to look more closely at the page of floor plans for the house.

She said, "So this room, your office, is actually *in* the colonial part of the house."

"Well, it is and it isn't. This would originally have been one of the garret rooms in the colonial house, but then in the mid-1800s they opened up this corner of the back wall and the roof so they could build on the Victorian addition, so now this room is kind of half-and-half." Like the rooms of the Victorian addition, it had undergone a total renovation in the 1980s, with the painted woodwork and the wallpaper to prove it; but the floor, though painted, was still the same wide-planked floor that had been here when this was just a garret room in the back corner of the old house, and I still got that wonderful walking-through-a-wardrobe-into-Narnia feeling every time I opened the old-fashioned paneled door in the wall behind my desk and stepped through into what felt like another century.

The spacious upstairs bedchamber that lay beyond that door had not seen many changes since colonial times. Large and square, it had a lovely feel to it with all its windows opened wide to let in the faint breeze that danced and rustled through the leaves outside, casting shadows over the floorboards and the dusty fireplace hearth. The air was fresh, the room was quiet, and I felt myself relax. In the older part of the Wilde House, this room was my favorite.

I was about to launch into a proper description of how this first house had been built, and what things had been altered, and how our new project was going to restore them, when the young reporter, studying her floor plan, cut me off with, "Which room was Benjamin Wilde's?"

From her tone, anyone would have thought him a living celebrity—someone with legions of fans who would line up to see where he'd slept.

I was still getting used to that.

Benjamin Wilde, I had learned, was our museum's claim to fame. A daring privateer, a dashing hero of the Revolution, and—if one could trust the portraits—devilishly handsome, he was largely why the Wilde House had been designated a historic building to begin with, and why funds had been donated for its restoration. Benjamin's descendant, Lawrence Wilde, may have become a fairly famous poet of his day and dined with presidents, but all these years afterward, Benjamin's was the name everyone knew. The man everyone wanted to hear about.

I smiled and told her, "Over here." We crossed the landing to the other upstairs bedchamber. This one was essentially the mirror image of the first—a square with two windows at the front and another in the side wall overlooking the green clearing at the forest's edge, where guests would soon be gathering to hear the speeches and take part in the official groundbreaking ceremony.

The room was plain, with nothing in it I would call remarkable, but still the young reporter seemed to revel in its atmosphere. She crossed the floor with reverence. But I thought I caught, within her voice, a hint of disappointment. "There's no furniture."

"It's all been put in storage. There's a bedstead that's original, and two chairs and a table that we know belonged to Benjamin, because during the Revolution, while he was away fighting and the British came to occupy his house, his wife wrote down a careful inventory of what was in each room. She must have thought the British officers would damage things, or steal them."

"Did they?"

"Not that we can tell. Most of the furniture that left the house left in the usual way," I said. "Sold off by later descendants who didn't want old-fashioned things." And who would have most likely been shocked by the prices colonial furniture fetched these days in fine antique stores. "We know where some pieces went, and we're working to get them back. But what we can't track down, we can at least replace, thanks to the records of Benjamin's wife."

She made a note of this, then looked around appreciatively at the peeling plaster walls and scarred wood of the paneling surrounding the room's fireplace. "So you're going to have this whole house restored to the way it looked when he was living here?"

"That's the plan, yes. With luck, we'll be able to have the museum officially open for visitors sometime next summer," I said, "but we have some ideas for special events in the meantime, so people can follow along with the project: a Christmas open house, maybe, and a plastering party in the spring."

"And ghost tours at Halloween?" Seeing my blank face, she said, "There's a ghost here, right?"

I couldn't tell from her tone of voice if she was being serious, so I kept my reply neutral. "I'm not aware of one."

"Oh. Well, you're new here. I'm new here myself, I just

moved here last winter, but I've had lots of people tell me things about the ghost."

I waited politely, but she showed little interest herself in sharing the tales she'd been told, so I agreed with her it might be fun to do a Halloween event, and on that note we moved on with our tour.

She didn't show much interest in that either, though in fairness it was getting close to noon and with the sun directly overhead the upstairs rooms were growing hotter. She began to fan herself again, and seemed content to briefly peek into the downstairs rooms and take a picture of me standing posed beside the massive old stone fireplace in the kitchen before we went out to join the others on the lawn.

The crowd, though small, was starting to assemble.

At its center stood the town of Millbank's mayor, a handsome man in his midforties with broad shoulders and a smile designed to charm. The young reporter fixed her sights upon him, shook my hand and thanked me for my time, and left so quickly that I doubt she was aware of my relief.

But someone was.

Malaika Moore, the current chairwoman of our board of trustees, sent a knowing smile across the space between us as she raised a hand to call me over. Standing in the sunshine, she looked elegant as always, the deep violet of her linen dress a perfect foil for the dark-brown tone of her skin, her closely clipped hair giving her a huge advantage over my own pinned-up hairdo that had started off this morning looking almost chic and now had wilted to a sagging mass of waves beginning to escape their clips. I tucked a strand behind my ear and crossed the lawn to stand beside her.

"Well," she said, "that's done. How many questions did she ask about your grandmother?"

I tried to recollect. "She didn't, really. She just asked about the family name, and moved on pretty quickly. She found Benjamin more interesting."

"Everyone loves Benjamin." Malaika smiled, assessing me with a calm look that didn't judge yet still had an opinion. "You look tired."

"It's just the heat."

"You're still not sleeping."

"I sleep fine." An outright lie, but I delivered it with confidence, and when Malaika let it pass I changed the subject. "We're supposed to have a ghost here, did you know?"

I knew what sort of glance she'd give me in reply to that, and so she did, replying dryly, "That's a local superstition. Don't believe it."

"Oh, I don't. But I should know about it, if it's common knowledge."

"Frank's the one to ask. He tells the story best."

I'd learned to trust Malaika Moore.

She'd been my brother's friend and, in a way, his business partner. Real estate lawyers like Niels needed good contacts, and in Malaika, the best high-end agent in this part of Long Island, he'd found a steady supply of referrals. They'd liked one another. Respect had grown into a friendship so firm that she'd transferred that goodwill to me when I'd come here, and when she had learned I'd be needing a job, she had wasted no time recommending one.

"I'm on the board of the local museum," she'd told me, "and we need a curator. Give me your résumé."

She hadn't told me that she chaired the board, but when I'd had my interview it had been clear she was firmly in charge. "We'd be lucky to have someone with Charley's qualifications," she'd said to the others, in front of me. "I think she's perfect for this."

It had not been unanimous. I knew at least two directors had not been in favor at first, and they'd made that plain to me since I'd been hired, but the others had welcomed me, solely because they, too, trusted Malaika.

It should have been her, I thought, making this opening speech to the crowd.

I eased the cotton collar of my light blouse from my neck,

where it had stuck from the damp heat inside the house. "Aren't we waiting for the contractor?" I asked. I hadn't met him yet, and so I didn't have a hope of recognizing him in the assembled group in front of us, but still I scanned their faces as I stalled for time.

"He couldn't come. He's working on another job," Malaika said. "He wants to get that finished off so he can start here Monday."

There was movement in the little crowd.

Malaika said, "It's time. You ready?"

"No."

She smiled and nudged me forward anyway, and told me, "You'll do fine."

❧

"Good speech," was Frank Wilde's curt review of my performance when he came to find me later. He was carrying an extra glass of lemonade. "You look like you could use this."

"Is it spiked?"

That earned a smile from him. Frank was an older man with features tanned and weathered from his years of farm work. He was stingy with his smiles. "It should be."

Frank was also a director on our board, by virtue of his being a descendant of the man who'd built the Wilde House, and a cousin of the woman who had willed it, with its wooded acres, to the town of Millbank on condition that they make it a museum. Many said it had been Frank who had persuaded her to do that, since Ophelia Wilde had never really been the giving type. Frank, they told me, always got his way, though I'd have said that came less from persuasion than from his refusal to back down once he had set his course. He wasn't like the mayor, who tried to charm his way through every situation. Frank was aptly named. He said exactly what was on his mind.

"You've done enough," he told me, with a pointed look at the untidy stack of paper plates I was collecting from the plastic-covered table where the cake had been. "Let Sharon and her girls do that."

I glanced across the clearing to the bustling red-haired woman who ruled over our few volunteers, and had them all now busy stacking chairs. "She has enough to do."

"She argued against hiring you as curator." His tone was dryly practical. He pressed the lemonade upon me. "Let her do her own damn job."

I wasn't going to win against a man who'd had his way for seventy-odd years, so I gave up and took the glass from him and thanked him.

He acknowledged this and looked at me assessingly. "I'm told you want to hear about the ghost."

"Oh. Right. Yes, the reporter from the *Herald* said we had one. Do we?"

"Well now, that depends."

"On what?"

"On whether you believe in ghosts."

"I don't." With someone else, I might have been less absolute, not knowing whether *they* believed, not wanting to offend them, but from what I knew of Frank I figured I was safe on that count.

His short approving nod confirmed this. "Good for you," he said. "My aunt, now, she wouldn't go into the old house at all. Always hearing things. Jumping at shadows. She used to leave Uncle Walt's lunch on the back step and whistle for him to come get it, when he was at work in there."

Frank's uncle Walt was the reason the house had come down to us in its preserved condition. A self-styled handyman, he'd also been a keen family historian, proud of his ancestry, and even after the family had moved to Manhattan and no longer lived in the Wilde House full-time, coming only in summer to make their escape from the city's heat, Walter had worked hard to keep the house standing. Or so we'd been told.

Frank had stories, and he loved to tell them. I had only been on-site a week, and I'd already heard at least a dozen of his tales.

"There was one time," he told me now, "my aunt came screaming downstairs saying someone was touching her hair, she could feel it."

"And nobody was?"

"Not unless you count spiders." He took a long drink of his lemonade. "Plenty of those in the house."

I agreed. I had seen them.

Across the clearing Sharon and her volunteers had finished with the chairs and were gathering, actively looking for what to do next. Frank appeared to have noticed this, too, because he gave another brief nod at my glass. "Drink up. Let's take a walk."

I'd already drunk nearly all of my lemonade, so I was able to empty my glass in one swallow and follow Frank as he set off toward the nearest path.

My favorite path, in fact, because I hadn't yet got lost on it. The property was riddled thick with walking paths that twisted through the woods. The longest, starting at the far end of the clearing near the parking lot, was crossed by all the others and could take you all the way around, if you knew which turnings to take, but I still hadn't conquered it. I managed better on this shorter path that wound down through the trees to the edge of the cove.

The trees closed above us. The air here was instantly cooler and quieter, and through the tangle of green leaves I glimpsed, in small patches, the blue of the bay.

It almost felt like nothing could intrude upon us here.

Frank said, "The story of the ghost has been around for generations, and every generation adds their bit to it, but I'll tell it the way I first heard it from my uncle Walt—the way *he* heard it at his great-grandfather's knee, so he said."

From what I could remember of Frank's family tree, his uncle Walt's great-grandfather had been the poet Lawrence Wilde, who'd likely told a decent story.

"Back before the Revolution," Frank began, in the same tone he always used when starting on a story, "back when we were fighting on the same side as the English, in the French and Indian War, Zebulon Wilde and his family took in a French officer, captured and sent to these parts as a prisoner."

"Zebulon Wilde," I said, checking my memory, "was Benjamin Wilde's father, right?"

"That's right. Benjamin was barely out of his teens at the time—twenty-two, twenty-three maybe—still a bit reckless, so his father kept him at work on the farm. Didn't want him to run off and join the militia. The one brother, Joseph, had already been halfway ruined by the war. Nearly killed, so they say, in the raid on Oswego, and never quite right in the head after that."

There were so many names to remember. I asked him, "Was Joseph the brother who went to the West Indies or the one who was a merchant in New York?"

"Neither. Joseph was the one who turned a traitor in the Revolution, and went up to Canada."

"A Loyalist? I don't remember hearing about *him*."

"Well, we don't talk about him much." Frank's voice turned dry, but when I glanced at him he winked. He knew that I was half Canadian. "Anyhow, here was this Frenchman, this officer, living right here in the old house with Zebulon Wilde and his sons. And his daughter."

I thought I could see where the story was going, but I let Frank tell it.

"The daughter," he said, "was a lonely young lady. She'd been set to marry a neighbor boy, one of the friends of her big brother Joseph, but he had gone up with her brother to work on the fort at Oswego, and when the French attacked them he was killed. That's what drove Joseph over the edge, they say: seeing his best friend get butchered in front of him. So Joseph came home half-crazy, and his sister—Lydia, that was her name—lost her fiancé."

Over our heads the leaves rustled and danced as a breeze

from the bay brushed my cheek like a sorrowful sigh, as though somehow the forest around us was listening, too, and recalling that long-ago loss.

"Then this Frenchman arrived," Frank said. "Handsome and charming. And Lydia, she fell in love with him. They kept it secret, of course. Had to. Zebulon wouldn't have liked that his daughter was sneaking around with an enemy officer."

"Maybe he ought to have thought about that before bringing the officer into his house to begin with."

"Maybe." The dryness was back. "But then we'd have no story to tell, would we?" Frank reached to take hold of a low-hanging whip of a branch that I otherwise would have walked into, because I was watching my feet on the path and not looking ahead. As he let it fall back into place he went on, "So the Frenchman and Lydia, they fell in love, and the plan was, she'd help him escape and they'd run off together. They had a boat waiting. But when the night came, there was no moon at all, so the officer, he took a lantern to light their way down to the water."

"And somebody saw them," I guessed.

"Are you telling this story?" asked Frank.

"No."

"Okay, then." The path took a turning and started a steeper descent and he waited to see that my footing was sure before going ahead as he picked up the thread of the story. "And somebody saw them. Her big brother Joseph, he saw that light passing his window, and he stopped them there on the path and he shot that French officer."

From all around us the trees sighed again as the breeze from the bay became stronger. The path here gave way to a series of wooden steps edged with a railing and softened with wind-drifted ridges of sand and old fallen leaves, and I followed Frank down to the second to last step, where I sat, as he did, with my feet only inches away from the clear shallow water.

This little cove—Snug Cove—had been where the Wilde

family's ships had once ridden at anchor before setting off on their voyages to the West Indies, where one of the brothers had married and settled and managed their business of trade. That was all long ago and forgotten. The only sails now were the little white sails of the yachts skimming over the bay on their way to Cross Harbor's marina.

The tide had come in. By this evening, the half-moon of pale sandy beach would be partly exposed, with the reeds and a handful of rocks at its edges, but now reeds and rocks were submerged and the small waves came furling toward us and flattened themselves into nothing. I slipped my feet out of my sandals and edged my toes closer, enjoying the cool of the small strip of sand on the soles of my feet.

"So, what happened to Lydia?"

"Well now, they say since her lover had died, and her brother had killed him, she just turned her face to the wall and died too, of a broken heart."

"And people think she's still haunting the house, do they?" One of the incoming waves reached to roll itself over my feet, but I barely acknowledged the brief touch of cold. I was thinking of how, even without the ghost part, the legend itself made a pretty good story, and one we could possibly use in our museum programming.

"Nope." Frank's short sideways look set me straight. "It's the Frenchman supposedly doing the haunting. The tale that's come down is, they buried him back in the family plot. Wanted to keep it a secret. No marker. No stone."

One more wave rolled in lightly and rose and surged over my feet, dragging sand from beneath them and tugging them deeper.

"So that's why some fools in this town think he still walks these woods with his lantern, the same as he did on the night he was killed," Frank said. "Waiting for Lydia Wilde to come follow him, so he can light her way down to the water."

LYDIA

S O THIS, SHE THOUGHT, was what she had been needing without knowing it. This one still, perfect moment when the whole world held in balance.

If she breathed, she feared she'd spoil it, so she held her breath and closed her eyes and tried to make it last, to mark the feeling so it would not be forgotten.

Round her knees, the water of the wide bay nudged her steadily with unseen currents, drawing in the tide, as though it sought to push her gently shoreward, but she held her footing firm against it and remained exactly where she was, her skirts drawn up and held within both hands, the tidy hemlines of her shift and cotton gown suspended just above the water.

The clouds were thin across the searing sky and yet they held a heaviness that signaled storms approaching. She'd been feeling it all morning, both withoutdoors and within, where with her father having gone out in the wagon before breakfast-time, her brothers had seen little need to temper their hostility.

They showed it in small ways at first: a slamming door, a clipped command. But by the time the sun had climbed above the trees and made the air inside the house too hot and thick to breathe, her brothers' sparring dance with one another had become an open argument.

If Mother had been here, she would have ended it. She'd never stood for fighting. She had raised four boys and buried three and, as she'd liked to say, there was a reason why her first name had been Patience. But she'd had a gift for making peace, and when there'd been a gauntlet dropped between the brothers she had stepped between them, picked it up, and neatly sorted it away as though it were naught but another bit of linen wanting laundering.

Their father had once said that had the English had the foresight to send Mother up to meet the French on the St. Lawrence, she'd have settled things so there'd have never been a war. She'd laughed at that, as had they all.

But that had been before Oswego, and before the laughter in their house had died and she had died along with it, and now no matter how the gauntlets fell and hard words with them, she would not be coming back to keep things tidy anymore.

A chilling wave slapped cold at Lydia's bare leg and caught the hemline of her shift, and so she gathered up the linen folds more tightly in her hands, still standing firm against the tide's insistence she return to shore.

They looked to her now, and she knew it.

"You are so like Mother," Benjamin would say—sometimes in praise, sometimes in irritation—and she knew that he and Joseph and their father and her older brothers looked to her to steady them. And so she tried.

But some days, such as this one, it felt too much of a burden to be shouldered, and she feared that she would stumble if she did not find her balance.

"I am trying," she said quietly, though none stood by to hear her, for she knew her mother's grave amid the trees above the cove would have been echoing all morning with the angry voices warring in the house, and with the hard and ringing sounds of Joseph's axe as he released that anger into action, stubbornly retreating, as he did these days, to silence.

There was no one there to give her any answer.

She stood her ground and raised her face, and waited for the storm.

JEAN-PHILIPPE

T HERE WAS A WOMAN in the water.

He had seen her for the first time when the wagon's nearside wheels had caught another rut along the road as they came round the headland, and the jolt had been enough to shift him from his frowning contemplation of the trees, and in that moment he had glimpsed the cool blue of what looked to be a bay.

The woman wore a yellow gown, and stood some little distance from the shore. That had seemed strange enough to warrant his attention.

Of the three men in the wagon, it appeared he was the only one who'd noticed her at all.

The heavy-shouldered driver who was now to be their jailer—or their "host," by the polite terms of this war—had for some time now been in conversation with the other officer, de Brassart, who seemed able to speak comfortably in English.

Jean-Philippe, who knew no English save for "Lay your weapons on the ground" and "Do not move" and knowing neither phrase would be of use in present circumstances, had found these few hours of their journey nothing but a waste of time.

He'd occupied himself in the beginning with a study of the man who had collected them. The English magistrate who'd been in charge of them at first had introduced the man as "Monsieur Wilde," a man of reputation in this colony. A man to be respected.

He was older, and the hair beneath his hat showed thickly white, his face more lined than Jean-Philippe's own father's, though his strong frame looked to be more powerful.

Whatever work he did, he used his hands. They had the calluses and strong veins of a man who did not use them just to hold a pen or glass of wine. And there was something in the man's straight-forward, level gaze that Jean-Philippe suspected might be honesty.

Which made a striking contrast to de Brassart.

In their time at Fort Niagara he had seen de Brassart many times, but never once in battle. Such a man knew well the ways to keep behind the men in his command so that he never shared their danger, while yet standing so his shadow blotted out their claim to any part of victory. A man who used his charm the way another man might use his sword, and with as deadly an effect.

In his years of military service, Jean-Philippe had learned the workings of a man like that so thoroughly de Brassart did not hold his interest long, and when the day's heat had begun to hang more thickly in the forest his attention had begun to drift among the shaded places on the narrow road between the trees.

Until those trees had parted, and he'd seen the woman in the water.

Now each time the trees grew thin, he looked for her, first idly then with growing curiosity.

Each glimpse, however brief, gave him a chance to add new details to his former observations.

She was slender. She had gathered up her skirts above the waterline. Her hair—what little he could see of it beneath her plain white cap—was dark. She might have been the age, he thought, of any of his sisters; he was too far off to tell.

She stood more still and for a longer time than any woman he could call to memory, as though she were fixed in place by some force yet invisible, within that clear blue water.

By the fifth time he caught sight of her, he had begun to envy her that stillness. He had never learned the way of it, himself.

"This one," he still recalled his uncle saying to his father once, "will never settle long enough to be a man of leisure. He was born to be a soldier." And like that, his course in life had been decided.

In the year of his tenth birthday he'd been taken on as a cadet within his uncle's company, where many of the officers were, like himself, Canadian. "We are not like the officers in Old France," he'd been warned. "There, men can pay to buy advancement through the ranks. Here, you must earn it. You must prove that you deserve to be promoted, on your merit."

He had proven it. His rise had been a steady one, helped by the European wars that cast their ripples over here and by the hard campaigns along the changeable frontiers that gave him countless opportunities to show his worth. He'd made full ensign by eighteen and now, at twenty-seven, he'd been two years a lieutenant in command of his own men, and in that time he could not call to mind a single day—not one—in which he'd had no task to focus on, no work to do, no orders needing action.

Until this day.

The English had removed him from his men. They'd had no right to. In the journey down from Fort Niagara to New York his English captors, holding to the terms of the surrender, kept the officers together with their men. But once he'd signed the paper giving his parole of honor at New York, the English all at once had broken faith, forgetting both the laws of war and their own word, and sent his men in one direction and him in another, over all of his objections. Not that any of his arguments had been of use. The only man within that room, besides his fellow prisoners, who'd understood a word he'd said had been an English captain who did not have the authority to alter what was ordered, but who'd merely passed him to the keeping of a New York magistrate, who in his turn had brought him, with de Brassart, to this wild part of Long Island and this morning had delivered them into the care of Monsieur Wilde.

De Brassart was using his charm to his benefit, but Jean-Philippe felt no call to be charming. He felt like a bundle of pelts being traded from one person on to the next without having a say in the matter or knowing his end destination. Uncertainty, he'd learned to deal with. Life was an uncertain thing. But he had never done well when deprived of all control.

He had kept what he could of it. Worn his full uniform, even the long white wool justaucorps, though if he'd been on patrol in this heat he'd have shed that fine coat first of all and gone just in his long-sleeved blue waistcoat. He'd shaved and he'd tied back his hair and he'd fitted his hat on as smartly as if he had been on parade, for wherever he ended up next he'd be damned if they'd see him disheveled. Nor would he allow them to break what control he yet had over his own emotions and drive him to anger.

The woman in the water was a welcome point to focus on at first.

But he could sense the subtle changes in the air within the woods and in the chatter of the birds that were the herald of a turning of the weather, and beyond the bay, above the strip of mainland, he saw darker clouds begin to roll and gather in a coming storm.

The woman stood unmoving.

Someone needed to call out to her, to warn her that the water was no safe place to be standing when the weather turned, but Jean-Philippe from his position knew he could do nothing.

In that moment, as the trees began to close again upon his view, the woman in the yellow gown became a vivid symbol of his myriad frustrations. He was powerless.

De Brassart turned and said, in French, "He says we're nearly there." De Brassart's smile, as always, did not touch his eyes, so Jean-Philippe felt no compulsion to return it.

"Good," was all he said. "Let's hope we beat the rain."

They didn't.

CHARLEY

I HADN'T EXPECTED THE RAIN. I'd been checking the forecasts for days now and keeping my fingers crossed there would be sun for the groundbreaking, and all the weather reports had assured me there would be, and they had been right. Any chance of a rainfall, they'd promised, was scant—only twenty percent—and if rain came at all it would be late tonight.

But the rain, having not read the weather reports, came exactly when it wanted to: just after five o'clock, when all the cleanup had been done and everybody else had gone and I was getting set to lock up the museum.

I liked to be the last one out. I'd always liked the ritual of locking up. Routines again, I guessed—my mother's influence. But there was something calming in the simple act of passing in an ordered way from room to room and making sure that everything was in its proper place, secure and safe.

Nothing in my life right now was any of those things, so it was good to feel, however briefly, I was in control of something.

I'd devised a route that took me through both conjoined houses in a logical progression, starting in the empty corner room downstairs, just underneath my office, in the colonial side of the house. From there I went through the big square room that had, in the old days, been known as the "keeping room"; passed from that into the front lobby with its broad door and big dog-leg stair-case, then into the other square downstairs room we called the parlor, and having now made sure the front of the house was locked tightly, I crossed through the parlor's back doorway into the colonial kitchen and buttery and up the narrow back stairs to the second floor. Here, in the two little storerooms set under the steeply sloped roof of the kitchen addition below, there was not much to check on or see, but the space opened up again as I stepped through into Benjamin Wilde's chamber and made my way—careful to step to the side of the one springy floorboard I didn't trust—over the landing and into my favorite room, where for a moment I stood and enjoyed the peace, liking the sound of the rain on the roof and the play of the rivulets chasing their way down the window glass.

The records from Benjamin's time had suggested that this was the room where his daughters had slept—he'd had three of them—and that was how we had planned to interpret it, but now I wondered if we couldn't maybe expand that to make space for Lydia Wilde's story, too. This was already going to be the most notably feminine room in the finished museum, and since we had nothing to tell us where Benjamin's sister had actually slept, we could speculate he might have given her room to his daughters. We'd still tell *their* stories, of course, but because they'd all lived quiet lives it might not be a bad thing to add in the tale of their aunt's tragic romance. The only thing people liked more than a ghost story was a good love story. This one was both.

It was just an idea, of course, and the trustees would have to approve it, but still, as I passed through my office and carried on fastening windows and turning off lights in the newer, Victorian side of the house, I was thinking of all the ways we could use Lydia's story—not only for Halloween, as the reporter had said, but for Valentine's Day.

I became so absorbed in exploring the possible angles that, by the time I came downstairs to the staff kitchen where the main back entrance was—the door I usually went out by—I was unaware of just how hard the rain was coming down until I realized that I couldn't see a thing beyond the windows. The sight of water sluicing at an angle down the windowpanes made me rethink my options.

There were spare umbrellas hanging from the coatrack, so that wouldn't be a problem, but umbrellas offered limited protection when the rain was coming furious and sideways, and since my car was parked out at the far end of the parking lot, closer to the front door of the old part of the house, it made more sense to go out that way and make a dash from there. I'd still get wet, but wet was preferable to soaked.

I locked the back door, switched the kitchen light off, and unhooked a pink umbrella from the rack, before starting over where I had begun—moving through what would be the exhibit space, under my office, and into the ground-floor colonial rooms. This time, though, while crossing the large keeping room, I heard something I hadn't before: a steady, repetitive squeaking of floorboards above me that sounded, in that empty, echoing space, just like footsteps.

I stopped, and the noises stopped, too, and I realized that was probably because they *had* been echoes. Old houses could be good at playing tricks with sound, and this house was older than many I'd been in. I wasn't about to become like Frank's grandmother, jumping at every stray sound and imagining ghosts.

Whatever the cause of the echo, it seemed to be confined to that first corner of the room because as I crossed the rest of it, there were no sounds above me. The shadowed front lobby was quiet, too, thanks to the nondescript carpet that some former Wilde had seen fit to install here between the front door and the stairs—a gray carpet, much weathered, that never looked clean. We'd be tearing it up in the new renovations, restoring the floor underneath, but for now it was working to soften my footsteps.

And that was a problem. Because when the creaking began again, over my head, I could not put it down to an echo. Especially when I stopped dead in my tracks and the sounds on the floor above didn't break stride, moving onto the staircase, taking the few short steps down to the first narrow landing, and turning…

In that moment my mind spun wildly. There wasn't anything

here anybody would want to steal, unless you counted my office computer and the somewhat obstinate coffee machine in the kitchen, and—

Now there were visible boots on the stairs. A man's work boots, attached to legs encased in faded jeans, that in their turn a few steps down were joined by a gray T-shirt and the chest and shoulders of the man who owned it.

One of the workmen, I thought in relief. He was halfway down the stairs now so I saw him full in profile, enough to see that he was not much older than myself, with the tanned skin of a man who worked outdoors and the imprint of a hardhat still compressing his short-clipped dark hair, the wires of earbud headphones trailing down to one front pocket of his jeans.

At the bottom landing of the staircase he made the ninety-degree turn to come down the final three steps and he noticed me then, with an equal surprise. His recovery, though, was more fluid than mine. "Oh, hey," he said, tugging the headphones from his ears and releasing a faint burst of wailing guitar before moving his hand to his pocket to switch off whatever device he'd been playing. "I thought everyone was gone. Sorry. Didn't mean to scare you."

In spite of the fact the umbrella was still tightly grasped in my hand like a weapon, I chose to pretend that I hadn't been scared. That I wasn't still nervous. But, as was my habit when facing a male stranger, I kept an eye on my possible exits and cautiously tried to establish if he posed a risk.

He was taller than me, broad and muscular, but not aggressive. He wasn't invading my personal space. He had stopped when he'd noticed me, and hadn't tried to advance.

"That's okay," I said, standing as straight as I could in a business-like posture. "You're one of the construction guys, I take it?"

"Kind of." He had a slow smile that seemed genuine. Friendly. Extending his hand for a handshake, he said, "I'm Sam Abrams."

I *did* relax then. "The contractor?"

"That's right."

Accepting the handshake I told him, "I'm Charlotte Van Hoek. Everyone calls me Charley."

"What do you like to be called?"

"Charley, actually." I was surprised he would ask me. No one ever had before. It made me take a better look at him.

Up close it was clear that his tan was not really a tan, but his natural skin tone. He had a nice face—dark eyes, straight nose, strong jawline. More handsome than ordinary, but not so handsome you couldn't look straight at it.

He had a nice handshake, too. Brief, firm, and self-assured.

Turning his left hand a little he showed me the bright-orange tape measure held in his square palm. "Just checking the width of a window. I'm done now. You locking up?"

"Yes." Since I'd already locked all the doors it was obvious he had his own key. "Which door did you come in?"

"This one."

The front door, behind me. Meaning all the others were still safely locked. I gave a nod and started to unfasten my umbrella.

"That's not going to be much help to you out there," he warned me. "Where's your car parked?"

"Over by the barn."

"I'll drive you over."

Under normal circumstances I'd have never gotten in a car with someone I'd just met, no matter how nice and harmless they seemed, but I knew Malaika spoke highly of Sam Abrams and since I trusted Malaika, I told him, "Okay." I was glad that I had, when we opened the door to discover the rain pelting down with a vengeance.

He'd parked his black pickup truck two steps away from the door, where the overhang sheltered the front stoop a bit, which explained why he hadn't been soaked coming into the house in the first place. And he'd been right: my pink umbrella didn't help me much at all as I sprinted around to the passenger side. I hadn't had to climb into a pickup truck since high school, so I wasn't very graceful as I hoisted myself up onto the seat. To my relief, he didn't seem to notice.

He was studying the windshield as he put the truck in gear. "What kind of tires do you have on your car?"

Once again, not a question I'd ever been asked before. "All-season radials. Why?"

"Old or new?"

"New last summer."

"You should be all right, then." He steered the truck around to slowly roll across the narrow gravel parking lot toward the farther end. "I wouldn't take the main road, though. It never drains right when there's this much water, and you don't want someone hydroplaning into you. I'd go the back way, down the shore road."

He sounded like Niels, looking out for my safety. *You sound like my brother*, I wanted to tell him. Instead I cleared my throat of the small lump that had just blocked it and said, "Okay."

"Have you driven on the shore road?"

"Once or twice." It wasn't a straightforward route. It had some twists and turnings, like the footpaths in the forest, and changed names at least once on its way down into Millbank.

I must have looked uncertain when he glanced at me because he said, "Well, that's the way I'm going. You can follow me."

He stopped alongside my blue Honda Accord and I thanked him and made the short dash to my driver's seat, happy to hear my car's engine behave when I started it. By the time I'd backed out of my spot, Sam had moved his truck into position to take the lead.

I wasn't nervous of driving in bad weather, but I was happy to have him in front of me as we rounded the two western corners of the large Wilde property, approached the grid of residential streets, and turned instead to take the sloping road that led us back toward the bay. We were within the trees again, and sometimes they closed over us, but every now and then they opened up to let the rain sweep in and made me grateful for the truck's red taillights.

He drove a little slower than he had to, putting his turn signals on well ahead of the corners we came to, and when we came to the place where the shore road—or whatever it was called here at the edge of town—passed underneath the shelter of the elevated highway that ran right across this north shore of Long Island, he pulled over to the shoulder, rolled his window down, and waved me up beside him to the stop sign.

I braked as I drew level with his truck and put my window down as well.

"Okay now?" Sam called over.

"Yes," I told him. "Thank you."

With a brief thumbs-up and nod he rolled his window up again and let me travel on ahead of him.

I didn't have too far to go. But once I left the underpass my full attention focused on the windshield and the road, and so it wasn't till I'd turned off and was halfway down the steep drive to the house and heard the friendly honk behind me as the pickup truck swished past that I discovered he had stayed behind me. Following me, possibly, to make sure I got safely home.

And because that was another thing my brother would have done, I found I had to sit outside a moment in my car, just by myself, until my cheeks were dry enough that I could blame their dampness on the rain.

Only a month ago, just walking into the house had been difficult. I'd almost conquered that now. It helped that my brother had only been here for a year, and that I'd only been down one time for a visit at Christmas, so I didn't have many memories of him in this place, and the house itself hadn't absorbed very much of his character. Nor did it really have much of its own.

Niels had never been fond of old houses. He'd inherited that from our mother, most likely, since she had been born and brought up in the same old stone farmhouse outside Quebec City where her family had lived for a hundred and seventy years. By her reckoning, six generations had weathered the same winter drafts in that house and she'd left it as soon as the chance had presented itself, taking a job at a bank in Montreal, where she had met my father. The first house they'd lived in as newlyweds, at Mom's insistence, had been clean and modern with no stone in sight. We'd always had new houses. Dad was no handyman, so when the gleam had worn off one house and things started needing repair, we'd moved on to the next. I'd enjoyed having new rooms to decorate, but to be honest I'd secretly loved that old stone farmhouse my French Canadian grandparents had never left, and my visits there had, I felt sure, been the start of my love of museums.

My brother had, by contrast, carried on just as my parents had and never bought a house if it was more than ten years old. Unlike Dad, though, Niels had never learned his limits when it came to wielding tools. He'd watched the home improvement programs on TV, and every home he'd lived in showed the scars of it.

The house he'd chosen here, in Millbank, was a plain two-story house with horizontal siding freshly painted the color of caramel fudge with lighter-yellow trim framing the neat rows of windows, the peak of the roof, and the flight of broad steps leading up to the wraparound porch. The porch, in my view, was its finest feature, unless you were counting its setting, because that was fine, too—it sat in a hollow behind and below the main street leading into the town, with tall trees to each side of it and a sloping backyard that was half-filled with reeds from the edge of the water where the mill stream widened into Messaquamik Bay.

The front yard had been graveled over when he'd bought it, which had suited Niels because he'd hated mowing lawns and it had made a perfect parking place for clients. I'd parked tonight where I always did, under the huge sycamore that sheltered the front porch, my headlights shining into the more lush back garden of his only neighbor, Mrs. Bonetti. Behind me, on the far side of a tall and tidy myrtle hedge that ran the length of the front yard, was nothing but a wide expanse of parking lot belonging to a restaurant that, in all the time I'd been here, had been under renovation, so the lot was always empty.

Sometimes the emptiness spooked me a little, especially since my apartment in Albany had been one of five in a big old house right in the center of town, so there'd always been someone close by.

But tonight I was glad of the fact there was no one to notice me wiping the tears from my face one last time as I dashed from my car to the porch in the furious rain.

Niels had "improved" the porch railing, which meant that it wobbled a bit as I raced up the steps and along to the side entrance, where he had added a fancy screen door that was fussy to open and took its time closing again, but I came through those obstacles without a mishap and, safely inside, took my coat off and shook it and added it to the collection that hung from the freestanding coatrack.

I turned to find Rachel, my niece, standing two steps in front of me. Though she was barely nineteen and petite, fully half a head shorter than I was, she still stared me down as though I was attempting to sneak in past curfew. She lifted one hand. She was holding my cell phone.

"You left this again."

"I know." I'd been at the museum before I had missed it, and by then there'd seemed no point in driving back here just to fetch it when I could as easily use the museum's phone. "Sorry, I thought—"

"I was trying to call you for over an hour before I found *this* on your dresser," she cut me off. "Gianni said there'd been an accident because of all the rain, and I heard sirens, and—"

I interrupted in my turn, but gently, because now I understood the reason for her irritation. She'd been worried. I was touched by that, and made a mental note to be more careful, more considerate.

"I'm really sorry." I'd have given her a hug, but Rachel wasn't much for hugging.

She had always been an independent kid. She'd been a tiny thing, just seven, when I'd first moved down from Toronto to live with Niels in Saratoga Springs. He'd fixed up an apartment for me over the garage, and I had driven the half hour down and back to university at Albany, and in the evenings and on weekends I had paid him back, in lieu of proper rent, by babysitting Rachel.

I would never have won prizes for my babysitting. Usually we'd spent the time together sitting on my thrift-store sofa watching movies on TV. She'd liked the scary ones the best, back then. She'd take whatever blanket I had thrown across the sofa back and wrap herself up tightly in it so that she could hide her eyes if things got too intense, and she would do the same thing if we watched sad movies, so that she could cry without my seeing her.

She hadn't let me see her cry at all since Niels's death, not in the whole time I had been here, but I sometimes caught a brief glimpse of that kid beneath the blanket, trying hard to keep it all together.

Reaching out, I took my cell phone from her hand. "I'll try not to do it again."

"Okay."

This little tiled area between the side door and the kitchen functioned as a mudroom and I left my wet shoes here as well, before I followed Rachel the few steps into the kitchen. Something smelled so good that, even if she hadn't mentioned Gianni, I'd have known that he'd been over.

"Ziti?" I guessed.

"No, lasagna."

Our neighbors were kind. At least once a week, Mrs. Bonetti made meals for us and sent them over with Gianni, her son, who at twenty-two still lived at home with her, working by day in the town's main street deli. If I'd been my niece, I'd have fallen for Gianni the minute I'd met him—he was stunningly good-looking with nice manners and a cocky sense of humor—but it all seemed lost on Rachel.

"Have you eaten yet?" I asked.

"Not yet. I wasn't really hungry."

But she'd set our places at the table with the fancy cutlery and wineglasses and place mats, and I found that touching, too, because I knew her well enough to know that meant she wanted company. I switched my phone off, washed up, and took over, dishing the lasagna out and opening the bottle of red wine she'd chosen from her father's stash down in the basement.

We hardly ever sat down at the table for a meal. It was partly a practical thing. There were only the two of us, and we were usually eating at different times, so it was simpler to pull up a stool at the breakfast bar and toss things right into the dishwasher afterward. And partly it came from us both being far too aware of the chair at the head of the table, and why it was empty, and who should be sitting there.

Missing my brother, for me, was a physical pain. Three months on, it still felt as though some vital organ inside me had been ripped away and the wound stitched up badly, the edges too ragged to heal; but I hid that wound under my everyday clothing, and because I looked, on the outside, the same as I always had, nobody saw I was no longer whole. If my mother were here, she'd have probably noticed, but we hadn't been in the same room since I'd gone up to Canada for the memorial service in May. And my parents, like Rachel, were dealing with wounds of their own. I'd be no help at all to them if I gave way to my grief.

So I angled my chair now to face it a little away from the head of the table, and smiled at Rachel. "So, how was your day?"

"Okay."

"You applied for that course?"

She corrected me. "Seminar. And yeah, I emailed the instructor, so I'll have to wait and see if she has room for me."

"And what was it about, again?"

"Transgressive women in eighteenth-century British fiction."

Which put an end to that, because there wasn't much that I could bring to conversations about English literature. My own degree had been in history, and while I loved reading I read differently than Rachel did. She reveled in identifying themes and analyzing structures, and wrote papers that examined Dostoyevsky's polyphonic style, on which I couldn't offer an opinion.

We ate our lasagna in silence a moment, but I could still tell that she didn't want silence. I'd always had an easy time interpreting her body language because she'd inherited so much of it from Niels. She didn't look like him. She took more after her mother, who'd been Niels's girlfriend and lived with him all through the years he was going to law school, before deciding she was not cut out for motherhood. She'd left them shortly after Rachel started kindergarten, and apart from Christmas cards from the West Coast the first few years, she'd dropped out of their lives completely.

I would have had trouble remembering what she looked like if it hadn't been for the fact she'd gifted Rachel with the same rich auburn hair, pale skin, and petite frame.

But the shrug and partial eye roll Rachel gave me, when I asked what else she'd done today, was pure Van Hoek. And I guessed who had earned the eye roll even before she said, "Tyler called."

She'd never had a high opinion of my boyfriend. It was mutual. Whenever they were in the same room, I felt like an arbitrator.

"Really? When was that?"

"At lunchtime. He 'forgot' today was your big thing at the museum."

"Yes, well, he's been busy with work."

"So have you," she said. "Don't get me started. He said he'd be out tonight, he had some dinner or something to go to. He said you could Skype him tomorrow at two."

I covertly studied her face while I sipped my wine. Her mouth had turned down at the edges, which meant that she was disappointed. And in more than just my choice of men. It was the same look she wore anytime an outing she'd looked forward to was canceled, or a treat she had been promised was forgotten in the rush of daily life. I cast my mind back over what we'd talked about this week, and what we might have planned.

And I remembered. I said, "It'll have to be later than two. We're still doing that whole Sunday brunch thing tomorrow, right? And checking out the new bookstore?"

The light in her eyes was my answer. And my reward.

I had wondered, when I'd first agreed to do this, whether I'd be any help at all to Rachel. She was practically an adult, even if she'd have to wait another two years, until she turned twenty-one, before she could inherit both this house and Niels's money in her own right. He'd set things up like that when she'd been five, and hadn't seen the need to change his will since then, because along with all the rest of us he'd never thought he'd die at forty-two. He'd been ridiculously healthy. When his heart had stopped, he had been in the parking lot outside his gym, just coming from a workout. It was dark. He'd fallen in between the cars. No one had seen him.

Rachel had called me a few hours later in tears, and the hours after that had been frankly a blur, but I'd been here by sunrise. I'd fielded the calls from the funeral home and from my mother in Canada, sorting things through, with my father still lying up there in his hospital bed, getting over his surgery, not yet aware.

I remembered the lawyer explaining that Niels had left everything, as we'd expected, to Rachel, but with the whole estate held in trust until her twenty-first birthday. My parents were named the trustees, which would work for the finances, but my mother had spoken aloud what we both had already known: "There is no way that your father will go back to Millbank. Even if his health allowed it, which it won't for some time yet, he just won't go. So there's the problem of the house, because I hate the thought of Rachel living there all by herself. And when she's off at university, someone needs to look after things."

I'd known what she was asking me to do, before she'd even put the words in proper order.

"Charlotte, I know it's an imposition, but do you think you could...?"

"Yes, of course," I'd said. "Of course I will."

There'd been no need to think things through. No hesitation.

And when Rachel smiled like she was smiling now, I knew I'd made the right decision.

With a nod she let me know we were still on for Sunday brunch and shopping. "I got us a reservation for eleven thirty."

"Perfect. Let's just hope this rain lets up by then. It's no fun driving in it."

"Did you see the accident?" she asked me. "Was it really bad?"

I shook my head. "We didn't come down the main road."

"We?"

"Sam Abrams, the contractor, told me the shore road was safer, so I followed him."

"Oh, is that the guy Malaika knows? The one who does the work on all her houses?" Rachel asked. "The Mohawk guy?"

"No, his hair's just cut normally."

"I didn't mean a Mohawk haircut, silly. Mohawk as in Native American. He's, like, about your age, a little older maybe, really built, short hair? He drives a big, black truck? I've never talked to him or anything," she said, "but he seems nice."

"He is. He's very nice."

"Nicer than—"

"Hey, go easy on the wine," I interrupted as she reached to pour a second glass. "You're underage. If Mrs. Bonetti comes over and finds you drunk, I'll get in trouble."

"Mrs. Bonetti won't care if I'm drinking wine. Anyhow, New York law says I can drink at home."

I'd tried that argument myself at her age, but I'd quickly learned that, when you argue with your brother and your brother is a lawyer, you get slammed by all the subclauses. The sad part was, I still remembered most of them. "Well, *technically*, it says that you can drink at home if there's a parent with you, or a legal guardian. And since I'm neither one of those—" And then I stopped, because I realized what I'd said.

Rachel glanced past my shoulder to the empty chair behind me.

Mentally I kicked myself. "I'm sorry."

"No, it's fine," she said. "I'm fine. You're right, I shouldn't have more wine. I've still got lots of reading to get finished before classes start." She set the bottle down and forced the little smile that hadn't changed since she was seven, and was just as unconvincing now. And then she rose and cleared her dishes off the table and retreated upstairs to her room.

Left alone, I reached over and picked up the bottle and filled my own wineglass. I filled it as near to the brim as I could. And I looked, in my turn, to the chair at the head of the table.

I said, "I am trying."

But if Niels was anywhere where he could hear me, he didn't reply.

LYDIA

T HE PATH UP FROM the cove between the trees had not yet
turned to mud before she reached its top, so it was only the
last dash across the clearing that exposed her to the fury of the storm.

Her skirts still gathered to her knees, she ran more freely and
had crossed the threshold of the kitchen doorway before she
became aware the room was crowded with more people than it
should have been.

She looked from Joseph, standing braced beside the hearth,
his face drawn and determined, to her other brother, Benjamin,
who had been sitting at the table but who stood as she came in, as
though to block her view. Or shield her.

Looking beyond Benjamin, she found her father's watchful
eyes and focused on them, making no attempt to hide the pain
and disbelief in hers as she asked in a tone she wished were less
unsteady, "Father?"

He was standing with two men behind him.

No, not simply men, she thought: two soldiers.

And not simply soldiers: two French soldiers. There was no
mistaking those white coats. They gleamed like vengeful spirits
in the dim space of the long and narrow kitchen, where the
ceiling beams hung low above them and the windows with their
heavy glass obscured yet further by the pelting rain let in a sickly
shaded light.

At first she had the dreadful thought her family might be prisoners, and fear rose up within her, swift and sudden as an unexpected
wave. It closed her throat and stole her breath until she noticed
that, although the Frenchmen wore their swords, their weapons

were not drawn. They stood at ease, hands at their sides, and watched.

Her father slid his gaze from hers. "These officers," he said, "have been assigned to me, on their parole of honor. They'll be staying with us."

"Staying *here*?" She glanced again at Joseph. "You cannot—"

Her father spoke sharply. "I can and I have. It's my duty." His tone, she knew well from experience, stopped all discussion and warned her to hold her tongue. Yet his stern eyes, when they lifted once more to her own, were not demanding her compliance. They were asking for her caution. "Lieutenant de Brassart speaks very good English. He'll serve as interpreter for his companion. You'll find them both gentlemen, and you shall treat them as such." In keeping with this order he stepped slightly to the side and made a formal presentation to the officers. "Lieutenant de Brassart, Lieutenant de Sabran, this is my daughter, Miss Lydia Wilde."

There appeared to be little enough to distinguish one man from the other apart from their long buttoned waistcoats beneath the white coats of their uniforms—one a bright scarlet with gold trim, the other a deep, vibrant blue. They both wore the same sharp cocked hats, had the same dark-brown hair fastened back in a queue, and were much the same height, being both of an age she'd have judged to be not far above Joseph's twenty-six years. But the man on the right, in the blue waistcoat, studied her silently as his companion stepped forward.

The man with the red waistcoat bowed while removing his hat in a gentleman's gesture.

His accented English was elegant. "Miss Wilde," he said, "we are most desolate to inconvenience you."

This was Lieutenant de Brassart, then.

Lydia did not consent to return his engaging smile, yet being mindful of her father's wishes, replied with a curtsey that any observer might think was respectful, and one she considered sufficient to answer both officers, since the blue-waistcoated one had by now also bowed—not as deeply or long as de Brassart had, but with the same sweeping off of his hat that seemed somehow more courtly than when her own countrymen did it.

She felt, in the moment they greeted each other, as if she were standing in water again, only this time more turbulent, pressing her in on all sides. At her back she heard Benjamin restlessly shifting his stance on the floorboards while Joseph stood wrapped in a silence so fierce it was practically audible, and she could tell that her father was waiting for her to say something to lessen the tension.

Her mother, she thought, would have known what to say; would have put everybody at ease.

She attempted her own slightly forced imitation. "It's no inconvenience. Do give me your coats—Father, you as well—and I will set them to dry by the fire."

As de Brassart turned round to translate this request to the other French officer, Lydia's father shrugged off his wet coat and stepped forward, his eyes warm with pride.

He said nothing to thank or to praise her, and yet she knew well he was pleased with her actions and speech as he handed the coat to her, watching her hang it on one of the pegs he had set at the side of the hearth for that purpose.

The hearth, in her childhood, she'd thought had been built by a giant, for only a giant, she'd reasoned, would need one so large. It would stand, said her father, long after the house and its timbers had fallen, and she did not doubt it. While Mother had lived, it had been the great heart of the house, always warm, but these past two years Lydia had come to learn it was not such an easy thing keeping a fire without letting it fall low or flare up too hotly.

It seemed too hot now, but that might have been simply because of the earlier heat of the day and the closeness and damp of the room with the rain beating down at the windows. She took care to see that her father's coat hung not too close to the logs in the grate, nor the iron pot set on its black hook above, in which rested a large rump of beef, stuffed with forcemeat and stewing with celery and carrots in water made flavorful with pounded cloves and red wine.

Her father leaned nearer and, pretending curiosity in what was in the pot, asked very quietly, "Where's Violet?"

Lydia replied as quietly, "Her head was aching badly, so after the milking was finished I sent her upstairs to get rest. I had no difficulty managing. Our dinner, as you see, is but a simple one."

"So simple you can cook it at a distance, I perceive." His tone was mild and yet reminded her he knew she had been out of doors and nowhere near the house.

"The weather was so hot, I needed air," she said. "And anyway, I did not leave the fire untended. Benjamin was here."

"And where was Joseph?"

She would not upset her father nor betray her brothers by revealing they had argued, so she turned her face away and answered simply, "He was also here."

Which had to satisfy her father, since the two French officers by this time had removed their coats and carried them across, as she had asked. Her father stood aside to give her room. The coats were long, of fine, white wool, and now that she was holding them she saw that they were different in that one of them—de Brassart's— had a collar faced in blue, and was itself lined all in white, while his companion's coat was collarless and lined in the same rich blue as his long-sleeved waistcoat.

She had heard the French were vain about their clothing and their uniforms, and looking at the coats she could believe it. Both were split below the waist along the side seams to allow for ease of movement, pleated full across the back to make them fashionably drape and swing, with rows of fine gold buttons and deep cuffs that turned back nearly to the elbow. And at each side, where the seams had been divided, there were buttons that allowed the inner corners of each panel of the coat, at front and back, to be turned upward from the hem and fastened so the soldier's leg was free for movement and the lining of the coat could be displayed.

A pretty thing to wear, she thought, for men who dealt in blood and fighting, musketfire and death.

The man in the blue waistcoat spoke. His voice was deeper than de Brassart's, less designed to charm, and more direct. It was a short speech but she did not know its meaning till de Brassart added, "Yes, of course, I wish to thank you also."

Lydia glanced at the other man but he was looking at her and she did not wish to hold his gaze long so she cast hers once more downward. "You are welcome."

Her father lightly touched her arm as though to show he understood what those few words had cost her. Then he spoke above her head to both his sons. "These officers will find it most convenient to sleep down here in your chamber. Both of you take what you need upstairs. Joseph, you can take the room beneath the eaves, and Benjamin, you'll share with me."

They knew that tone as well as she did, and they did not argue. Benjamin, always the first to do what was expedient, moved toward the doorway of the small square chamber at the kitchen's farther end. It had been his alone at one time, during those dark months three years ago when Joseph had been at Oswego, but when Joseph had returned to them—at least in body—later on that autumn, they had shared it once again.

He might have spent the morning trading angry words with Benjamin, but he said nothing now as he, too, ducked beneath the doorway of the small end chamber, re-emerging moments later with his few belongings in his hands. And then with Benjamin behind him, he passed stone-faced through the nearest door that led into the keeping room, and so to the front entry and the staircase, since to use the back stairs would have meant a walk the full length of the kitchen, past the gauntlet of their father and the officers.

And that was something, Lydia knew well, her brother Joseph would not do if it could be avoided.

It had taken him a full year to be able to be in the same room as their neighbor's hired hand, French Peter. And French Peter, being one of those French neutrals who'd been sent down by the British from Acadia, had never been a soldier so wore simple working clothes and not a uniform.

She knew if she was finding it this difficult to have them here, for Joseph it must be nigh on unbearable.

And that was why, after she'd waited in respectful silence while her father showed their new "guests" to their chamber, she took him aside in the moment of privacy after and said again, low, "You cannot do this. Joseph—"

"Is not made of glass. He's yet a man. He will not break."

And what of me? she almost asked him, but she closed her mouth upon the words because she saw her father's eyes and knew he was already troubled. Frowning slightly, she observed, "You do not want them, either, do you? Why, then—?"

"Come." He ushered her ahead of him across the kitchen to its other end, where at the farthest distance from the chamber given to the officers, the small square buttery stood partially closed in. The narrow back staircase was here, and the barrels of cider and ale and the bottles of spirits and wine, and the freestanding cupboards and dresser her father had built for their spices and foodstuffs and dishes. The buttery had no door in its wide and open doorway, but by standing in the corner by the dresser they could speak discreetly.

"Why?" she asked him, less accusing now.

His mouth compressed. "Your uncle Reuben had them sent to me."

She understood his problem then. There was no love at all between her father and his older brother, who seemed best amused when all the lives of those around him had been thrown into confusion.

Lydia had witnessed this for all her life, in small ways and in greater ones, and knowing well the hold her uncle had upon her father—upon all of them—it brought her pain to notice that her father was too bitter and ashamed to meet her eyes.

He said, "The magistrate's boy came this morning, before you had wakened. He did not say why, only that I was wanted. And when I arrived, I found *them*. And the magistrate holding a letter from Reuben assuring him I'd volunteered for the honor." He frowned at the floorboards. "What else could I do?"

"Nothing." Lydia, turning her anger away from her father to where it belonged, reached to take her spare apron down from its hooked peg on the wall at her side, and with calm, careful movements, she pinned it in place so it covered the less perfect folds of her gown. "You could do nothing, and neither can we, but endure what my uncle seems wholly convinced we cannot."

Over their heads, from the little room under the eaves just above, came the creaking of bed ropes and then the soft thud of bare feet being swung to the floorboards.

Lydia looked to her father, who'd noticed as well.

With a nod to the back stairs he said, "You had best go warn Violet, before she comes down. Reassure her there's nothing to fear. They *are* gentlemen."

Lydia clamped her mouth hard on the truth she knew well: that no Frenchman could ever be counted a gentleman. But as she turned from her father she heard the sharp edge to her voice, like the blade of a knife not yet drawn from a wound, as she answered him, "Then let us pray, for our sakes and their own, they take care to remember it."

JEAN-PHILIPPE

S HE WANTED THEM DEAD. Not just elsewhere and out of that house, but beneath the ground, dead, or else strung from the nearest available tree. He'd encountered such hatred before, but from men he had recently captured or wounded. This was the first time he'd met that same look in the eyes of a woman.

In truth it had caught him off guard, when she'd first met his gaze—and she hadn't done that till he'd thanked her for taking the justaucorps from him to dry by the fire. Beforehand and after, she'd seemed most determined to act as though he were invisible. He'd found that annoying. It wasn't that he was so vain as to think every woman should show him attention, nor even that he was accustomed to getting it, but for some reason he would have liked hers.

For his part, he'd had trouble noticing anyone else since she'd burst in upon them, her hair falling free of its pins underneath the plain cap that was soaked through in spots from the force of the rain, like the bright-yellow gown with its hem rather more wet than rain could have made it. He'd thought of a morning, more years ago now than he cared to remember, when he had been left at the edge of the woods to keep watch in the deadly gray hours before dawn, and all in his view had been dreary and dark, and the chill and the damp had crept through him so deeply he'd felt he might well turn to ice. And then sunrise had come—not a gradual brightening, but all at once, unexpectedly, piercing the clouds in a single, straight, glorious beam of clear light that had warmed him and brought his cold limbs back to life.

He'd felt that again at the moment she'd come through the door of the kitchen.

It could have been none other than his woman from the water, for the color of the gown was unmistakable. She'd been young—hardly out of her girlhood. Her feet had been bare and her cheeks had been bright and her smile had been wide, but the instant she'd caught sight of him and de Brassart, that smile had died.

He had not seen it since.

He had found that annoying as well, though he hadn't known why, so he'd focused his thoughts and attention where they should most properly be, on her father and brothers—for, given the likeness in feature and coloring, they were all clearly one family. And while the father appeared to be friendly, the brothers were yet unknown entities.

Jean-Philippe's life and career had depended for so long upon his ability to gauge the minds and intentions of men, that the measure he took at first meeting a stranger was usually true, but he trusted it more if he tested that first swift impression by careful and calm observation.

The younger brother had the air of recklessness that came with youth and arrogance. The way he'd stepped toward his sister when she'd first come in might have appeared to some a gallant move to place himself between her and potential harm, yet Jean-Philippe had seen it as a move designed to stop the woman in the yellow gown from interfering in a situation that the younger brother was enjoying. Not from cruelty or from spite, but in the way a hound kept tightly leashed enjoys the scent and promise of a new pursuit and new adventure.

He was taller than his older brother, with a cleaner line of jaw and eyes that held a quick and keen intelligence. A young man Jean-Philippe might have not minded having under his command a few years hence, once time and life had taught him caution.

But it was the elder brother with the lighter hair, the one who'd stood beside the hearth while they were in the kitchen, who would most need watching.

There was something in his quiet, steady gaze that was

unsettling. Jean-Philippe had often seen that same expression—or more properly, the absence of it—in the eyes of soldiers who had faced the darkness of a battle and been lost to it, consumed by it. Such men were unpredictable. Such men, in his experience, were dangerous.

At dinner in the afternoon the elder son had held his silence, although in all fairness it had been a mostly silent meal. Uncomfortable.

It had been, for Jean-Philippe, a disagreeable discovery to see this family kept a slave. He knew it was as common here as in Quebec—perhaps more common—but from the opinion he had formed of Monsieur Wilde he'd hoped…

But there she'd been, a tall girl with a slender build and deep-brown skin, her hair bound tightly back beneath a cap that matched her mistress's. She, too, had barely met his eyes, but when she had, it had been with a guarded watchfulness. She'd carried out the common dish of vegetables and meat at dinner but had set it down with a hard thump before retreating to the kitchen, where she'd stayed, leaving the family and their "guests" to serve themselves, which he had done with little confidence.

Nothing he'd eaten thus far in this province had led him to think that the food would be good. And observing how fiercely the woman in yellow had frowned while she'd seasoned it over the hearth, he'd been doubly wary. He'd tasted his dinner with caution…and found it surprisingly excellent. She'd cooked with wine, which he hadn't expected.

But then, there were many things here that he hadn't expected.

His mind, so used to danger, might indeed see threats where there were none. And yet, no man could live a day ahead of death for all the years he had without gaining the sense to know when things were wrong. There was something at play here, some deep current running a turbulent course through this house that had been here before their arrival, and as when he faced a new river he found himself seeking to study that current, the better to steer in it.

Over dinner it had become clear to him that he was not the only one there keeping a close watch upon the elder brother. Nor was he the only one relieved when, at the ending of the meal, the elder brother had done nothing more than push his chair back and excuse himself, and gone upstairs in private.

Jean-Philippe had marked the sound and the direction of the footsteps as they crossed the floor above, and while he did not know the layout of the upstairs rooms he knew the elder brother's was the room directly over the small chamber off the kitchen that he would himself be sharing with de Brassart.

Theirs was not a large room. Jean-Philippe had not found much within it that could occupy his time during the long hours that had stretched between their dinner and the evening meal, but having no alternative he'd focused on the tasks he could control. His coat had dried, and he had brushed it. He had polished every button, and the buckles of his shoes and belt, and then his sword.

A sword had never been his favorite weapon. He preferred a long gun or a hatchet in his hand, but the English had removed those useful things from him at Fort Niagara and allowed him only, under the surrender's terms, to keep his sword—a weapon, he presumed, that they thought fitting for an officer.

Like many things that came with rank its ornaments did little to enhance its practicality. The hilt was showy, done in silver figured with heroic scenes whose players he, from lack of education, did not recognize. His uncle, who had given him the sword some years ago, had not known either who the heroes on the hilt might be. The blade, to him, was more important, etched with the words: *Draw me not without cause; sheathe me not without honor.*

It wasn't a motto unique to this sword. Jean-Philippe had seen it writ on other blades as well. The only thing that marked this one as his was that his uncle had paid handsomely to have the name "de Sabran" etched above the motto in bold lettering. "A name that has long served the king," his uncle had reminded him. "See that you bear it proudly."

There was little scope for pride, he thought, in being made a prisoner.

But still he cleaned the sword and slid it back into its scabbard and arranged it on the mattress of his bed against the wall so he would have it at his back while he was sleeping.

That would not be for some hours. The rain was still pelting in fury against the small room's only window, but from what he saw of the sky and the cloud-filtered light he could tell it was late afternoon, not yet evening. His muscles and mind raised a silent and impatient protest against their continued confinement.

Not far past the window the watery line of the trees at the edge of the forest was beckoning. He found it galling to think he could not even walk outdoors now without asking permission. And worse, he could not even ask for permission without also asking de Brassart to translate his words.

It was maddening.

He almost never cursed aloud, especially when there were women standing in the next room within earshot, but the words he muttered now beneath his breath would have been impolite to translate.

She could not have heard them. Even though his chamber door stood open she was by the hearth, too far away. Yet from the corner of his eye he caught a swirl of yellow skirts against the floorboards as she turned to lift an iron cooking pot onto its hook with clanging force. And when she shot a glance at him it told him very plainly that she wished, as he did, that he was not here.

⤜⤝

De Brassart was taking his time getting ready for bed. He was one of those men who had rituals. Vanities. He was still carefully rolling his stockings when Jean-Philippe asked him, "What was it she said to you?"

"Who?"

"Our young hostess. At supper."

Their supper, just over an hour ago, had been a simpler affair than their earlier dinner. The woman in yellow had served them herself, and de Brassart had asked her a question she'd answered with firmness.

De Brassart now shrugged. "I asked if they owned but the one slave, and she said in fact they owned none, because one person cannot own another."

"She said that?"

"She did. Which proves that she knows nothing of the law, or that I did not understand her speech correctly. They have strange ways of expression here," de Brassart said. "Their English is not always proper English. Their words and turns of phrase are as corrupted as the French your people speak, and I confess some meanings may escape me."

Jean-Philippe let the small insult pass by, being used to the active disdain of those men, like de Brassart, who lived by their status and gains in the towns and frontiers of New France while insisting the ways of Old France were superior. He needed no man to tell him his worth, nor the worth of his colony.

"Perhaps," de Brassart said, "I can devise a better way for her to use that pretty mouth of hers, while we are here." His tone and smile left no room to misunderstand his meaning.

And that insult, while not aimed at him, was one that Jean-Philippe could *not* let pass. "That's vulgar talk, unworthy of an officer, and I would have you take it back."

"Or what?" De Brassart arched a lazy brow. "You'd call me out? Here, in this corner of a godforsaken colony? It seems a lot of bother." He'd have shrugged it off, but Jean-Philippe persisted, still more calmly.

"I would have you take it back."

"Oh, fine. I take it back, then. But the days will pass more slowly if I'm not to be allowed any amusement. Still," de Brassart said, "it is of little consequence. I cannot think we'll be here long before we are exchanged. There are sufficient English officers imprisoned at Quebec. I'm sure the governor is even now arranging a cartel."

A possibility, thought Jean-Philippe. Though no cartel would suit him if it did not also free his men. His thoughts turned once more, darkly, to their whereabouts and comfort, for he knew they might be lying in the open at the mercy of the rain tonight, or crowded on the stone floor of a prison plagued by rising damp and sickness, while he lay stretched full length upon a clean straw mattress on a sturdy bedstead with a blanket of good wool.

His thoughts grew darker still, and did not let him sleep. Not even when de Brassart had, at last, stopped fussing with his things and fallen silent for a while until beginning an uneven snore that, in its turn, seemed to awake the man above them, who began to pace the floor with careful steps as though he did not wish to wake the others from their sleep.

Jean-Philippe was used to being on his guard. He'd lived the best part of his life in camps and forts and battlegrounds, and while he might be ill accustomed to domestic life and to the noises of an ordinary family in the night, his senses still were tuned to know which sounds were ordinary and which meant a threat.

Above, the elder brother ceased his pacing and a door creaked open, quietly. The footsteps slowly and with stealth crossed overhead, and then as cautiously began descending the back stairs. They took their time. They paused, and came into the kitchen, where they paused again.

Within the chamber Jean-Philippe lay still and quiet, feigning sleep, but tensed in every muscle and aware of the man's presence on the other side of their closed door. His sword lay where he'd placed it, in its scabbard at his back, and he prepared himself to reach around and use it if it came to that.

The silence stretched.

De Brassart snored, and snorted once, and rolled.

And then the moment broke. The man within the kitchen moved away, his footsteps pausing farther off, then starting up more heavily, as though he'd put on boots. The kitchen door was opened, once, and shut with firmness.

Years of instinct told him that the danger, for tonight at least, was over. Jean-Philippe relaxed his body, but his mind took longer to comply. When sleep did finally come it brought not rest but troubled dreams, in which he was again back in that cold and dreary forest, keeping watch alone, his limbs like ice. Except this time when dawn arrived—still in that sudden spear of golden light—it swiftly moved away from him and even though he followed it and tracked it through the trees against the darkness, it stayed always out of reach.

CHARLEY

I DIDN'T REALIZE I WAS playing with my bracelet until Malaika commented, "You're going to break that."

She was right. It was made of glass beads strung by hand on a stretchy band, not meant to handle continual stress. I had made it at a sleepover in high school, with a friend who'd had a jewelry-making kit. I still remembered just how hard it was to keep those beads together in their pattern, neat and smooth, without them sliding off the other end and spilling out onto the carpet, but after hours of trying, I had conquered them, and more than ten years later those same beads were still in order.

Usually the bracelet lay buried under more expensive items in my jewelry box, and probably only Freud knew why I'd chosen to wear it today.

Maybe I'd needed some reassurance that one thing in my life was holding together the way that it should, because so far my Monday was not going well.

"So," I summarized, "we won't have windows?"

Sam Abrams raised one shoulder in a shrug that managed to be both accepting and apologetic. "Not the ones we planned for. Sorry."

Great, I thought. The first hour of the first day of our restoration work and I hadn't even made it to the door before discovering we had a problem.

I'd actually been happy for a moment when I'd pulled into the parking lot and seen the men at work already, with the little backhoe digging purposefully into the earth as it began to excavate a trench around the old foundation. Then I'd seen Malaika standing to the side, arms folded, talking to a dark-haired man I'd recognized as Sam from his broad shoulders and the deep tan of his muscled arms against his plain white T-shirt. If Malaika's frown of concentration hadn't warned me, I'd have known from Sam's expression as he turned to say "Good morning" that my morning wouldn't be remotely good.

Not that it was anybody's fault. The expert subcontractor whose job it was to deal with all the windows couldn't have foreseen he'd fall and dislocate his shoulder with such force that he'd need therapy and time before returning to his job. And I felt sorry for him.

But the delay Sam was talking about would mean our windows would not be in place by the time we had set in our schedule. And finding someone with the same credentials and experience who could step in to take over on short notice wouldn't be an easy task. Working on heritage buildings was a specialized skill.

Malaika's frown was fading. She was not so much an optimist as she was simply stubborn, and I'd noticed that she didn't get held back too long by obstacles. "Well," she said, "there must be an alternative. Let's think, now."

Sam was doing that already, thoughtfully taking stock of the windows on the second floor, eyes narrowing against the morning sun.

Now that I'd been told Sam was a Mohawk, I could see it for myself a little. Not that there was any one way for a Mohawk man to look—I knew that much from my time at the Hall-McPhail Museum planning reenactments and exhibits, when I'd worked in consultation with a few Mohawk historians, one of whom had been a blue-eyed blond.

They'd taught me, among other things, respectful terminology.

The oldest of the men had called himself Native American, the second had preferred the term Indigenous, and their younger colleague had assured me there was no collective term that everyone agreed upon, advising me the best thing was to learn which nation somebody belonged to, and refer to that instead. Which had made sense.

I knew that "Mohawk" wasn't what they called themselves in their own language, but I couldn't call the proper word to mind just at the moment. I was trying to remember it when suddenly Malaika's voice broke in.

"Sam, you could do this," she said, "couldn't you?"

Still looking up, he paused before he answered. "I was thinking about that." Another pause, and then, "Not all at once, like Jake would do, but if I took a couple every week and did them in the evenings, yeah, I think I could."

"And match the price?"

The corners of his mouth quirked upward briefly. "Tell you what. You buy me lunch, I'll match the price."

"Okay, then."

They shook hands, and that was that. Sam put his hardhat on again and gave us both a friendly nod before he walked across to check the progress of the backhoe and the workmen who were following behind it in the trench, doing more careful digging up against the stone foundation wall, with shovels.

Since Malaika was my boss, I didn't question her decision. But once Sam was out of hearing, I said very casually, "He's qualified to do that, is he? Carpentry?"

"You've seen the fireplace mantel in my dining room? He made that. And the dining table, too. If anything," she said, "he's overqualified. He's got a degree in architecture, too. Will you just stop with that poor bracelet? Have you had coffee yet? No? That's your problem, then. Let's get you some." She led me the few steps along the side walkway to where our staff entrance led into the kitchen of the already-renovated Victorian side of the Wilde House.

This kitchen, half the size of the older colonial one, had been "updated" back in the mid-1980s. The cabinets were white with wood trim and the counters were gold-flecked white Formica and the walls seemed to have trouble deciding if they were supposed to be beige or pale pink, so adjusted themselves to the lighting.

This morning, with sun coming in through the two windows—one at the back of the house and one over the sink—the walls had apparently opted for beige. A safe choice.

I privately suspected that the coffee maker was a relic of the 1980s, too. It made a lot of noise and steam but in the end what it produced was only faintly recognizable as coffee.

Still, this morning I was ready to accept caffeine in any form. I leaned against the counter while Malaika brewed a pot. While she was filling cups for each of us I ventured, "So, Frank told me all about the ghost."

"He likes that story."

"I did, too. In fact," I added, "I've been thinking." And I told her my ideas for the ways that we could use the story here at the museum for exhibits and events.

Malaika handed me my coffee with a thoughtful look. "I like it."

"Could I slip that into the agenda for the board meeting tonight, under 'new business'?"

"Sure. Just brace yourself," she warned me. "Sharon and her friends will fight it."

"Sharon would fight anything I suggested."

"True enough." She sugared her own coffee with a smile. "At least it livens up the meetings. I might even stay awake through this one."

✥

"I don't like it."

I wasn't surprised to hear Eve Downey echoing Sharon's objection. Eve was one of the two trustees who always followed Sharon's lead, although the second of them—Harvey—had probably turned things around in his mind and believed he was actually leading. Harvey was head of the Kiersted Group, named for himself, a commercial development firm that appeared to be somehow connected to everyone and everything in the area. Word was he had politicians as well in his pocket. The mayor and a congressman's aide both went golfing with Harvey on weekends. He must have learned his smile from them. It was practiced and a shade too broad and lacking any real conviction. He smiled at Eve now, flirting with her as he often did. In jeans, his cotton oxford shirt rolled to his elbows, with his hair too uniformly dark for someone on the other side of fifty, Harvey looked like what he was—a middle-aged man stubbornly refusing to let go of youth.

In that, he was a match for Eve. She looked amazing, and I gave her credit for the hard work she put into that—the perfect hair, darker than Harvey's but expertly done and done often enough that her roots never showed, and the tightly trim figure that showed the effects of her hours at the gym, and the makeup that didn't look heavy until you got close. But her jawline and neck were beginning to soften and let her down anyway, and I felt sorry for her about that, because she was the sort of a woman who wouldn't adjust to age well.

Sharon, on the other hand, had embraced middle age and the power it brought. Back in high school, she'd probably been the head cheerleader, queen of the popular girls, used to getting her way. But while Eve hadn't ever left high school, not really—she'd just moved from being a student to teaching them, only retiring a year ago—Sharon had moved on and upward, becoming the wife of a local policeman who now was the chief of patrol for the county. He seemed nice enough, and was certainly capable, but I suspected his rise through the ranks had been driven by Sharon's ambition. She knew how to lead from behind.

It was how she'd positioned herself even now, at the table.

The board of trustees for the Wilde House Museum met here, in the dining room on the Victorian side of the house. It was one of the few rooms downstairs that had kept its Victorian trappings. The ceiling had lovely crown moldings and plasterwork around a glass chandelier, and an elegant bow window draped with long curtains looked over the lawn to the edge of the trees, which were blending now into the darkening sky of the evening.

Not having a vote, I preferred to sit off to the side by the marble-faced fireplace and wait until I was called upon to supply facts or opinions, as curator.

This gave me the advantage of observing all the personal dynamics at the table. Field Marshal Montgomery, in the Second World War, had said something about soldiers needing to know how their own smaller battles fit into the bigger one, and I had learned this was useful advice, so I always tried now to take stock of the whole field around me before I marched onto it.

From where I sat, it was easy to see where the battle lines lay in the board of trustees.

Three trustees hadn't made it tonight to the meeting. Our legal adviser was sick, and one of my favorite trustees, a young single mother who owned her own fashion boutique on the main street, was still at her eldest boy's Little League game. And our most flamboyant trustee, Don Petrella—an actor who'd shot to cult status some years ago playing a crime-fighting vampire on TV—was off on a film shoot, as we had been told several times by his wife, who was also a trustee.

Rosina Petrella was little and likeable, one of those women whose age scarcely mattered because they were almost like pixies or fairies who seemed to be living on some different plane from the rest of us. She moved with fluttery grace and she smiled like she meant it. If she had a fault it was being *too* fluttery, too indecisive. But she was quick and the notes that she took of the meetings were nearly verbatim, which made her a great secretary.

And tonight she marked the neutral territory between the two factions of the board. Sharon and Harvey and Eve hadn't sat all together, but from their shared looks and the way they supported each other's opinions it would have been clear to an outsider they were a team.

At the head of the long polished table, Malaika sat coolly and calmly in charge, while Frank lounged in his chair to her right. Frank was no politician. If he thought a person was full of it, he let them know, by his facial expression if nothing else, and his muttered asides, if you managed to catch them, could be entertaining. Certainly they'd been amusing Tracy Chow, our treasurer, who had the seat across from Frank tonight.

Tracy and Harvey got under each other's skin. Harvey would have looked you in the eye and sworn he wasn't homophobic or a racist, but he seemed to make assumptions that proved otherwise and when he told a joke it was most often inappropriate. I'd been told that he had commented, when Tracy joined the board, that it was logical that someone of her ancestry had gone into accounting, and that Tracy had replied she hadn't been aware that people born in Idaho had any greater skills at math than anybody else. Which had made all the other trustees laugh, and from that point there'd been a thread of friction between Harvey and our treasurer, made stronger by the fact that Tracy's longtime live-in partner was a woman.

I might have been persuaded that, in Tracy's case, the problem wasn't Harvey's homophobia but his belief that every woman ought to be attracted to his manliness. He'd side-eyed me, as well, as though suspicious of a woman who refused to do his bidding when he smiled.

Malaika handled him with grace and skill. She let him feel important while not letting him take over. She was good at running meetings, keeping everybody moving smoothly through the night's agenda.

She had opened with the news about the window subcontractor and his injury, and there had been a quick vote of approval for Sam Abrams taking on the extra restoration work. There had been reports from Tracy on the new donations we'd received on Saturday from people at the ribbon-cutting ceremony, and from Sharon on the number of new members we had gained. Eve, with her teaching background, was in charge of education, and reported on her efforts to engage the local schools.

There'd been a minor bump when Frank had named the people

he had picked to join him on the subcommittee that would be in charge of vetting artifacts donated to and bought by the museum. "Lara," he'd said, starting with the trustee who was off at her son's baseball game, "and Tracy, and Dave Becker."

David Becker wasn't on our board, but subcommittee members didn't have to be. He owned a fine antiques store and had been the local auctioneer at one time, and still worked as an appraiser, which in my view made him an excellent addition to the acquisitions committee, but since nobody had asked my view I hadn't made a comment.

Harvey had made some remark about Dave's work and conflicts of interest, and Frank had fired back, "You'd know all about *that*, Harvey, wouldn't you?"

And then Malaika had settled them both and a vote had been taken, Frank's choices approved, and the meeting had moved on.

The next item on the agenda had been less contentious: a Fall Harvest Festival on the museum grounds.

This had been Sharon's idea, I gathered, a couple of meetings ago before I had been hired, and she'd lit up tonight when discussing it. "I've got the spinners and weavers, they're going to put on a whole demonstration, and six of the eight craft table places have already sold, so we'll probably want to add more. Isaac Fisher says we can use his little donkey for children to ride on. And Frank, you're still bringing your cider press?"

Frank had assured her he was, and when Tracy had asked where the apples were coming from, Frank had replied not to worry. "I'll call in some favors."

Malaika had added we'd need to apply for a permit for serving the cider, and Harvey had said, very sure, "*I'll* take care of the permits."

Eve had agreed to make up the promotional flyers. Rosina had said Don had offered to come dressed in character from his TV show. "He's always a big draw at Comic Con," she'd told us proudly, "and he figured people could make a five-dollar donation to the museum fund to have their picture taken with him."

Even though the discussion had gone on a little long, it had been nice to watch the board working in harmony, each member giving something, no one arguing.

But now we'd come to new business, and all that had changed.

"I don't like it," Eve told me again. "I mean, with respect, it just takes us outside of our mandate. We agreed—and you can read this in the package you were given when we hired you—we agreed our purpose was to show the role that Captain Wilde played in the War of Independence. Maybe you didn't read that part? But it's a very specific focus, and this proposal's asking us to go too far beyond that."

Not rising to her accusations of my ignorance, I only said, "I know what our mission statement says. But this still involves Captain Benjamin Wilde. He was living here, too, at the time."

Harvey came to Eve's defense. "But it's the wrong war, that's what Eve means. Captain Wilde didn't fight in the French and Indian War."

"That we know of," Malaika concurred without really agreeing. "Though some would say *that* war was really when our revolution began."

Sharon smiled the small condescending smile usually aimed at me, and with a turn of her auburn head asked, "Are we rewriting history? Or talking about whether this fits our mandate? Because I'm with Eve, I think this takes us too far off course."

Frank, who'd held his tongue this long, said, "Oh, come on. You're fine with Don coming dressed as a vampire to harvest days, you didn't think that was 'too far off course,' but you'll raise an objection to this?"

Sharon searched for an answer to that while Rosina replied that her husband's TV show was perfectly relevant. "Don't you remember?" she asked Frank. "In the opening credits each week they showed us that Don's character became a vampire *during* the Revolution."

He looked at her sideways a moment and drew breath to

argue, then closed his mouth firmly as though he'd decided it would be a waste of his time to debate a fictional vampire detective's connection to history. Instead he said, "Look, I'm the only damn Wilde at this table, and *I* think it sounds like a good way to draw people in."

Sharon paid no attention to him. She was looking at me when she countered, "You can't just start serving up legends and fairy tales as though they're facts. It's not right. It's misleading our visitors."

Harvey said, "Let's take a vote."

Predictably, it was three votes to three, with poor Rosina hovering a moment like a bird between two trees, forced to decide which branch to land on.

In the end she raised her hand for "No," and sent me an apologetic look. "I'm sorry, it's a nice idea, but as Sharon says, it's just a story, really. If we knew that it was real…if we had proof, then that would change things." Her glance darted from my face to Sharon's. "Wouldn't it?"

Magnanimous in victory, Sharon said, "Of course. When we find any proof Captain Wilde had a sister who had a romance with a captured French officer, then we can open this up for discussion again." But her tone made it clear she considered the chances of that to be almost as likely as finding a unicorn. "Shall we move on?"

I didn't let my face betray my disappointment. I had learned to pick my battles and I knew this was a minor one. It was the losing, really, that stung more than what I'd lost.

The meeting ended, and the trustees mingled briefly in the kitchen before leaving, one by one. Malaika touched my arm as she went out. "I'll see you in the morning."

Frank hung back and would have walked me to my car, but I was keen to have a moment on my own. "That's okay, go ahead," I told him. "I'll be fine. I'll finish locking up."

He gave a nod and said, "Don't let them get you down."

I didn't plan to. In the greater scheme of things, I thought, with all that I was dealing with, three board members who seemed bent on opposing me was hardly the worst problem I was facing. And whatever Sharon, Eve, and Harvey did, there were still seven members on that board who liked me well enough, and gave me their support. But knowing all that didn't take away my irritation.

I did my rounds and checked the rooms and doors and windows, seeking peace as always from the calm routine of putting things in order.

In my office I made sure that things were perfectly in place. I closed the blinds and cleared my desk of all the notes I'd used that day while I was writing my proposal for the board meeting. And then I reconsidered.

"You don't think I know my job?" I asked an imaginary Sharon and her allies, underneath my breath. "You don't think I'll find proof about the Wilde girl and her officer?" I took the notes out of the drawer again and stacked them firmly on the corner of the desk where I kept things I hadn't finished. "Well, just watch me," was my parting challenge to the empty air, and feeling satisfied with that I went downstairs.

The staff entrance door had to be locked from the outside. The security light here was on a motion sensor that sometimes acknowledged you were there and sometimes didn't, and tonight it had clicked on for thirty seconds before clicking off again, refusing stubbornly to "see" me even when I waved my arms.

It wasn't raining, but a bank of clouds still blanketed the moon and I was forced to bring my cell phone out to give me extra light so I could fit the key into the lock. The cell phone made a faint but useful flashlight, too, that helped guide my steps along the side of the house.

When the walls of the Victorian section gave way to the wider siding of the old colonial part, I slowed my pace a little and searched with the beam of my "flashlight" for the edge of the trench that the workmen had been digging. Finding it, I walked past it carefully but my foot still brushed a pile of excavated dirt and sent a scattering of pebbles bouncing down the hard bricks of the walkway.

And something, *not* a pebble, struck a half a step in front of me and landed with a small, metallic clink.

I stopped, and bent, and searched for it. A disc that nestled in my palm, its one side slightly domed, its other bearing a squared central bump, and made of a material that, even as I rubbed away the clinging dirt, I recognized as brass.

And then I brushed more dirt away and shone the cell phone light directly on it and I recognized exactly what it was. I'd catalogued enough of them when I'd been with the Hall-McPhail Museum.

It was a button, very old and showing traces still of gilt. A button that, back in the mid-eighteenth century, would have been part of a line of bright buttons sewn onto the uniform of a French officer.

I felt a tiny, thrilling tingle of discovery.

Suddenly a stronger light flashed on behind me. Startled, I looked back toward the side door and the motion sensor activated light above it. Nobody was there. The light shone brightly on the empty steps and walkway for a moment, then clicked off again.

The wind, I thought, or else a leaf.

But as I looked away, my gaze fell sharply on a smaller light that captured my attention.

It was shining at the dark edge of the forest, where there had been, moments earlier, no light at all.

Suspended maybe two feet from the ground, it slightly swayed from side to side as though in time with someone's steps. A clear light, burning warmly yellow like a lantern in a hand.

My heart leapt hard into my throat. I didn't realize that my fingers had closed tightly round the button in a fist until I felt the metal edges pressing cold into my palm. I didn't realize, either, that I'd made a sound when I had caught my breath. Until the light stopped moving.

My heart dislodged itself and dropped. Began to race against my ribs.

The light stayed there hanging a moment, then traveled away from me into the trees and the darkness, along the old path to the cove.

The same path I'd taken with Frank when he'd told me, "Some fools in this town think he still walks these woods with his lantern, the same as he did on the night he was killed. Waiting for Lydia Wilde to come follow him, so he can light her way down to the water."

LYDIA

H E'D LOST A BUTTON from his uniform. She'd seen him pacing slowly on the shaded strip of grass beside the house, as
though he knew exactly where the thing had fallen and, by force of
will, could make it reappear. But the gap remained along the long
bright line of buttons down the center of his rich blue waistcoat.

She guessed the loss would not improve his mood.

In the few days they'd been here she'd noted some differences
between the Frenchmen. The one who spoke English, Lieutenant
de Brassart, at least seemed determined to try to be charming,
as though he would have them think well of him, but the more
silent Lieutenant de Sabran appeared to care nothing at all what
they thought.

He was not impolite. He had manners. But while he was the
first to tell them thank you—in his language, not in theirs—he
never said it with Mr. de Brassart's gallantry, as if it mattered less
how one delivered such a sentiment than that the words were said.

A strange sort of officer, surely. Like one of the stones that
her father was digging this week from the orchard—unpolished,
unyielding, and always unpleasant to find in your way.

She had to grudgingly admit he had the height and form and
face to be a very handsome man. His nose was straight, as were his
brows; his jaw was strong, his gaze was steady. But each time she
met his eyes they held a hard expression that fell halfway between
anger and impatience.

Had it not been a ridiculous notion, she might have thought
she was annoying *him*.

And yet it was ridiculous, because their paths but rarely crossed.

He rose at dawn. She knew this because when she came downstairs each morning he was up and gone outside to walk, while yet his friend de Brassart lay abed. On their second day here he had asked, through translation, her father's permission to walk in the woods and her father had granted it if he would promise to keep near the house, for the terms of the French officers' paroles did not allow them to go farther than a mile from where they lodged without a magistrate's approval.

On those walks, Mr. de Sabran wore his sword. Joseph had raised a grumbling protest but their father had replied that by the terms of their surrender the French officers had been allowed to keep their arms. "Our officers, when captured by the French," he'd said, "are granted the same honor."

"I've seen how the French treat their captives," had been Joseph's forceful reminder. "And honor did not enter into it."

But as in all things, their father prevailed and his word was respected, and Mr. de Sabran had worn his sword.

He was wearing it now, as he paced at the side of the house with his head bent in search of that one errant button.

Lydia, reaching to harvest the beans from their trellis, glanced over a third time and drew the attention of both of her brothers who, just for this morning, were working together to mend the rail fence that encircled the garden.

Benjamin gave his quick grin. "Does he interest you?"

Joseph had once been the slowest of them all to show his anger. Now it flashed with violence as he set a post with force into the ground and asked his younger brother, "Do you ever think before you speak? She has an even greater cause than I to hate the French."

"I spoke in jest," said Benjamin. Already he was taking up the stubborn stance that meant he was preparing for a fight, or at the very least a war of words, and Lydia tried calming the unsettled moment as her mother might have done.

She told them, "Surely the offense, if there is any to be taken, would be mine to take. And I take none, for Benjamin is right. I find that officer of interest."

Which instantly made both her brothers stop their quarrel.

"Not for the reason you're thinking," she added, for it was an easy thing to read their shocked expressions. "But because he is so different from the other one."

Benjamin's smile returned, teasing. "You've grown up with Father and William and Daniel and Joseph and me, and yet you can find it surprising all men aren't alike?"

Joseph, in a former time, might well have teased her also. Now he only aimed a short nod at the pacing French lieutenant. "He's a Canadian, that's why he's different. The other's from France."

"Really?" Benjamin looked, as well. "How can you tell that?"

"The one with the red waistcoat and the white breeches and blue on his collar, his regiment came straight from France. The La Sarre. But *that* uniform," he said, and nodded again at Lieutenant de Sabran, "is not from any regiment. It's worn by those who serve in the Marine, as they are called. Their rank and file they mostly bring from France, but all their officers, or nearly all, are born and bred Canadian."

Lydia frowned. "The Marine? Do they serve in the navy, then?"

"No. They are land troops. They travel by water sometimes, but they guard the forts of the frontier and have a reputation, justly earned, for ruthlessness. It's said they send their officers as children to the Indians to learn their ways of fighting, and in truth to fight them is like fighting shadows in the trees."

She found this chilling, and yet curious. "Like Captain Rogers's Rangers?"

Joseph shrugged and did a thing he rarely did: he spat upon the ground. "If Captain Rogers was the devil, and the men he led were criminals."

He said no more, but drew back from the fence and went to fetch more rails.

Into the silence that was left behind him, Benjamin said

thoughtfully, "Well, that at least explains why they aren't friendly with each other."

"Who?"

"Our two reluctant guests. You've surely noticed?"

She shook her head, hoisting the basket of beans on her hip.

Benjamin leaned on the half-mended fence. "For men who speak a common language, they say little to each other. Now I know why. Like ourselves and the British, they're two different species of men altogether. And I'd imagine the French from France look on their loyal Canadian colonists with the same brand of disdain as the British do us."

౼౿

On Sunday afternoon, Mr. de Brassart proved that point with perfect eloquence.

In the parlor after dinner he arranged himself with practiced grace in one of the two high-backed chairs set near the fireless hearth and looked around appreciatively. The ornaments within the room were spare, but of good quality: an eight-day clock that counted off the moments with authority, a candlestick of silver set beside the inlaid ink chest on her father's desk, and still more silver gleaming from the sconces on the plastered walls that had been painted, like the shutters and the wainscoting, a calming shade of blue.

Lydia, sitting in her own chair by the window where the filtered sunlight cast few shadows, had just set a fresh, new page of paper on the boards she used for drawing, and was fitting a new black lead pencil in its holder when de Brassart sighed and said, "I have so missed the company of cultured men."

Lydia was clearly not included in that sentiment. She was the only woman in the room.

The only woman in the house, in fact, since Violet, having Sundays off, had gone as she did every week to the Cross Harbor meetinghouse.

Lydia herself had been, like all the Wildes, baptized and raised within the faith her English forebears had brought with them to Long Island, though the nearest church of that Episcopalian faith was down in Hempstead, and her father did not think it necessary to make such a journey save at special times like Easter and Epiphany.

But Violet's mother, while she'd lived, had been devoutly Baptist, and now every Sunday Violet carried on that same devotion, rising early, putting on her best blue gown, and joining Joseph in the small boat for the trip across the bay.

Joseph's weekly visits to Cross Harbor had been going on for years as well, but for a different reason: he spent Sundays in the dining room and parlor over Mr. Fisher's store, as he had done since he'd asked Sarah Fisher to marry him. She'd told him yes, and worn his ring of promise on her finger these four years, and written weekly to him when he'd gone to build ships at Oswego, and though Joseph had returned wrapped in a silence that had smothered all their talk of wedding plans, Sarah seemed prepared to wait.

That kind of patience was inspiring to Lydia, and totally beyond the reach of Benjamin, who even now was finding it impossible to sit still. He'd always disliked Sundays for their lack of entertainment, and he seemed to seize upon de Brassart's comment as an opening for argument.

"But surely French society," said Benjamin, his light tone edged with mockery, "is far more cultured than our own."

His tone made Lieutenant de Sabran, who sat in a fair imitation of Benjamin's boredom between the cold hearth and the door, shift his gaze very slightly, without too much interest, from where he'd had it focused for these several minutes past on the unchanging view of clearing, trees, and sky beyond the window. He glanced at Benjamin in such a way that Lydia felt certain he'd just taken the full measure of her brother.

But de Brassart took the words at their apparent meaning, and replied: "Society in France, of course, but I have been away from France so long I have forgotten what it is to see a shelf of books, much less a man who reads them."

He was speaking of her father, who had settled as he liked to every Sunday with a well-worn, calf-bound volume of *The Works of the Most Reverend Dr. Tillotson*, to read his favorite discourses and sermons.

Her father looked up from the page with indulgence. "You flatter me, Mr. de Brassart, but I'm sure that there are many men in Canada who read."

Still mocking, Benjamin amended this. "Just not as well or widely as the French."

"Indeed. They are not men of thought," de Brassart said. "They much prefer to run about the woods and fight what we would call *la guerre à la sauvage*, you know this term? *La petite guerre*, the little war, that would attack as a defense and strike and run away, and never in the open. This is not how we fight our wars in France. It is not civilized."

Lydia's intent had been to keep out of the conversation— not because she had nothing to say, for the truth was exactly the opposite, and in her family the women had always been given the same room as men to express their opinions—but because she didn't wish to interact with the French officers beyond her basic duties as the mistress of the house. Still, she found it hard to let a lack of logic pass unchallenged. "War, Mr. de Brassart, by its nature is not civilized, no matter how it's fought."

He disagreed. "It is of course a credit to your gentle nature that you think this, but this is why wars are left to men, for women always would be too kind in their hearts. And war has always been a necessary thing to guard our way of life."

She wondered what he would have thought if he had known just how unkind her heart was at that moment, but her father had already broken into their exchange.

He said, "My late wife, who was raised a Quaker, would have

set you straight on that point, sir, for she believed that war was anything but necessary."

De Brassart's frown was faint. "Forgive me, I am not familiar with this term, 'a Quaker.'"

"It's a faith, begun in England and quite common in these parts. A faith of fellowship, that holds that any conflict can be solved by peaceful means, and without violence."

"And your wife was of this faith?"

"She was."

"But you are not?"

"No." Taking up his book again, her father went on reading and the room fell into momentary silence.

The mention of her mother had made Lydia determined not to stir the waters further, but to calm them as her mother would have done, had she been here. The black lead pencil was secure now in its holder and she rested it upon the sheet of untouched paper, ready to begin, and broke the silence with, "What sermon are you reading, Father?"

He much admired the reverend's works and often shared the better lines by reading them aloud, which had, on many Sundays, been the start of very amiable discussions, as she hoped it would be now.

He faintly smiled as though he were aware of her intent. "This one is titled 'Of the rule of equity to be observed among men,' and the scripture is from Matthew, chapter seven, verse twelve. Benjamin?" He drew his son into the conversation. "Can you tell me what that is?"

Her brother shrugged. "I must defer, in all things biblical, to Lydia. She has the better memory."

It was true. She tipped her head a moment, thinking. "'Therefore all things whatsoever you would that men should do unto you, do ye even so to them.'"

"Yes, exactly." Her father spread the pages of the book. "And very appropriate to our discussion, for it is the Reverend

Tillotson's opinion that, as all men in God's view are equal, observation of this rule would bring peace to the world."

De Brassart said, "A pleasing thought, and yet God does not make men equal."

That brought Benjamin to life. He briefly rose and took another chair, from which he sent a pointed look toward Mr. de Sabran, who was gazing out the window once again and paying no attention. "You and he, you are both officers, and both of the same rank. You serve the same king. How is that not equal?"

Lydia repressed a sigh. She'd started drawing Benjamin because he was the nearest to her, but since he would not sit still she had to start again and use her father as her model. He was easier to draw, in many ways. His features weren't so changeable.

De Brassart spoke as if he were explaining to a child. "He is Canadian."

"Colonial, you mean."

"Yes, if you like. It is a difference of our birth, you see. A difference of our nature. I have told you how they fight. Not with the sword, but with the hatchet and the knife."

"Yet even you must own that, in these colonies, their ways of waging war are more effective." Benjamin leaned back. "A sword is fine when fighting in the open, but a tomahawk and knife are of more value in the forest."

Lydia, although she knew that Mr. de Sabran could not speak English and was unaware of what was being said, could not help glancing at him. And as though he sensed her movement his dark gaze left Benjamin and had begun to travel back toward her when she bent her head and fixed her concentration on her drawing.

She could capture a fair likeness of a person, but she struggled drawing hands. She could not manage them. She would have liked to have possessed the skill to draw her father's. They were capable and callused. They created things from nothing and could smooth a board or gentle the most skittish horse or rest upon her shoulder in a way that made her instantly feel safe.

They did not carry tomahawks and knives within the woods.

De Brassart said, "But it is not the weapons only. It is what a man has here, and here." He gestured to his heart, his head. "One cannot make a buzzard into a hawk. The officers of Canada, their blood is that of *habitants*, of farmers, and whatever they achieve, that will not change. Their children always will have one foot in the fields. In France, our social rank and reputation is inherited, an honor we can pass on to our sons."

Lydia knew Benjamin would have had much to say to *that*, considering their father was a farmer, but it was their father who replied first with a sound that fell between a cough and a short laugh, surprising Lydia and leaving the French officer astonished.

"I amuse you?" asked de Brassart.

"Not at all. No, it is only that you speak of reputation and of honor at the moment I am reading those same words here on the page. The Reverend Tillotson is talking of the inequalities of men, as you are, only he believes that what makes men unequal is no more than circumstance and health, and since those things are neither fixed nor constant, fortunes often turn, and men change places. Here," he offered, "let me read this passage to you, and you tell me if it does not perfectly apply: 'A disease may ruin the most happy and excellent memory, and make a man forget his own name; a little knock on any side of the head may level the highest understanding with the meanest; beauty, health, and strength, may be blasted by a disease, or a thousand other accidents.'" Her father's voice grew faintly rougher there, as though with memory, but he went on reading from the sermon with the firm conviction of a man who knew the words he spoke were true. "'Riches, and honor, and reputation, are the most slippery and brittle things that belong to us.'"

Whether de Brassart agreed with that, or even understood the finer nuances of language in that sentiment, she could not tell. Like Benjamin, he might have had much more to say in argument, had not Mr. de Sabran asked a question of him then, in French.

Mr. de Brassart shrugged and told her father, "Monsieur de Sabran asks for pen and paper, if you please, so he might write a letter."

The small request caught all of them off guard. There was a moment's pause before her father gave his answer. "Certainly," he said, and looked across the room at Lydia. "My dear, will you please see to that?"

She traded looks with Benjamin, then rose and set her drawing down and organized the necessary items on her father's desk. Mr. de Sabran rose as well and crossed to take his new seat, but when Lydia would have stepped back he stopped her with a quiet word and touched the sheet of paper she'd set ready for him, making a quick counting gesture with his fingers that appeared to indicate he wanted one sheet more.

She drew the extra paper from its place within the desk and laid it neatly on the first before retreating to her chair again and taking up her drawing.

He was too close for her liking, at the desk. She could look nowhere in the room now without having his blue waistcoat catch her vision. He'd replaced the missing button.

She had seen him in the midst of that task yesterday, while she'd been helping Violet with the cutting up and pickling of the watermelon rinds, and being that the door to the small downstairs chamber had stood partly open, from the kitchen she'd been able to observe him sitting at his bed's edge with his dark head bent in concentration, sorting through the contents of a small case made of metal that he'd taken from the cowhide pack he'd brought with him. The case appeared to hold the varied things he'd need for mending. He had found the size of button that was needed, bitten off a length of thread, and made the small repair with deft assurance before smoothing out the waistcoat and then brushing it.

She'd noticed that he was not as fastidious as his companion when it came to clothing, and his shirt cuffs and cravat were of plain linen, while Mr. de Brassart's were of lace—yet there was nothing in Mr. de Sabran's bearing or appearance to suggest that he was any less an officer. In fact to Lydia, of the two men, he looked the more commanding.

But perhaps that lay in how he had been raised, and trained. She thought of what her brother Joseph had said of the men of the Canadian marines, and how their officers were sent as children to live with the Indians and learn their ways. "They have a reputation, justly earned," he'd said, "for ruthlessness."

She could believe that from the hard, unyielding set of Mr. de Sabran's jaw as he bent above his letter. He wrote steadily and in what looked to be a plain, bold hand. And while he wrote, he frowned.

&

The problem with the letters was deciding what to do with them.

Had Joseph had his way, he would have thrown them on the fire. "They might say anything," he'd argued when he'd learned of them. "You don't know what intelligence he's passing to his friends."

Which had made Benjamin reply, "I doubt the French would care how many sheep are in our field. There's little else of interest or excitement he could find here to report."

The humor had been lost on Joseph. "It's a long walk down from Fort Niagara, and he's been through several of our camps. Who knows what he's seen *there* to catch his interest?"

Lydia had been too tired to step between them, but the next day, Monday, when she carried out the dinner pail to where her father was at work still digging stones to mend the wall between the apple orchard and the pasture, she could see that he was carrying the folded letters in the pocket of his coat.

She said, "You cannot send them, surely?"

"Circumstance," he said, "and inequalities."

"I do not understand."

The day was fair but very windy and she set her back against the chest-high drystone wall, letting it provide some shelter while she faced her father. He had been a fair-haired man when he was younger and whenever he worked hard enough to raise a sweat his face flushed red, as it was now, and yet his barrel-chested strength meant he was rarely out of breath. His voice was strong.

"If it were Joseph taken captive," he explained, "would you not want him shown the courtesy of having letters sent where he would send them?" He read the answer in her face and quoted very gently, to remind her, "'All things whatsoever you would that men should do unto you, do ye even so to them.'"

"I know." The wind had caught her apron and she held it down, her hand clenched in its folds. "I know, but it is very hard."

"If it were easy," said her father, "then no minister would ever have had need to write a sermon to persuade us we should do it."

With a small nod she acknowledged that, and looked away along the long uneven line of fence that subtly changed its course each year as every frost and thaw thrust up new stones from deep within the earth. New obstacles. "What are you going to do with them?"

"The letters? I will send them where he asks, but Joseph's right. We ought to first make sure they'll do no harm."

He used the dampened cloth she'd brought for him to wipe his hands and brow and took the dinner pail, investigating what it held. "Did Violet make this bread?"

She smiled because she knew why he was asking. "Yes, you needn't worry, it's not burnt."

"Your mother always said that oven had a temper."

She would not blame the oven. She would never be a baker and she knew it, but she would not let the conversation stray. "How do you propose to learn what's in the letters? You could never trust Mr. de Brassart to translate them."

"No." He'd found the seasoned chicken leg beneath the bread. "That's why I've sent Benjamin to hire French Peter."

French Peter lived not far from them and had a wife and children who, with other neutral French, had been resettled here from Nova Scotia by the orders of the king three years ago.

Her mother had considered that a travesty. "They are a peaceful people, the French neutrals of Acadia," she'd said. "They've done no harm." And when her husband in his more pragmatic way had answered that the British were most likely only trying to make certain that continued, she'd replied, "And how is justice served, I ask, by punishing a people for a crime they have not done, and might yet never do?" If there'd been any argument to make to that, her mother had refused to hear it, and when word had come French Peter and his family had been sent to settle near them, she had treated them with charity—so much so that, the day after her mother's death, French Peter had appeared upon their doorstep.

With her father deep in grief, it had been Lydia who had received French Peter's brief condolences. It had not been a comfortable encounter. She did not have her mother's gift for seeing past a person's nationality, and neutral French or no, he was still French.

"If ever there is anything I can be doing for you," he had said, his accent even thicker from emotion, "I will do it with a glad heart."

She'd replied that there was nothing they would need from him, and with a silent nod he had accepted that. And as he'd turned away he'd paused, and turned again, and said more thickly, "She was good to us." As though it needed saying.

Lydia had felt ashamed a few days later, looking back, because she'd known her mother would have asked French Peter in and made him welcome, and not stood stone-faced within the door and watched him walk away, his heavy shoulders stooped. But what was done was done, and time, as she had learned these past few years, did not allow for second chances.

If she'd treated him with disrespect, he'd done the very opposite to her since then. Whenever their paths crossed at Mr. Fisher's store or at the wharf or at the home of any of their neighbors who had hired him, French Peter always had a cheerful greeting for her, but as though aware there was a barrier between them he made no attempt to breach it.

She'd hoped she would be gone before he came today to see her father, but it was a warm day and her father took his time over the dinner pail. He had not finished with the chicken when she heard her brother Benjamin, behind her in the pasture, tell the sheep to move. They scattered in their lazy way and bleated as she turned to watch him weave his way between them with French Peter at his side—a slightly shorter man than Benjamin and doubtless twice his age, but with the solid build and browned skin of a man who earned his living by his labor. In the manner of his people he was dressed in woolen breeches and a sleeveless waistcoat over a plain shirt of weathered linen, with the same red knitted cap he wore no matter what the season, and the wooden shoes that, while they were unfashionable, served well in the fields and pastures without risking ruin from the mud.

Benjamin, as always full of energy, set both his hands atop the wall and vaulted it with ease. French Peter might have done the same; he had the strength. Instead he stayed securely on the pasture side and leaned his folded arms on the broad stones that capped the wall dividing him from Lydia, her brother, and her father. "You have a job for me, I hear?" He sounded pleased. "You need my help to dig the stones?"

Her father wiped his hand clean before offering it over the stone wall in greeting, and above their handshake answered, "Not exactly. I recall my wife said once that you could read. Is that right?"

The pleasure faded to regret. "Read? No, it is kind that she would say this, but I'm hardly speaking English very well yet, and to read it—"

"No, I meant in French. Can you read French?"

There was a brightening. "I can. My mother's father had some school and knew how to read and write, and he was teaching this to me when I was small. But why...?"

"We have some guests," her father said. "Perhaps you've heard?"

Of course he'd heard, thought Lydia. It was nearly a week now since her father had come back from Millbank with the captured officers, and news could not be well contained within a small community.

French Peter said, "The two lieutenants. Yes."

Her father drew the letters from his pocket. "One of them has written these, and I would like to know what they contain before I post them on."

"I see. So, not the stones?" French Peter cast another look toward the shovel and the other tools her father had leaned carefully against the tree behind him when he'd paused to eat his dinner. "Only this?"

"That's right. I'll pay you for the effort and your time, of course."

French Peter waved the offer to the side with one big hand. "No, I will do this for you without payment, it's not needed." And he held that same hand out to take the letters.

"If I'm not mistaken," said her father, "this first one is meant for Governor DeLancey."

With a nod French Peter read the brief address. "Yes, it says just that: 'To His Excellency the Governor of New York.'" Unfolding it, he read a moment, forehead creased in concentration. "Ah. He is complaining to the governor. You want that I should tell you in my own words, or in his?"

"Your own will do."

"Then he is saying to the governor it is not right the officers are separated from their men, that this is not what is agreed to in the documents signed at Niagara, and he is asking where his soldiers are now taken and if they are well, for he does not rest well until he knows this. He's asking that the governor will tell him at the soonest time that is convenient, and he signs the letter with a great respect, and says that he is humble and obedient and all such things, and then his name: Jean-Philippe de Sabran de la Noye, lieutenant of the Marine, prisoner."

Lydia hadn't expected to feel any sort of reaction at all, hearing Mr. de Sabran's words translated, and yet she could not help but feel a slight twinge of compassion that he might be worrying over his men, even if it surprised her that someone of his hardened nature would be like to worry.

"And so this one," French Peter said, shuffling the letters around so the second was topmost, "he sends to a nun, Sister Athanase, near to Quebec, at the hospital general."

That seemed to surprise even Benjamin, who raised his eyebrows. "A nun? Why on earth would he write to a nun?"

French Peter, having read through the first lines, gave a nod of comprehension. "Yes, I see. She is his sister. He is telling her that he is safe and that she should not fear for him, and he is hoping she is also safe and that the... I apologize, I do not know this word in English. For us, we say '*siège*'—it means when armies sit outside the walls and stop the help from coming and they wait to make the people fight or starve. You know this word?"

Her father cleared his throat. "It is the same in English, only differently pronounced. We would say 'siege.'"

French Peter thanked him. "So yes, he is hoping that the siege there will soon end and that it does not touch the hospital. He says that she should bring their mother also to the hospital so that if there is fighting they will both be safe. He says to do that right away, as soon as she will get this letter. And he says again that he is well and was not wounded, and is staying with good people, and he sends his great affection and he signs his name, but only that— he does not write 'lieutenant' after or say he is prisoner."

There was silence for a moment in the orchard and the weight of it was tangible to Lydia. She frowned, and was the first to leave the wall and take a step across the shaded grass. She suddenly had need of room to breathe.

French Peter said, behind her, "Anyway, that's what he writes." The heavy paper rustled as he folded both the letters on their creases and returned them to her father. "You are sure there is no other work you're needing me to do for you?"

Her father told him, "Thank you, no. There's nothing at this moment."

With a shrug, the other man looked past him to the almost-ripened pippins hanging heavily on all the trees. "Perhaps then when the harvest comes. Yours will be good, I think."

Benjamin shared that opinion. "A pity we don't have a cider press here. The nearest one, I think, is Mr. Brewster's, and I'll be carting these apples for days to him."

French Peter brightened. "A cider press? But I know where one is, very big—broken in pieces, but it can be fixed, and the owner I think will want little in trade for it. If you would like, I can show you."

"Well, I'd like," said Benjamin, pushing away from the wall in his turn. "Father?"

"Yes, go and look. And here, when you're done with that, take these on to Millbank, to your cousin. Have him seal them both and send them as enclosures in a letter to your brother in New York, with my instructions that he send the one directly to the governor, and use whatever means he can to send the other to Quebec." And handing the two letters over to Benjamin, Lydia's father thanked French Peter once more and bade him good day.

Benjamin hesitated. "I could carry these letters myself to New York."

"I have need of you here," said their father. "Your cousin will find somebody to carry them."

Lydia saw the swift flame of impatience sweep over her brother's face, but he did not argue, even if his "Yes, Father" was more biting than cordial.

Watching French Peter and Benjamin walking away again over the pasture, Lydia said gently to her father, "That was less than kind. You know he loves New York."

"I know. And if I thought he'd stay there I would send him there tomorrow and let William set him up in business. But a father knows the nature of his sons." His eyes were wise. "When Joseph was but small I knew he'd follow me into my trade and be a carpenter. Like me, he finds his happiness in building things.

William now, and Daniel, they were merchants from the cradle. What they crave are profits and the power that those profits bring. But Benjamin—" He looked across, as Lydia was looking, to where Benjamin was striding through the pasture, once more scattering the sheep. "What *he* wants is adventure. And his spirit and his recklessness will carry him to places far beyond New York, I fear, and far more dangerous." He seemed to stop himself from saying more. Crossing to his tools he took the shovel in his hands, preparing to get back to work.

She followed his example, picking up the empty dinner pail. She wondered if he knew her nature also, but she did not ask. Instead she asked him, "Father?"

"Yes?"

"Do you think General Wolfe will take Quebec?"

He dug the shovel hard into the ground and metal scraped on stone. "I hope he does, for I am ready to be done with all this fighting."

She was minded to agree. Except an hour ago Quebec, to her, had been another distant city full of faceless enemies, and now when she imagined it, instead of walls and guns she saw two women seeking safety in the hospital—a young nun and her mother.

Wars lay easier upon the conscience, Lydia decided, when you could not see the faces of the people you were fighting. And it was vastly easier to hate a man when you'd not learned his Christian name, or pried into his private thoughts and learned that he was human.

JEAN-PHILIPPE

I T WAS DIFFICULT, HE thought, to not admire the man.

Whatever might be broken in this family, Monsieur Wilde appeared unbowed by it. He was a large man, broad through chest and shoulders, and might easily have ruled his home by discipline and force, yet even a stranger could see that his children respected him not out of fear, but affection.

Jean-Philippe was not surprised. He'd watched the family closely since the day of his arrival and the more he'd seen of Monsieur Wilde these past few weeks, the more he'd found to like.

The two of them were very often up at the same hour, both rising earlier than others in the house, and every morning Jean-Philippe observed the older man would wash his hands and face and neck and do a thing that proved that, while he did not seem to go to church on Sundays, he was still a man of faith. He prayed.

"Amen" was the same word in any language. Monsieur Wilde said it quietly to end whatever brief and private lines he spoke before he faced the day. And then he worked.

In finer weather he'd be out the best part of the day and take his dinner in the field, but when it rained or blustered, Monsieur Wilde worked at carpentry. It was his trade, apparently, and he was skilled.

He'd built two shelves into the walls of the chamber that Jean-Philippe and de Brassart shared, so they would have more room to place their things, and he'd set pegs into the wall so they could better hang their clothes, and after that he'd made them narrow wooden chests to slide beneath their beds, with hinged lids that could lock, so their possessions could be stored with more security than simply in their haversacks and packs.

When Jean-Philippe had tried to pay him for this with some of the money they'd been given for that purpose, Monsieur Wilde had smiled and waved it to the side and not accepted it, but Jean-Philippe had stubbornly refused to take the charity. At last he'd cut a piece from his tobacco and held that out to the older man, who'd smiled again and taken it and clapped him on the shoulder with a friendly hand before he'd walked away.

An easy man to like.

Some part of that, Jean-Philippe knew, was nostalgia, for there was a quality about Monsieur Wilde that reminded him of other days, when he was but a boy of ten. Then, too, he had been far from home and hadn't known the language of the people who surrounded him.

That had been seventeen years ago, and the narrow-shouldered boy in his first uniform, who hadn't yet killed anything more deadly than a rabbit, seemed a very long way distant from the man he had become, yet he remembered his first summer's voyage westward from Quebec—the wideness of the water where the river met the lake; the deep green pathways of the endless forest, and the men who moved within it.

He'd felt sure he'd never lose his fear of them or understand them, but his uncle had assured him that he would.

His uncle had spent years among the Seneca himself—had been adopted by them when he had been cut off from his fellow soldiers on a raid and captured, and had passed three years among them. Rumor was he'd found a wife who'd borne his son before she and the infant both had died of smallpox, but his uncle never spoke of that. He did, though, hold the Seneca in high esteem, and when he'd taken Jean-Philippe into his care as a cadet within the service of the Troupes de la Marine, the first thing he had done was to present his nephew to those of his once-adopted family who roamed freely past the western limits of the maps along the wild frontier.

"I have no son," he'd said to Jean-Philippe, and something in his tone had made the boy believe perhaps the rumors had been true. "I have no son, but you are of my blood, my sister's child, and if you treat these people with respect and have the wit to learn from them, then what regard they have for me may, by extension, pass to you."

And so it had. When those Seneca had traveled from their summer village to the one they used in winter, they had stopped first at the fort and, by arrangement with his uncle, taken Jean-Philippe along. He'd viewed it as a great adventure—but by spring he'd come to know it was in fact a privilege, and his childish prejudice had given way to steadfast admiration and to gratitude. In that single winter he'd learned many things, and most of those he'd learned from the young man who'd been his older "brother" in the family he had lived with. Broad through chest and shoulders, with a power tamped by patience and good humor, that young man had taught Jean-Philippe by simply doing things that drew the boy's attention; drew him close enough so that the skill, once demonstrated, could be copied.

It was the same technique, he'd noticed, that Monsieur Wilde used with both his sons—or tried to use, for neither son showed any interest.

The younger of them had an energy that made him too impatient to observe and learn from anyone, nor did he have the nature of a farmer or a carpenter. The words that Jean-Philippe's uncle had once said of him would fit this younger man as well: *This one will never settle long enough to be a man of leisure.* Although whether he, like Jean-Philippe, was born to be a soldier was unclear. He had the boldness, but a soldier needed discipline.

The elder brother was the opposite, his discipline so deeply self-imposed he did not waver from a task once he'd begun it. Like his father, he seemed fairly skilled at carpentry. So far he had worked only at the smaller jobs, the fence rails mostly and the posts, but it was clear he had a builder's eye. There'd been a telling moment when he'd set a rail in place and not been satisfied, and taking up his axe again he'd shaved a little here, a little there, and squared the end to near perfection, sighting down the rail so he could set it true and level. It had only been a moment, yet his features had transformed from concentration and a craftsman's care, enough that Jean-Philippe with narrowed eyes had looked at him more closely and believed he'd glimpsed the man that this American had been before whatever in his life had left him silent and withdrawn.

That this withdrawal was a relatively recent thing was evident from how the others dealt with it—the younger brother trying to provoke with arguments, much as a small boy with a stick might try to prod a half-dead creature back to life; the father trying gentler means.

The Friday before last, Monsieur Wilde had gone out in the morning with his team of oxen and a full cartload of hay, and returned with the cart filled instead with what looked to be some great machine made of wood, all in pieces. He'd needed the help of both sons to offload the big beam and the jumble of odd parts and pile them next to the shed near the barn, and afterward the elder son had stood and looked a moment at that pile, and from the way his father had been watching him, so hopefully, it had been plain to Jean-Philippe that Monsieur Wilde had set that wooden puzzle at the shed by way of an enticement, like a hunter laying bait along a trail to draw his quarry out.

It hadn't worked. At least, not yet.

But it had made Jean-Philippe warm even more to Monsieur Wilde, who lately, when the midday meal was done, would rise and go outside and walk the little distance to the shed and, tying on his leather apron, take his tools in hand and set to work with the patient resolve of that Seneca man who'd sat years ago mending a break in a snowshoe or fletching new arrows until Jean-Philippe, curiosity burning, had asked the first question he'd learned in that language: "Can I help?"

There'd been a few times this past week when Jean-Philippe had felt that small boy stirring restlessly inside him, tempting him to ask Monsieur Wilde the same thing.

Instead, he'd asked de Brassart if he knew what the machine was.

"It's a cider press, apparently." De Brassart had been sitting in the room the family chiefly used on Sundays, leafing idly through the pages of a book and looking bored. "Our host has spoken much about it these past days at dinner. They have an apple orchard here, and harvest is approaching, so they found themselves a cider press."

Jean-Philippe had not wanted to sit. He had seen, through the half-open door to the kitchen, the black girl watching them suspiciously, so he'd crossed the few paces and opened the door fully to let her view them more easily, trying to calm any thoughts she might have that de Brassart and he were conspiring to do any harm.

Then he'd said to de Brassart, "If they want it ready for the harvest, they still have much work to do."

"And they are welcome to it." Stretching out his legs, the other officer had flipped another page. "Though our confinement here is tedious, at least the terms of the accord between our countries spare us being forced to serve as laborers."

Jean-Philippe hadn't found any comfort in that—both because he would rather have labored at anything than be condemned to do nothing, and also because he was darkly aware that the English did not always keep their agreements.

He hadn't had word of his men.

More than two weeks had passed since he'd written the governor, and there had been no reply. Monsieur Wilde had assured him, by means of de Brassart's translation, that both of the letters were sent, but for Jean-Philippe having to always rely on de Brassart to translate was also a source of frustration.

Often somebody would speak at length, and then de Brassart would summarize that in a sentence or two, making Jean-Philippe fully aware he was missing at least half or more of what people were actually saying, and since he would never have trusted de Brassart with anything else, he was little inclined to now trust him with turning *his* words into English, so he had begun to do what he had done as a boy with the Seneca: he'd set himself to learn by observation.

When they spoke to one another, he'd tried fitting sounds to common interactions. He had learned the words for "thank you" and the way to say "you're welcome," and the greetings for the evening and the morning.

And he'd learned her name.

It had not been an easy thing to learn, for those around her rarely called to her. But then, it seemed that there was little need to. She was always there.

Each morning when he came back from his walk she was already at the kitchen hearth. She served him breakfast—something he had never regularly eaten. He was used to dining at eleven in the morning or at midday, and having his main meal, his *grand repas*, at six o'clock in the evening; but here that evening meal was light and late, the more substantial dinner was not served till early afternoon, and taking breakfast had become a matter of necessity.

He also had been trying to acquire a taste for tea. At home it was used mainly to treat illness of the stomach, and was boiled black as tar. The tea she brewed for him was weaker and, with milk, was not entirely unpleasant. Even if it had been, he would have accepted it without complaint, since from what he'd observed she had enough to manage. Her brothers and her father never seemed to raise their voices to her, nor treat her with disrespect, but neither did they pay her the small courtesy of noticing how hard she worked to ease their days and smooth their interactions with each other. When the younger brother argued with the elder she would calm the one and cheer the other, keeping them apart by means that seemed completely natural, and all the while direct-ing the attention of their father elsewhere so he would not notice.

Jean-Philippe found it surprising that a man like Monsieur Wilde, who seemed to understand his sons so well, should fail to see the strain that it was causing his own daughter to be always taking care of them: part servant and part diplomat. It had to be exhausting.

But it had been from her father that he'd finally learned her name. One morning she'd been working in the garden and her father had called: "Lydia!" And she had turned.

And Jean-Philippe had marked the word. He'd stored the sounds within his memory: *Lydia*. And all that day he'd watched with care, and listened, and at dinnertime his patience was rewarded when her younger brother asked her to pass something down the table, and to capture her attention had begun by saying: "Lydia?" Again she'd turned. Her gaze had brushed past Jean-Philippe's and he had quickly lowered his to hide his satisfaction.

He had always liked to put a name to what he wanted.

It was not a name with which he was familiar. In fact he would have missed the times they'd spoken it before because it would have sounded as if they were saying *l'idéal*, a thought that made him smile faintly. Physically, at least, she was his own ideal. And even her dislike of him provided a distraction from his darker thoughts and troubles.

As did watching Monsieur Wilde at work upon the broken cider press.

Even if de Brassart had not told him what it was, Jean-Philippe would have been able to identify it for himself three days ago, when Monsieur Wilde had gone into the woods and felled a log and brought it back and had begun to fashion it into a massive screw, a part that had been missing altogether. The shape and function of the big machine became apparent to him then. They had one very like it at his father's manor farm.

This morning, Thursday morning, with the weather fair and fine for mid-September, Monsieur Wilde had set the shed doors open and was working just beside it, in full view of both his sons—the younger one restacking hay that had blown down the night before, the elder setting posts so he could fence around those haystacks.

Jean-Philippe had thought at first that Monsieur Wilde was trying purposely to draw his sons' attention once again, by pausing often, setting down his tools, and seeming to be puzzling over some piece of the cider press. But after half an hour it became apparent this was the first time the older man had seen a press of this particular design. By trial and error he had pegged the bottom platform into place, but now he could not figure out the way to fit the crossbars of the middle plate together to allow it to run smoothly up and down within the side posts' inner grooves, and his mild temper was beginning to dissolve into frustration.

Jean-Philippe stood in the deep shade of an oak tree at the forest's edge and felt that half-forgotten voice stir deep within him. *Can I help?* This time he knew the answer: Yes, he could. He knew the way machines like this were put together; knew the way they worked.

He glanced away and exhaled, hard, and fought that small voice with a stern reminder to himself that officers, when captured by the enemy, could do no labor. But he knew—before he'd even made the choice to leave the shadows and begin the walk across the sunlit clearing—it had never been a fight that he could win.

CHARLEY

Fʀᴏᴍ ᴡʜᴇʀᴇ I sᴛᴏᴏᴅ, in the deep quiet shade at the edge of
the trees, I commanded a view of the house and barn and the
clearing between them, still caught in the long stretching shadows that spread from the woods on the opposite side where the
golden pale edge of the brightening sky was beginning to show
now above the tall tangle of branches and leaves. The barn was
not original. Frank's uncle Walt had built it where he'd figured
that the old barn should have been, and time and weather had
done what they could to make it look authentic. It was only when
you got up close and saw all the twentieth-century details—the
nails and the hardware and too-perfect timbers—that you realized
it wasn't as old as it seemed.

Lots of things looked different when you got up close.

This place where I was standing, for example, was the same
place where the light I'd seen last night had seemed to pause, and
yet this morning I could find no evidence that anyone had walked
or stood here recently but me. And while I knew that I'd seen
something, I was less convinced of what I'd seen, and more inclined
to think it might have been a simple trick of light; perhaps a stray
reflection of the headlights from some car across the bay.

To prove I wasn't going to be swayed by superstition, I'd turned
my back to the trees and the path that wound through their green
shadows, but even though I knew that ghosts weren't real and
there'd be nothing sneaking up behind me, I was still uncomfortably aware of every rustle in the undergrowth and leaves as birds
and mice and squirrels went about their early-morning foraging.
Deliberately, I kept my focus forward on the clearing.

If I let loose my imagination, it was not too difficult to picture how this would have looked when Captain Wilde was growing up here with his parents and his brothers and his sister. In my mind I stripped away the whole Victorian addition, leaving only the colonial house with its plain white-painted walls and rows of square-paned windows. From the inventory, we knew there had also been a shed beside the barn, so I imagined that as well, and being mindful of the season added haystacks and a garden. I would have begun to add the animals and people, too, but the crunch of tires on gravel interrupted as a big black truck pulled in across the parking lot, destroying the effect.

I didn't mind. That truck was what I had been waiting for.

Sam was carrying his hardhat as he stepped down from the driver's seat, looking relaxed in his work boots and jeans and a well-weathered sweatshirt. He wasn't alone. He held the truck's door open for a moment and a small, smooth-coated dog leaped down and danced a joyous circle around his legs before falling into step beside him.

I would have thought that my dark-colored clothes and the shade of the trees and the fact I was standing here off to the side would have made it unlikely that someone would notice me, but Sam walked directly toward me.

"Good morning," he called, and the dog, having seen me by then, too, tucked quickly behind Sam's legs as though it wanted the added protection.

I liked dogs. I crouched low to make myself appear less threatening, holding out my hand palm down and with my fingers curled to reassure Sam's dog that it could sniff and get to know me without fear of being grabbed. "I didn't know you had a dog."

Which in retrospect seemed a ridiculous thing to say to someone you'd just met three days ago and didn't really know, but Sam didn't comment other than to say, "His name is Bandit. Bandit, come meet Charley."

At his voice the little dog edged forward, nudged my fingers with its nose, then ducked its head and bumped my hand in a wordless invitation. I obliged, petting its brown floppy ears, soft as velvet, and running my hand farther over the black-saddled back until the white-tipped tail was wagging. "He's a beagle?"

"Yep. And if you keep doing that he'll stand there all day long."

I smiled and gave the dog a final scratch behind the ears and straightened. Most dogs, off the leash like this one, would have wandered away to explore, but Bandit went right back to standing next to Sam, who told me, "You're here early."

"I'm a morning person." True enough, if not the whole truth, so I added, "And I wanted to catch you before your guys started their work today."

"Is there a problem?" He looked to be one of those people who lived life on such an even keel their faces rarely registered surprise, but I thought I heard the tiniest suggestion of it in his tone, so I was quick with my reply.

"No problem. I'd just like to ask a favor."

"Sure," he said. "What do you need?"

The antique metal button in my pocket pressed its shape against my fingers as I felt for it. "I'll show you."

Sam and Bandit followed me across the dew-damp grass to where the excavated trench was taking shape, the workmen having taken care to shore the trench up so the old foundation walls would be supported on the one side and the soil on the other side would not cave in.

I took my hand out of my pocket. Held it out to show him. "I found this last night, when I was locking up. I'm pretty sure it rolled out of that dirt pile. It's a button," I explained. "A really old one. Eighteenth century."

His nod held understanding. "And you think there might be more?"

"Well, maybe not more buttons, but more artifacts, or pieces of them. Yes. So I know this wasn't part of the original plan, but

I'd love to set up a place where we could sift through the soil before putting it back. Is that possible?"

Sam didn't see why not. "How do you sift it?"

"We usually use screens, about so big, with wooden frames."

His glance judged the distance between my two hands and he nodded again. "Do you want me to build you a couple of those?"

"That would be great. Thank you. Just let me know what they cost, and I'll—" I didn't get to say what I would do. A sharp ping from my pocket distracted me. "Sorry." I pulled out the cell phone and answered the text. "Just my niece checking up on me." I'd been expecting it. Rachel had still been asleep when I'd left the house, and although I'd left a note for her she still liked knowing I was where I said I was. "She keeps me on a short leash."

I had meant that as a joke, but Sam accepted it as reasonable. "Hard on her to lose her dad. It seemed like they were close."

"They were." I slid the button and my phone back in my pocket, processing what he'd just said. "You knew Niels?"

"We don't have many real estate lawyers in Millbank. In my line of work you do business with all of them. He was a good guy, your brother."

I found an excuse to look up at the roofline and shaded my eyes with my hand even though there was hardly the sunlight to warrant it. "Yes, he was." I had a feeling this would lead to sympathetic comments and condolences, and knowing that I really wasn't up to that, I asked him, "Have you lived here long, in Millbank?"

"Eight years. Why?"

"I've been told we have a ghost light in our woods." My tone was offhand. "Have you ever seen it?"

Not offhand enough, apparently, because his glance held interest. "Have you?"

"I don't believe in ghosts." I was speaking to myself as much as him. The place where I'd been standing by the line of trees looked innocently empty, and the climbing sun was shortening the shadows.

But I still felt braver having Sam and Bandit here for company. "I've got a pot of coffee on," I offered, "if you want a cup."

❧

The coffee maker had outdone itself this morning. Instead of its usual watery brew it had gone to the other extreme and produced something so strong I half feared the spoon might dissolve while I stirred sugar into my cup. Sam, apparently tougher than me, drank his black without any complaint. He stayed standing, leaning back against the counter by the sink while Bandit curled up by his feet, nose on the small round braided rug. I wasn't sure what the official policy was on having dogs in the museum's kitchen, but I knew two of our trustees, Don and Rosina, had brought their dachshund with them when they'd dropped by once to check on things. And Frank, when he came through the kitchen door ten minutes later, didn't seem to mind at all that he was greeted by the *thump-thump* of a wagging tail against the floor.

"New dog?" he asked Sam.

"Picked him up last month."

"Another rescue?"

"That's right."

"Looks a little calmer than the last one."

Sam looked down at Bandit, too. "He has his moments. But right now he's full of food. He's happy."

"Well, I'm happy, too, when I get fed." Frank smiled and looked at me. "And how are *you* this morning, kiddo? Fit for battle?"

"Always."

"Good. Because I've brought you ammunition." He was carrying a thick manila envelope, and raised it now to show me. "Uncle Walt's collected research for the book he never wrote about our family. After he died, my aunt packaged this all up and gave it to me. Thought I might want to finish his work for him." He moved to set it on the counter, saw my face, and said, "Relax. The originals are in my safe-deposit box. These are just copies."

Even so, I rescued the envelope from the damp countertop as soon as he set it down, and the thickly stacked papers inside slid and shifted their weight as I tilted it upright.

"You'll find all kinds of goodies in there," was Frank's promise. "Consider it a donation to the archives."

Our "archives" at the moment was the third drawer of the filing cabinet in my office, where we kept our copy of the inventory taken by Captain Benjamin Wilde's wife of the contents of the old house at the time the British occupied it in the Revolution, and a copy of the logbook of the *Bellewether*—Captain Wilde's most famous ship and the one with which he'd made his mark as a patriot privateer. And that was all we had. Most of the other documents having to do with the Wildes, I'd been told, were already in the possession of the local library. I hadn't known that Frank had any articles to add. "Did you tell Malaika you had these?"

"Oh, probably. I don't remember." He didn't seem concerned. "There's nothing in there about Benjamin that the historians haven't already said twenty times over, so there didn't seem any point in my bringing it in before, but I had a quick look at it last night and there *are* a few things about Benjamin's father and brother," he said. "And his sister. I thought it might help you get one up on Sharon." He glanced at Sam, including him with the brief explanation: "Sharon Sullivan."

Sam nodded in a show of shared and total understanding, as though no more needed to be said.

It made me feel a little better. "So it's not just me, then, who finds Sharon kind of...challenging?"

Frank said, "That's not the word I'd use, but no, it's not just you. Sam, here, could likely tell you lots of stories if he wasn't so damned diplomatic all the time. He did some work on Sharon's house a while back."

I thought I caught a smile behind the raised rim of Sam's coffee cup as he agreed, "She's challenging."

Feeling better still, I said, "Well, good. Then I'll try not to take it personally."

Frank assured me, "It's not personal. She's only sore because we wouldn't make Eve the curator."

"What?" This was the first I had heard of it. "I didn't know that."

"Oh, sure. When we started this thing Sharon figured eventually she'd be the big boss, museum director, and Eve would be hired as the curator, that was the plan. Until you came to town and Malaika suggested we might want to hire somebody with actual training." Frank reached past my head, took a mug from the cupboard, and poured himself coffee. He never seemed to mind the way it tasted.

I found I couldn't finish mine. I poured it down the sink and would have set the envelope aside a moment while I washed my cup, except Frank took the cup from me and said, "I'll do that. You go get your nose in Uncle Walt's research, and see what you can find. Just don't go too far down the rabbit hole," he warned. "My collections committee is having its first meeting here in"—he checked his watch—"forty-five minutes. You'll want to sit in with us. Dave's bringing cinnamon buns from the bakery."

Sam wondered aloud if this meeting was one that the contractor should be a part of, too.

"Nope," Frank said. "Nice try, though."

"I'll save you a cinnamon bun, Sam," I promised.

"The hell you will," Frank told me. "There won't be any to save."

"Well, then he can have mine."

Sam looked at Frank sideways. "She's nicer than you."

"Half the planet is nicer than me. What's your point?"

They were obviously comfortable with one another, so I didn't feel bad when I left them there, excused myself, and went up to my office.

I liked my little office in the mornings. The wide-planked floor and woodwork had been painted over gray during the renovations in the 1980s, and the wallpaper they'd chosen then was emerald green with floral twists of peach. But in the dance of light that filtered softly through the branches and green leaves outside my window, the effect was soothing and serene, like being underneath the sea.

The light was dim and quiet, though—the sun not risen high enough to let me read the papers Frank had brought me without switching on a lamp. I didn't want to spoil the ambience by using the strong ceiling light. Instead I reached behind me for the floor lamp in the corner. I knew I'd changed the lightbulb last week, so I was surprised that nothing happened when I switched it on. Until I noticed that it wasn't plugged into the wall socket.

With that fixed, I sat back and opened the big envelope.

Frank's uncle had been organized. He'd numbered every page in pencil in the top right corner, and he'd typed up a table of contents that served as a finding aid, letting me know what each section of pages contained. Benjamin Wilde's section, as I'd expected, was by far the largest, twice as long as that of his poetical Victorian descendant, Lawrence Wilde. The part I was interested in, though, was at the beginning: "From Reuben to Zebulon Wilde" in the table of contents.

Zebulon Wilde had been Benjamin's father. And if I hadn't known that to begin with, I'd have learned it from the handy family tree Frank's uncle Walt had made, his tidy printing leaning backward just a bit, but keeping to the lines he'd drawn and noting dates and places of the births and deaths and marriages of everyone he'd found. He'd obviously taken genealogy very seriously, and had footnoted each entry, citing sources.

Zebulon had been the youngest of four children—five, if you counted the first-named boy, Samuel, who had been born and died all in one day. There were two sisters after that, one who was written down simply as *Daughter, Unnamed*, which I took to mean her name had not yet been found in the documents, not that her family neglected to give her one. Then one more brother, named Reuben, who'd married and had at least one child himself. And then Zebulon.

Born at Newtown, Long Island, in 1697. Married Patience Hallett at the same place in 1722. Died at Snug Cove, 1765.

Almost seventy years of a life distilled down to three dates on a page. It was humbling to think that my own life, someday, would be summed up as blandly for some future reader, and probably then only if I got lucky and had a descendant who did something worthy of being remembered. Zebulon Wilde, by becoming the father of a Revolutionary War hero, had hit the jackpot—assured of a mention in every school history book, even if that was no more than his name. Not too bad for a man who appeared to have been, from a glance through this section of Uncle Walt's research, a farmer and carpenter. One of the documents copied here was a page from a receipt book for work he had done while in Newtown. *For work about stairs* read one line, and another: *For building a bedstead and putting up ledges and shelves*, and the still more ambitious: *For laying on shingles and building a barn*. He'd been paid in the way of colonial trade in both money and shares of the livestock and crops of the neighbors he'd worked for, *a good hog* and *winter wheat* being as useful as cash to a man in those times.

He hadn't stayed in Newtown, though. The last six of his eight children had been born here, at Snug Cove.

The family tree had them all listed in order of birth. First came William, whose name I had already learned. While he wasn't as famous as his brother Benjamin, he'd made a mark of his own on New York, being one of its wealthier merchants and shipowners, making a small fortune through his trade with the West Indies in defiance of the British laws that tried to put a stop to it. The next son listed, Daniel, had been William's partner in that trade. The family tree said Daniel had been married at Jamaica and had died at Hispaniola, so he'd evidently liked the warmer weather.

There were three sons after that, all with the same name, none surviving long. Samuel Wilde, born 1727, died 1727. Samuel Wilde, born 1728, died 1729. Samuel Wilde, born 1730, died 1731. Again, those spare numbers on paper seemed hardly an adequate record of all of the hopes and the loss and the sorrow that would have marked those painful few years for Zebulon Wilde and his wife. It appeared, for this family, that "Samuel" was not a fortunate name.

With the next son, they'd broken the pattern. And he had survived.

Joseph, born at Snug Cove, 1733. So then this was the United Empire Loyalist, as we in Canada called those who, in the Revolution, had stayed loyal to the British Crown, finding themselves fighting their friends and families in what could be argued had been America's first civil war. Frank had been right when he'd told me the family didn't talk much about Joseph—all he had here was a birth date, nothing more, the rest left blank as though they'd wanted to erase him. And if Frank was also right about the family legend, Joseph was the brother who had shot and killed his sister's French officer.

Benjamin came next in line, but I skipped over him and all his details, having memorized them all before the board had interviewed me for this job. I could recite his children's names and who they'd married and go down the line from there. That didn't interest me this morning.

What *did* interest me was the name that followed Benjamin's— the last child born to Zebulon and Patience Wilde, here at Snug Cove. Their only daughter.

Lydia.

Unlike her brother Joseph, she had been remembered by two entries: born 1739, died 1760—the source for her death date being cited as a letter in the Fisher family's personal collection, written June 11 of that year, which simply stated: *Zeb Wilde's girl was buried this day.*

According to this chart, then, she'd been twenty-one when

she had died. That hit me in a way the death all of those infants named Samuel hadn't done. They, too, were sad, but this seemed worse, somehow. For someone who'd survived all the hazards of childhood, who'd gathered the knowledge and life lessons and the experience to start her out on her path in the world, to be blotted from the record before she'd had any hope or chance of taking more than a few steps along that path, seemed cruelly wrong. And so unfair.

If I'd been motivated before by my desire to prove to Sharon I was smarter and more stubborn than she thought, then I was motivated even more right now by seeing those two simple, soulless dates bookending what had been the life of a young woman; and by knowing that, through research, I could fill the space between those dates with something that approached that woman's shape.

I'd have to wait, though. I could hear the door to the staff kitchen downstairs creak and bang above a cheerful rise of voices, and a half a minute later up the stairwell wafted one of the rare irresistible things that could draw me away from my reading—the scent of fresh cinnamon buns.

❦

Frank's way of chairing a meeting was much more laid-back than Malaika's. Declaring the dining room too hot and stuffy, he'd moved us outdoors to a shady spot under the trees by the parking lot, crafting an informal board table by dragging two picnic tables together end to end. At the center of these, in a large clamshell box, were the cinnamon buns that Dave Becker had brought from the Millbank bakery.

Dave was generous like that. I'd been in his antique store several times now since I'd moved here, and even when I hadn't made a purchase he had never let me walk out empty-handed, always giving me some little item—an egg cup or handkerchief—that he'd had tucked in the back of a cabinet or stuffed in a drawer;

and this morning without any arm-twisting he'd taken on the job of keeping minutes for our meeting. He set his pen down now. "So let's see if I've got this straight. I can keep doing appraisals for people outside the museum, the same as I've always done, right?"

"Right," I said.

"But if somebody donates an article to the museum, and needs an appraisal of what they're donating, for taxes, then I can't provide that appraisal."

"Right. That would be conflict of interest. I can't appraise either."

Museums weren't private collectors. Whatever we held was considered to be in the public trust, meaning when people donated things to a museum they expected us to manage and preserve them for the benefit of everyone, not hoard them for ourselves or, worse still, use them for our own financial profit.

There were rules for accepting something into the collection, and rules for taking care of it, and even more restrictive rules for how and when we could dispose of it, all written down in our policies.

Frank moved the meeting along. "I've broken down the inventory Captain Wilde's wife made of what was in the house when it was being occupied by Redcoats. On this first page, here, are all the things my family managed *not* to sell, the things that we held on to."

It wasn't a bad start. A four-poster bed that had been in the chamber of Benjamin Wilde and his wife, and two chairs and a small table matching the ones she had listed as being downstairs in the parlor; an old copper kettle, a soup tureen, six silver spoons and four candlesticks, and a long mirror, its frame carved and inlaid to match the description she'd made of *a looking-glass, brought by my husband a gift from Jamaica.*

Tracy, reading the list, asked, "And these are all in our storage facility?"

Frank replied, "If by 'storage facility' you mean my barn and the safe in Dave's shop, then yeah, that's where they are."

"And this second page?"

"These are the things that my family got rid of, but we have a record of where they are," he said. "Or where they're supposed to be. The dining room table, for instance—Lawrence Wilde donated that to his club in the city, and I'm pretty sure we can get them to donate it back to us."

"Some of these things are in other museums," Dave said. "What's the process there?"

Frank looked at me. "Charley?"

"Well, we could ask those museums to give us those items on permanent loan. And given the situation, we might persuade some curators to deaccession the artifacts from their collections so we can add them to ours. But there's no guarantee."

Frank accepted that. "And on these third and fourth pages, I've listed the rest of the things that we'll need to find, somehow."

The four of us read through the list, our easy silence challenged by the steady noises of the workmen digging a new section of the trench, and by the swelling whine and hum of insects stirred to life by the increasing heat of this late-August morning. My shirt had started clinging to my neck and back from the humidity, and I felt a deep sympathy for Captain Wilde's wife and other women of that period who'd spent their summers cooking over open hearths. *Two racks*, the list read, *two dripping-pans, eight iron pots, two spits, six pairs of pot hooks, three frying pans…*

A flash of white beside me made me jump, but it was only the fifth member of our small committee.

Lara Hollis Dennison was one of those rare people who could brighten any room that she walked into. A year younger than me, she was the single mom of four boys and the owner of Millbank's trendiest fashion boutique, which mixed things I couldn't afford with some quirkier pieces and vintage accessories. Very much Lara, in other words. Naturally pretty, she rarely wore makeup except for a bold stroke of eyeliner, letting her ivory skin glow on its own and her long wavy blond hair hang loose down her back.

Today, in a tunic of pale yellow linen worn over a crinkled white skirt, she was sunshine personified.

"Sorry," she said, sliding onto the picnic bench seat next to me with a cheerful disregard for any dirt she might be sitting on. "When I said I'd be late I didn't think I'd be *this* late, but the dentist was running behind."

Frank assured her it wasn't a problem, and in ten minutes flat he had brought her up to speed on what she'd missed, impressing me as always with his gift for cutting through the fluff to get to the essentials. "So now," he said, in summing up, "we're down to what we're going to have to beg, borrow, or steal."

I'd been studying the pages while he spoke, and now I pointed out, "Not all of these things have to be original antiques. In fact, there are some places where we're better off with reproductions. Like the kitchenware—if we're actually using the kitchen to do demonstrations, the way that we've planned, then we don't want to do that with artifacts. Lots of these pots and pans and the utensils and things, we can get reproductions."

Dave thought he could probably talk a few dealers he knew into donating some of the smaller things. "But when it comes to the big stuff, like some of this furniture, there's no way to get around it," he said. "No one's going to let stuff that old go for free. We'll have to pay."

Frank asked, "How much are we looking at?"

"For all of this last section?" Dave skimmed over the two pages with an expert eye. "Assuming we get maybe, what? A quarter of it donated?" He named a sum so large that it was sobering.

Frank whistled, low, and Tracy frowned. She said, "See, I'd been thinking we could set a list up like the library does for the books it wants to buy. You know, list all the things we want to get and people could adopt an item if they wanted. Donate fifty dollars and adopt a candle snuffer, or a chamber pot."

Frank told her, "Good idea."

"But," said Tracy, "if Dave's right with his appraisal—"

"My suggestion," Dave corrected her. "I'm not allowed to give appraisals."

"—then it isn't going to be enough," she said. "We'll need more money."

Lara, having helped herself to a cinnamon bun, took a thoughtful bite. "We could ask the Sisters of Liberty."

Tracy was shaking her head. "When they gave their donation to our restoration fund, they were very clear on how their bylaws capped what they could give each year for building preservation."

Countering with logic, Lara said, "But this wouldn't be about the building, would it? It's about the contents. And the contents will be used for education, and I'm pretty sure the bylaws don't cap what the Sisters give each year for education." Looking round at all of us, she gave a little shrug. "I think it's worth a shot."

Frank thought it through. "You might be right." He looked at Tracy. "Doesn't your better half cater their luncheons?"

"Not since they started to meet at the Privateer Club."

I had never set foot in the Privateer Club. It was one of the ritzier yacht clubs that fronted the bay, very modern, all windows and balcony railings. It sat on the opposite shore near Cross Harbor and often was easy to pinpoint from all the white sails dotted round on the water in front of it.

Lara said, "A couple of my regular customers belong to the Sisters of Liberty. And I heard one of them saying the other day that their next speaker had cancelled and they're on the lookout for someone to fill the September spot. I could pitch them a talk about Benjamin Wilde and this inventory we've got of his things, and how we're using it to track down what belonged to him and bring it home to Millbank. I'll bet they'd find that interesting."

I hadn't known Lara long, but I had known her long enough to grow suspicious when she turned her innocent blue gaze toward me.

"Who would give this talk, exactly?" I asked.

"You could," was her answer. "You're good at talking to groups like that. It'll be fun."

Frank was looking at me as though he knew there were few things that were further down my register of being "fun" than speaking to a roomful of strange women. I knew he wouldn't push me into doing it, but since it was, beyond all doubt, a very good idea, I consented.

"Fine," I said. "You go ahead and make your pitch, and if they say yes, I'll come do the presentation but I'm not quite in the same class," I said, "as the Sisters of Liberty."

Dave said, "I wouldn't say that."

"No?" From what I knew about them they admitted only those who claimed—and proved—direct descent from any member of the Revolution-era Sons of Liberty, which made them an exclusive club.

"No." Dave was very sure. "In fact, you could become a member if you wanted to."

He was really good, I thought, at keeping his delivery deadpan. So I played along. "Is that a fact?"

Frank gave the answer. "Yep." No trace of any humor. He was serious. "Our local chapter's president," he told me, "is your grandmother."

❧

The last time I'd driven the shore road, I hadn't seen much past the taillights of Sam's truck. This evening, without the rain, it was a different experience. Now I could see the broad view of the bay, as the curving road dipped into tunnels of trees and emerged again into the softening light. The road ran at a higher elevation than the shoreline in some places and at times I'd come around a bend and find that I was level with the roof of some expensive house built close along the water's edge, its sloping driveway gated.

These were few and far between, but when I passed the fourth one I slowed down deliberately, keeping my gaze forward in anticipation. One more bend to navigate, one more short closed-in stretch of arching trees, and there it was—the redbrick wall that rose along the roadside. Not a high wall, but enough to shield the property within from prying eyes and passing motorists. I couldn't see the house that lay beyond it, but that didn't matter.

I had seen the pictures.

Once when I'd been searching through the closet where we kept our family photos, on the hunt for baby pictures of myself with which to illustrate my "All About Me" project in third grade, I'd asked Niels to help reach a box down from a higher shelf, and we'd dislodged an album I had never seen before. A small black photo album that had tumbled down and hit me on the head.

"Ow!" I'd said. Then, as I'd looked inside the album, "Hey, it's you! What house is that?"

My brother had looked, too. "I don't know." He'd bent closer. "That's not me."

"Is too."

My brother had been twenty, home to visit us that week from university, but he'd still answered back, "Is not."

"Who is it, then?" Frowning, I had flipped the pages, looking at the boy who had a face just like my brother's.

Niels had guessed the answer first. "It's Dad."

We'd stood there in the closet looking through that photo album with a growing sense of wonder until Niels had reached to take it from my hand. "We shouldn't have this," he had said. He'd put it back where it had been, up on the shelf. "Dad wouldn't want us looking at it."

"Why?" I'd asked.

Niels hadn't been specific. "He just wouldn't."

But I'd gone back to that closet later, used a chair to stand on, and retrieved the album from the shelf to look at it more carefully. I'd seen the photos of my father, sometimes with another boy who looked like him, but taller; sometimes with an older woman, or an older man, or both. And very often with that house—that mansion, really—in the background.

I'd gone back to look at it the next day, and the next, until my mother had asked why I had been standing on the chair. I'd been a truthful child. I'd told her.

"Oh," she'd said. I could still remember. She'd been dusting. She had kept her back toward me for a moment while she'd concentrated on the beveled edge of the long mirror in our hallway. Then she'd said what Niels had said. "Your father wouldn't want you looking at that. It would make him sad."

"That other boy who's in the pictures with him. Is that Uncle Jack?"

"Yes."

"And are those his parents?"

"Yes."

My grandparents, I'd thought. It had seemed strange, because I'd only ever known one set of grandparents.

"And is that house the house where Dad grew up?"

"Yes. No more questions, now," she'd warned me, as we'd heard my father's footsteps coming up the stairs. And when I'd looked to find the album next time, it was gone. I never saw it after that.

My mother hid things like an expert.

But that didn't matter. I had seen the pictures. I'd remembered what was written on the sign above the gateposts. And the next time I'd been at my best friend's house, I'd looked it up on her computer: *Bridlemere*.

That's how I'd learned that the house had been built in the late 1940s for my father's father—my grandfather—Werner Van Hoek, on a piece of land that had belonged to my grandmother's family—my family—for six generations.

The driveway had come into view now, the gates framed by redbrick posts standing like guardians, the name of the house wrought in iron above them. I couldn't have counted the number of times, from my childhood till now, I'd imagined myself driving up to those gates and demanding they open to let me pass through, so that I could see with my own eyes where my father had come from. The home he had left behind.

This evening, given that chance, I did nothing. I simply drove by. And if Bridlemere's gates even noticed my passing, they didn't let on.

⤶⤷

"What *I* don't understand," said Rachel, scooping out the last piece of lasagna, "is how anyone could do it."

She was sitting at the breakfast bar and watching while I tidied up the kitchen counter, tucking takeout menus behind canisters and sweeping all the other papers into one of the deep bottom drawers, beneath the folded tea towels.

"I mean," said Rachel, holding to the subject like a pit bull, "Dad would never have disowned me."

"I don't know. That time you broke curfew and ended up getting in trouble with... What was her name?"

"Amy. And the policeman was really nice."

"I'm sure he was. I'm just saying, you came pretty close, there, to being disowned." We both knew I was only teasing, but I raised my glass to hide my smile so I'd at least look serious. I'd skipped the lasagna, myself, and gone straight for the wine. It was helping. "The only thing that saved you was the fact your dad had done the same thing when he was a teenager."

"My dad? My straitlaced, keep-it-legal father?"

"That's the one." I told her all about it, then, because I'd found it did us both good when I told these stories—sharing all the little parts of Niels that I held close, and passing them like legacies to Rachel. She was laughing when I'd finished, and that, too, was good. "Your grandfather," I promised her, "was furious."

"I can't imagine Grandpa being furious."

"You'll have to take my word for it."

"But see? That only proves my point. Your kids might make you really mad, but you don't go and cut them off. You don't stop talking to them."

"Well, I think with Grandpa and his parents, things were just a bit more complicated."

"How?"

I couldn't form an easy answer. Reaching for the wine bottle, I filled my glass again and thought about it, searching for the proper words.

There wasn't any simple way to talk of how wars had divided people's loyalties and shattered family ties down through the centuries. I thought of Joseph Wilde, the brother Frank had told me no one really talked about, not even now, his name and birth date all that had remained of him within the family record. When he'd taken sides against his brothers in the Revolution, I didn't doubt he'd been cut dead by all his family, as my father had been. Like my father, Joseph Wilde had traveled north to start a new life in another country. Like my father, probably he'd never seen his home again. A heavy price to pay, I thought, for following your conscience.

My father's conscience hadn't made him fight against his family. But it had made him refuse to fight the war they'd wanted him to fight; the war that had already killed his older brother, Jack.

My father's conscience had been speaking louder to him, I supposed, than any threats or arguments his parents might have made. And so he'd let it lead him north, to Canada, and they had not forgiven him.

It hadn't been a secret in our house, when I was growing up. My parents had a lot of friends who also had been draft resisters; who'd come up to Montreal the same year as my father, and who'd formed their own community around the same shared neighborhood. And even when my parents moved the family to Toronto after I was born, they all still stayed in touch and visited.

My mother had explained to me, the year I'd started school, in simple terms.

"There was a war in Vietnam," she'd said. "Your father's brother died there. Lots of people didn't think it was a good war to be fighting. If you didn't want to fight the war, you had to come to Canada, or go to jail. Your father's parents didn't think that he should come to Canada. They told him if he did, they'd never speak to him again."

"What did he do?" I'd asked, although I had already known the answer.

"He came anyway." She'd looked at me. "Sometimes, you can't make everybody happy."

I had learned, as I grew older, that my father didn't like to talk about the past. His past. He *really* didn't like to talk about his brother. These were like the sometimes unseen bruises that were left when you had fallen from your skateboard on your knees and, even though there were no scrapes or scratches, if you pressed your fingers on the spot it still hurt afterward for days. My father's memories of the past were like those bruises, and we took care not to poke them.

In my eighth-grade history class we'd watched a vivid documentary about the Vietnam War, and I'd finally understood in a more grown-up and complete way what it was my father and his friends had faced, and why they'd protested, and why it had been difficult for everyone involved.

But sometimes, honestly, I thought the simpler answer I'd been given as a child was still the truest one.

Sometimes, you can't make everybody happy.

"How," demanded Rachel, "was it complicated?"

With a shrug, I drank my wine and told her, "It just was."

Unconvinced, she said, "Well, it's a good thing that it will be you and not me at that Sisters of Liberty lunch thing. I'd tell Great-Grandma Van Hoek what I thought of her, right to her face."

There were no guarantees that I wouldn't be tempted to do the same thing, I thought. Even if, as the museum's curator, I'd have to be diplomatic.

My niece said, "I saw her once, you know. When Dad and I first moved here."

"Did you?" I'd only seen her in photographs.

"Yeah. She looked like a—"

"Hold that thought," I interrupted. My cell phone was playing a personal ringtone—the iconic whistling theme from a Clint Eastwood western—which meant it was Tyler. I answered and put him on video. "Hi."

Rachel rolled her eyes, slid from her stool at the counter, and left me alone to my nightly call.

Just seeing Tyler's face made me feel happier. When I'd first met him I thought he'd been way too good-looking to wish for. His smile had been perfect, his tawny hair cut just a little bit long so the curling ends gave it a sleep-rumpled look, and his blue eyes so clear and so blue in his suntanned face that for the first while I'd thought he wore contacts. But all of it, as I'd eventually learned, had been real. And that smile was for me.

I asked, "How was your day?"

"Not too bad. Yours?"

I told him, with help from a third glass of wine, just exactly how my day had been. And I threw in the highlights of last night's board meeting.

"Wow. Fun."

"Not really. But at least I'll get a break from it next weekend. Oh, and the hotel said that we can have the bigger room, the one that has the view. If I can pack the car the night before, I can drop Rachel at her residence and get her all unloaded and have time to make it down to the hotel to meet you there for lunch, is that okay?"

"About that," Tyler said.

The way he said it warned me.

"What?"

"Well, Bob from work…remember Bob? His wife walked out on him last month, and he's been having a hard time, so some of us decided we should take him to Atlantic City. Cheer him up."

"And?"

"And the guys decided that we're doing that next weekend." He could see my face. "I'm sorry," he said, sounding like he was.

"I'll make it up to you, I promise. We can meet up in the city anytime, right?"

"But I made the reservation. Like you asked me to," I said. "It's nonrefundable."

"I'll cover that, don't worry. Hey, you can still go and stay yourself. Go see a show, or something. Have a break, like you were saying."

"Ty."

He promised me again, "I'll make it up to you." And smiled the smile he knew would end the argument.

It wasn't that I didn't want to argue; that I didn't want to push the point and ask him why his boys' night in Atlantic City had to be next weekend, why it couldn't be the weekend after that, and why he felt it was okay to let *me* down but not his coworkers.

But when he smiled like that—his salesman smile—I knew his mind was set, and nothing I could say was going to change things.

"Fine," I said.

I said it once again when we were finishing the phone call, and he wanted to make sure I wasn't mad at him.

"I'm fine," I said.

And not long after that, when Rachel came downstairs to put the kettle on and found me standing at the sink, intent on scrubbing every bit of baked-on spatter from the glass lasagna dish, she asked, "Are you all right?"

"I'm *fine*," I said.

There was a pause.

"Okay, then," Rachel said. And very wisely left me on my own.

LYDIA

Y OU KEEP SCRUBBING THAT bowl," Violet warned, "you'll be wearing a hole in it." She'd just returned to the kitchen from gathering eggs and was looking at Lydia now with a mixture of mischief and sympathy. "All that poor bowl did was hold the man's breakfast. That's surely no reason to punish it."

Lydia straightened away from the basin and grimaced. "He vexes me."

Wiping the wooden bowl carefully dry, she set it with the others before glancing out the window at the place beside the shed where this past week, between the days of rain and wind, her father and Mr. de Sabran had been hard at work on the cider press. Today they were aiming to finish the caulking, her father had said, since the morning so far had been dry and what clouds they could see hung far off out to sea.

He'd seemed pleased to have help. It had left them astonished when Mr. de Sabran had set down his sword belt and shrugged off his waistcoat and, rolling the sleeves of his shirt to his elbows, had set about showing her father the way to position the crossbeam between the two sides of the cider press.

That had been all he had done that first day. With a nod he'd retreated and put on his waistcoat and picked up his sword, and exchanged a few clipped words with Mr. de Brassart, who'd seemed to be voicing a protest.

The next morning, though, when Mr. de Sabran had returned from his walk he had stopped to observe what her father was doing, and once again taken off both sword and waistcoat and lent his assistance.

"He knows what he's doing," her father had said, when he'd come in to wash before dinner that day. "He's no carpenter, but I'll not turn down a strong pair of hands when they're offered."

Her father had meant that short comment for Joseph, but Joseph had quietly let it slide by. Lydia, keenly aware of her father's frustration, had found herself growing increasingly grateful to Mr. de Sabran for helping him; but anytime she'd tried to act on this gratitude it had appeared to do nothing but increase the Frenchman's impatience.

This morning, when she'd tried to clear his empty bowl and teacup from the table, he had put her off with a short phrase in his own language and had picked them up himself and, rising, taken them across into the kitchen, to the basin, before heading out the door.

Which was why she had spent the past ten minutes scrubbing that same cup and bowl as though to clean off any clinging trace of him.

"He vexes me," she said again, to Violet. "He is always so ungracious."

"Well, Miss Lydia," was Violet's calm reply, "he's lost his freedom. Did you think that he would thank you for it?"

Lydia heard the rebuke in those words and accepted it, ashamed she'd needed the reminder that for people like herself, who'd had the fortune to be born and raised in liberty, its loss remained a hardship that they could not hope to know.

For years she had been ignorant of Violet's true condition, having grown up with the understanding Violet—like her mother, Phyllis—were free blacks. They'd been paid a servant's wage and never made to work on Sundays, and she'd known no differently until the year she'd turned eight.

That year, the funeral of her father's elder sister had drawn all the family back to Newtown. Well, not all, exactly—Phyllis had been left behind with Violet, and when Lydia had asked her father, "Why can't they come with us?" she'd received the curt reply, "Because they can't."

She'd been reassured by Phyllis, who'd maintained there were few places on this earth she wanted less to go than Newtown, and that being left behind on this occasion was no hardship but a blessing.

But that hadn't made it feel less wrong. And she'd missed having Violet to play with.

Lydia had met her father's brother for the first time at the funeral. He'd been only rarely talked about at home, and then but briefly, in the same pinched tones one used for speaking of unpleasant things. She'd understood why after meeting him. Uncle Reuben had been so unlike her father she'd have never known the two men were related.

His son, her cousin Silas, had been equally unpleasant. He'd been fourteen that summer, the same age as Joseph, though Joseph had already seemed a young man in his manners and physical build, whereas Silas had looked and behaved like a child who'd been overindulged. He'd been rude. He'd mocked their younger cousin Oliver, who stammered. He had slipped a silver spoon into his pocket at the table and, when Lydia had told him he must put it back, he'd done so with a sly smile that implied such things as theft were mere amusements. So she'd thought it only justice when, just after dinner, Benjamin had finally lost his temper and knocked Silas to the ground.

She hadn't heard the conversation that provoked it. She'd only seen Silas spin sideways and drop like a stone.

They'd left shortly afterward. And on the journey home no one had spoken at all until Benjamin finally had broken the silence. "He said when they were his, he'd sell them."

Without looking back, their father had replied, "They are not his. And he can make no claim to them until your uncle dies."

"And when that day comes," had been their mother's promise, "we'll do all we can to keep Phyllis and Violet safe."

Lydia, sitting in silence through all of this, had absorbed gradually what they were speaking of, and what it meant. And for days after that she had lived with a heavy place deep in her heart where a piece of her innocence had been torn out and replaced with the weightier truth of the world.

On the fourth day, her mother had taken her hand and they'd gone for a walk, through the cool of the trees to the path that led down to the edge of the cove where the tide, being in, lapped the shore with a shining, smooth surface that covered the tangle of reeds and dark rocks underneath. But she knew they were there.

She'd reminded her mother, "You said it was wrong to own people."

"It is. It is wrong. More than that, it's impossible." Squeezing her hand very slightly, her mother had explained, "One person cannot own another, darling, for our souls belong to us and God and no one else."

She'd been confused. "So Uncle Reuben doesn't own Phyllis and Violet?"

"He can only hold their bodies as a jailer holds a prisoner."

She had only vaguely understood, but she had known one thing with total certainty. "It is unfair."

Again her mother's hand had tightened briefly on her own. And then she'd bent and taken off her shoes and stockings, and had done the same to Lydia. "Come, let me show you something."

It had been a warm day but the water had been cold enough to numb her ankles as, beside her mother, she'd stepped into it. Beneath her feet the sand had shifted, changing to accommodate her, and when she had stopped to stand, it softly sank and swirled around her heels and toes and held her like an anchor.

Her mother, who like Lydia was standing with her skirts and apron gathered in her free hand, looking at the slowly drifting clouds above the blue horizon, had said, "When I'm feeling troubled and the weight of all my worries is a heavy thing to bear, I come down here, and in my mind I set each trouble on a wave and let it pass me by." She'd smiled down at Lydia. "You feel them passing?"

Lydia had felt those waves against her legs, and nodded.

Her mother had pointed. "Look there now, which trouble will you set on that?"

The swelling wave that moved toward them had but scarcely raised the surface of the water, but it had held darkness underneath it. "Silas," Lydia had said. "That wave is Silas."

"Then let's stand and let him pass us by. Good riddance to him."

But the darkness had been in the water still when that cold wave had passed, and nothing in the years between had managed to erase the threat of Uncle Reuben and her cousin Silas from their lives.

She knew it must be worse for Violet, but she'd never felt she had the right to ask how Violet felt.

She did not ask her now.

She only bent her head and answered, "No. You're right. Mr. de Sabran cannot enjoy being a prisoner. Perhaps I'm the one who is being ungracious."

"I didn't mean you had to treat him better," Violet told her. Moving up she dipped her own hands in the basin and began to wash them clean. "He's still a Frenchman. After what they did to Mr. Joseph and to—" With a sideways look at Lydia she caught the words back. "You don't owe them kindness. I just meant he had his reasons, too, for acting like he does." She looked where Lydia had just been looking, through the kitchen window to the cider press now taking final shape beside the shed. "At least he isn't idle, like His Majesty."

As if on cue, a series of by-now-familiar noises from the little chamber at the far end of the kitchen let them know Mr. de Brassart was just now awakening.

"His Majesty," said Lydia, dry voiced, "will want his toast and tea." And crossing to the hearth she swung the kettle into place above the low fire and began the preparations. She knew better than to ask Violet to do it, for if Lydia found it a challenge to mind her own manners while dealing with Mr. de Sabran, for Violet it seemed to be nearly impossible to walk the same floor as Mr. de Brassart.

He'd made a great show of accepting her father's reminder that Violet was not to be treated with anything less than respect, but his glances at times were so insolent Violet had come close to speaking her mind, and however sympathetic Violet might be to a person's loss of freedom, in his case she plainly thought it justice.

He had done himself few favors when he'd spoken up at dinner yesterday, starting badly to begin with by unwittingly asking about the one item of furniture in the whole house guaranteed to make them all fall silent.

"That's an interesting chair," he'd said. "Where was it made?"

He'd meant the chair that sat across the room, close by the window. It was curious in its construction, built upon an X-shaped frame instead of four straight legs, and with a leather seat slung lengthwise from the high back so its occupant, while well supported, did not sit completely upright. Her mother had adored that chair, since sitting very straight had caused her back to ache unbearably, and daily after dinner she had sat there with her needlework, the chair positioned just so it would sit within the light.

They had not moved it.

Lydia, aware the silence might stretch on forever if she did not speak herself, had said, "It is a Spanish chair. My brother Daniel sent it as a gift, from the West Indies."

That had roused Mr. de Brassart's interest. "Really? From where?"

"From Kingston, in Jamaica."

"He lives there, your brother?"

"Yes."

"I have a brother who lives in the West Indies also," he'd told her. "At Saint-Domingue."

Not knowing much about the islands or their relative positions, she had nodded in acknowledgment, content the conversation was no longer focused on her mother's chair. Until he'd added, "He has been there for many years, my brother. I have not seen his property, but he describes it in his letters very well. He has much land and many slaves. A great estate."

Violet had said nothing, though from the set of her jaw it had been plain she'd wanted to. Setting the platter of vegetables down with controlled force, she'd left the room. Joseph had frowned at his plate, and their father had frowned at the table.

But Benjamin, who never shied from confrontation, had sat forward and replied, "I should not reckon it a great estate if it was built upon the backs of others." His most charming smile had held a sharper edge of steel. "But what do I know? I am but a farmer's son," he'd said, "with one foot always in the fields."

Mr. de Brassart had smiled, too, very slightly, on hearing his words spoken back to him. Settling back in his chair he'd eyed Benjamin as any gamesman might eye a new challenger. "What is your own brother's business," he'd asked, "in Jamaica?"

Lydia had answered him, her tone cool as water poured over two dogs who'd been circling to fight. "He's the factor for our eldest brother's firm."

When she'd spoken, Mr. de Sabran's gaze had lifted with what might have been either interest or watchfulness, fixing on her face before moving on to de Brassart's as that man's attention swung back to her.

Mr. de Brassart had said, "You have many brothers, mademoiselle."

"I have four."

"Ah. Two here, and one in Jamaica, and the other…?"

"Is a merchant in New York."

"I see. He gathers merchandise and sends it to Jamaica, yes? And brings back from Jamaica things to sell here in New York? I should imagine he brings sugar, does he not? And indigo? And are these not produced by slaves? So then he also builds his business on the backs of others."

His logic had left no room for an argument, but Lydia had been aware of Benjamin beside her drawing breath to argue anyway, and so she had once more diverted him by asking him to pass the plate of vegetables, and used that action to lead into a discussion of which foods Mr. de Brassart had found curious and new when he'd first come across from France, and which had been familiar. Through their talk of corn and cucumbers, she'd seen Mr. de Sabran looking on with an expression that could only be described as disapproving.

And he'd worn that very same expression earlier this morning, when he'd spoken to her shortly and then stood himself to clear away his breakfast dishes.

Lydia, remembering that now, was frowning as she stirred the fire on the hearth. "It's been four weeks. Let's hope they won't be here with us much longer. With so many taken prisoner, the governor must surely be arranging an exchange."

Violet said, "I don't know about that. Mr. Fisher was saying last Sunday that one of the officers billeted over at Newtown had been here five years."

That made Lydia turn in dismay. "Five years?"

"That's what he said. Since the start of the war."

"Oh, I pray that won't happen to us." She would never be able to have these men here for five years, as a constant reminder of—

"God must be listening." Violet's words held a dry humor. Beckoning Lydia back to the window she pointed past Lydia's father and Mr. de Sabran, at work on the cider press, to the bright flash of a scarlet coat showing against the deep green of the trees, at the height of a soldier approaching on horseback. "Best put more water to boil in that kettle," she said. "We have company coming."

JEAN-PHILIPPE

D E BRASSART WAS AN idiot.

If Jean-Philippe had not been well aware of that already, he'd have come to that conclusion from just sitting here the past half hour and watching how the Frenchman interacted with the English captain. Fair enough, the English captain had so far been friendly; but an enemy, no matter how he smiled, was still an enemy.

The captain's choice to meet them in the room the Wildes called the "parlor," with its calm blue painted walls and silver sconces and the patient, homely ticking of the wood-cased clock, had plainly been designed to make them feel at ease and comfortable. More likely to converse.

That Jean-Philippe felt neither comfortable nor at his ease was not for want of effort by the captain, who had taken care to sit, not stand above them, and addressed them in near-perfect French with scarcely any accent. He was older than the other two men by perhaps ten years, of middle height, and with the kind of build that did not alter much with age but stayed forever lean and upright. His face was lean as well and there was nothing in his features that a man might find remarkable. His whole demeanor, like his voice, was even and straightforward.

Yet Jean-Philippe did not relax his guard.

In such a situation it was best to chart a neutral course and keep his face expressionless and not betray his comrades or their cause—a lesson that de Brassart had not learned, it seemed, in France.

"No, there were only four," de Brassart said now, listing off which regiments had been at Fort Niagara: "The La Sarre—that is my own, of course—the Béarn, the Royal Roussillon, and the Guyenne."

The captain, sitting at Monsieur Wilde's desk, dipped his pen in ink again and made a note of this. He had a tidy, careful hand. A man not unaccustomed to the art of writing. Jean-Philippe could picture him more easily in some dim office than upon a battlefield; although there, too, he would be careful. Someone who obeyed whatever orders he'd been given.

Such a man, when on your own side, was an asset. But he was not on their side.

The captain asked de Brassart, "And the Troupes de la Marine? How many companies were there?"

"That I would not know. You'd have to ask Lieutenant de Sabran."

The captain turned his head and looked at Jean-Philippe expectantly. Politely.

Jean-Philippe said nothing.

Privately, he felt glad he had chosen Monsieur Wilde's tall chair to sit in, since the angle of its back and arms allowed him to sit very straight while masking any tension in his body. He held himself as stoically as if he had been on parade, conserving all his energy in silence.

For an instant he saw something in the captain's eyes that might have been respect.

De Brassart said, "Oh, come now, answer the man's question. He can hardly be expected to arrange for an exchange of prisoners if he doesn't know our number." He looked to the captain with confidence. "There will be an exchange soon, will there not?"

"I believe General Amherst expects there to be one before he breaks camp for the winter."

As answers went, thought Jean-Philippe, that one took care to promise nothing. Which was fair. Negotiations between General Amherst and the Marquis de Montcalm—their own commander—would be slow. The couriers would have to take their letters across Lake Champlain and up along the forest trails and then by boat again down the St. Lawrence River to Quebec, and then return with the reply. It would take time. Meanwhile, the fighting season would be finished in a month or so, the soldiers on both sides retreating to their winter quarters. If there hadn't been a prisoner exchange arranged by then, he might be stuck here till the armies reassembled in the spring. And that would be a problem—for himself, and for the Wildes.

This family was already showing the strain of supporting them after no more than a month. If de Brassart and he had to stay through the winter, the Wildes could not manage it.

She could not manage it.

This morning when she'd served his breakfast she had been so tired there had been shadows underneath her eyes and when she'd sat a moment by the hearth those eyes had briefly closed—so briefly that he doubted she had even been aware of it. But he had seen.

And when she'd moved to take his bowl he'd tried to let her know she did not need to waste her energy in serving him, he'd do it by himself.

He'd done it badly. He had seen the crease between her eyebrows, seen her hurt confusion, and the stifled irritation that replaced it. Had he smiled, perhaps, and spoken kinder words, he might have smoothed the moment over; but the truth was, he'd been irritated, too.

They were a burden on this family, and on her. They should not be here.

"So you see," de Brassart said, "this is why Captain Whitlock—"

"Wheelock." The captain's correction was pleasant in tone.

"I beg your pardon. It's why Captain Wheelock needs this information from us. Being stubborn is a help to no one."

Jean-Philippe, unmoved, returned the captain's gaze with a reflection of the same unyielding expectation, waiting.

Captain Wheelock faintly smiled. And played a different card. From an inner pocket of his coat he drew a folded paper which he opened on its creases and consulted as though seeking to refresh his memory. "Lieutenant de Sabran is not required to tell me anything. But it would help if he would, at the very least, make me a list of the names of his men."

Jean-Philippe saw his own writing on the paper in the captain's hand, and recognized the letter he had written to the governor of New York. Mr. Wilde had told the truth then, when he said that he had sent it. Leaning back, he kept his tone flat and his face impassive. "Was there not a list already made?"

"Unfortunately not." The corners of the captain's mouth compressed the smallest fraction. Only briefly, but enough that Jean-Philippe knew his assessment of the captain had been accurate: a man with a decided sense of right and wrong, who disapproved when others broke the rules.

Such men, in life and war, took one of two roads and became either intolerant or honorable.

Jean-Philippe suspected Captain Wheelock was the latter. And seeing in the captain's face a flicker of discomfort, he ventured to reverse their roles a moment, asking, "But you do know where they are?"

"They will be either on Long Island, in Connecticut, or in New Jersey." Pausing, he admitted, "They might be in all three places."

"But how is that possible? The terms of our capitulation at Niagara clearly said our men and officers were not to be divided."

"I regret to say that Governor DeLancey had not seen that paper," said the captain, "or perhaps he would have made a different distribution. As it is, I cannot yet tell where your men have been disposed of. All the prisoners were sent away in sloops to different parts, but I shall know soon where they are by going round them."

Jean-Philippe did not relax his guard upon his features, but he knew his quiet anger must be showing in his eyes because the captain said, with understanding:

"I assure you General Amherst wishes to comply with all the terms of the capitulation, and with the agreement that was signed this winter past between your king and mine, regarding treatment of all prisoners of war. The general sent me here believing I'd find you together with your men, so we could give you funds to give each man the daily fourpence he's entitled to, with firewood and clothing. We did not expect—" He caught himself, and smoothing the frustration from his tone, said, "This is inconvenient for us both, Lieutenant. That is why I'm asking every officer I meet with here to list the soldiers under his command, so I can use these lists to bring things back into a proper order." With the letter to the governor still held within his hand, he raised it slightly. A reminder. "I had hoped that, since you showed such a concern for your own men, you wouldn't find this very difficult."

The anger simmered still, but what was done was done, and Jean-Philippe could understand that it was not the captain's fault. He held his hand out silently and Captain Wheelock handed him the pen and moved to make space for him at the desk.

"With their ranks as well," the captain added, "if you can."

He could. He wrote the thirty-two names swiftly, firmly, signed his name below them and returned the page.

De Brassart, when faced with the same request, wrote only two names on his list. "My second lieutenant and sergeant. Find either of them, and I warrant they'll make you a full and complete list of all my men."

If any other officer had said that, Jean-Philippe might have assumed he was concealing what he knew, but with de Brassart it could only mean he did not know the names himself. "My men," he called them, yet he did not know their names.

He noticed Captain Wheelock made that small betraying facial movement, tightening the corners of his mouth as though he disapproved. On that at least, thought Jean-Philippe, they could agree.

There was not much to settle after that. They had given their paroles already at New York when they had first arrived, and Captain Wheelock had the copies, so there was no further paperwork.

De Brassart, when informed that they could go, excused himself and bowed and left the room, but Jean-Philippe stayed where he was. This was his ground, while he was on it. He would be the last to leave.

As if he understood that, Captain Wheelock gathered up his things and rose and gave a short nod of acknowledgment. "Lieutenant."

Jean-Philippe stood too, aware that while this man was yet his enemy, his rank deserved respect. As did the fact they both appeared to share a common code of honor. "Captain Wheelock."

"Do you have sufficient money for your needs?"

"Yes."

"Because I can advance you more."

"I've no expense but room and board, and I have funds to settle that until November." He had done the calculations. "If we have not been exchanged by then, I will inform you what I need."

The captain smiled. "Perhaps your hosts will charge you less, since you seem to be paying them in labor, also." Likely he had meant that in a friendly way, a lightly joking reference to the fact that when the captain had arrived that morning, Jean-Philippe had not been in his uniform but in his shirtsleeves, working side by side with Monsieur Wilde. But the captain's words, phrased like that, seemed to imply Monsieur Wilde had been taking advantage. And Jean-Philippe could not allow that.

He said, in a tone that rejected the joke, "I am helping my host with his cider press."

Captain Wheelock, as though conscious of his misstep, said, "Of course." And then, "Forgive me, I meant no offense." He moved toward the doorway.

Jean-Philippe frowned. "Captain."

"Yes?"

Throughout their meeting, Jean-Philippe had taken care to keep his own gaze from too often drifting to the parlor window and the view it offered of the trees beside the barn, where for some time the younger brother had been climbing through the branches cutting clumps of berries to be tossed down to his sister.

It was clearly an old game with them, and Jean-Philippe could not help but be jealous of the laughter she gave easily to someone else.

He'd purposely not watched them long, in case his face betrayed his interest in her to the captain. It was never wise to let your captor see a weakness he could use against you.

Even now he did not glance toward the parlor window, though he wanted to. "What you just said...'Forgive me, I meant no offense'..."

"Yes?"

"How," asked Jean-Philippe, "does one say that in English?"

CHARLEY

M Y OFFICE WAS CROWDED this morning. Malaika had dropped by to give me some forms to fill out for the budget, and Lara had brought me a fan—an electric one, still in its box. "It's too hot in this room," she'd explained. "You need air."

More air and light and color was, in Lara's world, the answer to all ailments. And in this case she was right: my office *was* warm.

The sturdy window-mounted air conditioner that hummed out in the hallway did a decent job of cooling all the other upstairs rooms on our side of the house, but because my room still kept its older colonial footprint the door was offset just enough that the air didn't really flow through. So I'd welcomed the fan.

I'd also suggested that, given the heat, we should probably think about moving a bookcase from my office down to the room at the end of the hall that eventually would be our archives. We didn't have that many truly old books yet, but paper was better preserved in a cooler and drier space. And while Malaika and I had looked over the bookcases, choosing which one we should move, I had mentioned the papers that Frank had brought yesterday, and she had wanted to see them.

And that had led sideways, as things did, to us trading theories on Lydia Wilde and her captured French officer.

Lara said, "Parole of honor doesn't seem like something that should even work. To have captured officers walking around and not locked up in jail is just asking for trouble."

I told her it was just the way they did things in those days. "Not only officers. A lot of common soldiers, too, were billeted in private homes here on Long Island. They didn't have big prisons then, like we do now."

Lara still thought it sounded ridiculous.

Lifting the fan from its box she went on, "If an officer just signs a paper that says, 'No, I promise I'm not going to fight you until I'm exchanged,' what's to stop him from breaking his word?"

"Well...his honor."

"So one day I'm killing your friends in the woods, and the next day, because I've just signed this thing promising not to fight, I get to live in your house, and you just let me walk around? Really?"

"Pretty much. It worked both ways," I said. "The British officers who ended up as prisoners in Quebec were given freedom of the city there, and got to walk around and go to dinners and to dances. It was just how they did things. It meant something then, when a man gave his word."

By my desk, her attention now fixed on Frank's uncle's collection of papers, Malaika chimed in with, "*Some* men. There were liars back then, same as now. Just ask my five-times-great-grandfather. He nearly died fighting Redcoats because he'd been promised that if he would fight in the place of the son of the family that held him, they'd give him his freedom. It didn't work out that way. Speaking of which," she said, still looking down at the papers, "didn't Frank tell us Benjamin Wilde's family didn't hold slaves?"

"That's right."

Lara held up the fan. "Where do you want this?"

"Back here in the corner, I think. You might have to unplug the lamp."

Taking a look she said, "No problem. It's unplugged already."

Turning in my chair, I looked myself to where the lamp's plug lay beside the baseboard, on the floor. I remembered it being there yesterday morning, too...but then I'd plugged it in.

"Strange," said Malaika. Lifting a paper from the file, she passed it to me. "Seems like someone didn't get the memo."

What she'd handed me *was* strange, in light of what we knew—
or thought we knew—about the family.

Photocopied from a letter dated *Newtown, 16th April 1754*, it
read in a slanting and spidery hand:

Brother,

*I have learned of the loss of my property and will expect to receive
payment from you of forty-two pounds New York money to clear
this account as she was a skilled cook and not old. Violet now being
twelve by my reckoning I will reclaim her but if you desire her to
stay with you know that the price must be double what it was, to
be paid as before 1st July each year, for she is no more a child and I
would have her back or hire her to the best advantage.*

It was signed *Reuben Wilde*, who would have to be Zebulon
Wilde's brother. Lydia's uncle.

"You know what that is?" asked Malaika.

I nodded. "It looks like a slave lease."

The fan clicked on, and Lara set it to oscillate. "I know I'm
going to sound stupid for asking this," she said, "but what is a
slave lease?"

Malaika explained. "Slaves were looked on as property, valued
like livestock, so just like a person could rent someone's horse
if they didn't own one of their own, they could rent someone's
slave, too. It wasn't uncommon."

"It's sad, though," said Lara. She crossed to read over my
shoulder. "Do you think Frank knows about this?"

"I would think so," was my guess. "Frank doesn't miss much."

Malaika shrugged, elegant. "You'd be surprised what we
choose not to see."

Lara told her, "That's true. You know, back when I went
to school we never learned about us having slaves in the north.
It was all just the Underground Railroad and Lincoln, and how

we were good and the south was so bad, and then I read this article on slavery in Brooklyn and it said at one time New York had more slaves than any city except Charleston. And it blew my mind. I mean," she said, "it shouldn't have. I should have known of course we had slaves, too. The history was all right there, if I'd just looked for it."

"You liked the 'nice' story better." Malaika was matter-of-fact. "Most folks do. It makes them feel good." Looking at me she said, "That's why this might be a problem for you."

"Why?"

"If you're trying to broaden our mandate to take in the whole life of Benjamin Wilde, with his sister and all that, how much of his 'whole life' are you going to show?"

I could see what she meant. If there had been slaves here in the Wilde House, there were people who wouldn't want that to smudge their already bright image of Benjamin Wilde. But I looked at the lease in my hand and said, "All of it."

"Frank might not like that."

"I'll talk to him."

"Gird your loins first," was Malaika's advice.

Lara smiled. "Frank likes Charley."

Malaika said, "Honey, we all have our blind spots."

I looked up and laughed. "Thanks."

"I didn't mean *that*." She was laughing, too. "I just meant all of us have things we can't or won't see. Even Frank. He's so proud of his family, he might not... Well, don't expect miracles." Setting the open file back on my desk she rolled her shoulders, stretching them, and glanced at her cell phone. "I've got a showing in less than an hour. Are we moving this bookcase? No, you sit, we'll do it," she told me.

I knew not to argue. I sat where I was while the two of them emptied the small metal bookcase, maneuvered it into the hallway, and carried it down to the room we had chosen to use as our archives.

Returning the slave lease to where it belonged, I was closing the file when the fan stopped.

The air settled over me, heavy and thick and uncomfortably warm. *Great,* I thought. *Brand-new fan, and it lasts for ten minutes before it breaks down.*

But that wasn't the problem. The plug had dropped out of the outlet.

The holes of that outlet, I reasoned, were probably too large, or too loose. But no, when I bent down to push the plug in again, the prongs fit firmly and tight. The fan started again, and I felt the quick rush of air on my face. But I felt something else, too—the cold sweep of something that lifted the hair at the back of my neck, like the brush of a hand.

As I watched, the plug slowly, deliberately, worked its way out of the outlet again, and dropped to the floor, by the baseboard.

✧

I took the stairs two at a time, going down.

Why I went for the stairs in the first place and didn't just go to the room where Malaika and Lara were moving the bookcase, I didn't know. Nor did I take time to analyze. Maybe it was because they were way down at the end of the hall and the stairway was closer. Or maybe it was because I knew I probably looked like I'd seen...well, a ghost. And until the more logical part of my brain kicked in with the reminder there were no such things as ghosts, I didn't want to have anyone see me and ask what was wrong, because—

"Hey." Sam caught hold of my arms as I came barreling around the corner at the bottom of the stairs and nearly ran him over. As he steadied me he saw my face. "What's wrong?"

Sam's eyes were nice. Warm brown. Sincere. The kind you told your problems to. But not the kind you told that you'd been seeing things. I didn't want him thinking I was crazy.

So I forced a smile that might have fooled my mother.

"Nothing's wrong. I just came down for coffee." Which, now that I was down here, sounded suddenly appealing.

Sam let go of me and stepped aside as I moved to the counter, and I saw him slightly flex his shoulder.

"Sorry for running you over," I said.

"That's okay. Next time I'll know not to come between you and coffee."

My smile, this time, was real. "It can be dangerous. You want some, too?"

"Sure."

His boots, now entering my line of vision, were still relatively clean. He must have just arrived on-site. He didn't have the dog today.

I asked, "Where's Bandit?"

"Day care." Then, in answer to my look, he said, "No, really. I can't leave him on his own, he has anxiety. And there's too much going on today to have him here."

There was something kind of sweet about a manly man who put his beagle into doggy day care so it wouldn't be alone. I told him, "You can leave him in my office anytime, you know. I wouldn't mind the company."

An understatement at the moment, since I really didn't want to be alone up in my office. The logical part of my brain was still taking its time kicking in, leaving plenty of room to imagine what might have been pushing or pulling that plug from the wall. So much so that the thump of steps coming downstairs made my shoulders tense up.

It was only Malaika. "Hey, Sam. I thought I heard your voice down here."

In the exchange of "good mornings" and small talk that followed as Lara came down the stairs after her, I poured Sam's coffee and my own and fetched the Tupperware container I'd kept hidden in the cupboard. When I set it on the counter with Sam's coffee mug he glanced at it, then grinned. "No way!"

"I promised."

He looked like a kid with his cinnamon bun. A possessive kid. Lifting it up and away from Malaika as she leaned in closer to see what it was, he said, "Mine."

She assured him he could keep it. "I just have to look at those things and I gain ten pounds right on the spot."

"Better not watch, then." He bit off a mouthful and looked at me. "Thank you."

"You're welcome."

"I brought you something, too," he said, and nodded to the space beside the side door just behind him, where unnoticed by me until now, a wooden-framed screen leaned against the wall.

My turn to smile. "Oh, Sam, that's perfect!"

Malaika ventured, "Dare I ask?"

I told her, "I asked Sam if he could make a screen so we could sift the soil they're digging up, for artifacts."

"I made you three," he said. "The other two are in the truck."

Malaika's glance gently reminded me we hadn't run this through the proper budgetary channels for approval. "How much did they cost?"

"That's okay," I said, "I've got this. I'm paying Sam out of my pocket."

Sam shook his head. "I've been paid." And he lifted the cinnamon bun as his evidence. "I already had most of the pieces just lying around in the shed, they'd have gone to scrap anyway."

If I'd read his face right he was telling the truth, but if that was the case he took pride in his work because what he had brought didn't look roughly made. He'd built it almost exactly to the width I'd shown him with my hands, about two feet wide, and maybe six inches longer in length so it made a slight rectangle, with rounded handles at one narrow end. And he must have done some research on his own because at the other end, opposite the handles, he'd attached a hinged ladder-like "leg" that was built to lie flat on the back of the screen when it wasn't in use, and then

swing down and serve as a pivot supporting one end of the screen
so whoever was doing the sifting could work on their own simply
rocking it back and forth.

"I used quarter-inch mesh. Stainless steel," he said. "That
seemed to be what most other ones used. Was that right?"

"You just happened to have that lying around in your shed,
too?"

"Yep." Now he was fibbing, but he knew I knew it, his eyes
not even trying to be serious. He lifted his mug, took his first swig
of coffee, and couldn't entirely hide his reaction. He covered it
well, though, and I had to give him credit. When I'd made him
coffee last time it had turned out like the tar sands, and today the
coffee maker's mood had shifted so that mine, even with double
cream and sugar, tasted thin and weak as water. "Anyhow." He
set the mug down carefully. "I figured quarter-inch would let the
soil through fairly easily and still catch things like that old button
you showed me."

Malaika looked from Sam to me. "What button?"

"Oh." I hadn't meant to keep it secret from her, I'd just been
distracted by my reading of Frank's uncle's papers in the meantime.
"When I was locking up after the board meeting, I stumbled over
a button beside the foundation trench. Mid-eighteenth century.
Possibly French."

She connected the dots with her usual quickness. "As in a
French officer's uniform?"

"Possibly."

"Well then, I think we should definitely see what else is down
there in the dirt. Where's this button now?"

"Up in my office." I hid my reluctance to go back upstairs
when I offered to show her, then hid my relief when she shook
her head.

"Show me tomorrow. I've got to get going."

"And I need to open the store," Lara said, brushing by me with
a sideways hug. "I'll call you later with the verdict."

"Verdict?"

"The luncheon. The Sisters of Liberty. Didn't I tell you? I thought I did. Never mind. I had a talk with my clients," she summarized, "and they thought having us speak was a great idea. They said they'd talk to the powers that be and let me know sometime this afternoon."

"Sounds good." This time I knew my smile wouldn't have fooled my mom, but it felt fairly convincing and seemed to fool Lara.

So I was a little surprised when Sam, once we were left on our own in the kitchen, met my gaze knowingly. "Not your idea of fun?"

"What?"

"A Sisters of Liberty lunch." He was down to his last bites of cinnamon bun. "Are you sure you don't want any of this?"

I was sure.

"Well, don't worry," he said. "They're a nice group of women. They'll make you feel welcome."

All except one of them, I thought. My grandmother wouldn't be happy to see me. In fact, as their president, she might just veto the very suggestion of having me be their guest speaker.

But Sam, although he lived here, either didn't know my family's messed-up history or was too polite to mention it. "Too polite" was my guess, as I watched him diplomatically attempt another sip of coffee.

"You can pour it down the sink," I said. "It's awful. I know. The machine has a mind of its own."

He did as I suggested, rinsed the cup and washed his hands. "How do you drink this stuff?"

"I take caffeine any way I can get it."

"You're braver than me."

No, not really, I wanted to say as I watched him head back out to work, leaving me on my own in the house with whatever had pulled that plug out of the wall in my office. *I'm not brave at all.*

But I wasn't about to become like Frank's aunt, either, jumping at things that went bump in the night. Or the daytime.

I refilled my coffee mug, switched off the coffee machine, rinsed the pot out, and then—having delayed things as long as I could—I went back up the stairs.

In the door to my office I paused, and reminded myself that I didn't believe in ghosts. But just in case I was sharing my office with something that didn't care whether I thought it was real, I decided to play it safe. "Look," I said, speaking aloud to the empty room, "just knock it off, okay? Leave me alone."

Nothing answered, or moved, so I ventured inside. The plugs for the lamp and the fan still lay motionless on the floor next to the baseboard, behind my desk. Clearly I wasn't going to get anywhere by trying to plug them back in there, but the lamp was a necessity and I could really use the fan. The room felt stifling.

Picking up the lamp I crossed with what I hoped was nonchalance and moved it to another outlet opposite my desk. My fingers only shook a little as I plugged it in, and waited.

Nothing happened.

Reassured by that, I found a new spot for the fan beside the window, where its plug could share the power bar with my computer.

For the rest of the day, while I filled out the budget forms, dealt with my emails, and drafted a loan request letter to send to the other museums that held the few items we knew had once been in the Wilde House, my room remained obediently quiet. Nothing moved, apart from me, except the oscillating fan that sent its rhythmically repeating flow of cooling air across my desk and had a low-key whirring hum that muted the sounds of the workmen outside. So when my cell phone rang, the noise was jarring.

It was Lara.

❧

"The Sisters of Liberty? That sounds fun." Gianni Bonetti, the son of our neighbor, leaned back in his chair with a grin. He'd brought us meatballs and had stayed to help us eat them, and the three of us were sitting on the front porch of my brother's house now in the sultry warmth of this late-summer evening, while the colors of the sunset sky were softly overtaken by the deeper shades of blue. I'd once thought his mother was matchmaking, sending him over here, but I was starting to think it was Gianni's decision to play the delivery boy.

Twenty-two years old, he had a true Long Island accent—or, as he'd pronounce it, "LawnGUYland"—that turned all the *r*'s at the ends of his words into *ah*s and lengthened his vowels so *whatever* came out *whatevah* and *coffee* was *cawfee*, which I found adorable.

He also had a lady-killer smile and eyes for Rachel.

When she turned her gaze on *him*, he asked her, "What? I'm being serious. We used to cater their meetings before they moved out to the Privateer Club. They're a fun group of ladies."

"Ladies? Really?" Rachel challenged his word choice. "That's so patronizing."

He lifted his eyebrows. "I've heard you say 'lady.'"

"I say it ironically."

"Women, then." He shrugged it off and raised his arms to link his hands behind his head, a move that showed off his physique to good advantage.

I liked Gianni. He was a good-looking guy and he knew it, but underneath the cockiness he had a thoughtful nature and was smarter than he seemed.

He said, "I used to like to work their meetings. They had good presenters, really interesting. Once this lady—woman—came and talked about geology and how that ridge there, all of that was made back in the Ice Age, when the glaciers pushed the rocks down here and left them. That was fascinating. And another time, Sam Abrams—you know Sam, who's working up at your museum? Well, he talked about the architecture of the houses people lived in here during the Revolution. That was really cool."

I thought of Sam telling me this morning that if I spoke at a

Sisters of Liberty meeting they'd make me feel welcome. I hadn't known he was speaking from personal experience.

Settling back in the chair I had chosen, the old wicker rocking chair angled to face the road, I set it idly in motion.

My apartment in Albany hadn't had a balcony, let alone a porch, and I'd forgotten just how much I liked to sit like this, half-sheltered by the railing and the roof but with the whole outdoors before me in a panoramic view. The cooler air of evening felt revitalizing after my long day of working in the heat, and the summer sounds of insects singing in the reeds that edged the water of the bay behind the house rose on the breeze like music.

The sun had fully dropped from sight now. All along the ridge of darkened land that Gianni had just pointed out—the glacial moraine that formed the hills that gave this section of Long Island so much character—small lights had started twinkling on, like stars in the descending night. They were the lights of all the houses tucked amid the trees and winding roads that edged Millbank, some as old, or very nearly, as the Wilde House.

Watching those lights, I remarked, "I guess Sam's done work on a lot of old houses."

"Well, sure," Gianni said. "He was doing some work up at Bridlemere while they were meeting there, so that was cool, too, to see how he used antique tools. I mean, it isn't from the Revolution, but that house is *old*, you know?"

Tracing a finger through the condensation on the glass of iced tea I was holding, I cleared my throat and clarified, "The Sisters of Liberty used to have meetings at Bridlemere?"

"Oh, yeah. For years. They just moved to the Privateer Club this past spring." His shrug was pragmatic. "I think Mr. Kiersted made them an offer they couldn't refuse."

That didn't surprise me. For all he followed Sharon's lead on our board of trustees, Harvey seemed to like to throw his weight around in town. "Does the Kiersted Group own the Privateer Club, too?"

"Nah, but one of Mr. Kiersted's friends does. Owns the whole marina. So I'm sure Mr. Kiersted gets something for bringing him business."

Rachel thought that was unethical, and said so.

Gianni shrugged again. "You can't stop people doing what they do, you know? Some guys will always find a way to put an extra dollar in their pocket." But he did add, "It's a shame, though. I used to like working those meetings. Veronica did all the food. It was great. You won't get food like that at the Privateer Club."

Veronica, the daughter of the owner of the deli Gianni worked at, handled the catering side of their business. She was also the significant other of our museum treasurer, Tracy, and at my very first board meeting there'd been a tray of incredible canapes sent by Veronica, who had been testing new recipes for some upcoming event. Having tasted her cooking, I knew Gianni was right—any other chef probably wouldn't be able to match that.

But still, I felt relieved the meeting wouldn't be at Bridlemere. If I had to face my grandmother, at least it would be easier for this first meeting to take place on neutral ground. Besides, if it had been at her estate, there would have been no guarantee she'd even let me through the gates.

Gianni, though, had been through those gates. That made me curious. I asked him, "What is it like inside?"

"The Privateer Club?"

"No, Bridlemere."

"Big. Really fancy, old-fashioned, and big." Gianni lounged farther back in his chair and propped his feet carefully on the smooth top of the porch railing. My brother had "fixed" the porch railing when they'd first moved in, and you had to know just how to lean against it or else it tilted and wobbled, but Gianni appeared to have mastered the trick of it. "Too big for me," he said. "I'd rather have a house like the ones Sam talked about—you know, square house, square rooms, all the space you need and none you don't. I'd like to build a house like that, someday."

Rachel pointed out that, in a place like this, he wouldn't need to go to the trouble of building one. "There are lots of old houses in Millbank. You could just buy one and fix it up."

"Nah, I could never buy an old house. Might come with mice. Or a ghost. Hey," he said to me, "have you run into the soldier yet, up at the Wilde House?"

I answered a little too firmly. "No."

Rachel frowned. "What soldier?"

Gianni jumped in with the story and I let him tell it. He told the same version, or nearly the same, as Frank's—Lydia Wilde and the captured French officer falling in love, making plans to run off with each other, and being caught out by her big brother Joseph, who, seeing the light of their lantern pass by, had come out and confronted them there on the path, and had shot the French officer. But the way Gianni had learned the tale, Lydia Wilde hadn't died of a broken heart. She'd drowned herself in the cove. "She just followed him. Followed the light of her dead soldier's lantern, and he led her down to the water, and she walked right in."

One of the lights on the darkening ridge had begun to move— probably a motorcycle coming down one of the streets, but even so it made me feel uneasy and I looked away. I noticed Gianni, in his version of the story, hadn't given Lydia a name. She'd just been "Captain Wilde's sister." So I said, "Her name was Lydia."

"Yeah?" He looked at me with interest. "And the French guy? What was his name?"

"We don't know that, yet. I'm trying to do some research, though, so maybe I'll find out."

I recognized the look that Rachel sent me as the same one that my brother always used when I said something idiotic. "You do know it's just a story, right?"

"A lot of stories start from facts," I pointed out.

"I highly doubt you've got a ghost."

But Gianni begged to differ. "I've seen the soldier a bunch of times."

Rachel, her tone unimpressed, asked him, "Really? And what was he wearing?"

"You don't see the whole guy, you just see the light from his lantern. But trust me, it moves like a guy."

"Trust you?"

"Yeah." Gianni turned his head toward her and the angle of his chin was like a dare. "I'll take you up there now, tonight, and you can see him for yourself."

She faced him, too, and I was fairly sure that for the two of them, in that one moment, I'd become invisible.

"Nice pickup line you've got there," Rachel said. "I'll bet you get a lot of girls into the woods with you at night, with lines like that."

"I'll bet you scare a lot of guys away, with lines like that. Not me, though. I don't scare so easy." Gianni's grin flashed briefly in the dimming light. "Do you?"

In all her life, I'd never seen my niece back down from any challenge. And she didn't do it now. "I don't get scared by things that don't exist. You're on." She stood, remembered me, and turned to ask, "You want to come?"

"No, thanks." I stayed exactly where I was, securely in my rocking chair with my iced tea, and watched them leave in Gianni's car. I told myself I'd only stayed because I didn't want to be the third wheel, interfering in whatever was developing between them. But the truth was, I didn't feel nearly as certain as Rachel did that there'd be nothing to see. That they wouldn't find someone—or something—up there by the Wilde House, still walking the shadowy paths through the woods.

LYDIA

S HE WASN'T ALONE IN the woods.

She had known it for some minutes now, since she'd left the bright afternoon sun of the clearing around the small cluster of headstones and stepped again onto the path through the trees, and had glimpsed his blue coat through the branches behind her.

Before, in the time she'd spent pulling the weeds from her mother's grave, the clearing and woods had been empty and silent except for the trilling of birds and the buzzing of insects and now and again the swift rustling of some little creature across the thick carpet of moldering leaves.

Now, though, those rustlings had taken a rhythm that, although yet faint, confirmed someone was following.

Even if she had not seen his blue coat she'd have known it was him, because no shoes or boots would make sounds like that—only the softer-soled Indian footwear that Mr. de Sabran had taken to wearing these days when he went for his walks. It had taken them all by surprise when he'd pulled those strange shoes from his pack one day. Fashioned from deerskin and stitched all around, they were tied to the foot and not buckled, with flat, supple soles that had no added heels.

Mr. de Brassart, when asked by her father if he also had such shoes, had smiled with a trace of disdain and replied the Canadians of the Marine wore all sorts of strange clothing that was, in his view, unbecoming to white men. To which her brother Benjamin had pointed out such footwear gave a soldier an advantage, in that what the wearer lost in height and fashion he would gain in practicality. "He wouldn't leave much of a trail behind, no heavy footprints to follow," her brother had reasoned. "And they'd make so little sound, you could sneak up on your enemies and not be heard."

Mr. de Brassart had answered, as an officer and gentleman he had no wish to "sneak up" on his enemies. But with his words and tone he had implied Mr. de Sabran was no gentleman.

On that count, Lydia agreed.

That she heard him now behind her on the path, she guessed, was because he permitted it, and wasn't taking pains to stay concealed.

To test this, she stopped for a moment herself, and the rustlings—as she had expected—continued their sure pace toward her, and Mr. de Sabran advanced from the shadows and into plain view.

He seemed to be preoccupied; had seemed that way, she'd noticed, since the visit of the English captain yesterday. And when he saw her, he offered a brief and surprisingly courtly nod, and would have carried on past her had she not surprised herself further by saying, "Good afternoon."

That made him stop.

It was curious, Lydia thought, that she didn't feel threatened when standing alone with him here in the dappled half-light of the forest, so far from the house. She disliked him. Distrusted him. Wanted him gone. But she could not, in honesty, say that she feared him.

Not even when he turned his head and looked at her, his dark gaze level and direct.

He said, "*Bonjour,*" which she had come to know meant "good day" in his language. Then he frowned all of a sudden and said something else she did not understand, and made a gesture to her arm, and took a swift step forward and, without her invitation or consent, reached out to take her hand within his own. She might have made a protest had the shock not held her motionless, and had his touch not been so unexpectedly impersonal.

He held her wrist the way a doctor might, and turned it carefully, examining the spattering of red stains on her skin. She didn't understand at first why he should be concerned, until it dawned on her he thought she had been bleeding. He was looking for the wound.

He wouldn't find one. All her true wounds were so deep within her nobody would ever see them, and the stains upon her wrist and inner arm had not been made by blood.

Her voice, when she could find it, sounded harsher than it should have. "It's the rowan berries," she said. "I was only drying rowan."

She had spent two hours after dinner threading berries onto strings to be hung in the buttery to keep till they were needed. Messy work, it always was, and she had all but ruined her apron with the stainings of the juice, but then of course he would have had no way to know that. He'd been working with her father.

She could feel the calloused hardness of his hand, sunbrowned and strong beneath her smaller one. She pulled her own away and broke the touch, and said, "It's nothing."

There was no need to step back for he was doing that already, his frown darkening his features as he nodded once again.

Then in slightly cautious English he remarked, "Forgive me." Cleared his throat and added, "I meant no offense."

And turning, carried on his way and left her standing in confusion.

JEAN-PHILIPPE

H E HADN'T EXPECTED TO meet her at all; he had thought she was still in the house, hadn't noticed her leaving, but then his own thoughts had been elsewhere since yesterday. Learning his men were not only divided from him but most probably from one another, and scattered as prisoners over three provinces, had only stoked his dark sense of frustration, and most of today he'd been deep in that mood.

This second walk within the woods had been his own attempt to blunt the edges of that mood and lift its blackness.

Every forest had a different feel. The trees, the undergrowth, the fall of light between the leaves—these changed from place to place so that a man might know if he was in the north or south or west or east, and every forest had its own array of creatures, fierce and gentle, to contend with; but he always looked among them for the small familiar faces.

Like the little birds, the *grives des bois*, with their homely brown feathers and spotted white breasts and their quick black eyes, rustling along through the thick mat of leaves on the ground as they searched for the food to prepare them for winter.

This afternoon he'd found their single-minded actions calming, and he'd slowed his steps as he'd gone past the little clearing with the graves.

He'd found that clearing on his first walk, weeks ago. The little group of stones, so unexpected in this setting and so neatly kept, were calming to him, too. He liked to stand a moment there within the shelter of the circle of the trees, beneath the ever-changing sky, and think that while all men must die, even the smallest life—as witnessed by those three white stones that bore the same name and the sad brief dates—might be remembered.

And while pausing there he often said a prayer for those he'd lost himself, and being far from any church where he could light a candle to their memory he would count that prayer enough, and carry on his way content.

This afternoon he had not paused. He'd carried on so deep in thought he had not known that she was walking on the path in front of him until he'd overtaken her.

It had caught him uncomfortably off guard to realize he'd let his thoughts dull his awareness of what lay around him so carelessly. Soldiers died, as well he knew, for failing to be vigilant, and anyone who met him in these woods would view him first and always as their hated enemy.

She did. He saw it daily in her eyes. And yet, this afternoon she had been standing there upon the path as if she'd been expecting him. As if she had been waiting for him.

When she'd spoken first, although her tone had seemed more brave than friendly, he had seized the chance to try improving on his earlier attempts at conversation.

It had not gone well.

In fairness, when he saw a stain of that shade and intensity on someone's skin, he naturally assumed they had been wounded and were bleeding. It was clear she now considered him the next thing to a madman, grabbing hold of her as he had done and making such a fuss about a stain that, on close viewing, was apparently the product of some vegetable or fruit—perhaps the berries of the *sorbiers* he'd watched her harvest with her brother yesterday.

He grimly added "rowan" to his growing list of English words.

That list, for the time he had spent here, was shamefully small. In half the time, when he had been a boy, he'd learned enough words in the language of the Seneca to try to join their conversations, so he now had no excuse to not attempt the same. In fact, if he were honest with himself, he now had even more incentive.

He could start, he decided, by showing her father a leaf from a *sorbier* and asking if, in their language, they called it a "rowan."

The trees stood by the barn. It was a simple thing to snap a twig with leaves from one branch as he passed, but when he reached the shed he found that Monsieur Wilde was not alone.

With him, where the wide doors of the shed had been propped open, was a man of middle age—another farmer, from the look of his tanned features and his sturdy build. His clothes, though, were distinctively un-English, from his heavy wooden shoes to the red knitted cap he held and twisted in his hands while he was speaking. Both men looked so serious that Jean-Philippe, not wanting to intrude, cast the small twig aside and started past them to resume his work upon the cider press.

Monsieur Wilde called to him, and motioned him to come back to the shed, and then said something to the man with the red cap, who turned his head and said in French, "He says to leave that for today. He has another job to do."

His French did not possess the careful elegance of Captain Wheelock's. It was oddly rustic, but it also was, without a doubt, his native tongue.

To Jean-Philippe this twist was unexpected, and he might have answered with a question of his own, had not the other man continued, "He must build a coffin for my son."

The stranger's voice broke slightly on that final word, and there was no reply for Jean-Philippe to make then but the human one.

"I'm sorry."

"Thank you."

Monsieur Wilde was introducing them to one another, struggling a little with the names.

"Pierre Boudreau," said the stranger, above the brief clasp of their handshake. And then his gaze angled past Jean-Philippe's shoulder, and with a few final words to Monsieur Wilde he took his leave and walked away to the fields, with his shoulders bent heavily.

Jean-Philippe also glanced over his shoulder, to see what the stranger had seen.

And saw Lydia Wilde, who had newly stepped out of the woods, and was watching him back.

⤳

"He is not French." De Brassart seemed to find the thought amusing. "He's Acadian. Have you not ever seen one?"

"No." Jean-Philippe stood just within the kitchen doorway, looking out toward the shed. Pierre Boudreau was back this morning, deep in conversation with Monsieur Wilde.

At the kitchen table with his tea, de Brassart ventured, "That surprises me, for when I came across three years ago and landed at Quebec there were some there who'd just arrived as refugees. It made a stir. You must have seen them."

Jean-Philippe, unmoving, said, "It has been longer than three years since I was at Quebec."

"I thought you said your home was there."

"I said my family home is near the city."

"And you've not been back for more than three years?"

It would now be more than ten years, but he had his reasons that he did not wish to share. He only shrugged and said, "There is a war."

A cough reminded them the black girl—Violet was her name—was with them in the kitchen, and did not approve of them conversing overlong in French.

"She thinks we're plotting our escape," de Brassart said, and switched to English with an ease that only emphasized to Jean-Philippe his own deficiencies.

He frowned. And when he caught with his side vision the bright movement of a yellow gown as *she* entered the kitchen, he went out, and slowly walked across the crisp cool grass to join the other men outside the shed.

In English, very carefully, he said, "Good morning, Mr. Wilde."

He'd missed the older man at breakfast. Monsieur Wilde had risen even earlier than usual to work upon the coffin. He looked weary, but he smiled and returned the greeting pleasantly as Jean-Philippe dropped into French to nod a brief "*bonjour*" to the Acadian.

He knew it was a tragedy, what happened to those people. He'd heard tales of how the English had accomplished their removal from the villages and farms that had been theirs for generations—how the churches had been burned, and how the women on their knees had prayed for mercy and been herded with their children onto ships at point of bayonet, the men cast off in separate vessels, all of them condemned to starve and sicken in their exile for the "fault" of being neutral. And now tragedy had struck Boudreau again.

The coffin was completed. Made of palest pine and sanded smooth, it sat upon the bench where Monsieur Wilde did his work.

It was so small.

A tightness rose in Jean-Philippe's throat—he who had seen men cut down in battle with such frequency he'd thought himself immune by now to death.

He asked Boudreau, his voice quiet, "How old was your son?"

"He was four years old."

"His name?"

"René."

He marked this with a nod. "I'll say a prayer for him."

"Thank you." Boudreau, looking down, had his gaze fixed on Jean-Philippe's footwear. "You are the marine."

That surprised him. "Yes."

"Then maybe your sister the nun will say prayers for my son also. She being closer to God, He might hear her more clearly."

"I'll ask her."

Boudreau explained, "I read your letters. He"—nodding to Monsieur Wilde—"wanted to know what they said, before sending them."

Fair enough, Jean-Philippe thought. But he wanted to know

something. "How did he send them?" The one letter, he now knew, had reached the governor. But as for the one to his sister…

"He sent them both to his son in New York, who is very important and owns many ships. He says, 'Take the one letter direct to the governor, and see the other one reaches Quebec by whatever means possible.'" Nodding again to their host, Boudreau added for emphasis, "He's a good man."

"Yes. I know that."

If Monsieur Wilde knew they were talking about him, he gave no discernible sign of it. Nor did he seem to be bothered at all they were speaking in French. He was looking toward the house, blinking as men did when they tried not to show emotion.

For the second time Jean-Philippe turned to see Lydia, this time approaching them over the grass with a basket in hand.

She spoke only a few words in passing it to the Acadian, but what she said made his eyes fill, too, as he said, "Thank you," in English.

She said he was welcome—*that* much at least Jean-Philippe could understand—and not looking at anyone else she turned round, heading back to the house.

Jean-Philippe didn't want to betray his own interest by watching too long, so he glanced down instead at the basket in Boudreau's hand. There were eggs in the basket, a wrapped block of sugar, a bottle of what looked like wine, and a small sack of something that might have been tea.

"It's for my wife," the Acadian told him, his voice slightly roughened.

Unable to help himself, Jean-Philippe looked back at Lydia, walking away from them. "She is good, also."

"Yes," said the Acadian.

"Yesterday, though, when you saw her, you left."

"That was out of respect. Because I did not wish to upset her."

"Why would you upset her?"

Boudreau, bending down, took the pitiful coffin and set it

upon his one shoulder, and looking at Jean-Philippe told him, "You have much to learn, Marine, about this family."

And saying no more to him, thanked Monsieur Wilde and was gone.

CHARLEY

WILLIE McKINNEY, OUR STONEMASON, was hard at work in the trench that surrounded the Wilde House foundation when I came on-site. He was flirting with Lara.

I really liked Willie. A burly big Scot from the Isle of Arran, he had a great accent, a great russet beard, and a great sense of humor.

"You're finding more nails for my coffin then, are you?" he called up to Lara as she sorted through what remained on the sifting screen.

"Only a couple," she called back.

"Well, don't give up hope. Morning, boss," was his greeting to me. "You look fancy."

"I dressed her," said Lara.

"Well, that would explain it." And with a broad wink, Willie picked up his mallet and went back to sounding the walls, pounding on the foundation stones to see if he could detect any movement. He normally had an assistant at work with him—more an apprentice, I reasoned, who did all the side labor, fetching tools, moving thing, cleaning up afterward. I didn't see him today. "Sent him out for more sand," Willie said, when I asked.

Lara, still sifting, said, "Plenty of sand here."

"Not sharp sand. That stuff there's too dead," he replied. "It won't support weight like sharp sand."

"If you say so." Her tone was offhand but I realized, on seeing her smile, she was flirting back, and I'd have moved along out of their way if she hadn't said, "Come look what I've found so far. Just don't step in the dirt with those shoes."

Which was easier said than done. I rarely wore high heels, and when I wore them I wasn't entirely graceful. Keeping my balance, I stepped from the brick walkway onto the grass to examine her little collection of finds. There were three nails, including a lovely old forged one; two pennies, not old, and some pieces of porcelain that looked to be from the same plate.

Lara poked the porcelain bits and asked me, "Those are old, right?"

"I'm not sure. Dating porcelain can be kind of difficult, unless you know the pattern or you have a maker's mark, or you can get someone to carbon-date it. But they're not *new*, I don't think."

"They're pretty. I can clean them up and add them to the tray upstairs. You never know, we might find more." She looked me up and down and said, "You really do look fancy."

From the trench beside us, Willie chimed in, "Told you."

Lara smiled. "It still needs something, though. I don't know what. Just something."

"Work boots." That was Sam's voice, and I turned to see him coming up the path.

"Of course," said Lara dryly. "Just what every outfit needs."

"I'm serious." He had his own on, with the T-shirt, jeans, and tool belt that made up his daily uniform. "We're starting on the siding this week, and the roof is next, so if you want to stand around out here you're going to need some work boots. And a hardhat."

Lara made a face. "But not today, right? It would ruin Charley's hairdo."

Sam smiled faintly. "You look..."

"Fancy," Willie said a third time.

"Nice," was Sam's choice. "This your lunch day?"

"Yes."

He nodded, looking down. "The *shoes* are definitely fancy."

"Every woman," Lara told him, "needs a pair of power shoes."

"Is that what those are?"

"Yes," I told him, smiling back.

A bit of borrowed courage. And not only for the meeting with my grandmother.

❦

My office looked innocent. Empty.

I switched on the fan, which was still plugged in right where I'd left it plugged in. Cast a carefully nonchalant glance at the outlet across from my desk, to make certain the lamp had stayed plugged in, too. So I could safely assume that whatever had pulled those plugs out of the wall before, when they had been in the socket behind my chair, just had a problem with that one particular socket, and not with my lamp or my fan.

Good to know, then, I thought as I sat in the awkward, self-conscious way I did all things when I thought I was being watched.

Rachel would have told me I was being oversensitive. She would have looked around my office and assured me there was nothing there.

That's what she'd said to me this morning, before breakfast, when I'd come down after showering to find her sitting wrapped up in a blanket on the sofa, with the television on.

"How was the ghost hunting?" I'd asked her, trying not to sound too curious, and she had shrugged and told me, "There was nothing there."

I hadn't argued with her. Hadn't shared the fact that I had seen the phantom light shine in the Wilde House woods myself at night. Her life was mixed up enough at the moment, and right now she needed to go on believing that I was the steady, more practical one.

"You were out a long time," I'd said, "looking at nothing."

"Yes, well, Gianni's really stubborn."

She hadn't gone further with that, so I'd left it alone. And I hadn't asked how late she'd stayed out, because I had already known. I'd been sitting upstairs in my bedroom and reading, one eye on the clock, until I'd heard her come in at twenty-two minutes past one. *Then* I'd put down my book. Gone to sleep. I'd assumed she had, too.

Only seeing her sitting there wrapped in her blanket this

morning had made me less sure. It was how she had sat as a little girl when we'd watched movies that scared her or made her cry. And while the blanket this morning had not been the same one she'd had in her childhood, she'd still worn it in the same way, like her personal armor—a signal for me to tread carefully.

Rachel was one of those people who didn't like being approached when they felt upset. True to our family, she held things inside, so if she was bothered by something that Gianni had done or concerned about school starting or simply missing her dad, I'd have no way of knowing until she decided to tell me.

It might have been none of those things, I'd acknowledged as I'd glanced toward the TV. She had just started watching a movie that would, on its own, have been cause for the blanket—an old haunted house thriller, older than me. We had watched it together a couple of times, but this morning while eating my breakfast I hadn't been in the right mood.

"It's too creepy," had been my excuse.

"But the ghost isn't trying to hurt anyone, he's just trying to right an old wrong."

"It isn't what he *does*. It's the idea that he's *there*."

She'd shrugged again, the way she always did when she'd decided that I wasn't making sense. On-screen, the hero of the film, having just lost his wife and daughter in a car crash, was returning to his now-empty apartment, standing lonely at a window, looking out while distant echoes of their voices and their laughter tugged his memory.

Rachel had retreated in her blanket; drawn it up and close around her head and shoulders like a winter shawl. "Sometimes," she'd told me suddenly, "I wish there really were such things as ghosts."

And then I'd understood.

I'd understood the blanket, and the movies, and I'd known whose ghost she wanted to be there with us. I'd wanted him there, too.

But it was one thing to think about ghosts in the abstract. It was another to be sitting here now in my office, on my own, and feel the crawling sense of certainty that I was not alone.

To distract myself, I picked up the notepad where I had been jotting down prompts for my speech, but the feeling grew so strong that I couldn't bring myself to look up from the paper. With the notepad clenched within my hands, I kept my focus fiercely on the few lines I had written until all the words were blurred, because I knew—I *knew*—that if I dared to lift my gaze above the notepad's edge there would be something there to see.

It was a sudden, all-consuming dread.

I felt the thudding of my heart inside my rib cage; felt it pressing upward until it was hard to breathe, and so I caught my breath and held it.

Go away, I told the thing that stood in front of me, in silence. *Please, just go away.*

The oscillating fan swung back and swept a puff of cooling air across my desk that ruffled the loose pages of my notebook and the damply curling strands of hair that clung against my neck. And then it passed me by.

My office door, which had been standing fully open, creaked a little on its hinges. Paused. Then creaked again, and in a slow arc so deliberate that it seemed controlled by someone's hand, it swung and closed itself.

And gently, very quietly, the knob clicked shut.

❧

The Privateer Club didn't strike me as the kind of place that any self-respecting privateer would ever frequent. It was bright and airy, all light wood and windows, with white curtains and white tablecloths and views of the white sailboats moored along the slips of the marina.

Here and there were accents of bright brass and summer blue, and Lara had made sure I'd fit in perfectly by dressing me in patriotic tones—the cool white blouse that flared above the blue-striped skirt, and those red high-heeled "power shoes" that clicked across the polished floor as I walked to the lectern.

I hadn't needed to rely on them for confidence, so far. The Sisters of Liberty, as Sam had promised, had turned out to be a remarkably welcoming group. They had greeted me warmly and given me lunch and had put me at ease. And for all that I'd worried, my grandmother wasn't among them.

I didn't know why, and I hadn't asked. All I was sure of was that there was nobody here who resembled the photographs I had looked up on the internet over the years. My relief had been blunted by faint irritation she hadn't been even a little bit curious to come and see what I looked like. She was this group's president, so there was no way she wouldn't have known I was coming to speak today. Whether her absence was meant as a snub or was simply her way of avoiding me, I didn't care.

Really. I didn't care.

I reminded myself of that as I smiled out at the roomful of faces and started my talk.

That was easier, too, than I'd thought it would be. I had a projector, a screen, and a slideshow, and organized notes. By the time I had outlined the Wilde House's history and started explaining how Benjamin Wilde's wife had written a full room-by-room list of all the home's contents to keep them from being destroyed or removed while the house had been occupied by British officers, I'd hit my stride and felt fully relaxed.

"It's so rare. We're so lucky to have this," I said as I clicked to the next slide to show them an image of one of the document's pages. "Most inventories were taken after someone died, so they don't necessarily tell us where things were when they were in actual use. We don't know, for example, if a painting or table that's listed as being in an upstairs room was being used in that room or had been moved there for storage. And in many cases there are no inventories at all, so when a family gets divided—"

Here I stopped, and paused a moment because something was

occurring at the center of the room. People were rising, moving, murmuring, and shifting to make space for someone new to take a seat. A late arrival, with distinctive short white hair, a flash of jewelry, and a stylish lilac pantsuit.

There was no mistaking who it was. Even without the fuss everyone made and the way they all parted for her with such deference, Elisabeth Van Hoek just had the kind of face you recognized.

I met her cool eyes levelly a moment and then let my gaze move on. My hands were shaking slightly but I knew that was adrenaline—the classic fight-or-flight response. I wasn't going to give this woman who'd disowned my dad the satisfaction now of seeing me do either. Resting my hands on the top of the lectern, I picked up as smoothly as possible where I had paused.

"So when a family gets divided, their possessions get divided, too, and we don't have a record left of what was lost, or where it was originally in the house. That's why, when Captain Wilde's wife made this inventory, she was giving us the most amazing gift—a snapshot, in a way, of what the whole house looked like on that day. And we can try to re-create it."

There, I thought. I had my balance back. I carried on through the remaining slides, explaining how we meant to go about refurnishing the house, retrieving some items from where we knew they'd ended up, and buying others where we could, and filling in the gaps with custom replicas and reproductions.

"We'll be appealing to the public and inviting them to sponsor or donate the things we need, and we're looking at getting some inter-museum loans, but that still leaves us with this amount we'll need to raise for the purchases." Showing the next slide, the breakdown of finances Dave had projected, I said, "I do realize you've been very generous already in giving to our restoration fund, and I'm aware that your bylaws set limits on what you can give for that purpose. We really appreciate all that you've done. But this would be a separate project, meant for education." Education was central, I knew, to the Sisters of Liberty's mission, so I let the emphasis of that one word hang a moment. "We'd be very honored," I told them in closing, "to have your support."

With those words, my attention had settled again on my grand-mother, and for the second time she looked right back at me. It was impossible to guess what she might be thinking.

Then the woman who'd first introduced me came forward again to the lectern to thank me, and after that several more women approached to discuss the museum and what we were doing. They closed up the space between me and my grandmother. Offered me more tea, and let me refocus on why I was there.

So I spent the next few minutes chatting, and making new social connections, and trying to be less aware that Elisabeth Van Hoek was sitting three tables away. And next time I dared to glance over, she wasn't. The chair where she'd sat was pushed back at an angle and empty, and scanning the room I caught no glimpse of her lilac pantsuit. My grandmother, as she had been for the whole of my life, was not there.

⌘

"I thought you might be needing friendly company," Malaika said, explaining why I'd found her in the parking lot outside the Privateer Club when I'd finished with the meeting. She'd been sitting with her car door open, talking on her cell phone while she waited for me. Now she slipped the phone back in her purse and stood gracefully, shutting the car door and locking it. "Let's go and sit on the boat."

She was always surprising me. "You have a boat?"

"It's more Darryl's than mine," she said, naming her husband. "You can't keep a mariner away from the water, and I figured letting him have this was better than having him off on a big ship for months at a time."

"Was Darryl in the navy?" I had only met her husband once—a tall and quiet man who'd kept his focus on the barbecue and left us to ourselves.

"Not the navy. The merchant marine," said Malaika. "He came out of King's Point the year we got married, and went out to sea on the freighters, but when the kids came along he didn't want to be gone so far." Like me, she was wearing high heels, but she stepped with more certainty onto the long sun-bleached wooden dock edging the water. "Then he was a New York harbor docking pilot, but that got tough, too. Lots of guys were getting laid off back about ten years ago, and I was doing okay with my real estate, so Darryl just decided he would rather do his own thing, work his own hours as a maritime inspector. That," she said, "is how we ended up with *this*." We'd stopped beside a slip that held a fair-sized sailboat, maybe forty feet in length. "Darryl inspected it for somebody who ended up not buying it, and he just couldn't let it go."

I didn't know much about boats, but I could sympathize with Darryl. This one did have graceful lines that made it stand out sleekly from its neighbors.

It also had a chrome-and-canvas canopy that gave us shade as we climbed aboard. Malaika asked, "You want to go below, or sit up here?"

"Up here, please." The breeze felt refreshing after the confines of the Privateer Club's luncheon room.

Malaika settled back into the curve of molded fiberglass that formed the bench seat facing me. "How did it go?"

"Really well. Their education committee is going to discuss it when they meet, and let us know."

"No, I meant how did it go with your grandmother?"

"Fine." Because she looked less than convinced I explained, "She came late and left early, so that made things easier."

"What did she say to you?"

"Nothing." I shrugged it off. "Guess that was better than having her yell at me."

"I told you not to worry. She's not going to go off on you in public. When she speaks to you, she'll be polite."

I doubted she was ever going to speak to me, and said as much. "She cut my father dead, and never said a word to Niels while he was living here, so I can't see her changing now. Why would she?" Without meaning to, I turned my gaze across the deep blue water of the bay where sunlight danced and glittered in a thousand points of light. On the opposite shore I could just see the steeply pitched roofline of Bridlemere sheltering deep in the trees like a recluse. "We're no longer her family."

"Family," said Malaika, very firmly, "doesn't work like that. A family's not some club you join or get kicked out of. Lord knows I have cousins I'd be happy to disown, but even if I did, they'd still be family."

"I'm just saying. If she wouldn't talk to Niels, she isn't going to talk to me. He was the peacemaker."

"Oh, I don't know about that. You've been doing all right yourself, keeping our trustees from killing each other."

"You're doing that," I pointed out. "I'm the reason they're fighting, remember?"

"You don't think they'd fight if you weren't here?" She sent me a look that knew better. "Frank and Sharon have been trading words since I first got involved with the historical society. And Harvey and Don, so I'm told, have been mad at each other since middle school. Some fights are rooted so deep they're a force you can't stand against. Best to get out of the way."

"Yes, well, Sharon won't let me get out of her way."

"She's a difficult woman," Malaika agreed. "But you're managing her fine."

I'd managed Sharons every day in high school. I'd just never figured out how to make friends with them. I wasn't even sure they had friends. Followers and allies, yes, like Eve and Harvey, but that wasn't truly friendship.

Friendship was somebody letting you sit on a sailboat to cheer you up after you'd first met your grandmother.

It was working. I was gradually relaxing to the gentle rocking of the boat, the creaking of the mooring ropes, the rhythmic slap of water on the hull below. I'd never spent much time on boats, apart from being taken out from time to time on the old wood-and-canvas two-man kayak that my dad had kept in our garage. I'd been too small to be much help—he'd done the paddling—but I'd always liked the feel of being buoyed above the water, and the soft splash of the paddles as they dipped into the river. I'd loved that kayak, but eventually it had started leaking and my dad had disassembled it into its canvas bags and it had sat and gathered dust until at some point it had ended up at Niels's house in Saratoga Springs. I'd seen it there in his garage when I had first moved down to stay with him. "I'm going to get it fixed," he'd said. "We'll take it on the lake." We never had. For all I knew, it was in pieces in its storage bags still, somewhere in his house. He'd left a lot of things in pieces.

As though following my thoughts, Malaika asked, "How's Rachel doing? Is she ready to go back to college?"

"Sort of. I mean, she's all packed up and organized. Whether she's mentally ready or not, I don't know."

"It might do her good to get back into a routine."

"It might." I looked away from Bridlemere and let my gaze slide down the shoreline, almost down to Millbank, until I saw the patch of tall reeds and the arching trees that framed the caramel-colored siding of my brother's house, its back toward the water. "I'm not ever really sure what's going on with Rachel. She just lets you in so far, you know?"

She sympathized. "She goes back this Saturday, right? Well, at least you'll be getting a night in the city. Are you and your man going to take in a show while you're there?"

"He can't make it," I said. "He had something come up." I was careful to keep my tone light but she glanced over anyway, making me wish I was wearing my sunglasses as I deliberately searched the small harbor for something to draw her attention to.

Several slips over, a gray-haired man seemed to be readying a smaller sailboat to take it out onto the bay.

He looked so familiar I shielded my eyes from the brightness with one hand to see better. "Isn't that Frank?"

"Where?" She looked too. "No, that's one of the Fishers—I don't know which one. Maybe Jim. There are three brothers, I always get them mixed up. But you're right, there's a family resemblance. The Fishers are one of the old families here, like the Wildes. They all married each other. They used to own most of Cross Harbor, the Fishers. They owned this marina, too, until a year ago."

"Really? What happened a year ago?"

"Harvey decided the Kiersted Group needed more waterfront property." Her side-eye spoke volumes. "When Harvey decides that he needs something, he won't give up till he gets it."

Having dealt with Harvey too, I felt a little sorry for the Fisher brothers, and it must have shown on my face because Malaika said, "No need to feel too bad for them. They still have millions in the bank, they just don't flash their cash around."

The undetermined Fisher brother—who still looked like Frank to me, from this distance—had by now cast off his lines and was easing his little boat expertly out of its slip. It was hardly the size of boat I'd have imagined a millionaire owning.

"Now, Harvey," Malaika went on, "is all flash. Guess which boat here is his?"

That was easy. I pointed it out. "That one." The only one that demanded you see it, admire it, and pay it attention. It wasn't a sailboat at all but a motor yacht, pointed and sleek with a narrow black stripe that sliced hard through its shimmering reflection in the water of the harbor and set all the smaller boats' reflections wavering and trembling.

The Fisher brother's boat seemed unimpressed. Sail up, it tilted slightly without slowing down, still nosing its way purposefully toward the open water.

I could see, just beyond it, the curve of Snug Cove and the rise of the shore where the Wilde House sat waiting for me in the woods. And even though Malaika was my boss, I knew I couldn't sit here on a break forever. Lunch had ended half an hour ago. I needed to get back to work.

But I sat five more minutes, enjoying the sunlight and breeze and the bright sky above, watching that one small sailboat head out. It had no cares or worries, no meetings to keep, no brave faces to wear, and no pledges to honor. It moved fast and freely, so fast that soon I could see only the speck of the boat and the white slash of sail reaching up and I envied it, riding the blue of the water and leaning with confidence into the wind.

LYDIA

S HE SAW THE SAILS at sunrise.

She'd been sent up to the field to fetch the mare, although perhaps "sent" was too strong a word. Her father had done nothing more than ask her if she'd go, because the mare would not come willingly to any of the men but led them all a tiring chase, whereas for Lydia she came directly, took the halter quietly, and let herself be led downhill as meekly as a lamb.

To Lydia, it was a welcome chore. These first days of October had been busy ones that kept her in the garden cutting squash to dry and harvesting the beans for seed and digging her potatoes. There'd been pies to bake and pickles to be scalded—she had left the last to Violet, who made pickles best of any she had tasted—but the garden on its own had wanted more hours in the day than she could give it, and the digging left her shoulders sore, so it had been a great relief to start this day by simply walking up along the orchard wall into the upper field to find the mare.

Her father had a mind to go to Hempstead to Aunt Hannah's, and the mare would take him there and back more swiftly than the wagon team. She was a gray, a four-year-old with something of a filly's mischief glinting in her eyes as she stopped grazing, raised her fine head, and watched Lydia approach.

"There'd be no point," was Lydia's advice. "I've neither will nor energy to chase you so you'd have to play the game alone, which would be little fun."

The mare flicked one ear in acknowledgment of this and gave in gracefully, and although she did not step forward, she at least stood still and did not run. Lydia wasn't entirely sure herself why the mare favored her, but they had shared this rapport from the very first day that her father had brought the mare home as a yearling. Just as a horse could sense a nervous rider or a cruel one, it appeared that the mare could sense Lydia already carried a full share of troubles and did not need more. Whatever the reason, the mare bent her head to the halter and made no complaint and submitted herself to be led.

Not that Lydia was in a rush to be leading her anywhere just at the moment. The day, being only begun, was still peaceful; the chill of the air making mist of her breath as the sun ventured up from its bed into view, sending pink and gold streaks spreading over the eastern sky.

Here on the upland where the land had been well cleared, she had a view not only of the bay but of the wider Sound, and of the ships that came and went continually between New York's harbor and the sea.

Benjamin had come here often as a boy to chase his dreams of grand adventure, studying the passing ships so that he could, like Joseph, know the types of vessels by their varied shapes and rigging, be they brigs or sloops or bilanders or snows. He'd watched them for so long that he could name most of the New York ships on sight, amazing Lydia, who only recognized her brother William's four: the *Bellewether*, the *Honest John*, the *Katharine*, and the *Fox*.

Of these, her favorite was the *Bellewether*, because although the smallest of them all it was the prettiest and swiftest.

"She will run before all others," had been William's explanation of the sloop's name. "Like the sheep we bell to lead the flock."

"You've spelled it wrong," their mother had said mildly as she'd read the brave name painted on the hull. "It is spelled 'bellwether,' without the second *e*."

"But '*belle*' is French for 'beautiful,' and she is surely that," had been his answer.

And she was. Built to outrun the privateers that prowled the trade routes, she had turned the tables on them many times and carried her fair share of captured ships as prizes into New York's harbor, but the true prizes for Lydia had been the letters carried from Jamaica from her brother Daniel, and the gifts and parcels that he regularly sent, which, since their mother's death, had been one of the few bright things their family could look forward to. The sight of the *Bellewether*'s sails sweeping past in the Sound was a sight that, on most days, brought Lydia joy.

But this morning, the sight of sails sliding below her and into the bay brought a darker confusion.

Those sails were the *Bellewether*'s, but they'd been set strangely. In this uncertain light, moving through shadows and mist on the dark water close to the shore, she appeared to have no more than half a mast, less of her rigging, and dangerous, jagged holes scarring her deck.

Lydia, who had been stroking the mare's warm neck, stilled her hand. And then she moved it and took a firm hold of the mare's tangled mane, and in one scrambling motion she hauled herself up, clinging to the mare's withers and urging her into a quick walk at first, then a run, down the slope of the field, racing home with a warning.

Because on the heels of the *Bellewether*, gliding now into the bay, sailed a second ship—larger and darker and trailing the wounded sloop's wake like a predator.

&c∞

The men who came ashore to them were Spanish.

Her father, from her warning, was already dressed and waiting just outside the open kitchen door. He'd given up his plans for Hempstead and instead told Benjamin to ride the mare around the bottom of the bay through Millbank and up to Mr. Fisher's at Cross Harbor so that Mr. Fisher, in his turn, could have word sent to William in New York. "He needs to know his ship has been brought back in this condition."

They'd had a better view now of the *Bellewether* between the trees as she'd gone past to drop her anchor in the cove below them, and it seemed a miracle that she was still afloat. She'd had her tall mast snapped in two and was missing two-thirds of her bowsprit, her sails and hull damaged, her rigging much shattered.

"I'll ride into New York myself," had been Benjamin's answer.

"No. Leave Mr. Fisher to send someone. I'll need you back here."

There'd been, as usual when Father used that tone, no point in arguing, so Benjamin had done as he was told. As too had Lydia, when she'd been told to keep back in the kitchen out of sight, with Violet.

Joseph had come down to join their father on the threshold of the open door. Mr. de Brassart had been yet asleep in bed. Mr. de Sabran, though, had stepped through from his chamber to the kitchen and despite the fact he did not speak their language and could not have known the cause of this new tension in the household, he apparently had sensed that it meant trouble, for he'd dressed in his full uniform and taken up position between Lydia and Violet and the door, as though preparing to defend them from whatever might attempt to enter.

Lydia, to her surprise, felt safer for his silent presence. But she did not like to be kept back where she could not see what was happening, where she could only hear the brief words Joseph and her father were exchanging, low, with one another.

"British?" asked her father.

"No," said Joseph. "Those are not the colors of a British ship."

"What colors are they?"

"I don't know." Then, "They're putting four men in that boat. They'll outnumber us."

"We have four men."

"Only two we can trust." Joseph's tone was agitated, and their father noticed.

"Go inside," he said. When Joseph did not move at once, their father laid a firm but gentle hand upon her brother's shoulder.

"Go. It will be fine. They've brought the *Bellewether* back home, I doubt they're anything but friendly."

He did not relax his guarded stance, though, even after Joseph had obediently left his side and sullenly retreated past them all into the front part of the house. Nor did her father go to meet the strangers as they came ashore but stood and waited, holding to the high ground so that when their leader reached them he was winded from the climb.

Lydia, by taking one step closer to the kitchen window, could just see the figures crossing from the woods toward them. If there had been four men in the landing party, two must have been left down with the boat, because she only saw two men approaching now—the one in front with black hair and a short clipped beard, wearing a black coat faced in scarlet; and the man behind him taller, dressed in gray, and with skin darker brown than Violet's.

Both men appeared to have empty hands. Neither was holding a weapon.

"Good day!" called the bearded man, cheerfully. "I look for señor Wilde."

Her father, standing so he blocked the doorway, spoke with caution. "You have found him."

"I'm glad. This is not a small hill that you have, and my legs are not used to the land." He spoke English with ease, and in spite of his words and his breathing seemed physically fit, in the prime years between youth and middle age. Neither as tall nor as broad as her father, he nonetheless stood as his equal and, facing him over the threshold, thrust out his right hand. "An honor, señor Wilde. I am Domingo del Rio Caballero, *capitán* of *El Montero*, this beautiful ship you see down in the bay with the not-very-beautiful one of your son's, at the moment. And this is my—how do you say it in English? First mate, is it not? Juan Ramírez."

Her father shook the black man's hand as well. "Mr. Ramírez. And Captain—?"

"Del Rio," the captain supplied. "I regret we could not take

your son's ship the whole way to New York, but it's not so safe
for us, you understand. The English may not be at war with Spain
but they still like to seize our ships and ask forgiveness after, and
we've had a very tiring voyage these past days and are not looking
for a fight."

The emphasis he put upon those last few words made Lydia
suspect he'd seen beyond her father and had glimpsed the armed
French officer who stood within the shadows of the kitchen,
though she could not know for sure.

Mr. de Sabran had not moved.

Her father said, "Captain del Rio, I am grateful you have
brought my son's ship back to us. But I confess I'm curious how
you came to possess it in the first place?"

"Ah. *That*," the Spaniard said, "is a good story. And good
stories, so my father always told me, become better ones when
told with food and drink." His grin, what she could see of it, was
self-assured. "May we come in?"

~~~~~

It was, if not the oddest group to share a meal, at least the most
unlikely one. At one end of the table sat her father in his customary chair with Joseph at his right hand, and then next the
two French officers, and rounding out the table's other end the
Spanish captain and his first mate, who was evidently—from his
introduction and the fact he used a surname—a free black, and
so around again to Lydia, who couldn't help but think that if the
English Captain Wheelock were to turn up at that moment in his
scarlet coat, their keeping room would hold the Old and New
Worlds fully balanced.

She found it increasingly obvious, looking at Mr. de Sabran,
which side of the scales he belonged upon. His manners were
the plainer kind, and what his movements lacked in grace and
elegance they gained in pure economy, so that he looked more
like her father and her brother than the Europeans. The only thing

he did that they did not was use his own knife from his pocket when he cut and ate his food—the same small, curved, bone-handled knife he made use of for various purposes—but this one habit that had seemed so strange to her at the beginning now seemed entirely normal. Mr. de Brassart and Captain del Rio and Mr. Ramírez all handled their cutlery in the same fashion and brandished their cups with a similar flair, as though bred to a dining room finer than this one, with plates made of porcelain, not pewter and wood.

To be fair, no one yet had complained of the meal. Since the uncommon hour made it too late for breakfast and still a few hours too early for dinner, it had been a scramble for Violet to make them a meal on short notice. She'd curdled some cream with sweet wine and a grating of cinnamon, serving it warm to the table, and thickened the porridge of Indian meal they had eaten at breakfast and fried it in cakes drizzled thick with molasses, brought pickle and cheese from the cellar and rounded it off with two pies of the first apples picked from their orchard, still fresh from her baking of yesterday. Even with Lydia helping it had been a great deal of work to assemble, and Violet—who rarely withheld her opinions—would normally have raised a protest against the disruption of her day's routine. But she hadn't said a word, seeming distracted by her fascinated study of their guest Mr. Ramírez.

He was returning the favor, his gaze seeking Violet on several occasions, but it wasn't obvious whether he watched her because he considered her pretty or because he viewed her with sympathy.

Surely there must be a range of emotions a free black man felt when he looked at a slave.

Lydia didn't know much about free black men. They were an oddity, even in larger New York. In her memory there'd only been two who had come to this part of Long Island: one last year, who'd stopped at Cross Harbor to preach at the New Lights Church, and one a few years before that—a bootmaker who'd briefly set up his business in Millbank only to leave so discreetly and in such great haste there were many who still felt convinced he'd been stolen away.

Neither man, though, had looked like this Spaniard, who could not be older than forty, his close-clipped hair dark with no sign yet of whitening, shoulders as broad as her father's beneath the fine gray fabric of his coat that at its turned-back cuffs was trimmed with silver cord and buttons, with a narrow fall of lace across his dark-brown hands.

Lydia had thought Mr. de Brassart might in his turn raise a protest against being made to share the meal and table with a black man, but in keeping with the day and its surprises he had not. Instead, the whole of his attention had been captured by the Spanish captain, whose name he had recognized.

"You wouldn't by chance be," de Brassart had said when they'd been introduced, "the great pirate Captain del Rio made famous in all of those stories by Madame MacPherson?"

Del Rio had smiled and corrected him. "Great pirate *hunter*. And no, he's my father."

"Is he? My mother devoured those tales. And you must resemble him strongly, for you look exactly how I would have pictured him from the descriptions."

The smile had become a grin, brilliantly white against the trimmed black beard. "But my father will tell you he's much more handsome."

"He is still alive?"

"Very much so. But now he leaves all the adventures to me and to Juan, here. Now Juan, he could tell you some stories, and true ones. He sailed many years with my father."

But de Brassart, predictably, hadn't asked anything of Juan Ramírez.

And Captain del Rio had proven that he could tell colorful stories himself, like the one he was telling them now. "So on the fourth night, we fell in with—this is how you say it, yes?—we fell in with the *Bellewether*. This ship I know and recognize, because I have done business many times, señor, with your son Daniel. So we keep in company with her all night, since on the sea it's good always to have a friend beside you. With so many English ships around, it's better not to be alone."

De Brassart asked, "Why would the English bother you? Your kings have signed a treaty of neutrality."

The Spanish captain even shrugged with style. "We are not at war, but the English still capture our ships, and whatever we carry they say that we carry for you, for the French, you see? Then by declaring our cargoes French property they can condemn them and claim them and keep them for sale, so they capture our ships and they carry us into their ports and they take all our cargoes. They give back our ships, but our profits…" He shrugged again, raising one hand in a gesture as though he were scattering unseen coins into the empty air. "Two times I've been carried now into Antigua, and if it continues this way I cannot make a living," he said, "and besides, it is very annoying."

Joseph, who'd kept silent so far, spoke up unexpectedly, and in the tone that Lydia knew carried trouble. "Are you saying, Captain, that the British have no honor?"

Del Rio reached toward the center of the table with his knife to take more salt and used the movement to glance sideways at her brother as though noticing him there for the first time. That single glance appeared to take her brother's measure, and she felt a quick flood of protective feelings that she just as quickly sought to stifle, lest they do more harm than good, for Joseph lately rose to anger if he sensed that he was being treated softly.

As she pulled her gaze deliberately away it caught and clung a moment to the silent, level one of Mr. de Sabran, directly opposite. He was frowning, as he often did, and yet this time there seemed to be no anger in it, only what appeared to be the kind of concentration that a man might give a puzzling thing he sought to understand.

She broke the contact as Del Rio gave his answer to her brother: "No, of course I would not say this." With a faint curve of his mouth he added lightly, "I am saying war can be a complicated game of many moves and many players, and a man must guard his backs."

She saw the lowering of Joseph's eyebrows and she intervened to keep the interchange from turning to an argument. She said, "Forgive me, Captain, but you have not finished telling us your story." As he looked to her with interest, she reminded him, "You had just met the *Bellewether* at sea."

"Ah. Yes. This was at night, as I have said, and in the dark all things are hidden, so we sail the night in company with her and all seems well. But when the dawn comes, the light shows us all is *not* well, that the *Bellewether* has suffered much from some attack. And when we come up close enough to call to them, we see there are not many men aboard that ship, and those we see are not the men that we expect to see aboard the *Bellewether*, you understand. They are men who sail with Big-Headed Tom." He paused his narrative to ask, "You know this name?"

None of them did, so he elaborated. "All of us who sail in the West Indies know this name. He's not a good man. Very violent." To de Brassart, with more emphasis, he said, "*He* is a pirate." Then he reached and slid his knife point once again into the salt. "He is a plague to all my countrymen, to all us Spanish. When he takes a ship he kills each man aboard, her crew and all her officers. He has killed many friends of mine. So when I see his men on board the *Bellewether*, this is not good."

He knew the way to spin a tale and keep the listener in suspense. He salted his food in the pause, and sliced it with precision.

"So," he said, "I talk with Juan, and he reminds me Daniel Wilde has always been a good man and an honest one, and so we think we should not let his brother's ship be kept by pirates. But how to take it back—this is a problem."

Lydia knew that the *Bellewether*'s crew numbered near fifty men, but a ship that had been captured would be running with a prize crew put aboard her by the capturer, and prize crews were significantly smaller, sometimes ten or fewer men. She pointed out, "Your ship is larger than the *Bellewether*."

"It's true. I sail on *El Montero* with a hundred men and eighteen guns, but these I could not use to full effect on this occasion."

She was puzzled. "But why not?"

He smiled. "Because, señora Wilde, your brother's ship it was already very damaged, and if I had fired a shot at it myself, if I had made another hole in it, that would not have been wise. You cannot tell a friend, 'Come, look, see how I've saved your ship, it's at the bottom of the ocean.' I don't think he'd be so grateful."

She could see his point, and smiled herself at how he'd stated it. With such a man, she thought, it was impossible to not be slightly charmed.

She was still smiling when her eyes again met Mr. de Sabran's, across the table. He did *not* look charmed, though it appeared this time his frown was aimed directly at the Spanish captain.

Unperturbed, Del Rio carried on. "Then I remember that the men aboard the *Bellewether*, they do not know we will not harm that ship. So I…well, in my language we say *tirarse un farol*, yes? The words mean exactly to show them a lantern, a light, but a false one, like when you are playing at the cards and you make someone think that you carry the king when you only have deuces."

Her father translated. "You bluffed."

"If that is the same meaning, then yes," said the captain. "I bluffed. I tell Juan to knock open our gun ports, to show them our teeth, and we fire at the same time our deck guns and muskets, but just at their rigging because it is already bad. And they think we are truly attacking them."

De Brassart nodded. "And so they surrendered."

The Spanish captain looked at him as though he did not understand the word, his eyebrows faintly drawn together, but from what he said next Lydia assumed it was the concept of surrender that was foreign to him. "No, of course not. No man would surrender in such circumstances. But he might run, and this is what they tried to do. It is unfortunate for them," he said, "that no ship is as fast as *El Montero*."

Lydia owned that the Spanish ship might have had an advantage in that quarter, with the *Bellewether* so badly mauled and poorly handled, but she knew that if her brother's ship had been in fine condition there was none upon the seas that could sail faster.

From good manners she said nothing, though she shared a glance along the table with her father, who had evidently had the same thought, for his eyes danced in the way they did when he was trying not to smile.

He said, "Well, we are grateful to you, Captain, for returning her. I hope it did not cost you any men?"

"It cost one man a finger, and another has a new scar on his shoulder, but I give thanks to God the rest of my crew are all well."

De Brassart asked, "What of the pirate crew?"

"They did not do so well. There were I think eleven of them to begin with, and when it was finished there were only seven we could find." His tone was light, as though it were lost nails that he was speaking of, not human lives. "We put them down together on a little island we were passing, very scenic, with a little bay like this, you know, for swimming. If they're careful of the sharks."

She couldn't tell if he was being truthful, but she didn't care at all about the pirate crew. She only asked, "And did they tell you, Captain, what became of those who'd been aboard the *Bellewether*?"

He had told her already, she knew. He had said that when Big-Headed Tom took a ship, he killed everyone on it. But some of those men had been sailors she'd known, and she wanted to be very sure.

"No." The Spaniard's eyes leveled on hers with a blend of directness and sympathy. "No, they did not tell me." But his voice and his expression told her he had known, as she herself knew.

Lydia looked down, and thought of all the men who'd started

on that voyage several weeks ago, and would not now be coming home—the brothers and the sons and husbands—and she found the knowledge very hard.

Del Rio said, "But I am happy to have brought the *Bellewether* back to your house." He helped himself to one more piece of apple pie and added, "And to have as my reward this pleasant company and such a banquet. This one here with the apples is particularly excellent. My compliments, señora."

"They are owed to Violet, not to me," she told him.

"To Violet? Ah, your cook. Then I will have to have her tell *my* cook the way that this is made, I think."

The fact that he'd referred to Violet as their cook—as someone skilled at what she did, and not a piece of property—made Lydia increase her good opinion of him, and she offered, "Those are apples from our orchard, Captain. I am sure that we could spare you some."

"You have an orchard here?" He looked up from his plate and took a keener interest. "Because I still have room within my hold if you would like for me to take your harvest for you to the markets. They would bring a handsome price for you."

"But not at English ports," said Joseph.

The Spaniard turned to him. "I'm sorry?"

"You have said you will not sail to English ports," was Joseph's clipped reply, "and it's against our laws to send provisions to be sold at any other."

"Ah. Because there is a war, you mean." A casual wave of the fork in his hand dismissed such things as trifles. "There are many neutral ports where I could carry your apples, if you would prefer it."

Her brother asked, "Neutral in whose view?"

His voice held a challenge and Captain del Rio's gaze shifted to match it, and it was like watching a sword blade of steel sliding out of a decorative scabbard.

"Your king views the ports of my country as neutral, señor," he replied, "and since you seem to hold him in such high esteem I am sure you would share this view?"

Lydia looked to her father, who seemed unaware how the mood of the table had changed, so she hastily stepped in herself.

"It's kind of you to make the offer, Captain, but my eldest brother carries a commission to supply our troops at Albany, and always sends a good part of our harvest there directly. What remains, we use ourselves. Though I am certain, as a token of our gratitude," she told him with a pointed look at Joseph meant to make him hold his tongue, "we could at least give you a bushel as our gift, so that your cook may make you pies."

His eyes returned to her, and with relief she watched the challenge in them change and warm again to gallantry. "They will not be as good as these, I think," he said. "But I would be most pleased, señora Wilde, by such a present." He took his cup in hand and faced her father, his good-natured smile resurfacing. "Although I think before we have done anything, we need to find a place to put your ship."

❧

They beached the *Bellewether* that evening, when the tide was at its highest in the cove.

She did not see it done. However well-behaved the Spanish captain and his first mate might have been that morning, Lydia had reasoned she could not expect the same of *El Montero*'s crew. And having seen a ship careened before, she knew it would take many men to haul the battered *Bellewether* into the shallows and run her aground upon the sand, then drag her farther up beyond the water's reach and tilt her so she lay half on one side.

And while all those men were at liberty down in the cove, she'd decided her presence would be a distraction—if not for the men, for her father and Benjamin, who'd feel the need to look out for her safety.

She stayed instead with Violet, in the house. Her father had instructed Joseph to remain there also, saying it was simply to protect the women, even though they all were well aware it was to spare him the uncomfortable experience of being thus surrounded by a group of strange men—armed men—speaking in a foreign language. Joseph had accepted this arrangement with a nod, and gone upstairs to pace his chamber.

Both of their French prisoners had kept within the house as well. Mr. de Brassart settled in the parlor with a book as he so often did, but Mr. de Sabran stayed planted firmly in the kitchen with his chair drawn up to one side of the hearth, watching the closed door and windows as though he were waiting for trouble.

Violet at last said to Lydia, "He's vexing *me*, now. I can't do my work with him under my feet."

While she sympathized, Lydia knew there was no way to easily shift him, and if she were perfectly honest she wasn't inclined to. Although she disliked and distrusted the French, she was forced to admit that his sitting there made her feel safer.

And when heavy footsteps approached and a shadow passed outside the window and there came a knock at the door, she looked first to Mr. de Sabran and waited for his nod before she crossed over to answer it.

French Peter stood on the threshold, his red woolen cap in his hands.

It occurred to her she did not know his last name. Her mother had known it, and greeted him always as Mr. Whatever-it-was, but to Lydia he was French Peter and only that, and tonight all of a sudden that felt like a failing. She could say no more than, "Good evening."

French Peter, returning the greeting, asked after her father. "I must... There is something I need to discuss with him."

Lydia told him, "He's down at the cove. There are quite a few men down there now. Spanish sailors. They've brought back a ship of my brother's and now they're careening it, so you may want to wait."

"No. Thank you, no. I will find him and speak to him now." And he thanked her again, put his cap on his head, and before stepping back from the threshold spoke past her and into the kitchen, addressing the man who still sat to the side of the hearth. He said, "*Bonsoir*, Marine."

And to her surprise Mr. de Sabran replied almost pleasantly, "*Bonsoir*, Monsieur Boudreau."

She asked her father later on that night, when both French officers had taken to their chamber and the rest of them were readying themselves for bed upstairs, if he had ever learned French Peter's surname.

"It is Bowdro, I believe," he told her.

"Boudreau?"

"Very possibly." He laid his waistcoat neatly on the clothes-press without asking why she wished to know.

She was not certain what she could have told him. Only that it shamed her slightly knowing that a stranger had observed French Peter's name when she had not.

Benjamin, already in his bed and half-asleep, said, "His arrival was well-timed tonight. I might have lost an arm if not for him."

"Not quite an arm," their father answered dryly.

"Well, I might at least have had a bruise," amended Benjamin. "That spar was twice as tall as me. French Peter caught it as if it were no more than a sapling." Then he seemed to catch himself as though he'd heard what he'd just said, and in the silence that fell afterward he rolled himself more tightly in his blankets. "Anyhow," he finished, "I am glad that he was there."

Lydia hoped it was not all a wasted effort, and she told them so. "It sounds as if there's little of the ship that may be salvaged."

"That," her father said, "will be for William to decide."

They could but wait for William's answer and instructions. After Benjamin had ridden to Cross Harbor and so passed the word, arriving home again midafternoon, they'd seen the sails of Mr. Fisher's small sloop heading out along the far shore of the bay into the Sound, away toward her brother's dock in New York harbor so he could deliver him the news.

"Till then," her father said, "we have our own concerns. And I am glad to hear you find French Peter helpful," he told Benjamin, "because he will be helping in the orchard with our harvest."

Benjamin rose halfway on one elbow, more awake. "Beginning when?"

"Tomorrow morning."

It was after sunset and that left her only candlelight to view her father's features by, but still she saw their firm and stubborn lines.

She looked at Benjamin, and he at her, and neither of them dared to ask the question that was uppermost in both their minds, and yet their father heard it notwithstanding, for he told them both, "Your brother has done well enough these weeks with the French officers."

Lydia said, "But we had no choice, with them. And with French Peter—"

"He has lost a child." Her father's tone reminded both of them he knew the pain of that. "He wants to pay me for the coffin, but he has no money of his own, for as a refugee he has been forced to live on charity. So if he seeks to pay me with his labor I cannot deny him that. Sometimes," he said, "you must allow a man to be a man."

He said no more, but Lydia thought long about those final words.

She turned them over in her mind while she lay in her bed that night. And she was thinking of them still when, early the next morning, she watched Mr. de Sabran fit the final pieces to the cider press, his dark head bent in concentration.

Maybe, she thought, that was what he sought to do when he threw all his focus into work, as he was doing, as though idleness were something he did not know how to manage. Maybe he was seeking to remind himself—remind them all—that while he was a prisoner at the mercy of his keepers, far from home and from his purpose, he had not yet ceased to be a man.

⁂

The wind had changed.

It held the black-hulled *El Montero* captive at its anchor in the bay, although the Spanish captain did not seem concerned. "No, no," Del Rio said, "it's not a problem. We are flying now the colors of the—" Breaking off, he looked up at the green-and-white-striped flag that flew above his mast, and asked Mr. Ramírez, "What are these ones?"

And Ramírez answered in a clear deep voice, surprising them by speaking English, "These ones, *capitán*, would be the colors of a merchant who is Portuguese."

"You see then," Del Rio returned, "we are Portuguese, just at these times. And the English and Portuguese, they are good friends, yes? So we will be fine."

He was—as seemed to be his habit—right. They had attracted some attention, with their sleek black hull and Spanish bottom, sheathed in lead to guard against the worms that could destroy a ship in warmer waters. But while a couple of their neighbors had rowed up from Millbank or over from Cross Harbor for a closer look at *El Montero*, it was the sad *Bellewether* that truly held their interest, and her father having called across to one of them a version of how she had been so damaged, word was passed along and heads were shaken at the loss of men, and lively curses called down on the English pirate who had brought the ship to ruin.

And then William had arrived. Not by the sea, but by the forest road, on horseback.

Violet, coming from the milking, saw him first. And entering the kitchen said to Lydia, "Your brother's here," in tones that didn't hide the fact she'd never had much time for William. She was like her mother, Phyllis, who had many times remarked that, for a man who liked to stand and talk as much as William did, he never truly stood for anything. Which wasn't wholly accurate. He stood for many things, but in a shifting way. He was the perfect model of a man of business, showing to all men the face they wanted most to see. With men of learning, he would mirror their own interests, speak of books and of philosophy, and yet with men who worked along his docks he could as easily share stories that would curl a barmaid's hair, and leave both groups convinced that here, indeed, was someone they could trust and like. A man like them.

It was a gift he'd had since birth, so Lydia believed. Everyone saw what they wanted in William, their parents included. Like many a firstborn, he had a strong look of their father which gained as he grew—the wide chest and broad shoulders and height that allowed him to walk with authority. That likeness had saved him from trouble a number of times, so their mother had said. "I'd look down at his little face," she'd once told Lydia, "and it was just like your father was looking back up at me, and goodness knows that I've never been able to stay angry long with your father."

Their father, who'd been sitting there at the table, had smiled and replied that he'd never himself known a boy who could argue his way out of hidings with more ready eloquence. "Made me feel all but ashamed of myself that I'd so much as thought about discipline. And *that*, my dear," he had said to his wife, "comes entirely out of your nature, not mine."

And in truth, had the Fates schemed to take all her mother's intuitive features and twist them to turning a profit, the end result would have been William.

Lydia never knew whether the William she saw and knew well was the same William anyone else saw, but neither did she let it bother her. He was still her brother, as he'd always been, and as he reined his horse beside the barn and looked round to see her approaching, his smile was warm and familiar, and as he dismounted he gathered her into the same brief, rib-bruising embrace that had marked all their greetings since she had been small, and it lifted her feet from the ground.

"I'm too big," she protested.

"Never." His grin showed off fine, even teeth for a man who in but a few years would be forty. His clothes were fine also, though not ostentatiously so—tailored neatly, expensively, of dark-gray wool lined with silk that was doubtless from one of his shipments.

"You look well," she told him.

"And you." Looking down, he made a show of brushing one obstructing strand of fair hair from his eyes to clear his vision as he added, "Every time I see you, you get prettier."

Rolling her eyes, she assured him, "I'm too big for *that*, too."

"What, compliments?"

"Flattery." Glancing away she took note of his horse and her brows drew together in puzzlement. "Isn't this Henry's new gelding?"

"It is." Henry Ryder, their cousin, lived down with his wife and two children at Millbank, and kept the post office there. "My own horse," William said, "cast a shoe as I came into Millbank last night, so I stopped at Henry's and supped and slept there, and he gave me the loan of this beautiful lad for the day, while the blacksmith attends to my mare." Leaving the horse at the rail of the fence he stood straighter and stretched out his shoulders and asked, "Where is Father?"

"In the orchard, with the others."

"Others?"

"Benjamin, and Joseph, and French Peter, and"—she hesitated, only for the smallest moment—"one of our French officers."

"Oh yes." His features sobered. "I'm sorry indeed that you've been so imposed upon. I tried my best to intervene when Silas told me what was going on, but Uncle Reuben has his own channels of influence, I fear, and there was nothing I could do." With cautious eyes he asked her, "How is Joseph?"

"He is managing."

If William had suspicions she was guarding Joseph's privacy and honor by concealing the true state of things, he did not press the point but only asked, "And you? How are you bearing up? It cannot be so easy for you, either."

A part of her was longing to confide in him and lean again into his strong embrace and tell him no, it was not easy. But she was a woman now, and not a child, and so she only shrugged her shoulders and assured him, "I am managing, as well." Her thoughts were turning to a different subject anyway. "When did you speak to Silas?"

"What?"

"You said that Silas told you," she reminded him, "about his father sending us the officers. When did you see him?"

"Silas," said her brother dryly, "is a frequent visitor upon my doorstep these days, now he's settled in New York."

"He's not in Newtown any longer?"

"No, since early this past spring he's had his lodgings not three streets from us, and it's the rare week when he doesn't come around to see us once. Especially at mealtimes." He could evidently read her thoughts without her saying anything, because he said, "I know. He's not my first choice of associate. But he *is* family, Lyddie, and there would be talk were I to shun him."

"Let them talk," she told him. "He's a loathsome little toad."

Behind them, Violet, who had come out of the house and walked across the clearing, having nearly reached them, caught that final phrase and answered it with feeling: "If you're speaking of His Majesty, he's back there in the parlor. And if he wants more tea he'll have to up and make it for himself, because I'm done with him this morning." With a nod that was just clinging to the edges of politeness, she told William, "I'll go up and let your father know you're here." And without breaking stride she walked on by and passed beneath the rowan tree and headed up the lane toward the orchard.

William arched his eyebrows, looking down at Lydia. "The king is in our parlor?"

She corrected him. "She means Mr. de Brassart. He is one of our French officers, and Violet cannot stand him."

"Well," said William, "now you have me curious. A man she dislikes more than she does me? I have to see this creature, or I'll not believe it." With a grin, he took her arm in his and set their backs toward the barn. "But first, come show me what the devil's happened to my ship."

⚘

The tide was ebbing, giving the assembled party on the beach a broad expanse of drying sand to walk on as they made their circuit of the stranded *Bellewether*, her shattered hull careened with care. It seemed so wrong to see her hauled so far out of the water where she'd run so freely and so fast; to see her leaning here upon her side like some great racehorse that had faltered and collapsed and could no longer bear the struggle it would take to stand.

The sight was sad, and Lydia was feeling it more deeply than she'd thought she would. To William, standing not far off, it must have been a devastation.

In the span of time since she had brought him down here to the beach they had been joined by Benjamin and Joseph and their father, come directly from the orchard. And their father, in his turn, had hailed the Spanish captain and his mate, who'd rowed across obligingly, arriving onshore not ten minutes before Mr. Fisher, their neighbor—who having delivered their summons to William in New York had found himself stranded there due to the contrary winds, and been forced to return by the road, as had William—rowed over himself from Cross Harbor, with Sarah, his daughter, as passenger.

Normally Lydia would have delighted in having a visit from Sarah. They were of an age, had played often in childhood, and grown into easy companions. But on this particular day, all of Sarah's attention was given to Joseph, while Lydia's focus stayed fixed upon William.

He'd accepted in silence the news that the captain and crew he had hired for the *Bellewether*'s voyage were probably dead. Hard news for him, surely. The captain had been a close friend. But apart from his tightening jaw and a nod he had made no reaction.

And now, as he surveyed the wreck of the ship that had once

been his pride, everybody was watching, and holding their own words with quiet respect.

William stood and looked a moment longer. "Well," he finally said, "at least she did not lose her life without a fight."

"No hope of rebuilding her?" Benjamin's tone angled upward to make it a question, though all of them well knew the answer.

William, in fact, did not bother to voice it aloud, only gave a slight shake of his head in reply and said, "She'll be a hard loss. Although it's the loss of her cargo that will be the hardest, I think, for my partners."

Here Captain del Rio cut in with an elegant cough and the comment, "Your cargo, señor, is not lost."

William turned as though he had forgotten the Spaniard was there. Even Lydia, if she were honest, had only just realized how close to her Captain del Rio was standing, which might either be a tribute to his gentlemanly manners or his stealth. He smiled. "There was, as you have said, much fighting, and I cannot fight well with a ship so heavy, so the cargo it was transferred to my own ship, *El Montero*. It is there still, and I can assure you, very safe." The look he cast on William now was plainly from one man of business to another. "But since I imagine it cannot be any use to you to have it now returning to New York, from where you sent it, I'd be glad to carry it again for you to the West Indies. It is not so good, of course, for me to sail into an English port at these times," he admitted with a dry glance toward Joseph, "but our Spanish ports are neutral."

William met the captain's gaze and seemed to think on this a moment, then replied, "A most kind offer, Captain, and one I'll be happy to accept if we can come to terms agreeable to both our interests."

Lydia had braced herself for Joseph to express his own opinion of the Spanish and their "neutral" ports, the way he'd done before, but he said nothing. When she ventured to look round, she saw why. Joseph wasn't listening.

He'd stepped clear of the little group and was now standing

close beside the *Bellewether*. She watched as he lifted one hand to the broken hull.

William, who'd been talking to the Spanish captain, stopped midsentence.

Lydia found she was holding her breath. She felt all of them there on the beach—except maybe the Spaniards—were doing the same thing, not daring to stir, in case somehow the moment would break and be lost.

Joseph, still with his back to them, ran his hand slowly along one broad, sea-weathered board. Then he tilted his head in a way she remembered and sighted along it, not paying attention to anything else. In an easy and confident tone she had not heard him use in three years, he said, "It could be done, you know. She's not past saving."

She was unprepared for the quick swell of tears in her eyes and she blinked hard to keep them back. Turned to her father, and found he was looking at William, and she could see clearly the strain of the silent emotion that touched both their faces—the unspoken question that was being asked and, as silently, answered.

At last William, very casually, told Joseph, "You'd know best. How many weeks would it take, by your reckoning?"

Joseph, with his hand still on the ship's scarred hull, replied with a small careless shrug that was, again, a gesture none of them had seen in far too long. "That would depend how many men I had to work on her."

"But you could do it?" William asked, and once again they held their breaths and waited.

Then, "With tools and time, yes," Joseph told them.

"Good. That's good," said William, and he looked away from Joseph as though something in the angle of the midday sunlight hurt his eyes. He sought their father's gaze again and shared a glance that knew the weight and meaning of his words. "For tools and time, and even men, are but a small expense if, in the end, what we have lost can be restored."

JEAN-PHILIPPE

S HE'S PRETTY, IS SHE not?" The big Acadian had come to stand
beside his shoulder.

Jean-Philippe, for one unsettled moment, thought he might
have dropped his guard and so betrayed his thoughts, but when he
swiftly turned from his appraisal of the figure in the yellow gown,
he saw he need not worry.

Boudreau's focus was on something else entirely as he went on,
"Despite all that, you can still see the lines of her, the beauty of
her, yes? There was no faster ship in New York's harbor."

It was coming on to dinnertime. They'd walked back from the
orchard not along the lane but by the forest path, where it was
shaded still and cool. And where the path had turned to follow
close along the cliff top and the trees had thinned to give them a
clear view down to the cove, they'd stopped and Jean-Philippe
had studied the small group of people gathered now beside the
broken ship.

He could not count the times he'd stood like this, concealed
on higher ground, and looked down on an adversary, measuring
their strength before a battle. And their weaknesses.

He watched for interactions, always. Sought to learn who truly
held command, and in this instance it was clear that of the seven
men upon the beach the one in charge was Monsieur Wilde, for
even though he had stepped back behind the younger man in
gray, the others there all looked to him while speaking, as though
seeking his approval.

The man in gray would be the eldest son, the one who'd come
this morning, for in build and stance he was the younger image

of his father. And his brothers had now fallen into their role as subordinates to him, although the youngest had not shaken off his restlessness and gazed, not at the ship before him, but toward the tall masts of the Spanish ship now riding to her anchor in the bay.

The middle brother had, to Jean-Philippe's surprise, a woman with him—young, fair-haired, and dressed in blue.

At first he'd wondered if she was the eldest brother's wife, but it was obvious her whole attention was upon the troubled one, and any man who held himself as proudly as Monsieur Wilde's eldest son would never have stood by and let his wife show such great favor to another without trying to reclaim it for himself. And a few more minutes' observation had left Jean-Philippe convinced the woman dressed in blue must be the daughter of the other older man who was now standing talking to the Spanish captain, who, in turn, was standing close to Lydia.

Too close.

"Yes, very pretty," Jean-Philippe replied, in level tones. "But tell me, who are those two people there, the woman and the older man?"

Boudreau said, "The Fishers. Mr. Fisher keeps the big store at Cross Harbor, with his children. That's his eldest daughter, Sarah."

"And what is she to the middle son?"

"She was—she is—his fiancée, though whether they will marry now is something God alone can know."

"Why?" Jean-Philippe looked down more closely at the young blond woman in the blue gown, with her feelings for the troubled son so obvious in how she held herself so close beside him; how she watched him. "Tell me, what was it that happened to him?"

Boudreau hesitated, shifting where he stood as though uncomfortable, and Jean-Philippe looked back at him.

"You told me I had much to learn about this family," was his challenge. "Teach me, then." He made a guess. "He has seen battle, that one, yes? And he did not cope well with it?"

It was the right approach to take to make Boudreau begin to

speak, his tone and stance defensive. "Joseph was not sent up to Chouaguen to fight. He was a peaceful man and not a soldier." With a frown he added, "So I think there is no shame that he has struggled with it afterward. Were you there?"

"At Chouaguen? No." That would be three years ago. That summer he'd been sent with a detachment of his men to the Ohio Valley. "No, I was not there." He'd heard the stories, though. He always heard the stories.

It had been a famous victory, the attack upon Chouaguen— "Oswego," as the English called it. Since he was a boy that fort had stood upon the south shore of the lake—begun in wood and fortified in stone, an English blight upon their territory. It could not be allowed to stand, and his superiors, Monsieurs Coulon de Villiers and de Rigaud, deserved to bear the honor of attacking it, together with Montcalm. While he disliked Montcalm, he could not fault that victory. The campaign had been well planned, well executed, and a great success.

But from his own experience he also knew that battles did not end with the surrender of a fort. For common soldiers and civilians, the most dangerous of times came in the aftermath of that capitulation, when storerooms were plundered and liquor was drunk and the victors and their native allies, who held to their own rules of war, took control.

So it had been, according to the tales he'd heard, at Fort Chouaguen.

He looked now at the middle Wilde son—Joseph—and asked quietly, "What was he, then, if not a soldier?"

Boudreau paused again, as though he still did not feel comfortable with this discussion, but at length he said, "He was a shipbuilder."

This made good sense to Jean-Philippe and fit with what he had observed, although it went a step beyond his own suspicion that the young man had once been a carpenter. A shipbuilder had skills that were more specialized.

Boudreau went on: "He worked at the same shipyard as the son of Mr. Fisher, and the two of them were friends, like this." The big man held two fingers up, pressed close together. "This is what I'm told, you understand, by Madame Wilde, for I did not come here myself until just before Joseph went to Chouaguen. I saw him only two times before he and his friend, Moses Fisher, went north to that place." He shrugged. "These were difficult times for this family. For the Fishers also, because they were intertwined— the Fisher girl, there, being Joseph's fiancée, and Moses Fisher having asked Miss Lydia to marry him, it made their leaving very sad. And then of course, when Joseph came back as he did, that was more sad."

"And Moses Fisher?" Jean-Philippe imagined he already knew the answer but he asked the question anyway, aware his tone had hardened. He had not thought he could feel so deep a jealousy for someone he'd just heard of. But he did.

Boudreau sighed heavily. "Well, he did not come back at all. And that was very terrible, because it was while Joseph was beside him that his friend was killed, and he was there to witness it, and that I think is what has left him broken most of all."

Jean-Philippe, his thoughtful gaze upon the straight back of the woman in the yellow gown who stood so still upon the beach below them, could not help but wonder whether Joseph was the only one who'd been left broken by the death of Moses Fisher.

Joseph Wilde was moving. He had stepped away from Sarah Fisher and the others and was now approaching the careened ship.

Jean-Philippe, observing this, asked, "What was he like, when you saw him those two times, before Chouaguen?"

"Who, Joseph?" Boudreau shrugged again. "A quiet man, but happier. Then, he could laugh. They all could. But they had her then as well, you understand. Their mother," he explained, when Jean-Philippe glanced briefly over, questioning. "May God be with her," Boudreau said, and crossed himself with deep respect.

"She has not been dead long?"

"Only a year. There was a storm. A tree fell. For a time it seemed she might recover, but..." The big man's voice trailed off in sadness, then he simply said, "God takes those souls he loves the best."

Jean-Philippe was less convinced of that. He'd seen men die who would not have been greatly loved by God, but he did not share his opinions, knowing Boudreau had just lost a child.

On the half-moon curve of beach, the mood had shifted. There was tension now—he saw it clearly in the way they all were standing.

Joseph Wilde had raised his hand to touch and test the boards of the ship's hull.

As if on cue the birdsong stilled above them in the trees, and all the leaves hung quietly a moment, as though waiting.

Boudreau, having taken little notice of the latest movements on the beach, had looked away instead to where the waters of the wider bay showed blue between the gaps amid the tangle of the woods. Now he said, "The wind is changing."

"Yes," said Jean-Philippe, still taking in the family scene below them. "I believe you may be right."

CHARLEY

THERE'S A STORM COMING."

Strange thing to hear on a perfectly cloudless October day. Stranger by far when the warning was given to you by a vampire.

Adjusting his teeth, Don Petrella stepped out of the booth where, for most of this morning, as part of our Fall Harvest Festival, he had been posing for photos with fans for five dollars. He glanced skyward, adding, "A *big* storm. My scar's acting up."

I liked Don. I'd been too young to watch his show back in the day, with its crime-fighting vampire detective, but he had been famous enough that I'd seen him in interviews, and I remembered. Back then he'd been lean, dark, and dangerous-looking, and viewers had voted him "Sexiest Man on TV" two years running. His waist might have thickened a little, his eyes showing hints of the puffiness men sometimes got when they drank to excess, and his hair might have silvered to gunmetal gray, but when he shot me that lopsided smile, I could still see the sex appeal.

Rachel, on learning that Don was a Wilde House trustee, had said, "Lucky you. He's really hot."

"He's a grandfather."

"So? He's still hot."

I'd conceded the point. "But he seems like he's pretty high maintenance."

She'd glanced at me then without comment, and gone back to helping fold laundry, but I'd caught the edge of her smirk.

"What?"

She'd shaken her head. "Nothing."

"Rachel."

"It's just that I'm trying to picture how bad he must be if *you* think he's high maintenance."

"I'm not sure I know what you mean."

She had rolled her eyes. "Look who you're dating."

"Who, Tyler? He isn't high maintenance."

"Oh, really?" She'd caught Tyler's cadence in a pretty good imitation: "Hey, babe, can you make me a sandwich? Can you take my car for an oil change? Can you move your whole life half an inch to the left, babe? You're blocking my light."

I had tossed her a T-shirt. "Come on, he's not like that."

She'd said, "He's *exactly* like that, and you know it."

At that point, she'd only met Tyler a handful of times, and I'd still held out hope that I'd get them to like one another someday.

But I wasn't so sure anymore after how she'd reacted on Labor Day weekend, when I'd taken her back to college.

She'd been quiet for most of our drive to the city that morning, but after I'd helped her to carry her boxes and suitcases up to her dorm room she'd sighed and said, "Look, I've been thinking. I know when you asked me a couple of weeks ago if I'd have dinner with you guys tonight, I said no, but I understand Tyler's important to you, so I'm changing my answer. I'll do it."

I'd looked down, pretending that there was a wrinkle I needed to smooth on her bedspread while I tried to figure out how to respond. Rachel knew me too well. She'd said, knowing the answer, "He bailed on you, didn't he?"

"Well..."

"He's not coming."

"He had something come up with one of his friends," I had said, and I'd tried to make it sound as though the thing that had "come up" was more important than a boys' night in Atlantic City.

Rachel hadn't bought it. "He is *such* an ass."

I'd known there wasn't any point in arguing. I'd taken her for lunch instead, the two of us alone, and then we'd snagged last-minute tickets to a Broadway show, and after that I'd dropped her at her dorm again and spent the night all by myself in the fancy, expensive hotel room that wasn't refundable.

Tyler had offered again to repay me when he'd called the following night, but I'd shrugged it off. "No, it's okay."

"Well, we'll go somewhere nice for the long weekend. My treat."

"It can't be that weekend."

"Why not? Rachel's going up to spend time with your parents, right? To celebrate Canadian Thanksgiving? So you'll be on your own."

"I'll be working. That's our Fall Harvest Festival weekend, remember?"

He hadn't remembered, or so I'd assumed from the change in his tone. "So then when will I see you? I have to work weekends the rest of September, you know that."

"We'll figure it out," I had promised, and he'd let it drop. Which was good, because I'd had enough on my plate these past weeks.

I'd had meetings to deal with our Fall Harvest Festival plans and more meetings to deal with our annual budget, and in between I'd been working with Frank to track down all the furniture and smaller items his family had given to other museums. At least three of those donations had been made over a century ago, but we were making progress, and most of the curators I'd spoken to were happy to arrange to let us have the items back here to display, on what amounted to permanent loan.

The only one who'd been a bit resistant was the curator/director of a large historic house museum in New Jersey. According to the records, he'd acquired the "Spanish chair with leather seat" that had been listed in the inventory, but despite repeated emails and three phone calls I'd heard nothing back from him.

On all of those calls his assistant had answered and seemed very helpful and nice, and the third time I'd called she had offered apologies. "I don't know why he hasn't called you back yet. I'm so sorry."

"Maybe I could just email *you* all of the details, and then you could pass those on. Would that be easier for him?"

"It might."

As she'd started to give me her email address I'd said, "Hang on, I just need a pen." There'd been everything else on my desk at that moment, but nothing to write with. Not even a pencil. I'd bent down to open a drawer, and repeated, "Hang on."

Modern phones weren't designed to be cradled between ear and shoulder like old phones had been. Mine had kept slipping as I searched my desk drawers. No luck.

Then I'd straightened.

The voice on the phone had asked, "Are you still there?"

I had stared at the top of my desk. At the pen that was now sitting perfectly placed on the neatly stacked papers that filled the same space where, a heartbeat before, there'd been total disorder.

I'd answered her carefully, "Yes, I'm still here." She had told me her email address. I had copied it down. I'd said, "Thank you."

And then, having ended the phone call, I'd said it again, only this time the words had been meant for whatever it was that was sharing my room: "Thank you."

There'd been no answer. No cold brush of air, no mysterious footsteps, no movement at all. But I'd known that I wasn't alone.

I'd begun to accept it. I still hadn't wrapped my mind comfortably around the concept of ghosts, but I'd come to that level of compromise where I no longer denied they existed. I just hadn't let my thoughts dwell on that too long.

And then had come the morning when I'd opened up my office door to find a pair of steel-toed work boots on my desk, beside a brand-new yellow hardhat.

Those, I'd guessed, had *not* come from the ghost.

The boots had been brand-new as well. I'd put them on and tied the laces tightly, put the hardhat on, and gone downstairs.

Outside, I'd found Sam working on the scaffolding his men had set up all along the north side of the house.

"Okay," I'd said. "I take the hint."

He'd grinned. "I only told you twenty times." He'd looked down at my feet. "They fit all right?"

"Like they were made for me. How did you know my size?"

"Well," he'd said, "yesterday when I was eating my lunch and you tried to sneak past without letting me see you were wearing your running shoes…"

"Oh." I had shaded my eyes, looking up. "You saw that?"

"Yes, I did. And you left some nice footprints right there in the mud. So I measured one."

I'd said, "I'm usually better at not being seen."

"I'll remember that."

"Anyway, thanks. Let me know what I owe you."

"I'll invoice you."

I'd known he wouldn't, but I'd let it pass. I'd glanced along the scaffolding instead, and said, "It's looking good."

"It's getting there."

His crew had started working on removing all the north end siding, sorting out the clapboards between those too damaged to be used again and those that didn't need replacing. With the timber frame exposed, Sam could make structural repairs and reinforcements where they needed to be made.

We had been lucky with the weather.

For the whole month of September there'd been hardly any rain at all, just days of warmth and sunshine, and this first week of October had been following the same path.

Lara, coming up the walkway from the parking lot that morning, had shown from her fashion choices that she'd started to embrace the fall. Her woven sweater held the warmer hues of autumn, and her knee-high boots had been fringed suede.

She'd whistled at my boots and hardhat. "Hey, great outfit. Very *Vogue*."

"Thank Sam," I'd said. "He picked these out."

"Good eye," she'd praised him, careful to keep clear of all the scaffolding so that she could avoid both falling boards and safety lectures.

I'd begun a silent mental countdown, waiting for our stone-mason to magically appear, as he'd begun to do whenever Lara turned up on the work site. I had only counted to eleven when I'd first heard Willie's heavy steps, and then his cheerful Scottish voice had greeted Lara, "Morning, gorgeous."

"Morning."

Willie, I knew, had been making good use of the warm weather. Having found all the places where water had made its way into the stonework and washed out the lime mortar over the years, he'd drilled into those voids and filled them with fresh mortar and was now back to the job of repointing the faces of all the foundation walls. He'd also trimmed his beard and had been wearing shirts that looked as though they had been newly ironed. With a smile for Lara, he asked, "Come to help me with the pointing up?"

"As tantalizing as that sounds," she'd told him, "no. But I *do* have a favor to ask you. And you, Sam."

Sam, who had begun to sidle off along the scaffolding, had turned halfway around again. "What kind of favor?"

Lara hadn't been put off by his suspicious tone. "For our Fall Harvest Festival we have a wheelwright coming out, and there was supposed to be a blacksmith, but the blacksmith had to cancel, so the wheelwright's on his own, and I was thinking it would really be much better to have more than just one craftsman, you know, giving demonstrations. So—"

Here Willie had cut in with, "So you thought a handsome Scotsman with a hammer and a chisel might be just the thing you're wanting?"

"Yes." She'd answered his flirtation with a warm smile of her own. "And Sam, Malaika says you have these antique tools, and she said if you'd be our woodwright for the festival, she'll let you have that leaded window she's got in her shed. The one you wanted."

Sam had briefly smiled and pulled his work gloves from his belt so he could put them on. "I'll think about it."

He must have decided the window was worth it, because when I'd arrived on-site this morning for the start of our Fall Harvest Festival, he had been here already, dressed in an old-fashioned work shirt and trousers that, although not purely colonial, still looked a lot more in tune with our period than Don Petrella's TV costume.

Don had me looking toward the blue sky now, too, searching for storm clouds.

I didn't see any.

But Don assured me his scar never lied when it came to predicting the weather. "You don't always see a storm coming," was his sage advice as he made sure again that his vampire teeth were in place before heading back into his booth.

He was one of our best-loved attractions today, second only to Dennis the donkey, who, over in the shade beside the barn, was giving rides to children in a patient, constant circle. Dennis's owner, Isaac Fisher, was one of the Fishers Malaika had told me about when we'd sat on her sailboat—the family that once had owned most of Cross Harbor. The family resemblance between him and Frank was even easier to see when they were standing close together, interacting with the ease of men whose ancestors had intermarried over generations. They were working as a team today, since Frank had set his cider press up over by the barn as well, where he could demonstrate the way it worked and hand out paper cups of cider to the people lining up for donkey rides.

The length of that line was apparently bothering Sharon and Eve. The barn was their domain—its airy, dim interior decked out with tables lined with crafts for sale by local artisans, while all down one wall Millbank's Spinners and Weavers Club hosted a display that showed the steps of turning wool to cloth, complete with an actual sheep at one end and a loom at the other. Which Sharon felt—as she had said at least three times already—should draw bigger crowds of people than a donkey.

Frank had pointed out that bringing in the donkey had been Sharon's own idea, but that hadn't helped.

I'd stayed out of the argument. In fact, I'd stayed out of the barn as much as possible and focused on the great swirl of activity outdoors. There was a storyteller over by the picnic tables, keeping people entertained. A pumpkin-carving booth beside another one where kids could try their hand at making scarecrows. And Harvey, always keen to be the center of attention, had rented a full reenactment uniform and was dressed as an officer of the Revolution, right down to the wig and the sword and the high polished boots, strutting around with a false air of leisure to let everybody admire him. He'd strutted across my path too many times today for me to think it was purely coincidence. With Eve and Sharon confined to the barn, I suspected they'd deputized Harvey to keep a close eye on me so they could pounce if I made a mistake. The plan, I gathered, was to gather evidence to back their claim I wasn't the right person for this job. I hadn't acknowledged their constant surveillance but I was aware of it, so when I saw Harvey now standing a few feet away with his back to me, talking to Willie and Sam and the wheelwright, my first instinct was to go straight past, and quickly, while he was distracted.

Then I heard what he was saying.

"But with these zoning changes, now, the mayor's just gone right off the reservation." Looking straight at Sam he added, "No offense, Chief."

I stopped walking. "Harvey," I cut in, my voice professionally level, "could I see you for a minute?"

All four men had turned their heads to look at me, but Harvey seemed the most surprised. "Sure."

Leading him a little distance off till we were out of earshot of the others, I said, "Look, I can't control what you do on your own time, but when you're here representing our museum, could you please try not to be a total racist?"

Harvey's eyebrows rose. "Excuse me?"

"What you said just now to Sam—that was completely disrespectful."

Harvey looked at me like I was crazy. Then he told me so. "You're nuts. Sam didn't mind. Besides, I told him, 'No offense.'"

The condescension in his tone was making it a challenge for me not to lose my temper, but I managed somehow. "First," I shot back smoothly, "Sam is way too nice to tell you if he minds. And second, anytime you need to make a point of saying 'no offense,' it means that what you're saying is offensive." I was done, so I dismissed him with, "Just don't do it again, okay?"

And then I walked away.

I'd pay a price for that, I knew, but there were some points that, for me, were nonnegotiable.

Willie, having spotted Lara over by the donkey rides, had set his tools down for a break and gone across to see her, and the wheelwright was explaining to an interested family how to fit a metal tire on a buggy wheel. But Sam had time to spare me. He'd been working on one of our old upstairs windows, I noticed—efficiently killing two birds with one stone as he demonstrated old techniques and tools while getting necessary work done.

They weren't the first windows the Wilde House had known. In our weeks of sifting through the excavated soil, although we hadn't turned up any more French buttons, we'd found twisted fragments of window lead and a few broken bits of blue-green glass from the diamond-shaped quarrels of the casement windows that would have been on the house originally when it was first built, but at some point in the eighteenth century—possibly when Zebulon Wilde had returned to the old house from Newtown to raise his own family here—those casement windows had been taken out and replaced with twelve-over-twelve double-hung windows, and one of these now lay supported across two old sawhorses while Sam refitted its muntins.

I felt ashamed for ever having doubted his ability to do such specialized repair and restoration. I couldn't imagine any subcontractor doing a more expert job. His hands kept up their movements, sure and certain, even as he raised his head. I think he'd only meant to smile and nod and say hello. Instead he looked more closely at my face and asked, "Is something wrong?"

"I just came to apologize for Harvey. He can be so…" Words failed me. "Culturally insensitive" seemed too tame and too polite, but what I wanted to say wasn't very professional.

Sam's smile showed briefly. "Yeah, well. I've dealt with guys like Harvey my whole life."

"You shouldn't have to here, though." I could feel my own frustration breaking through a little as I noticed Harvey, in his flashy costume, heading back toward the barn and Eve and Sharon. "It's not right," I said. "You shouldn't have to just stand here and take that kind of—" Once again the word I needed wasn't one that I could say while working.

Sam seemed capable of filling in the blank. "Are we still talking about me?" he asked. I looked at him, and met his understanding eyes. He said, "Don't let them make you crazy." Then, as if he knew I needed to make light of it, he added, "Or is it too late for that?"

I smiled back. "It's a little late."

"Then here." He handed me a hammer. "Help me put this frame together. You'll feel better if you hit something."

I did feel better, though I had to give my hammer up five minutes later to a little girl who, stopping with her family to observe what Sam was working on, was keen to help. For someone who'd been called in at the last minute to demonstrate, Sam did a decent job of it. He knew how to explain things, how to keep people's attention—how to teach, and make it memorable.

I was as absorbed in his talk as the little girl until a hand brushed the back of my neck and I jumped.

"Hey," said Tyler, surprising me more just by being here than he had done with his unannounced touch.

"Hey!" Recovering from my initial disbelief I leaned into his hug. "What are you doing here?"

"Since you won't let me take you somewhere fun this weekend, I thought I could bring the fun to you." He flashed The Smile. "You do have restaurants here, right? We can go to dinner, maybe catch a movie, then tomorrow we—"

"Tomorrow I'll be here," I told him, "cleaning up. But you can come and help with that."

"Since when do you work Sundays?"

"Since you've known me. When we have special events, I work the days and hours I'm needed, Ty. You know that. And this is our big fall—"

"Harvest weekend. Yes, I know." He looked around at the activity. "Good crowd. You've got good weather for it."

I didn't bring up Don Petrella's scar and its prediction that a storm was on the way, because he'd already changed focus. With his left arm still around me, Tyler held his right hand out to Sam, who'd finished with his demonstration. "Hi," he said, and introduced himself, and added, "I'm the boyfriend."

Sam, above the handshake, said, "I gathered that. Sam Abrams."

"You're the contractor."

"That's right."

I always found it interesting watching men meet other men. It was an almost primal and subconscious thing, the way they took each other's measure, marking out their relative positions in the hierarchy. I'd watched while Tyler did this countless times in business and in social situations, but this was my first time watching Sam. While Tyler used his tone of voice and body language and his posture, Sam achieved the same thing with his eyes alone—his level gaze that held a quiet confidence and knew its worth and wasn't all that easily impressed. He didn't change how he was standing and his voice remained polite.

But it was Tyler—taller, dressed in more expensive clothes, and speaking with more force—who broke the contact first and looked away, then asked me, "How much longer do you have to stay here?"

When I told him we'd be done at five, he pulled his phone out. Checked the time. The last time I had done that, not too long ago, it had been ten past two. I was about to offer him a tour when he said, "Tell you what, babe. Let me have your house keys. I'll go down and get unpacked and take a shower while I wait for you."

I'd thought he'd stay on-site awhile—he'd heard me talk so much about the Wilde House and the work that we were doing, but he'd never seen it. But he was already holding his hand out and I knew if he didn't want to stay, there wasn't any point in trying to convince him to. I handed him the keys and deftly hid my disappointment.

Willie, returning to take up his tools just as Tyler was walking away, remarked, "Either that lad's a fast worker or you are, if he's got your keys."

Sam said, "That was her boyfriend."

"Ah." Willie grinned. "What does he sell, then?"

The sun speared my eyes and I shaded them. "What makes you think he sells something?"

"Well, does he?"

I admitted, "Yes. Insurance."

Willie's grin broadened, and taking his mallet in hand he said, "There you go."

He winked and got to work, and left me wondering what it had been that tipped him off. I didn't get a chance to ask, because by then another group of visitors was gathering, and Sam and Willie and the wheelwright started with their demonstrations. And I was distracted by Frank's whistle.

Frank had one of those distinctive whistles—sharp and short and through his teeth—that carried right across the clearing.

When I turned my head to look toward the barn he raised his hand to call me over.

In the grass around his antique cider press the wasps were hovering with stealth, attracted by the pungent apple pulp that clung to all the working wooden pieces and collected in the sloping tray below that caught the cider. A few wasps had also laid claim to the apples still stacked in round bushel baskets up against the barn wall in the shade beside Frank's chair, but with a careless hand he brushed them off and chose a few more apples to run through the press.

I chose my steps more carefully, not wanting to be stung.

Frank acknowledged my arrival with a short nod. "Keeping me a secret, are you? From your boyfriend," he said, when I looked at him blankly. "You didn't bring him over."

I knew Frank was a watcher. He noticed things. And that meant he would have noticed that Tyler had only been here a few minutes, so I didn't need to explain. "Sorry. Next time."

"It took me a minute to figure out that's what he was. Thought at first he was selling you something. But listen—" he began.

I interrupted him, the opposite of listening. "What *is* it about Tyler that makes everybody so sure he's a salesman?"

Frank paused. "Isn't he?"

"Well, yes, but—"

Frank assured me, "Nothing wrong with selling stuff. I've got a bunch of salesmen in my family going generations back, and so does Isaac, there. And listen, that's what I was going to tell you. Isaac says that all the old sales registers from Fisher's store, the old store at Cross Harbor, were donated to the library. Benjamin Wilde would have had an account at the store, so I'm thinking that maybe those records would help us in figuring out what he had in his house at the time."

"Good idea." I'd met the librarian. She'd seemed approachable. "I can go take a look at them this week."

"Isaac also says he's got a painting," Frank said, "of the *Bellewether*."

Benjamin Wilde's famous ship had been widely immortalized. We had two paintings of it in our budding collection already.

"But *this* painting," Frank told me when I raised that point, "shows the ship being built. And it came from this house."

I considered this. "Really?"

"Yep. The story goes Isaac's great-grandfather bought it from mine at the auction."

I knew about the auction but it took me half a minute to sort the generations of Frank's family into place so I could put a name to his great-grandfather, who'd been—if I worked backward—the great-grandson of our famous Captain Benjamin. He'd also been the second son of Lawrence Wilde, the poet, who had given all his children great, romantic names, like...

Arthur. That was it, I thought with satisfaction: Arthur Wilde. He hadn't had his father's writing talent nor his great-grandfather's daring, but he'd left his own mark on the history of the house. In the early 1880s he'd lost four of his six children in one week to typhoid fever. Grieving, he had blamed the cove and its "unhealthy" air, and hastily moved his surviving children and his wife to a more modern townhouse in Manhattan, leaving the Wilde House shuttered and empty for all but a few weeks each summer, for years. It was during this time, with the costs of his Gilded Age Manhattan lifestyle increasing, that Arthur had auctioned off some of the Wilde House contents, specifically things that had been owned by Benjamin Wilde and would bring a high price. Arthur's auction was one of the prime reasons we were now having to track down the long-missing items snapped up at the time by museums and private collectors.

If Isaac Fisher had a painting that had been sold in that auction, chances were that it was something we would want. Especially if it was of the *Bellewether*.

"Do you think he'd let us have it?" I asked Frank.

He shrugged. "Don't know. But knowing Isaac, I doubt he'd have brought it up in conversation in the first place if he wasn't thinking of a deal. He's an old fisherman, Isaac. He likes to bait his line and throw it out there, see what happens. But you never want to take that bait too soon, or else you're done for."

"Good to know." I filed that fact away.

"And if you want to come out on the right side of a deal with Isaac," Frank advised, "it never hurts to do a favor for him. Like right now, he's been walking round in circles with that donkey for a couple hours. You could just wander over there and offer to step in so he could have a break. He'd like that."

I looked toward the line of children waiting for a donkey ride on Dennis, who was plodding after Isaac Fisher in a steady circle.

Frank said, "He doesn't bite. Dennis, I mean. And he wouldn't be the first ass you've dealt with today."

I turned around a little bit defensively because at first I thought that he was talking about Tyler, but he winked and told me, "Saw you putting Harvey in his place. I'm guessing he deserved it."

"Yes," I said, "he did."

"Well, then. If you can deal with Harvey, you'll have no trouble with Isaac. He's a pussycat."

In retrospect, when I had walked across and talked to Isaac Fisher, I wasn't sure "pussycat" was how I would describe him, unless that included grizzled, wily barn cats that had fought their way through several lives and earned the notches on their ears to prove it, and could spot fresh quarry by the faintest twitch beneath the hay. But he was grateful for the break, as Frank had said he'd be, and in the end Dennis and I got along so well that I was sorry to hand his reins back an hour later.

I did, though. And keeping Frank's advice in mind I didn't bring the subject of the painting up with Isaac. I just gave him Dennis back and went to have a break myself, and hoped whatever goodwill I'd just gained would help us come out, as Frank put it, on the right side of the deal.

Under the trees that ringed the picnic tables, snacks and drinks had been set out for visitors to buy. Malaika's husband, Darryl, reigned over the barbecue where hamburgers and hot dogs sizzled, sending plumes of tantalizing, stomach-tugging scents upward to catch the cooling breeze. One wafted my way and I changed my course because of it.

Malaika, standing next to Darryl, handed me a hot dog bun. "You're making friends," she said. "I've just had Isaac Fisher telling me how nice you are."

"That's good," I said. And told her why. I finished with, "So even if he doesn't want to donate the painting, he might at least go easy on the price. And if the Sisters of Liberty give us that grant, we'll have money to buy it."

I saw the brief look Darryl sent to Malaika, and noticed the glance that she gave in reply. They could speak without words, like my parents could, and I envied that. Envied the easy way both of them seemed to be always connected, each strong in their own self but stronger together. Most times when I saw them "talk" to each other like that, I imagined how wonderful that must feel, being so fully in sync with the person you loved.

But today, I was focusing more on what they might be saying, because I felt certain I knew. And it wasn't good news. "They've refused us the grant," I guessed. "Haven't they?"

Darryl set a hot dog on my bun as consolation, as Malaika nodded. "Their treasurer called me last night, but I figured that the news could wait. You had enough on your mind for the weekend."

Deep inside my pocket, my phone vibrated to tell me that I had a call. I took a look, saw it was Tyler, let it go to voicemail. Then I used the time it took to put the mustard on my hot dog to collect my jumbled thoughts and try to turn them to the positive. Because, although I'd hoped my presentation had persuaded them, I'd known from the beginning that my grandmother had power and prestige here. And she wasn't on my side.

I didn't bother asking why they'd turned us down. I knew.

Instead I said, "Well, that's okay. We'll find some way to raise the money."

Once again my phone vibrated, and again I let it go. Tyler should understand why, I thought. He'd lectured me enough times on why he couldn't answer a personal call during working hours, and since I was standing right now talking to my boss it wouldn't be at all professional to answer.

When my phone went off a third time, though, I reasoned that it might be an emergency. I said, "Excuse me," to Malaika, stepped away, and answered it.

"You have to come home *now*," were Tyler's first words. I could hear exasperation in his tone.

I tried to keep him calm. "I'm sorry, but I can't. I have to—"

"Rachel's here."

That stopped me. Rachel was supposed to be en route to join my parents in Toronto for Canadian Thanksgiving. They had sent her down the plane tickets. Her flight, if I remembered right, should have been in the air by now. "She can't be."

"Well, she is. She just walked in with suitcases and everything and all I did," he told me, heated, "all I did was ask why she was here, and she ripped into me."

"Is she okay?"

"*She's* fine. But I don't need this, babe. I really don't. You have to come home *now*. I mean it."

My stomach sank below the crushing weight that came with knowing that my weekend would now be completely taken up with trying to keep Tyler, Rachel, and my parents on an even keel while fielding arguments and explanations. "Let me see what I can do."

Behind me, Darryl said, "Hey, Don! You want a burger?"

Turning back around, I saw that Don Petrella had now sauntered over to the barbecue in search of something more sustaining than a vampire's normal diet. "Sure," he said, and took his teeth out. "Make it two."

Malaika asked, "And how is your day going, Don?"

"Pretty good." He rubbed his shoulder. "Scar's been acting up, though. There's a storm coming. A big one."

Pocketing my phone I smiled tightly, and beneath my breath I answered, "You have *no* idea."

⤳

Rachel sat very still, facing her window. The trees in the backyard blocked most of the view of the bay but the branches would dip now and then in the changeable wind and stray flashes of evening light dancing across the blue water broke through, making patterns of shadow and light on the ivory-striped wallpaper. I wasn't sure Rachel noticed.

Niels had done the same thing when emotions got the best of him—he'd withdraw inside himself so deeply he'd be unaware of everything around him, sitting there unmoving like a thick-walled tower with its drawbridge up. He'd never wanted anyone intruding then, and knowing Rachel had inherited my brother's moods I was about to close her bedroom door again and give her privacy instead of going in, but as I started easing the door shut she spoke.

"I'm sorry."

Pausing with my hand still on the doorknob, I said, "That's okay. You don't need to be sorry."

Tyler, I knew, wouldn't have agreed. He'd been hit full force with her anger and frustration. He had told me where she'd told him he should go. "You need to talk to her," he'd said, "because there's no excuse for that."

But clearly he had missed the full significance of what I'd noticed right away when I'd come in. She hadn't just brought suitcases, the way you did when staying for a weekend. She'd brought everything—her bedding and her pillow and her laundry basket packed with smaller items wrapped in tissue, and a cardboard box of books.

"Was someone driving her?" I'd asked, because she didn't have a car.

"What?" He'd been irritated, but he'd said, "She took a taxi. What difference does that make?"

"Did she carry all this in herself?"

"The driver helped her. What—"

I'd interrupted him with, "Ty. Just stop a minute. *Look.*"

He'd looked. And slowly reached the same conclusion I'd already come to. "She's left college?"

Rachel didn't want to talk about it.

I could tell, from standing in the doorway of her room right now and looking at her, that she wasn't ready to discuss why she'd come home. She needed time, and understanding, and the space to work things through in her own way. I fought the urge to hug her, knowing that would only make her more uncomfortable. Instead I asked her, "Is there anything you need?"

A pause. And then she shook her head, and even though the movement was a small one it allowed a single tear to squeeze through her defenses and escape the corner of her eye. It trailed a jagged path down her pale cheek, and hurt my heart.

"It's going to be okay," I promised. Then, because I saw that she was trying hard to pull that drawbridge up again, I left her on her own with, "If you need me, I'll be right downstairs."

Retreating, I'd found Tyler waiting downstairs in the kitchen. He'd brought a six-pack of the beer he liked to drink and had one open in his hand, half-finished. "So much for our dinner plans."

I stopped and shot a glance at him and had to bite my tongue. I wanted to say they'd been *his* dinner plans, not ours. *My* plans had been to eat in tonight, on my own—preferably wearing pajamas while watching an old TV movie. I wanted to say that plans changed all the time, and the mark of a grown-up was learning to deal with that. But I knew that if I lost my temper his would only rise to match it and I didn't want to spend my evening arguing. Instead I said, "That's okay. Mrs. Bonetti brought over potatoes and sausages yesterday, I still have those. I'll make salad and we can have wine. It will be just like going out."

Tyler's tone knew better. "No, it won't."

We ate in silence—though his brooding didn't stop him

finishing the roast potatoes without asking if I wanted any more. But food, as always, helped his mood, and as I stood to clear the dishes he said, "I've been thinking. Maybe this is good, that she's dropped out."

"I don't know if that's what she's done."

"But if she has, it makes things easier. For us, I mean." He set his knife and fork across his empty plate and passed it to me. "That's why you came down here, right? To take care of the house for her until she finished school. So if she's finished, you won't have to stay so long. Okay, so maybe she'll need you around a few more months until she finds a job and gets a bit more settled, but then you can come back home."

"It's not that easy," I reminded him, and standing at the sink I let the taps run for a moment, having learned the water always came out scalding hot to start with. "The museum hired me for a two-year contract."

"So you'll break it. After all the trouble you've had with the board, they shouldn't be surprised."

"It's not the whole board giving me the trouble, only three of them. The rest of them are nice. I like the job."

"It's just a job, though. Anyone can do it."

That point stung. It wasn't that I thought my skills were special, but I *did* have skills. And knowledge. And experience.

We'd had a game when I was young—an upright plastic cylinder with sticks poked through it in a kind of web, with several marbles balancing on top of them. You'd play by taking turns to very slowly and strategically pull one stick out while trying not to let a single marble drop. It wasn't possible, of course. You couldn't keep those marbles on that shifting web of sticks forever, and eventually one player drew the stick that made them all come crashing down. I hadn't thought about that game in years, but now, with all the things that I'd been balancing myself today— not just with the Fall Harvest but with Sharon, Eve, and Harvey, and the disappointing news of the Sisters of Liberty turning us down, and the separate arrivals of Tyler and Rachel—I couldn't help feeling my own web of sticks was precarious, just at the moment. And Tyler, who should have been keeping me balanced by giving support, was instead pulling out the remaining sticks, one by one.

"Well, thanks." I tossed the cutlery into the sink. It made a satisfying crash. "I'm glad you think so highly of the work I do."

"Whoa, slow your roll, babe. Don't get all defensive. What I meant was, it's a little place, it isn't the Smithsonian. They'll get along without you."

With my focus on the fork that I was washing, I replied, "I don't break contracts. I'm not leaving until mine is done."

"But that's just—"

"Besides," I cut him off. "I can't leave Rachel now."

"Oh, I see. But you can leave *me*."

"What?" I turned. "I haven't left you."

"Haven't you?" He didn't try to smooth things with The Smile. In fact his features were the furthest from a smile I'd ever seen them, and his eyes had hardened, challenging. "Because it sure as hell feels like I'm doing this all on my own, right now."

And that was it. He had pulled the last stick and whatever I'd held in the balance came tumbling down. "Listen, I'm not the one who decided to cancel the weekend we *did* plan and go to Atlantic City instead, so don't even—"

His turn to cut in. "That," he told me, "was different."

"You're right. You know why? Those were buddies from work. This is family, Ty. *Family*." My anger had raised a big lump in my throat but I forced the words through it. "You don't turn your back on your family." The thought of my grandmother made me drive that point home harder. "Especially not when they need you."

"Yeah, well, I have needs, too, you know."

I heard Rachel's voice say in my mind, "He is *such* an ass," and I admitted in silence he could be, sometimes. In a purposely calm voice I said, "Ty, don't ask me to choose between you and my family."

His chair scraped the floor as he stood. "I'm not asking you anything."

Watching him gather the few things he'd brought with him, I wasn't sure how I felt. Surprised, maybe, this was the way things were going to end. But the thing that surprised me the most was discovering I didn't care. When I'd stopped caring, I wasn't sure. I only knew that, as he turned away from me, nothing inside me stepped forward to call him back.

And then the kitchen door banged shut behind him.

That door had been one of my brother's first handyman projects here, and it had never hung perfectly level. The bang left it even more crooked, askew on its hinges like everything else in my life at the moment.

I heard Rachel's steps on the stairs. By the time she came into the kitchen I'd forced myself back to the dishes as though things were normal, as though Tyler's car wasn't audibly gunning away up the driveway.

She asked, "Did he just break our door?"

"Not really." I fitted the last plate to dry in the rack with precision and pulled the plug, watching the water drain out. "It was already broken."

LYDIA

There were some things that could not be repaired.

She'd learned this small and sad truth in the months and years since Joseph had returned home from Oswego. At first they had been thankful he'd come back to them unbandaged and with all his limbs, and walking; that his outward wounds had healed so soon and left no scars. But they had come to realize that where Joseph had been broken was on some deep, inner surface that could not be seen and was beyond the reach of any doctor. And along the broken places bits of who he had once been had fallen and been lost, like all the tiny chips of porcelain that had scattered in the ashes of the hearth the time her mother had once dropped a cherished platter, so that even though her father had with patience and determination pasted it together so the seams but barely showed, there still remained, along those seams, small voids and tiny imperfections where those chips had once been that could never be recovered.

To a stranger at their table it appeared the platter had been cleanly mended.

She knew otherwise.

He did not call out often from the nightmares anymore but she still knew each time they plagued him from his restless wanderings. And when his demons came by day she knew that, too, from how his eyes would brighten and his breathing grow more rapid as his body tensed beneath whatever pressures were assaulting him.

But sitting as he was now, with her drawing pencil in his hand, his papers spread out tidily across the empty dining table, it was to her as if one of those small bits had been found among the ashes and retrieved with care and fitted into place again.

She'd always liked to watch him draw his plans for ships—the lines so straight, the measurements meticulously reckoned—for beneath all that precision lay an artistry she much admired.

The Spanish captain found it of great interest. Drinking brandy with her father in the chairs across from Joseph he leaned forward on the table as he watched the plans take form. "You mean to lengthen her?"

Joseph, at work, seemed too deeply absorbed to be rude or suspicious. "Yes. She's been practically severed already just here. There'll be no cost or effort to add ten more feet for an increase in cargo space, and," he remarked, "she can carry more guns."

"Guns are always a good thing," the Spaniard agreed.

At his side, her father took a sip of his own brandy—a rare thing for him. He seldom drank and when he did preferred the rum that Daniel sometimes sent them from Jamaica, but on this day the Spanish captain had brought brandy from his private store, by way of saying thank you for their hospitality, and so her father had indulged.

She knew that Benjamin would have outdone them both had he been there, for he loved brandy, but he was not there and she did not know where he was.

She knew where Mr. de Sabran was. He had not come in to dinner either, which had not surprised her since he did not seem to care for being in the captain's company, and Violet had reported that when she'd gone to the orchard with the dinner pails she'd found him hard at work there with French Peter.

This had irritated Lydia for reasons she could not explain. "And Benjamin is with them?"

"No. He wasn't there." And turning, Violet had said, "But I wouldn't tell that to your father."

Lydia had been in full agreement. While she'd never told a falsehood to her father, she had learned it wasn't necessary to share every truth, if by not sharing it she could avert an argument.

They'd gone a full day now without a voice raised in the house, although she could not say how long it would continue, having noted that Mr. de Brassart seemed even more bound to speak his mind with little care or thought for consequence when he was drinking brandy.

Its presence had enticed him to stay with them in the keeping room when all the dinner dishes had been cleared away and Joseph had begun his drawings.

Lydia had mending to be done, including one of Joseph's bedsheets that had torn along its seam from all his turning in the night, so she'd retired from the table to the comfort of her mother's chair beside the window, where the light was best for sewing, and from where she could observe the four men and their conversation without having to take part.

Her father being mellowed by the brandy told the captain in good humor, "That's a useful skill you have, sir. Being able to read drawings upside down."

"A man in these times must have many skills." Del Rio grinned. "I am better with the charts of the sea, to tell the truth. A drawing like this one I would leave to Juan. He understands such things. This was his trade before he came to sail with my father."

De Brassart asked, "So he was never a slave?"

Captain del Rio's voice held, as it had once before, that hard edge of cold steel as he slid his gaze sideways to look at the Frenchman. "He was born a free man, and so he remains." He paused before challenging Mr. de Brassart with, "You as a boy read the stories of Madame MacPherson, yes? And so you greatly admire my father. Then you should, I think, remember why he never fired on galleys. Why he hated the corsairs."

De Brassart shrugged. "I do recall that he did not approve of slavery."

"Not approve?" The Spanish captain's mouth curved as he raised his cup and briefly drank. "He says it is the evil of our age, and we are none of us unstained by it, and all of us will answer to our Maker in the end. This is a truth," he said, and gestured to the room around them. "All these things we have—these clothes, this drink, even this colony—we build these things on stolen land with stolen lives, and turn their blood to gold to fill our ships. This is a truth my father knows. It's why he stays now in his garden and no longer guards the *flota*," he concluded, naming the great Spanish treasure fleet that had for generations crossed the wide Atlantic.

Joseph's pencil stopped its course across the paper and he looked up, frowning. "But *you* guard it, do you not?"

Del Rio raised one shoulder. "I am not so good a man. But like my father, I will never fire on a ship that carries slaves. And like him, I know I will face my judgment. God may forgive some of us for all that we have done, but there are others who, I think, will not be easily forgiven." Then, as if he felt the tone had grown too solemn, he raised his glass and told them, "This is why I drink my brandy now, you understand, while it is possible."

He did a good job drinking. There was very little brandy left for Benjamin when he returned toward the ending of the afternoon. He poured the last of it into a cup and lifting it asked Lydia, the only other person then remaining in the room, "No lectures, Mother?"

"Don't say that." Her tone was sharper than the sewing needle that slipped painfully into her thumb as she misjudged a stitch in the worn waistcoat she was mending. "I'm not her."

"I know. I'm sorry. It's the chair," he said, and offered no more explanation knowing none was needed, for they both knew well enough who should be sitting there. "Where's Father?"

"Carting apples from the orchard. He could use your help."

"I'll help unload them." Drinking deeply he said in an offhand way, "I've been aboard the Spanish ship."

She knew it was a confidence, not something he would lightly share with anyone. Behind the closed door to the kitchen came the clanking sounds of Violet scouring the milking pans, and from the smaller chamber on the far side of the wall Mr. de Brassart's snores were keeping rhythm, but this was a rare and private moment with her brother, so she set her mending down upon her lap and gave him her attention.

He said, "She's beautiful." His eyes were shining with the light they only held when he was speaking of a ship. "Not like the *Bellewether*. Not like she *was*, at least. But beautiful. Ramírez took me over her from stem to stern. You know that, in his youth, he was a shipbuilder? That's how he came to know the captain's father. He was telling me of some of their adventures."

"And so now you wish to run away to Spain and be a pirate hunter?"

He acknowledged her light tone by smiling slightly. It had been a warm day for October so there had been no need to light fires in any hearth besides the great one in the kitchen, but the daylight had begun to soften and a chill would settle soon in all the shadowed corners of the room from which sunlight had withdrawn, so Benjamin in silence bent to stack the wood in readiness upon the iron dogs within the fireplace.

When he paused this long, she knew that he was gathering his words; that what he said next would be serious.

He said, "Do you remember when I made a tunnel in the snow and Joseph stood on top to test its strength, and it collapsed on me?"

They'd all been very young, but she remembered.

"It's like that," he told her. "Every day. It's like I'm being smothered. Like I'll die if I don't find a way—some way, it scarcely matters how—to just get out." He turned his head, eyes seeking hers, imploring her to understand. "I wasn't meant to be a farmer, Lyddie. I was meant to have a different life."

She understood, she truly did, but, "So was Joseph," was her soft reminder. "So was I."

"I know, but—"

"We can't always choose our lives."

"And if life hands us choices? What are we to do then?" He

had set the fire ready and it wanted but a spark to start it burning. As he straightened, he seemed taller and his tone was filled with new resolve. He said, "I need to ask a favor."

⟨❧⟩

Her father watched the Spanish sails that having filled this morning with the first fair wind were passing now like some pale ghost glimpsed through the screen of autumn trees. She knew he would keep pace with them along this path as long as he was able, and would climb the hill to stand above the meadow from where he could watch those sails until they were a speck of white upon the wide blue of the Sound, bound for a wider, bluer sea.

So she kept pace with him in her turn, knowing he'd find comfort in her being there.

She had not thought he would say yes when she had faced him privately to plead her brother's case last night, for all she'd argued reason.

"How often in his letters," she had asked, "has Daniel said he misses us and wishes it were possible for us to pay a visit? He'll be happy to see Benjamin, and Benjamin will benefit from both the voyage and the time away. And it is only for the winter."

It had helped that, near to suppertime, Mr. Ramírez had expressed his formal wish to stay behind and help with the rebuilding of the *Bellewether*—a wish that she suspected had as much to do with Violet as with anything, because although he had remained the model of a gentleman he could not take his eyes from her.

Captain del Rio had approved the plan. "I can return in April, or in May, before the *flota* sails again to Spain."

"And," she had told her father afterward, "he's promised to bring Benjamin back home with him, if Daniel has not already arranged another passage. Though in honesty he'll be much safer on a Spanish ship than he would be on one of ours. The French don't fire upon the Spanish."

"*We* do, if you can believe Captain del Rio. And pray tell me, if the captain is avoiding British ports, how is it he intends to carry my son into Kingston harbor?"

She had not worked that through herself, so she could only tell him, "He knows Daniel. They do business with each other. They must have their ways."

Her father had said nothing, only grunted. He'd been standing with his back to her.

"Did you not say," she'd prodded him, but gently, "that you must allow a man to be a man?"

"I did. But Benjamin—"

"He is a man. If you deny him this, you may yet keep him here another year, but in the end," she told him, "in the end he will leave anyway, and carry his affections with him when he does. Is that what you would wish? Is that"—she'd drawn a breath, and played a card she did not like to play, though it held truth—"is that what Mother would have wanted?"

When her father had not answered she had gone to him and placed her hand upon his shoulder, knowing that he'd needed it. "The captain is an honest man. He will look after Benjamin and keep him safe."

This morning in the cove, the captain had made her that very promise. "I will see he does not come to harm," he'd told her privately. "With my own hands I will pass him very safely to your brother at the Mount."

Which must, she'd thought, be what the Spaniards called the town in their own language. She had said, "We call it Kingston."

For the barest blinking of an eye, Captain del Rio had appeared confused by that; but then he'd smiled and said, "Yes, Kingston. In Jamaica. Yes, of course." And then he'd bent with gallantry to kiss her hand, and gone to join her brother to be rowed across to *El Montero*.

It had all been worth it, she decided, to see Benjamin content and happy, full of life. He'd hugged her hard.

"I'm in your debt," he'd told her.

"Yes, you are. And don't forget it." She had kissed him back. "Now go. And try to be a little careful."

He had grinned and winked and said, "I'm always careful." Yet of course, when *El Montero* set its sails and turned them to the wind, he had been standing square upon the deck, already looking out toward the limitless horizon.

And for a long time, on the hill above the meadow, she stood now beside her father while he did the same, until the tiny sails of *El Montero* could no longer be distinguished from the line of low clouds closing in a haze above the distant water.

The wind blew cold. Her father turned.

He was not one for sentiment. He only said, "It's past time I got started on the cider."

And their footsteps sounded hollow on the hard earth of the hill as they began the walk back down.

❧

Mr. Ramírez was a quiet man of careful habits. His arrival scarcely made a ripple in the running of the house. When he had tried arranging payment for his room and board, her father had replied whatever help he gave them with the ship would be enough, since he had only filled the bed that had been filled before by Benjamin, and ate no more than had her brother.

Even Violet had remarked how little trouble he had given, and in truth he'd been a help to her, for in the mornings and the evenings when she did the milking he would walk with her and carry the filled pails to spare her shoulders. He would talk to her, and twice he'd made her laugh—a sound that Lydia had not heard often since the death of Violet's mother, Phyllis.

Phyllis hadn't laughed much, either, but she'd been a force to reckon with, and she and Violet had made a small circle all their own within the larger family—closed to all but them, and filled with warmth and love so fierce Lydia wasn't sure how Violet had stayed standing after Phyllis had been taken by the fever. But she had.

She had her church meetings on Sundays and they seemed to give her strength, and she had all the family there for comfort—though of course while there was love there, too, they couldn't fill the place of her true kinfolk, nor was Lydia convinced that they were properly her friends.

"There is a line between us," Phyllis had once told her, on a day now long ago when she had wanted Violet to come play with her, and Violet hadn't felt inclined to.

"Now, Miss Lydia, my Violet wasn't put here for your plaything." Phyllis, standing at the kitchen hearth, had not brooked any argument. "When we've done all our work the time beyond that is our own, and no one else has any right to it." The poker in her hand, she'd drawn a line straight through the ashes of the hearthstone at her feet. "There is a line between us, just like this. You might not see it, might not feel it, but it's there, and don't forget it, 'cause there's those of us that never get a chance to."

Looking down at that hard line across the stone between them, Lydia had felt a sudden sadness she could not express. "Can nothing get across it?"

Phyllis seemed to weigh her answer, then she'd offered one word. "Freedom."

And the truth of that had been one of the hardest lessons Lydia had learned.

She might think that Mr. Ramírez was too old for Violet, but she was still glad Violet was, for the moment, no longer alone.

Mr. de Sabran appeared to have found a new ally as well in French Peter. With the harvest finished in the orchard they'd been working with her father making cider, and their conversations drifted now and then across the clearing while she did her chores outside. She did not understand a word they said, but it seemed to be friendly.

And this morning while she'd harvested her beans for seed she'd glanced up from the garden and to her complete astonishment Mr. de Sabran had been smiling.

Not at her—he had been saying something to French Peter, his attention focused mainly on the cider press. But still, he had been smiling. And that simple act had made his face a thing she barely recognized.

His teeth were even. Very white and very straight although the smile itself was lopsided, so wide it carved deep lines in both his cheeks and made his eyes crease at their edges. He looked younger. He looked—

Then, as if he'd known that she was staring, he had turned his head and for the briefest, stomach-dropping instant, he had turned that smile on her. Her hand had itched to hold a pencil that would let her somehow capture it, but with one polite, quick nod he had looked away, returning to his conversation and his work.

Since that moment, she had found herself innumerable times now glancing up from her own work to see if she might catch him smiling in that way again. She hadn't, but she noticed he looked more relaxed today than she had seen him; more at ease with both their company and his surroundings, as though he were there by choice and not by force of circumstance.

Which made what happened next the more regrettable.

It was, as always, Violet who first saw they had a visitor, and called out from the kitchen to tell Lydia, "That looks like Henry coming now."

It was. Her cousin Henry Ryder was her father's sister's son, and like his mother had bright copper hair that made him easy to identify. He was her brother William's age and had a wife and children, but the similarity between them ended exactly there. Henry was "straight as an arrow," as William once called him in tones that implied it was more a defect in his character than a true compliment.

He kept an inn at Millbank and he ran the local post from there, which meant he always had the finest horses, like the dappled mare he rode today.

"She's beautiful," was Lydia's first greeting from the garden fence as Henry drew alongside and dismounted.

"She is. And fast. I'm thinking I should let her run the Hampstead races in the spring." He smiled and bent across to kiss her cheek. "But I was needing a fast horse to bring you the good news."

They sorely were in need of some. "What news is that?"

"Quebec has fallen."

Lydia's reaction was not what she had expected it would be. It *was* good news, she reasoned. Joyous news. A blow against their enemy, a victory in the name of all those men who like her brother and like Moses had paid dearly for it. Yet her own emotions at that moment were like waves that struck the sand in crossing patterns, overlaying one another in a swell and surge and backwash until all that she could feel was deep confusion.

Henry held a newspaper toward her. "Here. It's Monday's *Mercury*. It came this morning by express."

She took the paper numbly from his hands, and read. The news had come, it said, via a letter from a gentleman in Louisbourg, to someone in New York. There was a time when she'd have read the words with satisfaction. Now some phrases seemed to rise toward her in a darker ink and snagged her thoughts uncomfortably: *A most bloody Engagement...pursued them to their Sally-ports... ravaging and destroying the country.*

"A brilliant victory," Henry called it, as he gave his mare's gray neck a cheerful thump. "It is a shame that General Wolfe was killed, but as the correspondent says a death like that is glorious and almost to be envied more than pitied, and he's won us a great prize. I knew you would be pleased to hear of it. As will my uncle."

"Yes." The word came flatly. "Let me take it to him."

She could not recall a stretch of grass that had seemed half as long as that she had to cross to take the newspaper to where her father stood positioning a barrel at the cider press, while Mr. de Sabran attended the great wooden screw mechanism and French Peter scooped a new measure of freshly cut apples into the machine.

As she neared them they all stopped their work for a moment, and Mr. de Sabran gave one of his nods and surprised her by saying in accented English, "It's nice how you're wearing your hair today."

"Thank you," she said, automatically.

French Peter said something in his own language and Mr. de Sabran replied, and then smiled in the way she'd been waiting to see again.

She looked away. "Father, Henry brought this." Without more explanation, she passed him the newspaper.

Wiping his hands on the rag he'd tucked into his belt, he frowned faintly and watching her face asked, "What is it?"

"News." Lydia turned. Then she thought better of it and turning back, looked to French Peter and asked, "Will you tell him, please, I'm very sorry to hear of it? Tell him I hope that his family is well."

Then she turned once again, so she'd not have to see that smile fade from the officer's face.

❦

It seemed strange and inhospitable to drink in celebration with the French lieutenants also standing with them in the parlor. Even though her father turned it to a toast including all, "That we may see a quick end to this war," the wine felt cold and tasted oddly bitter.

She was glad to set her cup down on the little table in the corner, and to take a seat.

Mr. de Sabran also sat, continuing to read the letter Henry had delivered to him, sent from Captain Wheelock, written tidily in French. Uncertain which disturbed him more—that letter or Quebec's surrender—she knew only that he had withdrawn into his attitude of deep reserve, reverting to his customary frown.

Beside her, Henry, from politeness, had moved on to other news that might be counted less offensive to their involuntary houseguests. "You know they've issued warrants in New York for the arrest of James Depeyster and George Folliot?"

Both men were well-respected merchants in the city, friends of William's. "No," she said, "I did not know."

"It's all the talk. Their ship captain has fled or else he'll face a charge of treason."

"For what action?"

"Why, for trading with the enemy." Her cousin's mild expression seemed to think the answer obvious. "I'm told that our new admiral means to end the Monte Cristi trade, and twice now Mr. Kennedy, who keeps the New York customhouse, has published advertisements for informants to come forward should they know of those engaged with it, so any merchants who persist in breaking laws," he said, "must face the consequences."

Henry knew of many things that Lydia did not. He had been educated well, yet he was able to explain things in a way that did not make her feel ridiculously ignorant, so while with someone else she might have kept her lack of knowledge hidden, she dared to ask Henry, "And what is the Monte Cristi trade?"

He told her, "Monte Cristi is a harbor on the Spanish side of Hispaniola. You recall that Hispaniola, though a single island, is divided—with the one side owned by France, the other owned by Spain? Well, let's say I am Monte Cristi harbor," he proposed, "and this space here, between our chairs, marks out where Spanish territory ends, and France's starts. Then you, my dear, can be the French harbor of Cap-François, for truly the two harbors are this close together on the map." He hitched his chair a fraction closer. "In the Monte Cristi trade, a ship might take out papers in New York to carry its provisions to another British port—to Kingston, say—but then it sails instead to Monte Cristi harbor."

Lydia said, "But, since Spain is neutral, surely that is not illegal?"

"To drop anchor there? Of course not. Nor to even trade in merchandise, providing it includes no banned provisions, such as flour," he said. "But that is not what this ship in my harbor here intends. Because the truth is Monte Cristi harbor is naught but an empty bay, constructed with one purpose: an illegal trade with

France. And so the ships that anchor here offload their cargoes onto smaller ships, and send them round this bit of land to you." He passed his cup of wine across the arms of both their chairs and placed it in her hand, to illustrate how it was done. "So now you have whatever I've brought down to sell to you—and trust me, it most often *is* provisions—and you send me back, by way of those same smaller ships, my payment and new cargoes of French sugar and molasses and whatever else we have arranged." He held his hand out for his wine cup and she passed it back to him. "These will of course be certified as Spanish by false papers, and so legal to be brought back to be sold here in New York." He drank. "You see?" he asked. "It's simply done."

She frowned, and worked it through. "But these provisions that the Monte Cristi traders sell the French, are those not sent to feed the armies fighting ours?"

"Exactly," Henry said. "That's why the admiral means to put an end to it. Apparently he's stepped up his patrols."

Her father added his approval, and said, "William is well out of that. With Daniel in Jamaica they can profit more supplying king and country than can those disloyal men who do their trading at the Mount."

She raised her head.

Across the room, Mr. Ramírez briefly met her gaze before his own skipped sideways like a pebble striking on a stone. She heard again the parting promise of the Spanish captain: *With my own hands I will pass him very safely to your brother at the Mount.* And the flicker of confusion in Del Río's eyes, so quickly overcome, when afterward she'd talked about Jamaica.

Now, although she had a dreadful feeling she already knew the answer, she still asked her father in a tone she hoped was calm, "What is the Mount?"

"Another name for Monte Cristi," he replied. "*Monte* is the Spanish word for 'mountain,' so our men call it the Mount."

"I see." She saw more than she wanted to, but knew she could not share it with the others. Not with Henry, not with Joseph, and above all not her father. Not until she'd had a chance to ask her brother William—to his face, so she could watch his eyes and see the truth of what he answered—what he'd gotten them involved in.

"Henry," she asked carefully, "may I please have more wine?"

JEAN-PHILIPPE

THE WEEK HAD STARTED well enough.

He had been glad to see the Spanish captain and his ship depart, and not entirely surprised to see it carry a new passenger, for he had marked the way the younger son looked always at the sea. Nor had he been surprised to see Ramírez left behind.

He'd thought that it might happen when he'd seen Ramírez and Del Rio talking with each other very earnestly one evening, and from how the men had shaken hands it had seemed a farewell was in the offing.

He got on well with Ramírez, who spoke decent French as well as Spanish and, from what Pierre had said, good English. He had always got on well with men who did their work without intruding needlessly upon his own.

Ramírez evidently felt the same way about interference, for one evening when the Spaniard had been sitting at the parlor table looking over Joseph Wilde's drawings for the ship repair, de Brassart had come close behind his shoulder, peering over, while Ramírez sighed and waited.

"Have you built a ship before?" de Brassart had inquired, as though prepared to offer his advice.

"Only a hundred. More or less," Ramírez had replied, with a politeness that was somehow not polite, and had made Jean-Philippe feel kinship with the man.

Pierre agreed he was an interesting character.

"It is a shame," Pierre had said to Jean-Philippe the next day as they'd worked together in the orchard, bringing in the last of the large harvest, "that Madame Wilde is not still alive to meet him, for she would have much enjoyed to see a free black man with such an education. She was not like others of her faith, you understand."

"What faith is that?" Though Jean-Philippe recalled de Brassart telling him that Madame Wilde had not shared the religion of her husband, he could not remember what she had been, other than a Protestant.

"The Quakers, they are called. I don't know why, I did not ask. She said above all they believe in peace, but I am not so sure because they cast her out for marrying a man who, while he was not of their church, was also peaceful, so I think they are not altogether good. She also said that, while they don't believe in slavery, in their church the blacks are not allowed to sit with whites, they have to sit off separately, and this she could not reconcile. Madame Wilde," he said, "believed we all are equal under God."

Which might explain, thought Jean-Philippe, why the girl Violet seemed to be respected in the household, and why Monsieur Wilde would let Ramírez share his room and treat him as though he were any other man despite the color of his skin. "All right," he said, and twisted one more apple from its stem, "but why then do they keep a slave?"

"Who, Violet? She is not their slave."

He frowned. "Then she is free?"

"No, you misunderstand me. She is not *their* slave," Pierre explained. "She is the slave of Reuben Wilde, Monsieur Wilde's older brother." With a strong arm he pulled one branch down until it nearly cracked and added, "He is not a man, I think, who'll ever see the gates of heaven. He will go the other way. He is as different from Monsieur Wilde as night is from day."

There were men who drew their pleasure—and their power—from the suffering of others. Jean-Philippe had met them on the field of battle and as frequently behind it, men who reveled in manipulating lives the way that others, in their idle hours, might set a starved and beaten dog upon an even weaker one for sport.

And when Pierre began describing Monsieur Wilde's older brother, Jean-Philippe knew he was such a man.

"He lives at Newtown, to the west of here, much closer to New York, and has an orchard there much larger than this one, with slaves to work it. Violet's mother, Phyllis, she worked in his house," Pierre said, "from the time that she herself was young. I was not here, of course, in those times, and she was already dead before I came here, but I heard this story, all of it, from Madame Wilde. She told me once that Violet's mother was the bravest woman she had known. Braver than many men. And so I asked her why, and so she told me, and so now, Marine," he said, "I will tell you, so you will understand this family."

Bending one more branch, he stripped the fruit from it with expert movements. "Violet's mother, Phyllis, kept the house of Reuben Wilde. And one day he complains she's tried to poison him, and so he has her put into the jail; but in a week or so the jailer and the sheriff of that county come to tell him she is very sick, and he must take her back again. Except then he discovers she is sick because she is with child. With Violet. And she will not tell him who the father is. He beats her, very brutally, and still she will not tell him. So he takes her to the garret, to a very small room, very hot, and there he keeps her, and he starves her and he beats her, and forbids the others in his house from helping her at all. She would have surely died, but for a neighbor who could hear her cries and brought her food when none could see. And then one night this neighbor, she sees Monsieur Wilde—our Monsieur Wilde—has come to fetch two sheep, I think it was, that he was owed for work he had done for his brother, and he's brought his team of horses and the wagon. And so the neighbor, she helps Phyllis leave the house unseen, and helps her to the wagon where the sheep are, and she hides there and stays hidden all the way here to the cove."

"And then what happened?"

"Well, when Monsieur Wilde has stopped his wagon and

comes back to get his sheep, there's Phyllis facing him, and telling him she won't be taken back—that he will either have to help her, or she'll walk straight down that path into the water of the cove and drown herself, because she will not bring a child into the world to be raised at the mercy of his brother, in his brother's house." He gave a shrug. "And so they helped her."

"But his brother surely figured out where she had gone."

"Of course. They did not try to keep it secret, for in such a place as this it is not possible to keep a secret. First they told his brother they would pay the price of Phyllis and the unborn child, to keep them here, but Reuben Wilde is not a fool, and knowing that they then would turn around and give her freedom, he instead made an arrangement that pleased nobody but him and kept them under his control: he let them hire her, for a large price that they paid him every year—and Monsieur Wilde still pays this price, and more, for Violet. But she is not free of Reuben Wilde, and he can change at any moment this arrangement, and reclaim her. And if he should die, she will be passed to his son, Silas, who from all I hear is just as evil in his heart. So Madame Wilde, she told me even though he's of the devil, every day she said a prayer that Reuben Wilde would never die. And so do I," Pierre concluded, grimly.

Jean-Philippe stayed silent for some minutes. Then he asked, "How long ago did Phyllis die?"

"I don't know. I think Violet had perhaps eleven years, or twelve, so it was maybe seven years ago. She has not had an easy life, that little one. But now at least you know why she is here."

"Yes," Jean-Philippe said. "Thank you."

He felt no need to share the reason why he held the views he did about the wrongfulness of slavery, but it made him glad to know that Monsieur Wilde and his family seemed to share that same opinion. He saw their interactions now with more perceptive eyes. He gained new admiration for the quiet strength of Violet as she went about her daily chores. He paused now with new understanding at the simple gravestone marked with one name: Phyllis, standing neatly kept among the others in the clearing in the forest. And he added to his own prayers in the mornings and the evenings the blunt wish that Reuben Wilde, as undeserving as he was, would never die.

Death had, indeed, seemed very distant to him earlier today.

It had been one of those October mornings when the sky had spread above him like a perfect jewel, bright blue and cloudless, and the air had held a crisply pleasant chill that made it comfortable to work even in sunshine.

He had been a child when he had last made cider. He'd forgotten the sharp rush of smells, the sweetness and the almost-rotten richness and the way it lingered everywhere. He had forgotten, too, the way the cider tasted freshly pressed, before it had fermented. Before time had changed its purity to something stronger. Harder.

"You are like my sons," Pierre accused him. "You will drink by half more than we put into the barrels."

"It is thirsty work," was Jean-Philippe's defense, but he obligingly put down the wooden cup he'd used to catch the running cider and moved back to turn the handles that would tighten down the press. From that position he had a clear view of Lydia within her garden, working with an admirably single-minded steadiness.

She'd changed her hair. She normally pulled all of it straight back and off her face and bound it simply, letting part of its coiled length hang down beneath the plain white muslin of her cap. But on this morning she had not been so severe with it. He liked the fuller, softer waves of brown about her forehead and her temples.

"So," he told Pierre, "it would be useful for me, while I'm here, to learn more English, so that in the future I can speak to those I capture."

"You are maybe overconfident, Marine, to think you will return to war."

"I'll be exchanged eventually." With a shrug he said, "So then in English, tell me, how would you tell someone that it's nice, the way they wear their hair today?"

Pierre's glance held amusement. "This is how you deal with men you capture, eh? You compliment their hair? It's very threatening and very tough, I'm sure it leaves them terrified."

He hadn't had much cause for smiling since coming here, but Jean-Philippe felt his features relaxing now into a genuine smile at the other man's dry remark, and without meaning to, he looked again toward Lydia.

And found her looking straight back at him.

Once he'd been hit an inch under his heart with a bullet—there had been no pain but he'd lost all the wind from his lungs and been knocked right off balance, and what he felt now felt like that. This time, though, despite its swift and sudden strike, the feeling was decidedly more pleasurable. As he sent a nod across the clearing to acknowledge her, his smile of its own volition broadened like a schoolboy's.

He was letting down his guard, he knew, allowing the Acadian to witness where his interest—and his weakness—lay, but for some reason, standing in the sunshine with her watching him, he'd ceased to care.

And it appeared to aid his cause on this occasion, for Pierre said, "Fine, I'll teach you."

Waiting until Monsieur Wilde had gone for a new barrel and was out of earshot, Pierre told the English words to Jean-Philippe and made him speak them back again, correcting him. "Yes," he said finally, "that's good. That is right."

Jean-Philippe repeated the phrase silently within his mind, in rhythm with his work, until he was distracted by the faintly distant hoofbeats of a fast-approaching rider. Then his instincts overrode all else.

His hand dropped for his sword before remembering it was not there. Since he'd left off his morning walks in favor of more useful work, he'd found it far too cumbersome to carry, and more commonly than not now left it lying in his chamber near the box that Monsieur Wilde had made him, underneath his bed.

With one glance he surveyed the clearing, taking note of where the members of the Wilde family were, and calculating just how quickly he could move to cover them and shield them from attack. But when he would have stepped between Monsieur Wilde and the angle of the clearing leading to the forest road, he heard a brief, untroubled call from Violet in the house, and from the way Lydia rose from working in the garden, turning without fear toward the woods, he knew the rider would be somebody she welcomed.

"That," Pierre said, when he asked, "is Monsieur Ryder. He is the son of Monsieur Wilde's sister."

So her cousin, then, thought Jean-Philippe as he watched Lydia lean forward and accept a kiss of greeting from the newcomer. The man would be ten years his senior, maybe. Nearing forty. He was ruddy faced with russet-colored hair and rode a fine-legged mare of dappled gray. "He lives nearby?"

"At Millbank, yes."

He'd brought her what appeared to be a newspaper, and evidently it had been intended for her father because she had folded it into her hands and was now coming over. As she neared the place where they were standing by the cider press a wayward breeze caught one soft strand of her dark hair and lifted it against the lace edge of her cap, reminding him what he had planned to say.

And when she greeted him, he said it. "It's nice how you're wearing your hair today."

She thanked him, and Pierre in French said dryly, "So that you can speak to those you capture, was it?"

Jean-Philippe smiled and with equal good nature returned, "I am practicing."

Lydia had looked away from them both as she handed her father the newspaper, and after a brief exchange of words started to leave.

Then she paused. Turning back to Pierre, she said something in quiet tones and her expression was solemn and troubled. He caught the word "sorry" and then the word "family," and then without meeting his eyes again she walked away.

Pierre translated.

And Jean-Philippe, with a weight closing in on his heart, stood as straight and as still as he could while Monsieur Wilde confirmed what he already knew must be so.

⌘

He did not drink the toast, but set his cup of wine untouched beside him on the parlor table as he took his seat again and went on reading Captain Wheelock's letter.

It said nothing of the battle of Quebec, having been written by the captain some few days before the news had reached this province, but it dealt with something nearly as disquieting.

De Brassart, sitting in the armchair next to his, assumed the captain's letter could be only on one subject: their exchange. "For surely in the fight we will have captured English officers who must now be returned. It is regrettable of course that we have lost Quebec, but let them try to hold it through the cold months that are coming—they will die from that as soon as from our guns— and in the spring we'll strike them hard from Montreal and take the city back. And Montreal, you must admit, is a more lively and diverting place to pass the winter."

Jean-Philippe, for his part, was not thinking of diversions. He was thinking of the men whose blood now stained the Heights of Abraham, for from the newspaper's description of the battle that was where the armies must have met. Reportedly their own side suffered sixteen hundred casualties—three times those of the English—and both generals had been killed. He had not liked the Marquis de Montcalm, but death upon a battlefield was still a death deserving of respect, however little the man might have earned it living.

"What does Captain Wheelock say?" de Brassart asked.

"He does not write of an exchange." That he would write at all was something Jean-Philippe had not expected. When the Wildes' cousin, Monsieur Ryder—who, Pierre said, also kept the post in this vicinity—had asked for him by name and then produced this sealed and folded letter, tidily addressed in careful handwriting, it had seemed suspect. But as he had read, he'd understood, and had been grateful for the courtesy. "The captain's in New Jersey. He has traced some number of my men, and writes to tell me where they are, and whether they are well."

"I see." De Brassart, vaguely disappointed, raised his drink. "That's decent of him."

"Yes."

"You don't look pleased."

"My sergeant is in the hospital. In New York."

"Ah." De Brassart drank his wine as though digesting that small bit of news. "I shouldn't worry. I am sure the English will look after him."

"The English are the reason he is there. He was attacked."

"Well, we were all attacked."

Jean-Philippe did not waste breath explaining this attack had happened here, more recently. There was no point discussing things with someone like de Brassart, who stood always at the center of the world in his own view and measured all events in terms of how they hindered or advanced his needs. The injuries of others would, to him, be of no consequence.

To such a man, Quebec was nothing but a cold place in a country not his own, and since de Brassart learned of its surrender he'd said nothing to suggest he'd even thought about the starving people now within its walls, who having struggled through the months of English siege were now held hostage in their own homes at the mercy of an occupying English army.

Jean-Philippe, whose childhood home was not far past Quebec along the St. Charles River, found that he could think of little else. He'd asked de Brassart earlier, when they'd been shown the newspaper account, "Does it say anything about the general hospital? The one outside the walls?" Of course it hadn't. It had only listed names of the main officers who had been killed or wounded in the battle, nothing more.

There was no one who could tell him if his sister had received the letter he had written when he'd first arrived, or if she'd brought their mother down to join her in the general hospital, or if they had been overrun by the invading English. All he knew was that Quebec had fallen one full month ago exactly, and in all that time while he'd been unaware, his family had been in harm's way and suffering he knew not what indignities, and he was here and powerless and able to do nothing that would help them.

Nothing.

So instead he gathered his frustration with a purpose and he focused on the one action he *could* take—the one person he could help.

He told de Brassart, "You will help me speak to Monsieur Wilde."

Their host was understanding, if a little hesitant when asked the question. He replied, and with a shrug de Brassart translated, "He thinks there's nothing in the terms of our parole that will prevent you going to New York, but if you are to go more than a mile from here the law says you must have somebody with you, and permission from the magistrate. Permission he can get for you, but he does not know who just at this moment can accompany you."

Jean-Philippe acknowledged that would be a problem, with the younger son now gone, because the older one would hardly be a candidate—not with his history, and his troubled temperament. And Monsieur Wilde could not take time so easily away from all his work.

They were all looking at him now. Across the room, where Monsieur Ryder had been playing some strange sort of game with Lydia by passing her his wine cup and receiving it again above the armrests of their chairs, she had now straightened in her seat and was regarding Jean-Philippe directly with what seemed to be a purpose of her own.

And then she said, "I will."

He understood those words, and knew their meaning.

But to make her purpose still more clear she looked toward her father and she told him, "I will go."

De Brassart, unaware no translation was needed, turned the words to French and added, "There, you see? That ends your problem."

Jean-Philippe was less convinced. While refolding his letter on its creases with precision he looked carefully at Lydia and was inclined to think from how she held herself, so resolute, that she had business of her own to see to in New York. And that might prove a problem for them both.

CHARLEY

"You're on a mission," said Malaika, watching from her front porch as I climbed the long flight of stone steps toward her, "I can tell."

Her house was in an older part of Millbank on a street that wound uphill along the side of an embankment, with the houses sitting higher up amid the trees, so once you'd reached her sidewalk gate you had to turn and climb again. Her front steps had been landscaped very prettily, but there were twenty-two of them. You had to be intrepid.

Still, I liked the fact that she was within walking distance. Everything in town was within walking distance, really. I had left the car at home today, enjoying the perfection of the crisp fall afternoon, the sky a clear, pale blue against the mounds of trees with turning leaves that painted all the hillsides shades of gold and russet red.

Malaika's lawn was still a vibrant green that nearly matched the shutters of her big white-painted house, its broad porch angled for a stunning view across the road and rooftops to the sunlit park and millpond at the center of the town.

The porch had wicker chairs with deep, inviting cushions, and I sat and caught my breath and told her, "I've been at the library."

"Of course you have. How else would you spend Sunday afternoon on a long weekend when your boyfriend's here?"

"He isn't."

"What?"

"He isn't here. He left last night." I set my weathered tote bag down and took the glass of water she had poured me from the pitcher on the glass-topped wicker table by her own chair. "And he's not my boyfriend, anymore."

"Oh, Charley. Well then, since you're walking, let me fix you something stronger." She stepped inside and came back in a minute with tall glasses of what looked like fruit juice.

"What's in this?" I sipped experimentally. It tasted of tequila.

"Secret recipe." She settled back. "You need to talk?"

If she had asked me that five minutes earlier, I might have told her no, that I was fine. But with the comfort of her presence and her front porch and the potent drink, I found myself unloading all the details. "I don't know," I said, in summing up. "Maybe I made a big mistake, but—"

"No, you didn't." She was very sure. "If he was right for you, you wouldn't be so calm right now. You'd be curled up somewhere crying your eyes out." With a long drink from her own glass she said, "When you find the right man, you'll be devastated if he walks away."

Dryly I said, "Something to look forward to."

She smiled. "No, what I mean is, when it's right, you really know. You feel it. There's no 'maybe' anywhere."

"Is that how you felt when you met Darryl?"

"Honey, when I first met Darryl he was dating my good friend. It didn't take, it didn't last long. He thought she was just too wild, and she liked her men more exciting. So did I, in those days," she admitted. "But there was just something, and the more he came around, the more I noticed it. The more I liked it. When they called it quits it hit me hard. And then my friend told me, 'Malaika, just be honest with yourself. You know you want to call him, so go call him.' So I did." She took a drink, the ice cubes clinking in her glass. "Sometimes the right man just sneaks up on you."

I couldn't picture Darryl—six-foot-something, handsome— sneaking up on anyone, and told her so. "But if I find somebody half as nice as Darryl, I'll be happy."

"You will," she assured me. "Like my friend said, you just have to keep it honest, with your man and with yourself. Men aren't so complicated—what you see is what you get. But sometimes what we see is what we want to see, and not what's really there. And that's what gets us into trouble."

I considered this, acknowledging that I'd been seeing Tyler for a long time through a filter that had blurred his imperfections.

All of us, Malaika had once told me, have our blind spots. And that made me suddenly remember why I'd come to see her in the first place.

As I reached down for my tote bag I could feel the faintest first effects of alcohol, reminding me I also should have eaten lunch. But this was more important.

"I found Violet," I said, pulling out the sheaf of photocopied pages I'd been busy gathering. "Remember Violet, from the slave lease in Frank's uncle's files? Well, I had time this afternoon, you know, so I thought it would be a good thing before our next board meeting if I just went and looked through all the records from the Fishers' store—the ones that Isaac Fisher said his family had donated to the library, to see, like Frank said, if we could find any account for Captain Benjamin that might show what he bought there. And I did." I slid those papers from the pile to show her. "These are his accounts, they're really interesting. They even tell us what his favorite kind of tea was. But," I added, pulling out a second group of stapled sheets, "the Fishers kept a separate ledger at their store for black people who shopped there." They were not the only storekeepers to keep a so-called "Negro register." I'd come across them several times before while doing research, and I knew Malaika wouldn't be surprised by its existence, but, "There's Violet," I said, pointing to the page. "Right there. See? 'Violet, from Snug Cove.' She shows up in 1754, and the last entry is 1760."

Malaika took the papers from me, reading through them. "There's a Phyllis here from Snug Cove, too."

"I think that's Violet's mother. In the letter Reuben Wilde

wrote his brother—wait, I've got that here as well." I rummaged for my copy. Found it. "He says, 'I have learned of the loss of my property' and then he says he expects to be paid because she was 'a skilled cook and not old.' And then he goes on to talk about Violet and how she's now twelve and he wants to be paid double or he'll reclaim her. So I think it's possible Violet was hired out here with her mother, and then when her mother died she was kept on. Phyllis," I said, to bolster my argument, "is in the Fishers' store records beginning in 1742, but then she disappears in 1754, right when Violet starts turning up. And Reuben Wilde wrote this letter in April of 1754. So it would all tie in, if Phyllis *was* Violet's mother, and that was the year that she died."

"Have you shown this to Frank?"

"No. I'm working up to it. I'm going to, though," I said. "I'd like to bring it up at the next board meeting, but I think it's only fair to let Frank know in private, before that."

Malaika agreed. "Better you than me, though. He won't like it. It's part of the legend of Benjamin Wilde that he never held slaves, so to learn he grew up in a house with them will be a hard thing for Frank to accept."

"Like you said, though, it comes back to honesty. Really, it—" I broke off, losing my train of thought as an animal streaked past the porch in a brown-and-white blur, plunging headlong into the tangle of flowering groundcover. "Is that Bandit?"

Malaika said, "Yes. We're not sure what he's doing, when he does that. Sam thinks he's chasing moles."

"Sam's here?" I hadn't seen his truck, but then I wouldn't have. The driveway access to Malaika's house was from a side road that dead-ended in a cul-de-sac around the back.

"He must be. He probably came by to pick up the window."

It took me a minute to make the connection. "The window you bribed him with, so he'd come help at Fall Harvest?"

"The very same."

"Must be some window."

"It is," she said. "Come have a look for yourself."

The beagle had skidded a little way down the hill and now popped up again out of the flowers and with a quick wag of his tail bounded off again, leading us around to the backyard, where we found Sam and Darryl loading something large into the back of Sam's truck, near the shed.

Malaika said, "Hang on, now. Charley wants to see my window."

Sam corrected her, "*My* window." But he stood aside to let me see, and then I understood why he had wanted it.

"That's beautiful," I said, because it truly was. Victorian, and round, and huge—at least four feet across—it had been crafted of cast iron, with six petal-shaped glass panes all set around a central circle so the whole thing, with its flaking ivory paint and deeply beveled edges, looked like an enormous flower.

Malaika said, "I got it from an old hotel upstate that they were tearing down, and ever since I put it in the shed Sam here's been hatching schemes to take it off my hands."

He grinned and didn't bother to deny it. "Hey, you offered it. I wasn't going to tell you no." Securing it within the truck bed, he flipped up the tailgate. Taking off his gloves, he looked at me and asked, "She's got you working on a Sunday?"

"It's a social call." My thoughts felt slightly fuzzy. "Well, a little bit of work, but mostly social. We've been sitting on the porch. Malaika made us these amazing drinks."

"Uh-huh. They didn't have tequila in them, did they?"

"Maybe."

In her own defense, Malaika said, "I didn't make them strong."

"Uh-huh," Sam said again. And then to me, "Well, when you're ready, let me know. I'll drive you home."

"Oh, that's okay," I told him. "I can walk."

But half a minute later, I was pretty sure I couldn't. "Sam?" I asked him. "Can you drive me home?"

"Sure thing."

Malaika must have fetched my tote bag from the porch, because

Sam handed it to me to hold before he reached to clip my seat belt buckle safely into place. "Okay?" he asked.

I wasn't. Everything was spinning, and my face had gone all tingly, and I felt a little bad for Bandit, relegated to the narrow back seat while I took his place, but all I said was, "Yes."

The drive was mercifully short.

Sam came around, opened my door, and unfastened my seat belt for me. As he helped me out, I said, "I don't think I can move my eyebrows. Is that normal?"

"Yep."

It seemed an easy thing to walk across the yard with him beside me, and his hand beneath my elbow kept me steady as I climbed the porch steps. Rachel let us in.

"Is she all right?"

"I'm fine," I said.

She leaned in close. "Your eyes are shiny."

"Are they?"

"Really shiny."

And then I was lying on the sofa in the living room, and somehow I'd been covered by my favorite crocheted blanket with the fringes.

From the kitchen I heard Rachel's voice, and Sam's. *Oh, good*, I thought. *She's been polite and asked him in for coffee.*

And although the world was still spinning around me, it felt strangely peaceful. So I fell asleep.

❧

It was a good thing that the next day was a holiday.

When I arrived at work on Tuesday morning Sam was working on the scaffolding. I put my boots and hardhat on and went around to talk to him. "I don't think I said thank you."

"Yeah, you did." He grinned. "About ten times."

"Oh. Well, that's good. Because I really do appreciate it."

"Anytime. Malaika mixed those drinks for me and Darryl,

once. I think there might be video, somewhere." The clapboards had already been removed along this section of the old house wall, exposing the underlying sheathing boards that Sam was now examining for rot or insect damage. We'd been fortunate. The structure of the house was fairly sound.

"And I'd be fine," I said, "with Rachel looking after Bandit for you." I'd reminded her that since it was her house she didn't need to ask for my approval, but she had insisted on it anyway.

She'd gone all through it yesterday. "He said he'd pay me for it. He'll drop Bandit off here in the mornings and come by to pick him up, and he'll bring food and everything. He's really so adorable. The dog, I mean. Did you know he's a rescue beagle?"

I'd remembered Frank and Sam had used the term the day I'd first encountered Bandit, but I'd just assumed it meant that he'd come from the pound.

Rachel had set me straight. "They use them to experiment on. You know, in laboratories. Sam says they use beagles because they're so gentle and sweet-tempered they won't even bite you when you're hurting them. And after a few years when they 'retire' the dogs, some labs give them to rescue groups who try to find them homes. Sam says that Bandit didn't even know what grass was when he got him. It's his second rescue beagle. He had one before, a girl dog, but she ended up with cancer and he had to put her down. So he got Bandit."

"Beagles," Sam said now, as he stood squarely on the scaffolding, "don't like to be alone. So she'll be doing me a favor."

"What about the doggie day-care place?"

"Nah. There's a Labradoodle there that's always picking on him. He'll be better hanging out with Rachel."

I was not completely fooled. I knew he'd talked to Rachel for a while, because she'd told me that he had. "He's really nice," she'd said. "He listens."

So I knew he knew that Rachel wasn't finding this an easy time, and I suspected Sam just figured she and Bandit were a lot alike in needing some companionship from somebody who understood and didn't push their boundaries.

Whatever his true motivations, it was an inspired move.

When I came down for breakfast the next morning, I found Rachel up and cuddling Bandit on the sofa. She was still in sweats and hadn't washed her hair, but for the first time in four days she was awake before lunch, so I chose to count it as a sign of progress.

"It's called situational depression," Gianni said that evening, leaning on the fence that lay between his mother's garden and our graveled yard. "I looked it up. It's rough, but most people come out of it fine without needing meds. She just needs time."

I asked him, "Did she tell you what went wrong at school?"

He shrugged. "She couldn't concentrate. She couldn't read the books, and didn't want to. She just wanted to lie down and cry and sleep a lot, she said. Between us, I don't think she wants to be a lawyer. I think that was for her father. And now he's gone, she ain't sure what she *does* want."

I had left that conversation feeling Gianni had just saved me all the fees I'd have been charged by a psychiatrist for that same diagnosis, and in keeping with his wise advice I'd given Rachel space.

I had enough to keep me busy. At the end of the week when Frank chaired the next meeting of our acquisitions committee, I drew him aside afterward for a talk and explained what I'd found about Phyllis and Violet, the slaves who had lived at the Wilde house for almost two decades.

He listened in silence at first, with his head down. He read through the papers I handed him. Then he swore, once, but with feeling.

I thought he might need space, too, but all he said was, "I'm guessing you'll want to bring this up next week at our board meeting."

Frank liked directness, so I was direct. "Yes."

He nodded, and thrusting the papers toward me said, "Do it."

He didn't go back to his car straightaway, but walked off on his own through the woods on the path that I knew from experience led to the old family graveyard. I'd been there a few times myself. There weren't many stones left—most had fallen or broken or been lost to time, and the few older ones that survived had been gathered and propped on a central stone monument topped with a carved bust of Benjamin Wilde gazing fearlessly over the cove to the waters of Long Island Sound, where he'd sailed as a hero.

I knew Frank went up there from time to time. He kept the grass trimmed and straightened the stones when they needed it. And while he might not believe that his ancestors left any ghosts behind, I had a feeling he still had a few things to say to them on this particular visit.

He kept to himself for a few days but by the next week he was back to his regular pattern of coming on-site to keep up with the work being done.

The engineer had been here, too, inspecting the repairs to the wood sheathing and the timber frame, and having met with his approval part of Sam's crew were now on the north side of the house replacing siding, while the rest were on the south side of the roof removing shingles.

It was not a job I would have wanted. Even though the south side of the roof, above the kitchen lean-to, wasn't pitched as steeply as the front, you had to be a certain kind of crazy, I decided, to spend all day walking on an angle over thin boards that in places had been rotted through by insects and neglect and years of damp.

I had a clear view from my office window of the workers on the roof. One was a woman who worked with a steady competence that didn't make me worried, but one of her colleagues was a guy who looked younger than Gianni, with a hipster beard and hair tied in a ponytail beneath his hardhat. He moved like a mountain goat—a very reckless mountain goat. It made me nervous every time he crossed my field of vision.

So the day I heard the crash and yell and looked up just in time to see a hardhat disappearing through a dark hole at the far end of the roof, I knew whose hardhat it would be.

I don't remember pushing back my chair and dashing through the doorway from my office into the old section of the house. I only know I reached him first.

I found him standing on both feet within a shaft of sunlight spearing through a jagged hole in the sloped ceiling of the room above the buttery. Dust danced wildly in the dimness, sparkling in and out of shadow as it sifted from the opening above his head. It covered him. It settled in his beard and on his shoulders.

"I'm okay," were his first words to me as I raced in. "I'm good, man." He repeated that, as if he was amazed to find himself unhurt. "I'm good."

Above us came a quick, deft fall of footsteps on the rafters and Sam's face appeared within the new hole, blocking out the light. "What happened?"

"Man," his worker told him, looking up in awe, "it was like someone caught me. It was awesome! But I'm good."

Sam didn't care how awesome it had been. "I'm getting Rick to take you to the hospital," he said, "to get checked out. And when you work for me, you wear your safety gear, you got it?"

"Got it." With a glance around the room, as if he half expected there'd be someone else to see besides the two of us, the bearded worker moved his hands to test them. "Cool," he said, and sauntered past me.

He had dropped his hammer. Or, to be more accurate, his hammer had smashed through a floorboard near where I was standing in the doorway, and was stuck there with the metal head embedded in the splintered wood, the handle angled upward.

Sam could see it, too. "Hang on," he said, and shifting he maneuvered himself through the hole and dropped down with a solid thud that raised another swirl of dust. "A good thing it was just his hammer, not his head."

He tried to ease it out, but like King Arthur with his sword stuck in the stone, looks were deceiving. It was really stuck. The floorboard lifted with it, and I heard the ripping sound of wood, and then Sam pointed to the gap now showing where the floor-board's end had been, and asked me, "What is that?"

I looked. It was a small cloth bag, or what was left of one, and when I saw what it had once contained I knew this hadn't truly been an accident.

❧

"And this," I told the members of the board, "is what we found."

I set the tray down carefully that held the remnants of the little bag and all its contents, cleaned and catalogued.

Malaika had known this was coming. So had Frank and Lara. But most of the others were looking at me like I'd lost my mind.

I didn't blame them. To the average eye, the things that I was showing them looked more like things someone would throw away on purpose, not a find of any true significance: thin brass pins, several bent iron nails, small glass beads, a few fragments of pottery, oxidized lead shot, and two flat, triangular, water-smoothed stones that looked something like axe heads.

I attempted to put things in context. Not knowing what every-one's level of knowledge was when it came to the historical facts of the slave trade, I started with the Portuguese and rapidly moved on to, "So a large part of the slaves who ended up here in America came from what's now Nigeria on Africa's West Coast, and most of those were either Igbo or Yoruba, and in the Yoruba culture there's a god, Eshu-Elegba, who is kind of like a trickster god. He mediates between the gods and men and carries messages between the worlds, and he guards all the crossroads and all thresholds. And a slave here in America would follow the religion of their ances-tors and if they were Yoruba they would leave specific offerings for Eshu on their thresholds. Archaeologists aren't sure if these were meant to protect those inside the room, or harm those who might try to enter, but when you find these near windows or at doorways, what it means is there were probably slaves living in that room."

"Probably," Sharon said, archly. "Not certainly."

"Well, no. But then we've got all this to add to it." I'd spent a lot of time getting my evidence organized. Now I presented it piece upon piece like a lawyer constructing a case.

I started with the copied pages from the "Negro registers" of Fishers' store, with entries for a Phyllis and a Violet, of Snug Cove. I'd done some digging in the New York Public Library and found they had the personal accounts of Reuben Wilde for 1743, detailing money owed him by his brother *For the hire of Phyllis and her child*. And then, the coup de grace, I'd found the will of Reuben Wilde, that listed Violet in the property he passed to his son, Silas, when he died. "And he died in the summer of 1760," I told them, "so that's why our Violet stops showing up in the store registers over at Cross Harbor."

She'd been "reclaimed" by the cousin of Benjamin Wilde— Silas. I hadn't found much on him, yet, but Violet, if we could believe all the documents, would have been eighteen years old at the time. And Benjamin, who wouldn't captain his first ship till later that year, would have been twenty-five.

"There's no doubt in my mind," I said, "Benjamin Wilde grew up in a household with slaves. What we need to decide now is, what are we going to do with that knowledge?"

Eve wasn't sure we should do anything. "Like Sharon said before, I think this takes us too far off our mandate."

Sharon nodded firm agreement. "That's right. First you want the legend of the French ghost, which not only is a legend but has no connection whatsoever with our Captain Wilde. And now you try to sneak this whole slave angle in. I just don't think you even understand what you were hired to do."

I let the insult pass. "I think that I was hired to oversee the start of a museum in the home of Captain Wilde that shows the story of his life and legacy."

She argued, "But what you're discussing now, with this"—her gesture took in all my papers and the box of artifacts—"you're talking sixteen years before the date that we've decided we're depicting in this house, the date of Captain Wilde's inventory."

"Well," I said, because I had been giving this some thought, "I think the inventory's useful when it comes to our refurnishing the house, I do agree, but if you're saying that one day's our only point of reference, then it really can't be Captain Wilde's museum."

"What?"

"He wasn't even here," I said, "the day they did the inventory. He was off at sea. We'd have to make this the museum of his wife and children, and just tell their stories. Or, to tell the truer version, it should really just be a museum of the British occupation, because on the day they took that inventory there were British officers in charge here, so we really ought to tell *their* story—have their maps and charts and things spread out around the rooms, right?"

Sharon's tone turned icy. "I do not appreciate your sarcasm."

"It isn't really sarcasm. It's logic. If our mandate is to tell the story of the captain's life, we should tell all of it. We shouldn't just redecorate the past to make it look the way we want it to."

She was starting to say something else, but Frank had reached the limit of his patience and he cut her off. "Enough. We all know, don't we, what the right thing is to do? A show of hands, who thinks we ought to use that upstairs room to honor those two women that my family tried pretending never lived? Don, get your damn hand up. There now. We good? Then let's move on."

Across the table, Tracy tried to hide her smile. She always liked it when Frank lost his temper and shut someone down. She coughed, and brought the others up to speed with what our acquisitions committee had been dealing with.

"This painting Isaac Fisher has," said Harvey, "are we sure we're going to get it?"

Frank replied that I was working on it.

Sharon sniffed and got her own back, just a little. "Well, I hope she does better with that than she did with the Sisters of Liberty."

I let that one slide by harmlessly, knowing I'd won the real battle this evening. Besides, I was already forming ideas of how we could come up with alternate funding to pay for the furnishings that we still needed.

"Security," Don put in, "for this year's Halloween ghost watch. Who's going to give up their evening?"

There were various excuses and vague murmurings around the table.

I asked, "What's the ghost watch?"

"Oh," Rosina said, "that's only what Don calls it. It's not anything official."

"Every Halloween," Malaika told me, "people drive up here to park and party in the woods, so they can try to see the ghost light."

"It's a nuisance," Eve agreed. "And now that our board's officially in charge of the museum, it's our problem, not the town's."

And Sharon said, "My husband said he'd try to get a few off-duty boys to come and help us out, but it's a busy night."

I looked around at all of them. "So...wait. We're going to have a lot of people coming up here Halloween night, on their own, and we don't even have to advertise?"

Malaika smiled, catching on. "What did you have in mind?"

❧

Gianni met the cars as they were entering the parking lot. "I'll bring my pumpkin," he had promised, and he did—a plastic orange pumpkin bucket like the one I'd carried as a kid at Halloween around the neighborhood.

"Hey, welcome to the ghost hunt!" he was greeting every new arrival. "Parking by donation, give whatever you feel comfortable with." Parking by extortion, I thought, watching him in action. To one driver he said, "Really, Tony? Really? You feel comfortable with that? You want your girl to see how cheap you are? Yeah, there you go. That's better."

As the couples—they were mostly couples—left their cars, a

little bit uncertain still what they'd just wandered into, they were met by Don, resplendent in his vampire teeth, who handed them a paper bag for garbage and a photocopied map of all the pathways and then started them along their way. "Be careful!" he called after them, each time. "You never know what might jump out at you."

I knew what would jump out at them. First Lara, dressed as Lydia, would pass them in a pale and tattered nightgown with her hair all tangled up in imitation seaweed as though she had returned from being drowned.

Then one of Gianni's friends, another waiter from the deli, in the role of Joseph Wilde, would stumble from the bushes and accost them with a toy rifle in hand and ask them, "Have you seen my sister?"

Harvey, who had rented the same reenactment uniform he'd worn for our Fall Harvest, would be skulking around through the trees pretending to be the lost Revolutionary War soldier who'd been guided by the ghost to safety, urging anyone he saw to watch out for the British.

And if anybody made it to the graveyard, they'd find Frank up there to tell them, in his practical but chilling way, the story of the fatal love affair between young Lydia and her French soldier, leaving those who'd heard the tale to find their own way back again along the dark and lonely path between the trees where every leaf that scuttled in the wind became a footstep just behind you.

By the time the moon was high and it was nearly midnight, we must have had eighty people, maybe more, assembled near the picnic tables in our clearing, enjoying the ghost-shaped cookies and hot chocolate that Tracy's partner, Veronica, had set up there. We'd been lucky—since her family owned the deli she'd been able to persuade the town to waive the license fee so we could serve the food and drink without a problem, and the deli had provided the refreshments free of charge.

One of the women standing closest to the house let out a shriek.

"It's him!" She pointed to the woods. "Look, there he is!"

And everybody turned—including Lara, Gianni's friend, and Harvey, who had finished with their acting parts and come back, still in costume, to join in the general fun. They turned and saw a small light, swinging slowly like a lantern in a hand, move through the trees along the far edge of the clearing.

Frank, who'd also left his post by now and stood among us, to the side, surprised me with his flair for the theatrical. "Now, everyone stay *quiet*," he advised. "Don't want to spook him. He's just looking for his Lydia, to lead her to the cove."

Nobody spoke. Nobody moved. The light swung silently along, then turned away along the path that led down to the water.

Well done, Tracy, I thought, looking at Veronica, who winked.

A collective breath of satisfaction rippled through the onlookers, as conversation started up again. Within a half hour we were wrapping up, the tables wiped, refreshments packed away, the people leaving as they'd come, in couples.

One big middle-aged man with a leather jacket and a neck tattoo reached for my hand and shook it heartily. "I tell ya, I've been coming up here thirty years to see the soldier's ghost, and I ain't never had a better time than this."

When Gianni came back from the parking lot, his smile was wide. "You shoulda seen them. People shoving tens and twenties at me. We must have a grand in here." He held his plastic pumpkin bucket up.

We carried it into the kitchen. Tracy, as our treasurer, did the official count.

"Nine hundred eighty-seven dollars," she announced. "And twenty-five cents." She had scratched her face a little on her journey with the lantern through the woods, but she was smiling. "That's *so* great."

"It really is," said Harvey, looking genuinely happier than I remembered seeing him, as though he had been caught up in the spirit of our shared success. He clapped me on the shoulder. "Good job. Good idea."

Frank observed this with a lifted eyebrow, then in private tones advised me, "Hell hath frozen over. Watch your step."

But it felt nice to have the group's acceptance and approval for that moment.

Nice, too, to know that Frank, Rosina, Don, and Lara were out front and waiting by the parking lot to see that I got safely to my car. I could hear their voices as, alone inside the house, I started with my ritual of locking up.

This time, I walked the same route backward, starting with the upstairs rooms to get them over with. "I'm coming in," I told the empty air as I walked through my office door. "Don't scare me."

Nothing moved.

"Thanks." Quickly moving through into the old part of the house, I checked the upstairs chambers, being careful of the patched floor in the little northeast corner room, where Sam had also now repaired the wood frame of the sloping ceiling.

Violet and Phyllis's room, as I'd taken to calling it. Nothing moved here, either.

As I descended the narrow back stairs to the buttery I could hear everyone's voices outside with a comforting clarity. Lara was laughing.

I crossed through the parlor and checked that the front door was bolted securely. Passed on, through the keeping room into the corner room under my office that would, from the floor plans, have once been a small chamber just off the kitchen.

The window here looked to the side of the house, to the woods where I'd once seen the ghost light myself, and tonight as I turned I thought I caught a glimmer of something again through that window, out there in the dark.

I shouldn't have stopped, I knew. I should have carried on doing my rounds and ignored what I'd thought I saw. Left it alone.

But I didn't.

I took a step nearer the window, and looked.

It was there, gleaming brightly beyond the dark glass. I leaned closer. Cupped my hands against the glass so my reflection wouldn't interfere. The light went out abruptly like a candle flame extinguished.

As I pulled back from the glass, it came to life again.

And that was when I realized it was a reflection, too. It wasn't shining in the woods at all. It was behind me.

In the doorway.

As I spun around my heart shot up and started pounding at my collarbone.

The light was there. The light, and nothing else.

I couldn't move. I thought the light moved upward as though somebody had lifted it to see me better, then it lowered. Traveled on away from me, with nobody to carry it.

It seemed to disappear into the plain wall of the corridor beyond the door. A wall that had been built with the Victorian addition.

But when Lydia's French officer had lived here, there had been no wall. He would have walked straight from this room into the kitchen, and I knew that if I had been braver—if I'd forced my feet to move and gone around myself to look—I'd find the light there moving now, across the old and empty Wilde house kitchen with its long-cold hearth.

LYDIA

H E WAS CARRYING THE lantern.

It did make the walking easier, the sun not being up yet and the woods alive with small and furtive rustlings. Every dropping of an acorn seemed the footfall of a predator, and though she knew this path so well she could have walked it blindfold, she was grateful for the warmly swinging light of that one candle in its glass and metal box.

Her father, having gone ahead, called back to them that Mr. Fisher's sloop was there and waiting as he had arranged.

She'd have much preferred to go by land, but Father had explained he could not spare the beasts nor wagon, nor could he afford just now to hire ones from Henry, but since Mr. Fisher owed him for the shelves he'd built last summer, this would cancel out that debt and serve their purpose.

"This is very precious cargo," said her father to his friend. "See you take care of it."

"You need not fear," was Mr. Fisher's answer. "As for the other, though, I've half a mind to dump it in the Hellgate." But he nodded a terse greeting to the man who held the lantern next to Lydia. "Good morning."

Mr. de Sabran echoed those words in reply in his deep voice, but said no more than that, and handing off the lantern to her father he helped Lydia to board.

The tide was at its highest point, and soon it would be turning, with a wind set fair to carry them straight into New York's harbor. Mr. Fisher's single-masted sloop looked very small against the darkly looming shadow of the *Bellewether* beyond it, but she knew that it had speed, and they would be at William's dock that afternoon.

She had not realized just how long the hours between would be.

The other times she'd sailed with Mr. Fisher she had been with Joseph and with Moses, and the men had talked among themselves and left her little to do other than to watch the passing shoreline and enjoy the sense of freedom. Except Moses was not here now, and each glance from Mr. Fisher made it plain exactly where he laid the blame.

It did not help that on this day Mr. de Sabran wore his full and proper uniform, with shoes and stockings and the long white coat with its blue lining. With his hat set low above his eyes, hair fastened back, sword at his side, he somehow became less an individual and more a symbol on which Mr. Fisher focused all the hatred that he felt for those who'd killed his son.

She understood. She'd felt the same at first, and Mr. Fisher had not had the chance, as she had, to observe the better qualities of Mr. de Sabran.

So she could only do her best to keep the tension at a manageable level by diverting Mr. Fisher when she could with conversation.

With the cold and wind and salt spray she was growing hoarse and welcomed their arrival at the Hellgate, with its swift and shifting currents that required Mr. Fisher's full attention. And then they passed into New York's harbor, and there was no need to talk.

It was a sight that always filled her with excitement and with awe, although she would not wish to live in such a place. There were too many buildings—houses closely pressed together in a row along the shoreline, stretching farther to the north each time she saw it, spires of churches rising here and there amid the rooftops, and the solid walls and towers of the star-shaped fortress sitting for protection at the bottom of it all.

The harbor was itself a city built of ships—high masts and sails of every shape, tall ships and small, some riding at their anchors, others riding on the wind, all crossing paths and navigating boldly around one another so she was convinced that there would surely be a great collision. But there was none. Mr. Fisher brought them through the shadow of a giant British man-of-war, its colors flying crisply in the wind, and steered between a swiftly moving privateer brig and a rowboat full of raucous sailors, and delivered them in safety to the wharf.

She knew the way from there.

"Some men may build their mansions in the meadows," William had once told her, "but a city's beating heart lies in its markets and Exchange, and in the wharves and docks that keep them well supplied with their life's blood of trade."

Accordingly, his own house was in Dock Street, flanked by finer shops and counting houses. And in truth the street was like some pulsing vein of life, filled with the noise of clopping hooves and creaking wheels and voices chattering above a constant flow of people from so many walks of life and varied places she would not have been surprised if Mr. de Sabran in his white coat drew no attention. But of course he did. Two women they were passing drew aside as though he were the very devil, and a carter going by them with his wagon tipped his hat and called down crude "congratulations" on Quebec's surrender, but Mr. de Sabran neither broke his stride nor paid them notice. Like her father, with the manners of a gentleman, he walked between her and the muddy street, and as they crossed the road he gave his arm to her to help her keep from stumbling in the wheel ruts. She released his arm as soon as they had crossed, but she remembered her own manners enough to say, "Thank you," and received his brief nod in reply.

William had married well. Deborah, his wife, being the daughter of a judge, had brought money and connections to their union that helped William rise in both respectability and wealth. His house was built entirely of brick, a full three stories high, its windows sashed and glazed with finest glass. And since Lydia's last visit, he had added at least one more servant to his household.

The girl who held open the door to admit them was not someone Lydia recognized, though it was clear she'd been told to expect their arrival.

Not blinking an eye at the sight of an enemy officer there on the doorstep, the servant stepped back for them and said to Lydia, "Mr. and Mrs. Wilde are in the parlor, miss."

They weren't alone. They had another visitor, a tall, well-built young man who stood as Lydia and Mr. de Sabran entered. Had it been another person, Lydia might have believed he'd stood to show respect, but she knew "respect" was not a word that ever featured in this man's vocabulary.

"Cousin Silas." She was much relieved to hear her own voice held the proper notes of coolness and composure. Though she did not offer him her hand he held his own out notwithstanding, knowing it would be the height of rudeness to refuse him, and she was too well brought up to behave rudely in her brother's house.

The light brush of his kiss across her knuckles was a victory, and his mocking eyes made sure she knew he knew it. "Cousin Lydia."

Before they could say anything of note to one another, William intervened, and coming forward took her two hands warmly in his own, erasing Silas's unwelcome touch before releasing her to greet the man who stood behind her, patiently observing.

"Mr. de Sabran," said William, with his usual good memory for names, "I'm glad to see you once again. How was your voyage?" Then he caught himself, and said, "Of course, forgive me, I forget you don't speak English," and to Lydia's surprise asked something briefly in what sounded to her ears like French.

Mr. de Sabran made a short reply in that same language.

Still surprised, she turned to William. "When did you learn to speak French?"

"I can speak several languages."

Deborah, his wife, confirmed this as she rose from her chair. "It's true. So long as no one wanted to converse more broadly than 'good morning,' 'how are you,' 'did you enjoy your voyage,' and 'what is the best price you can give me for your cargo?'" With a smile, she leaned to embrace Lydia. "His French may sound impressive, but I should suspect that with that phrase he's reached the limits of his knowledge."

Lydia liked Deborah, who in age stood nearly halfway between Lydia's own twenty years and William's thirty-six. She was golden-haired and elegant and graceful in her movements, as befitting the society in which she had been raised, but she was fair of mind and quick to laugh and kind. She held her hand now to Mr. de Sabran as William introduced them, then she turned again to Lydia and said, "But you'll be wanting to refresh yourself, I should imagine, won't you? Have you eaten any dinner?"

They'd had cheese and bread and apples on the sloop, but Deborah did not seem convinced that much would carry them until the supper hour.

"I'll tell our cook," she said. "She can, I'm sure, make something light for you. Will you have tea as well? Or one of William's ships has lately brought us some fine chocolate, if you'd rather that."

Lydia was not altogether keen on chocolate, but she'd watched Mr. de Sabran force his tea down every morning and pretend that it was pleasant, and she guessed he would be grateful for a change, so she said, "Chocolate, please."

The same girl who had let them in the house now saw them upstairs to their rooms. Mr. de Sabran's was on the floor above hers. Still, when Lydia had washed her face and hands and smoothed the wildness from her hair and brushed her gown's folds into order, she emerged to find him waiting for her on the landing. He'd been standing leaning with his shoulder to the wall, but as she exited her room he straightened, gave his short and customary nod, and fell in step behind her on the stairs.

Down in the parlor, Silas had entrenched himself in one of the fine armchairs by the window, the curtains newly drawn against the fast-descending evening.

William's house was furnished to reflect his status as a man of consequence. The walls of his parlor were hung with a rich, painted paper brought over from England, the draperies matching the blue of the floral design, and the oil-burning lamps in the sconces set on every wall were reflected by round shields of mirror and silver.

The pot for the chocolate was silver as well, as indeed was the tray that it sat upon, holding a large dish of very small cakes, and the cups they were given were fine painted porcelain.

She wondered what Mr. de Sabran thought, faced with opulence after their own plainer home. She had given no thought until now what his own home might be like, although she supposed she'd assumed from what Joseph had said of the men of the Troupes de la Marine, and the image she'd shaped in her mind of Quebec, that he'd come from a more rustic background. Yet he did not look out of place at all, here in this room drinking chocolate, the porcelain cup held in his hand with an ease that surprised her.

Not out of place, but not at home.

He was keeping apart from them, as was his usual way—sitting off to one side in a chair she suspected he'd chosen because it afforded him views of the door and the window at once.

Joseph did that, too. It was an instinct gained from having been in battle, she suspected, so a man might then see the approach of any danger.

William tried a few times to include Mr. de Sabran in their conversation by addressing him in slow and simple English, speaking over-loudly, until Lydia was moved to comment, "William, he is French. He is not deaf."

Beside the window, Silas smiled. "Indeed. I should imagine that his hearing will be very sharp indeed while he is in our city. There is much news to be gathered here."

Lydia looked at him. "If you suspect him of being a spy, you have no one to blame but your father, for thrusting him into our midst in the first place."

As the words fell out she knew she'd made a fool's mistake. She saw within her cousin's eyes the gleam that had, from childhood, meant he was about to twist the knife. And so he did.

He smoothly said, "I'm sure my father did not think it would be a great burden for you, since you've had the room to spare within your house these twenty years to shelter others not your family. If he was mistaken, if it *is* a burden, you have but to tell me. I am sure he would be happy to relieve you of your guests," he told her. "All of them."

The threat, though velvet-toned, was clear, and Lydia reproached herself for having selfishly forgotten Violet's safety was not something she had any right to put in jeopardy.

She cast her eyes down, swallowing her pride to show him deference. "It's no burden."

Deborah deftly moved the talk to other things, while Lydia exchanged a glance of shared frustration with her brother. With all his wealth and influence, he could do nothing either; only hope, as did they all, that Uncle Reuben would not choose to change the rules of their arrangement.

Turning from William she noticed that Mr. de Sabran was studying Silas. His features, impassive, gave nothing away of his thoughts, though she would have been interested to know them.

She wondered, too, what the French officer saw when he looked at her brother.

She'd always believed she saw William more clearly than most, but what she'd learned from Henry of the Monte Cristi trade had left her vision fogged with doubts.

If Daniel *was* in Monte Cristi, not Jamaica—and the more she cast her mind back over what Captain del Rio had remarked, the more she felt sure it was so—then William had much to explain, though she knew she would not get the answers she needed this evening.

Her brother had risen and looked as though he were preparing to leave. "That's the problem with this time of year," he complained. "It's too cold not to have a fire, but then you're always drowsy. I'll just take a walk to clear my head. No, Silas, stay and keep the ladies company. I won't be long."

Since William knew—and in many ways shared—her opinion of Silas, she wasn't sure why, when her cousin had risen to leave as well, William would tell him to stay. But this wasn't her house or her parlor, and she could do no more than try to control her tongue and not shame Deborah by causing an argument.

She found it difficult.

Silas hit all of her sensitive points with his questions. He asked after Joseph. He feigned interest in how their family was managing after her mother's death, probing the places he knew were still hurting and raw. And when that failed to get an appropriate rise from her, he turned the subject again to the captured French officers.

"I must say, I was unaware," he said, "that they could travel."

"Well, they can. With the permission of a magistrate, and if they are accompanied."

"It seems unkind of Uncle Zeb to put this burden onto you, with all you've been through. Could he not send Benjamin?"

She thanked her day of traveling for having slowed her brain enough to give her time to analyze his words before replying. It was obvious his sympathy was insincere, but there was something… Benjamin, she thought, with sudden certainty. He did not know where Benjamin had gone. Perhaps he'd heard a rumor but he did not *know*, and looked to her now to confirm it.

She denied him that. "I'm glad to come. It has been far too long since I've seen Deborah and the children. Are they hiding?" she asked, turning to her sister-in-law, and the talk then shifted to her tiny niece and nephew who were staying for the night at Deborah's parents' house.

"They can be very noisy," Deborah said in summing up. "We didn't want to inconvenience you while you were here." Which was a fair enough excuse, if slightly spoiled by her quick glance at the corner where Mr. de Sabran sat in silence. Had she been a mother, Lydia knew she too might have thought it would be best to shield her children from the presence of an enemy beneath their roof. And it was only for two nights.

Silas seemed surprised to learn she was not staying longer. "It must be important business then, to bring your French lieutenant all this way for such a short time."

He was digging again, furtively, just like a sleek destructive creature in the garden seeking hidden roots on which to feast.

She knew what was bringing Mr. de Sabran to New York. He had told them, through Mr. de Brassart's translation, that one of his men had been wounded and was now in fear of his life, and she knew William had made arrangements himself to accompany Mr. de Sabran in the morning to visit the wounded man. But Silas needed to know none of that, so she only replied in her most offhand way, "I don't bother myself with the business of men."

From the front of the house came a knock at the door and a murmur of low voices out in the entry hall and then the house-maid came into the parlor, a message in hand.

"It's from William," said Deborah, on reading it. "He sends apologies but he has met with a friend and accepted an offer to sup with him. No, Silas, *do* stay."

It was one of the longest, most wearisome evenings that Lydia could call to mind. She would gladly, when supper was done, have excused herself under some pretext and gone up to bed, only she became gradually certain that Deborah was actually trying to keep Silas occupied—keep him from leaving the house.

And when Deborah sat down at the harpsichord and asked, "Come, Lydia, sing us a song," there was a faintly pleading light within her glance.

Lydia disliked singing on demand. She sometimes sang in private, and she knew her voice was passable, but had it not been for her sense that Deborah truly needed her to sing just now she never would have risen from her chair and done so.

Nor would the song Deborah played have been Lydia's choice—the "True Lover's Farewell," full of sentiment.

And yet she sang it, all five verses, and would have gone on to sing another song had William not returned, his long coat carrying the scents of pipe smoke and stale wine and the cold night wind from the harbor.

"Silas, good, you are still here. We are in sore need of a fourth for cards," he said, then looked to Deborah. "If, my dear, you do not mind?"

"Of course not."

"Lyddie, I shall see you in the morning," William promised. With a nod to Mr. de Sabran, he left them once again, this time with Silas trailing darkly in his wake.

A moment later Mr. de Sabran stood also, bowed and said, "Good night," to them in English, and went upstairs to his room.

When he was out of earshot, Deborah said, "He's very surly, isn't he?"

"So might we be," was Lydia's reply, "if all our friends and loved ones were now dead or captured, at the mercy of the enemy, and we could neither give them help nor comfort."

"I just meant—"

"He has a sister and a mother at Quebec. I should imagine that his thoughts are turned to them now more than to our entertainments."

Deborah smiled. "That's twice you have defended him," she pointed out. "He does not strike me as the kind of man who needs defending, or would welcome it." She laid an arm along Lydia's shoulders in a hug. "And you are far too tired for me to tease you. To the contrary, I owe you thanks for helping me keep Silas out of mischief."

So her first suspicion had been right, thought Lydia. "What mischief did we keep him from?" she asked. "And where did William truly go this evening?"

Deborah shook her head faintly, still smiling, and said, "I don't bother myself with the business of men. I have heard that's a very wise policy."

Lydia, for all she acknowledged those were her own words given back to her, was less inclined to obey their advice.

⤺

Next morning she rose early when the house was still in darkness and went downstairs to find William in his study. He had always liked to seize this time of day to do his work.

"May I come in?" she asked.

"Of course." He stood as she came in, and crossed to move a cane-backed chair for her so that it would be closer to his own, beside the bookshelves.

This had always been her favorite room in William's house. It was not large. Its windows did not look upon a view of any consequence, but only on the brick wall of his neighbor's house, across a narrow lane. It had few fineries—the walls were plainly paneled and the curtains unremarkable, the mantelpiece above the fire as straight and simple as they came without any adornment. William's writing table and the chairs had been made by their father so they were more functional than fancy, and the only painting on the wall was of a field, with horses.

She knew why this was her favorite room. It felt like home.

And here, so she imagined, she was closer to her brother's true self than in any other place.

He told her, "You're up early."

"I've a question I would ask you."

He sat back and interlaced his fingers, studying her across the little space that lay between them.

She imagined she could see the wheels and gears begin to turn within his mind, and before they could put his thoughts too far in motion she asked simply, "Where is Daniel?"

She had left the question open with a purpose—so that she could watch his eyes in the few seconds before he replied. It was not ever easy to be certain when her brother was untruthful, but she'd long observed that sometimes there was just the barest flicker in his eyes, like that in Father's eyes when he was calculating sums in silence in his head.

And there it was.

He said, "Why, he's in—"

"If you tell me Daniel is at Kingston, and it is not true," she interrupted smoothly, "know that I will not forgive you for it."

William stopped. He looked at her a moment longer. Then, like the negotiator that he was, he walked around the question. "Why would he not be at Kingston?"

She was not about to play that game. "Is he at Monte Cristi?"

"If he is, why should it matter?"

"You know why." She let the words hang there reproachfully between them, leaving space for his apology.

But he did not apologize. He shrugged off her discovery of the fact that he and Daniel were engaging in illegal trade with, "Honestly, it is no crime."

"The king may view it differently."

"The king's ships also trade at Monte Cristi," he replied, "though they are free to sail from England with provisions for the Mount and take back sugar and molasses without being charged the tariffs that we must pay here. It's the tariffs," he said, "that are criminal. All of these acts passed in Parliament telling us where we may sell our provisions and where we may buy our molasses and setting high tariffs that only apply to *our* cargoes, not theirs, so their ships out of English ports can reap the riches of trade in the Indies while our New York ships are harassed on the seas, seized, and sold in their admiralty courts. It is not to be borne, Lyddie. No, any act passed in Parliament should apply equally to all the king's subjects, not seek to raise one and lower the other. That is unbearable."

"So you would trade with the enemy."

"I trade with Spain. What Spain does with the cargoes I sell to it, I can't control." While his words had the strength of defiance, his gaze could not hold hers.

She felt calm in her anger. "You know where those cargoes

are sold. Does it not even bother your conscience that those same provisions are sent to support and feed those who killed Moses? Who nearly killed Joseph?" Her voice nearly broke and betrayed her then. "William, how could you?"

"You don't understand." His tone was gentle. "It is business. War affects it less than you might think. Those men in Parliament in London, they are lining their own pockets by this same trade with the French. It's not our politics that trouble them," he told her, "it's our profits."

She cared nothing for his profits. "There are laws for a reason."

He shrugged. "When a law is unjust it becomes a man's duty to stand and oppose it."

"Then stand and oppose it alone," she shot back, "but give thought to the people you force to stand with you."

His frown told her he wasn't following, so she collected her temper before she said, "Father sent Benjamin down to meet Daniel. Do you know why? Benjamin wanted to go, and he asked me to help persuade Father, so that's what I did."

"Lyddie."

"So now that's on my account, too," she told him, "what happens to Benjamin."

"Nothing will happen to Benjamin."

"How do you know? Henry said the admiral means to stop the Monte Cristi trade, which means there will be men-of-war patrolling there. How do you know that Benjamin won't suffer for it? Had he gone to Kingston he'd be fine, but if he's found at Monte Cristi, William, he could well be pressed into the navy, and what then?" She knew he'd heard the stories told by New York men who had been taken up and forced to work on ships of war, and none of them were pleasant.

William only asked her, "Henry knows this?"

"What, that you and Daniel have been trading with the French? Of course not. All he did was tell me how the Monte Cristi trade works, and the rest I reasoned for myself."

"And Father?"

"No, of course he doesn't know," she said, impatient. "It would kill him. Nor does Joseph know that he is working to repair a ship that will be carrying provisions to the men who stole his life." She straightened in her chair and faced him, firm. "And he will never know this, because you are going to stop it."

"Lyddie."

"I am not a fool," she said. "I don't pretend to think our family matters to you half as much as do your profits."

"Lydia."

"But," she told him, "you must give your promise that the *Bellewether* will never sail to Monte Cristi harbor. You must promise, William. Joseph needs this. You know how he needs to do this work. But if you sail that ship to Monte Cristi, then you might as well destroy him and be done with it."

He met her gaze again and this time held it. "Fine."

"I have your word?"

"You have my promise."

"I intend to hold you to it. And we'll have to hope that Joseph does not learn of you and Daniel by some other means." A sick thought struck her, and she asked, "Does Silas know?"

"No."

"How can you be sure?"

"Because I shared a bottle of Madeira last night with him for that very purpose, to discover what he knew. Our cousin does not hold his drink well," he said. "It deprives him of caution and inflates his arrogance, and you can then learn whatever you like before he even realizes he's being questioned."

She noted that William was speaking now in a confiding way he'd never used with her, and that emboldened her to ask, "And why were you questioning him to begin with? Why last night?"

He paused. Perhaps because he felt some guilt for lying to her earlier, or for exposing all of them to dangers they did not deserve, his next words had the simple ring of truth. "There's an informer in our city, named George Spencer, who would see us all arrested and claim his reward."

She remembered Henry telling her that advertisements had been posted lately in the papers for informers to come forward to report on any merchants who were trading with the enemy.

"I'm not alone in what I'm doing, Lyddie. Even the governor—well, let us say if George Spencer comes forward without any penalty, it will affect half the men of New York. So last night we all met at the coffeehouse. That's where I was over supper."

"And why you told Deborah to make certain Silas stayed here."

"He would have followed me otherwise. You know what Silas is like."

"Yes." Of course, she thought, William would never have thought what effect it might have upon her, upon Deborah, to have to bear Silas's company for all that time.

William carried on, "Silas has been a great nuisance since taking up lodgings in Sloat Alley, and it occurred to me he, like George Spencer, might have been too close to our warehouses, so when the meeting was over a few of us thought it was best to find out. That's when I came back round here to fetch him." He shrugged as though that were the whole of it. "And he knew nothing."

"For now."

"True, but after today, any would-be informers will think twice before coming forward."

"Why?"

"Because," he said, "we mean to make such a spectacle of Mr. Spencer that none will forget it. Don't look like that. He'll not be harmed much, just shaken."

"For telling the truth."

"There are times when the truth would be best left untold." William's eyes warmed until they became once again the same eyes of the brother she'd long known and loved. "You are young."

She did not feel young. She stood. Smoothed her skirts. "It must be time for breakfast."

"Most likely." He seemed to be faintly aware something vital had shifted between them, and much like a plasterer seeking to smooth over a tiny crack, sought to pay her a compliment. "You've changed the way that you're wearing your hair, I see. It's quite attractive."

He was the first of her family to notice, although she'd been wearing it this way for nearly two weeks. Since the day Mr. de Sabran had complimented her on it, and smiled.

"Thank you," she said. She paused. "Where is this house where the injured French soldier is billeted?"

"Only a few streets up, near Coentjes Market." He twisted around in his chair to glance back at the clock on the mantel. "I nearly forgot about that. I'm supposed to be taking your officer there at ten thirty."

"I'll take him."

He offered no argument. No doubt, she thought, he was glad to be free of the burden, so he could attend to his own affairs.

And though their chairs hadn't moved since they'd started their talk, at that moment he somehow seemed farther away.

JEAN-PHILIPPE

H E SHOULD HAVE BEEN watching the harbor. He should have been noticing how many ships were there, and of what nations, with how many guns. He should at the very least have been applying himself to a study of this single street, but he wasn't. Instead he was studying her.

She'd been quiet since breakfast. She was a quiet woman by her nature but he knew that this was something more.

He'd thought at first it was her cousin who'd upset her. He had marked the man's name when her brother made the introductions: "Mr. Silas Wilde, my cousin," who could only be the Silas Wilde he'd heard of from Pierre—the son of Monsieur Wilde's unpleasant older brother. And if Pierre was convinced that Monsieur Wilde's brother, when he died, would find himself in hell and not in heaven, Jean-Philippe could have assured him that the son would join him there. In all his life he'd only met two men with eyes like that, and he would not have wished to turn his back on either of them.

Understanding William Wilde had taken him more time, because the man refused to take a constant shape. Instead, much like the quicksilver that backed a mirror, he reflected anyone who faced him. It was only when you stood off to the side and watched him speak to others that you saw the subtle shifting, even with his sister. With his wife. Perhaps he'd never had a single form, or had forgotten it as he'd matured, and acting from self-interest he had altogether lost the art of keeping to one character. He was not heartless—his affection for the women was not feigned, but love from such a man would always have its limits at the boundary of his own needs and convenience.

That was why the women had been left all but alone last night with Silas Wilde, when any man who truly loved them never would have left them unattended. Worse that he'd stayed out so late, long past the hour when Jean-Philippe in any other circumstance would have excused himself and gone upstairs, having endured a day of travel with a man who clearly hated him, compounded with some hours of conversation which did not include him, and which even if it had been in his language would have left him at the limit of his tolerance for everyday society. But even he, who knew the women only slightly, could not in good conscience have abandoned them.

He could not have abandoned *her*. He'd seen her face, however closely she had tried to school it, and he saw what it was costing her to maintain her politeness. He had seen her struggle just as hard to do the same with him, when he had first arrived. From time to time her cousin Silas would say something that brought angry color washing to her cheeks but she would skillfully suppress it with a gesture or a movement and her voice, although it lowered once, was always calm. He found her quite remarkable.

He'd known the very moment that she realized—as he'd done some minutes earlier—that William's wife was purposely attempting to detain their cousin at the house, and he'd watched them work together to accomplish it.

The song had been an unexpected benefit. He had not known she sang. She did not sing around the house as Violet did. Perhaps, he reasoned, she had not of late had cause for singing. But her voice was high and clear and very beautiful to listen to. He'd had to guard his features well to keep his admiration hidden. For her brother to make his return at that moment, depriving them all of a second song, had seemed a thoughtless intrusion.

That was, to be honest, the single descriptive word that suited William Wilde best: thoughtless. It seemed probable that something he had said or done had caused his sister's change of mood this morning. At breakfast he'd been too solicitous and she'd been too reserved, and although he'd stood close beside her in the entry hall, presumably to give her last directions, she had scarcely looked at or acknowledged him while she had tied her bonnet.

Jean-Philippe, in that respect at least, could sympathize, since it appeared he also was invisible to her this morning. When they'd crossed the street he'd paused to offer her his arm as he had done the day before, but she had walked ahead without his aid, not in the manner of a snub but with the faint distracted frown of someone wrapped in troubling thoughts. The sky, as though to echo that, was dark with clouds. The day was cold.

He was not bothered by it, being well protected by his woolen uniform, but she was wearing what he guessed was her best gown—a pretty, ruffled thing, all over flowers in bright colors, but not warm, and only covered by a cloak that was unlined and had no hood.

Luckily they had not far to go. The house was only a few minutes' walk from William Wilde's, close by a bustling market. On the ground floor was a shop that offered, judging from its window, wines and brandies—no doubt carried into New York on the many merchant ships that now lay anchored in the harbor. But along the side, behind the shop, a door admitted them into the private residence.

The woman who came down the stairs to meet them was of middle age and dressed in widow's black. She welcomed Lydia in English, but to Jean-Philippe she spoke in French so flawless it was evident that it was her first language. He recalled her name from Captain Wheelock's letter, and returned her greeting with, "Good day, Madame de Joncourt."

Wheelock had explained that the de Joncourt family had long had the favor of the governor, did work for him, and took in special lodgers. *When your General von Dieskau was so gravely wounded, being taken prisoner four years ago*, so Wheelock had continued, *he was cared for by Madame de Joncourt, so I thought you would approve my*

sending her your sergeant also, that he might there convalesce in greater
comfort than he would in jail.

It was indeed a house of comfort.

Stepping in, he felt surrounded by its warmth and scents of
bread and coffee, raising childhood memories that were height-
ened when, on entering their upstairs parlor, he found a gathering
of girls in curls and petticoats and one lone boy, who might have
been his sisters and himself when younger. And to add still further
to the feeling he was on familiar ground, the man now rising
from his chair to greet them was an officer of the regiment of
Guyenne, gold buttons shining brightly on the red-cuffed sleeves
of his white coat, and a fine expensive powdered wig tied back
beneath his gold-trimmed hat.

"Louis de Preissac de Bonneau," was how he introduced
himself. He was a captain.

Jean-Philippe paid him the proper honors and returned his full
name, "Jean-Philippe de Sabran de la Noye," then stepped aside
and added, "And may I present to you Mademoiselle Wilde."

"Mademoiselle." Bonneau bowed deeply, smiled with charm,
and spoke to her in English while Madame de Joncourt turned to
Jean-Philippe.

"We were just having coffee. May I bring you some?"

"I'd see my sergeant first."

"Of course." She broke into the captain's conversation with,
"Captain Bonneau, will you take the lieutenant up to see his man?"

Bonneau said, "Certainly," and gallantly excused himself from
Lydia. "Come, it's this way."

Jean-Philippe followed, glancing back just once to make sure
Lydia was settled in the parlor with the others. Just the slightest
glance, but it did not escape Bonneau.

"She will be fine." His tone was sure. "Madame de Joncourt
takes great care of everyone beneath her roof, particularly pretty
girls. She guards her own as if they were the gold and she the dragon.
And believe me, I've the scorch marks to bear witness to it."

As they climbed the narrow staircase Jean-Philippe tried hard to call to mind the faces of the three de Joncourt girls who had been in the parlor. He could not. But they'd seemed young, and he remarked on that.

"The eldest is near twenty," Bonneau told him. "Jeanne. A lovely girl, but fonder of a red coat than our white ones, I'm afraid. Her youngest sister, Phila, is but ten, and still a child. And Rachel, in between them, is sixteen. A girl so young, in my experience, is apt to think on love when you are minded to less-lasting pleasures, so it's neither nice nor kind to sport with them." The captain's glance was speculative. "How old is your mademoiselle?"

Jean-Philippe, to any other man, might have replied she was not his, but in the face of Bonneau's easy charm he found himself responding with a shrug instead, defensively. "I've never asked."

They'd reached the upper floor. Along the corridor, toward the end, a door stood open. Inside, in a bed heaped warm with quilts, the sergeant lay alone, his bandaged head against the pillow. He was sleeping.

Bonneau stayed within the doorway. "There's a chair there you can pull across to sit beside him. I do that some days. He never sleeps for long. The pain," he said, by way of explanation, "will not let him."

Frowning, Jean-Philippe asked, "How long has he been like this?"

"Like this? I could not say. They only brought him here two weeks ago. Before that he was in the prison hospital, but Captain Wheelock—you have met him? He sent orders that your man should be moved here instead. He is a good man, Wheelock."

"He would seem to be."

"No, you must take my word. I've been here for a while, and of the English soldiers I have dealt with he has been the best of them." Bonneau nodded toward the bed. "Your sergeant is a good man also. I don't think I've yet heard him complain."

"It's not his nature to complain." Taking the plain rush-seated chair that had been set beside the window, Jean-Philippe moved it with quiet care across so he could sit as Bonneau had suggested, at the bedside of the wounded man. "His name is Jacques Le Roy, but he is called La Réjouie."

It was a long tradition in the army—common soldiers having second names that they were called by, often given to them for some trait of personality. His sergeant's meant "the cheerful one," because he always smiled.

"It suits him well," Bonneau agreed. "Though with more time here he may grow as disagreeable as me."

Beneath the light tone Jean-Philippe could hear an edge of truthfulness, and glancing up asked, "How long have you been here?"

"I was taken the July before this past one, up at Carillon. The English general gave me leave to go to Montreal to put my few affairs in order first, but naturally I had to come back down here to surrender when I'd finished, and I've been here ever since, waiting to be exchanged. If any good comes at all from our loss of Quebec it will be that there are enough officers taken on both sides to force a cartel," he said. "But it's a damnable paradox, having to wait for your enemy's victory so you can get back in the fight."

A man who felt his own frustration, then.

The sergeant stirred. His eyes were coming open.

"Well," Bonneau said, "I will leave you two to talk. I'll see you downstairs after."

Jean-Philippe took little notice of the other's leaving. His attention was already on his sergeant, who was struggling to raise himself as though he thought it disrespectful to be lying down when in the presence of an officer.

"No, rest," said Jean-Philippe. "Lie still."

"I can do little else, in honesty." La Réjouie grinned feebly. "I am like a child." His ribs were obviously hurting him. He shifted to relieve them before going on. "I told him you would come, you know. That other one, the captain here, I told him you would find out where I was and come to see me. 'It may not be easy,' that was what he told me, and I said to him, 'You don't know my lieutenant. Wait and see.' And here you are."

It was a touching thing to know that you had earned a good man's trust. "I'm sorry that I took so long."

"No matter. I can barely keep the days and weeks in order." With a motion to his head, La Réjouie said, "Everything gets jumbled up together. I can't even tell you what today is."

"It's the second of November."

"Is it? Truly? Well, you see I should be grateful for this injury, because it makes the time of my captivity fly by." He coughed, and tried to hide his wince.

"You've reported to the English how this happened?"

"I have told them, yes." A smile. "I can't say whether any of them wrote it down."

"Tell me."

"They were marching a detachment of our men toward some place called Hempstead. I was at the back, as is my place, and when we came to where the road bent on ahead and none could see, an English corporal and one of the private soldiers of their escort came behind and one of them—I couldn't tell you which it was—dealt me so hard a blow across my back with the butt of his firelock that I fell there and could neither move nor call for help. And having me then at their mercy, both of them, still with their firelock butts, began to beat me. I lost count at thirty blows."

"They meant to murder you?"

"I did not think to ask them their intent," the sergeant answered with his usual good humor. "But I expect my purse was of more interest to them than my life, because they took that with them, even though it only held a crown, two dollars, and some coppers."

"And they left you there for dead?"

He shrugged. "One did return, and held his hand above my mouth to see if I still breathed, but being less than trusting by this point I held my breath, and being satisfied that I was dead he gave me one last blow upon my stomach and departed."

Jean-Philippe could feel an echo of that blow in his own stomach, where deep anger had begun to burn.

As if aware of this, La Réjouie said, "I was found by local people, and they cared for me and saw that I was carried back here to New York, to Dr. Talman, who has treated me most expertly and with great kindness." As though he were speaking to a child needing reassurance, he remarked, "There are good people here as well, sir."

"Yes," said Jean-Philippe. "I know there are. But I will see the ones who did this to you brought to trial and punished. I'll see you get justice."

He'd have promised more, but already the sergeant's eyes were drifting closed again, his bandaged head turning with heaviness against the pillow as the urgent sleep of convalescence claimed him.

Jean-Philippe sat half an hour after in the chair beside the bed, but seeing that La Réjouie was not about to waken he rose quietly and left the room.

Downstairs, he found a newcomer had joined the gathering in the de Joncourts' parlor.

Captain Wheelock, rising now to greet him, could not possibly have known just how unwelcome Jean-Philippe found the mere sight of that red uniform.

In French, the captain asked him, "You have seen your sergeant?"

"Yes. Have you?"

"No, I'm afraid I only got back yesterday. I have been in the Jerseys."

"But you are aware what happened to him?"

Wheelock raised a shoulder and admitted, "I've heard some of it."

"Then let me tell you all." Aware that there were children in the room, he drew the English captain to one side so they'd have privacy to talk, and there repeated what La Réjouie had said to him, concluding with, "I will expect that charges will be laid."

"Yes." Captain Wheelock's frown seemed genuinely troubled. "I should never wish for such a crime to go unpunished. I'll let General Amherst know of it. You have my word."

He had the sense that Captain Wheelock's word would not be lightly broken. With his anger damped down to a place where he could keep it well controlled, he told the captain, "Thank you," and they took their seats among the others.

He was careful not to look too soon toward the woman who in fact drew all his interest, though he caught her flowered gown just at the corner of his vision. He tried purposely ignoring it, as much as he ignored that she was talking to Bonneau. He could not have understood their conversation anyway, because they spoke in English, so instead he focused on their hostess, who had brought him coffee. And her son, who seeming much the age that Jean-Philippe had been when he'd first joined the Troupes de la Marine, was chafing at the need to sit politely in his chair.

This one will never settle long enough to be a man of leisure...

Smiling faintly at this shadow from his boyhood, Jean-Philippe acknowledged him with one brief nod, upon which the lad must have felt emboldened to speak up in his clear voice.

"Captain Bonneau says you were raised among the Indians."

His mother cautioned, "Robert, that is not the way to start a conversation."

Jean-Philippe could see no harm in it, and said as much. "Captain Bonneau exaggerates. I spent a winter living with the Seneca, when I was near your age, but that is all."

"Without your mother and your father?"

"Yes, it was myself alone."

Evidently this held some appeal, and yet the boy asked, "Were you not afraid?"

"Of course. We always fear what we don't know. I was a long

way from my home, and it was coming on to winter, and I did not speak the language." As he said those words he wryly thought again how life had brought him round full circle. "But the people I was with were very kind."

The boy, uninterested in kindness, wanted stories of adventure. "Did you learn to dance a war dance?"

"No. It was not time for war," he said. "We hunted, and I learned to make things."

"What things?"

"Snowshoes. Arrows. Shoes and leggings that work better in the woods to keep your feet and legs warm."

Only one of those held any interest for young Robert. "Did you have a bow and arrow of your own?"

"I did."

Respect at last. The boy said, "I would like to live among the wild men, too."

"They are not wild," said Jean-Philippe. "They're every bit as civilized as we are. Maybe more so."

"But they torture people."

"So do we. Have you not seen an execution?"

"No. Maman won't let me."

Jean-Philippe took the reminder there were some things children did not need to learn too early. "Well, when you have seen one," he said simply, "you will know we have no right to call another nation cruel." He paused to drink his coffee, and then added, because ignorance was always to be fought, "I still have friends among the Seneca. Their nation is a part of a great federation, the Haudenosaunee. They have government and rule of law and farms and houses, just like us. Before we came, they also had great towns, big forts, but we have ruined those. The miracle is that they will still speak to us at all. Remember that, if you should get your wish to live among them."

The boy's eyes had grown wide. "I will." He sat a little straighter. "And I will not be afraid."

"Good. You'll find most people, when you get to know them, are not what you were afraid they'd be. They're only people."

He'd been unaware of anyone else listening until Madame de Joncourt said, "That is a lesson for us all. But, Robert, do not think to run away from home just yet to live among the Seneca, or I will have to send Lieutenant de Sabran to track you down and bring you back to me again."

Her elder daughter joined their conversation with, "Or Captain Wheelock. He has also spent time in the northern forests, have you not?"

The captain smiled. "In campaign tents. It's not at all the same. And please don't give me anybody else to find. I'm afraid I shall never be able to make a complete list of those I'm already in charge of. The jailers have no general list, and several of the prisoners were taken from the barracks and the jail here without anybody leaving a receipt, and several others in the Jerseys have been carried off by flags of truce," he said, "from Philadelphia. No doubt they are already on their way to the West Indies."

The boy Robert asked, "What is a flag of truce?"

"A ship," Wheelock explained, "carrying prisoners of war to be exchanged, and so it flies a special white flag to let everybody know that it is not to be molested, and it also carries papers that can prove it has permission from our government to sail to a French port. At least, that's what it's meant to be. Except these days more often it's a ship whose owners have done nothing more than buy the white flag and the papers for a secret fee, so they can sail around our laws and sell their cargoes to French ports. If they have a prisoner aboard, so much the better, but if not, they'll carry anyone who can speak French."

The youngest of the girls now gave a solemn nod that bounced her curls. "Like Monsieur Laine," she said. "That's what he does. He gets to ride on ships, and always brings back sugar."

In the small, uneasy silence following that statement, Captain Wheelock raised a hand of reassurance. "I heard nothing of that.

Honestly, unless your Monsieur Laine is on my list, I have no room within my brain to mark his name. It's filled already with the names of several hundred prisoners and one ensign named McDonald we've apparently misplaced."

He seemed uncommonly relaxed within this house. And then he turned and smiled down at the young woman beside him and she smiled back, and Jean-Philippe then knew exactly what Bonneau had meant when he'd said the de Joncourts' eldest daughter was more fond of red coats than of white.

There must, he thought, be twenty years in age between the English captain and young Jeanne de Joncourt, but the captain's heart showed plainly in that moment. Jean-Philippe could not help wondering if his own face revealed that much when he was watching Lydia.

It made him more determined not to look in her direction now.

He did it so effectively she had to say his name twice over before he reacted to it. As he turned his head she said in very careful French, "Please leave."

An unexpected order. He was less than sure how to respond till Jeanne de Joncourt laughed and spoke to Lydia in English and corrected her by giving her the proper words in French, and then he understood, but he gave Lydia the space to save her dignity and ask it over.

"May we leave, please?"

"Certainly." He stood, and took his leave, and thanked Madame de Joncourt once again.

Bonneau said, "Come, I'll walk you out." And downstairs while they waited for Madame de Joncourt to fetch Lydia her cloak, Bonneau said low and privately, "Don't worry. I will keep your sergeant company, and send you word if he grows worse."

"If he grows worse, he'll need a priest."

"You know they are illegal in this colony."

"So I am told."

The faintest smile. "I'll see if there is one that can be found among the Irish."

"I am in your debt." *There are good people here as well,* La Réjouie had said. And that reminded him he owed a debt to someone else. "Tell Captain Wheelock that the ensign he says he's misplaced, Ensign McDonald, is a prisoner of the Seneca near Fort Detroit," he said. "At least, that's where he was when I was taken at Niagara."

Bonneau looked at him. "You're sure?"

"I'm sure. I saw him there myself."

"I meant you're sure you want to tell him?"

"Captain Wheelock is a man of honor. And his list is long enough."

Bonneau's smile this time was more broad. He aimed it straight at Lydia as she approached them, wished her a good day in English, and turned one last time to Jean-Philippe. "Keep well, Lieutenant de Sabran. I'll see you in the spring when we reclaim Quebec." Clapping one hand firmly on his shoulder he said, "Oh, and by the way. Your mademoiselle? She's twenty."

With a wink he stood back while Madame de Joncourt let them out into the street and closed the door behind them.

It felt colder than it had been, with a raw wind that chased sharply down this narrow lane between the houses, and he knew if he could feel it cutting through his heavy coat then she, with her light cloak, would feel it keenly, so his mission then became to guide her quickly to her brother's house, where she'd be warm.

For all the missions he had led, this should have been an easy one. He'd led his men by night through fields more treacherous than this—the slow, mud-churning wheels of carts and wagons crossed by swifter, finer carriages were nothing when compared to rolling cannon fire. And crowds, no matter how large they might be, were nothing when compared to enemies concealed by shadows.

That there *was* a crowd, growing more raucous by the minute, should perhaps have been a warning to him.

But as he prepared to cross the street she took his arm of her own choice, before he'd offered it, and he looked down at that and she looked up at him, and that left all his senses fully occupied.

He'd always thought her eyes were blue. In fairness she had rarely ever looked directly at him, and the few times that she had she'd looked away, not held his gaze this long. But now he saw with clarity her eyes were green, the color of new leaves.

And he forgot the cold, the wind, the people pushing all around them, and the chaos of the rolling wheels and skittish horses.

When the first brick struck his shoulder he was unprepared.

His first thought—that it had been thrown at him on purpose—quickly vanished when he saw that many in the crowd around them were now foraging for stones and clods of mud and broken bricks and any other refuse they could find, their voices rising, their attention fixed upon the cart now drawing near to them, a frightened-looking man of middle age crouched in its open back, exposed to all their fury.

Jean-Philippe had seen men carted through the streets before. He knew how swiftly any crowd could turn to open riot.

Acting from instinct he angled his body so it would shield Lydia's, sweeping her back into the recession of a doorway that, while closed, would give her shelter. Pressing close, he wrapped himself around her so the blows would strike him first.

They did. Repeatedly. A clump of mud and small stones that had missed its target struck and shattered on the doorframe and he felt her jump and start to tremble, so he bent his head and murmured words of reassurance, low and calm over the wailing of the injured man, and all the ugly shouts of his tormentors.

Fear, he knew, was mostly in the mind, and he would spare her that. He'd long since learned to channel his own fear to action, so it was surprising to him now to feel it twist within his chest—a fear not for himself, his safety, but for hers. It lingered even when the mob had passed them by, the angry tumult growing fainter down the street, and there was no more danger.

Stepping back, he gave them both the space to breathe. Her face was pale, and she appeared to still be shaking but she only drew her cloak a little tighter as though wanting him to think it was the cold, and he had seen enough cadets who did not wish to show him weakness that he recognized her brave attempt to seem more strong in front of him, and though he was not fooled by it he understood her need to make the effort. Having satisfied himself she was unharmed, he waited for her to collect herself sufficiently to leave the sheltered doorway, then he offered her his arm again, and once again she took it, holding tighter to him this time, and they crossed the street in silence.

But the feeling, strange and new, stayed firmly lodged beneath his ribs, as though once having taken hold it was now part of him, and he had no idea what to do with it.

We always fear what we don't know, he'd told the young de Joncourt boy.

And walking now with Lydia's gloved hand upon his arm, her warmth beside him, Jean-Philippe admitted there was truth in what he'd said. Because in all his twenty-seven years, with all that life had dealt him, he had not known anything like this.

CHARLEY

THE TAXI WOULD HAVE flattened me if I'd been looking to the right, but as it was I had just time enough to leap back, out of range.

Niels always said the way to tell a true New Yorker was to watch the way they crossed a street. "They're always three steps off the curb to start with," he'd say. "Daring cars to hit them."

I was not a true New Yorker. I stayed safely on the sidewalk till the light had changed, but even so it could be an extreme sport, crossing streets in New York City, and today I needed to take extra care because of what I carried.

Sam had built a custom crate for me—exactly measured, light, and narrow—adding wooden handles at the sides to make it easier to carry, but even something built as well as Sam could build it wouldn't have been able to survive a speeding taxi, and until the day was over what was *in* the crate officially belonged to Isaac Fisher. So I took my time.

The fact that I had Isaac Fisher's painting in my hands was an achievement in itself, and Frank had made sure everybody knew it. "In my whole entire life," he'd told the board, "I can't remember Isaac giving anything to anybody. Well, he gave me chicken pox, but even then he argued I should pay him fifty cents for all the time I got to spend home sick from school. So, well done, Charley. No one else here could have done it." He had gallantly left off the "told you so" he could have added, because he *had* told me I should go alone to Isaac Fisher's house.

I'd thought that I should take Malaika with me. "She's so good at doing deals."

"And that's exactly why you shouldn't take her. Never set two salespeople against each other."

And that had reminded me. "How *did* you know that Tyler was a salesman?"

"Tyler who?" But he'd been smiling. "Kiddo, there are salesmen in this world, and there are salesmen. There are ones like Lara and Malaika, honest ones that want to treat you right so they can have your business back again. But then there are the ones with shiny shoes, and smiles from here to here, as slick as snake oil. Guess which kind your Tyler was?"

I'd had to smile myself. "His shoes *were* shiny."

"Yes, they were."

"What kind of shoes does Isaac Fisher wear?"

"Well, that depends," he'd said, "on who he's dancing with." He'd poured himself a cup of coffee. "If it's you, he'll probably wear good, old-fashioned loafers."

"Why is that?"

"You're nice." He'd said that gruffly, in the tone he used when giving out a compliment. "And to old guys like me and Isaac, nice girls are about as rare and powerful as Kryptonite."

I wasn't sure that Isaac Fisher thought of me as Kryptonite, but he had worn his loafers when he'd met me at the door. He'd made me tea, and we had sat together in his kitchen talking for an hour or more, about his family and Cross Harbor and the old store, now long gone.

And then he'd said, without my even prompting him, "That painting, now. I think it ought to be at the museum, and I'd like for you to have it. Can you give me a receipt, though, for my taxes?"

I had promised him I could, once it had been appraised.

When I'd reported all this to the trustees, Sharon had jumped right on that. "And who," she'd asked, "is going to pay for this appraisal? If you hadn't put Dave Becker on your acquisitions team, we could have gone to him, but now we can't, is that right?

It would be a conflict. So, we'd have to pay an outsider, and where will we get money to do that?"

She'd thought she had me in a corner, I could tell, and it had given me a lot of satisfaction to be able to reply, "I have a cousin in New York who owns a gallery, and she said she would do it for us free of charge. If," I had added calmly, "that's all right with everybody?"

I had hugged the beauty of that moment for as long as possible. I'd even gone the long way home on purpose, right past Bridlemere, to show those gates I wouldn't be intimidated.

Not that they had noticed. At nine o'clock at night this time of year it was already good and dark, and there'd been no lights on at all that I could see within that mansion sprawled along the water's edge.

My brother's house had been a different story. Every light had been ablaze, Sam's truck was parked beside the tree out front, and Bandit met me at the side door to the kitchen. Or, to be specific, at the open place where the side door belonged.

Sam had his tool belt on. "Good timing," was his greeting. "I could use an extra pair of hands."

Obligingly I set my briefcase down, shrugged off my coat and draped it on the nearest kitchen chair, and turned to help. "You didn't have to do this."

"Yeah, I did." He handed me the hinge pins. "It was bugging me. Now here, I'm going to hold this up. If you'll just drop those pins in…perfect. Thanks." As I stepped back he gave the pins a final tap in with his hammer, swung the door shut, and surveyed it with the eye of a perfectionist. "Almost."

If there was any kind of flaw I couldn't see it, but he knocked the hinge pins out again and handed them to me. "Just need to mortise in this hinge a little better."

While he got his chisel from the toolbox on the floor, I looked around. "Where's Rachel?"

"Skyping with your mom."

"My mother Skypes?"

"Seems like it."

Mortising a hinge appeared to take a lot of patience and restraint. He made the small cuts with his chisel, set the hinge in place and screwed it firmly back into the doorjamb, and then took the door in both his hands and said, "Okay, let's try again." This time it seemed to suit him better. Even so, he rummaged in his toolbox for a hand plane and shaved off the slightest bit along the inner edge below the lock plate.

I glanced up toward the ceiling, wishing I could listen in on Rachel and my mother, hoping it was going well. My mother had Opinions when it came to education, and specifically on people dropping out of it. I knew because she'd voiced them all to me, at great length, these past weeks. I ventured, "So, have you heard arguing or yelling?"

Sam assured me that he hadn't. "It's been pretty calm."

Bandit, curled up in the corduroy dog bed that Rachel had bought for him and which had become a fixture now under our table, appeared to bear witness to this. Then again, he might just have been tired. It was after nine thirty and long past the hour when he should have been home.

Sam was checking the fit of the door again, swinging it wide to make sure it was up to his standards. He had to be tired, too. He'd been on the roof of the Wilde House when I had pulled into the parking lot early that morning, and after the regular workday was over, when I had been putting together my notes for the board meeting, he'd still been clearing things up, making sure that the site was secure for the night. He'd been driving out just as the first of the trustees drove in. I'd have thought, after dropping by here to get Bandit, he would have gone straight back to his place.

Although now I thought of it, I wasn't sure where Sam's place was. I knew that he had one. I also knew it had a shed that was either incredibly large or had magical properties, because it seemed anytime I mentioned anything, even in passing, that I wished we had at the Wilde House—a good pair of shutters, a shelf, or a step stool—he'd turn up the next day with one he'd found "lying around in the shed." And for things he considered a favor, he only took payment in food.

So I looked at his work now and asked, "Can I make you a sandwich?"

He promised me there wasn't any need. "I grabbed a burger. And besides, you're out of bread."

"Oh."

Rachel, coming through the doorway from the hall, remarked, "I tried to call you earlier to see if you could pick some up on your way home, but it's a little hard to call you when you don't have *this*." She held my cell phone out, accusing.

"Sorry."

She seemed more resigned to my forgetfulness this evening than upset by it. "How can you not even know that you don't have it with you?"

"I was busy getting ready for the meeting."

Sam closed his toolbox, unbuckled his tool belt and set it on top, and asked, "Good meeting?"

"Great meeting."

I told them why. "So that's two victories, really," I finished up. "Getting the last word with Sharon, and getting that painting in spite of my grandmother."

Sam said, "You've lost me, now. What did your grandmother do?"

"You remember. We asked for a grant from the Sisters of Liberty, to help us fund acquisitions. They turned us down."

"And you think your grandmother did that?"

I sent him a sideways glance. "She *is* the president."

"Maybe in name. But she doesn't do much with them anymore. Not since the spring. It would be her vice president running the show—Carol Speck. And *she's* good friends with Sharon." Standing there looking so casually male in his T-shirt and jeans he hardly seemed the sort of guy who'd notice who was friends with whom, but when I asked him how he knew, he said, "Small place like this, it pays to figure out how people are connected so you don't get into trouble."

Rachel nodded understanding. "Dad said the best thing to do is assume everybody's related until you learn differently."

I felt my forehead crease faintly as I tried absorbing Sam's words. "So you think that this Carol…"

"Speck."

"You think that she was the reason the Sisters of Liberty turned down our funding request?"

"I'd believe that before I'd believe that your grandmother did it."

"And why is that?" I hadn't meant for the edge to creep into my voice. It just did.

Sam shrugged. "It's not her style. She's too much of a lady."

A short silence followed his words until Rachel said coldly, "She wasn't too much of a lady to miss my dad's funeral."

Sam looked from Rachel's face to mine. "I've obviously hit a nerve. I didn't mean to. Sorry."

With a small smile I explained, "It's a pretty big nerve. Kind of hard not to hit it."

He looked as though he was about to say something else, but then he didn't, and things might have ended there except I asked, "Why since the spring?"

"What?"

"You said she hadn't had much to do with the Sisters of Liberty since the spring. Why?"

"I don't know. She got sick, I think. Nobody saw her in town for a while. She still doesn't come out of the house much."

"She came to see *me*," I said dryly, "that day at the Privateer Club, so she can't be a total hermit."

Once again he seemed about to say something, but I saw him rethink that impulse. "Anyway," he said, and lifted Bandit's leash from where it hung beside the door, "I'm going to get this troublemaker home. Thanks, Rachel. Charley, see you in the morning."

Bandit dragged his heels a bit, and since Sam's hands were full with leash and toolbox I stood there and held the door for them, which gave me time to notice something. "Sam."

"Yeah?"

"This isn't the same door."

"That's because the old one was just an interior door," he said. "This one will actually keep out the weather."

"But it can't have cost nothing," I pointed out. "And if you tell me you just found this lying around in your shed, I'm not going to believe you."

It would have been an easy thing to miss the slight curve of his mouth because it came and went so quickly, but his eyes still held the smile. "You won't, huh?"

"No."

Accepting this, he said, "Okay, it wasn't in the shed." He let the dog go first as they stepped out onto the porch, and then he turned and told me, "It was in the basement."

"Sam."

"No, honestly. I had it left over from another job. It didn't cost me anything."

He clearly wasn't going to let me pay him back, so I could only say, "Well, thank you. We really appreciate it."

"Anytime." He briefly eyed his handiwork from this new angle, by the porch light. "*My* grandmother," he told me, "had a theory about doors. Whenever things were going wrong, she'd have my stepdad come hang a new door for her. He'd tell her she was nuts, that doors were doors, but she'd say no door ever opened exactly the same as the last one, the new one was always that little bit different, and anyway it never did any harm to walk through a new door now and then, and see where you end up."

I thought about that for a minute. I thought about what he'd been actually trying to do for us, hanging that door on this house where right now it seemed everything was going wrong; and I thought how incredibly thoughtful and nice he was, and how inadequate any reply I could make was, to thank him. And by the time I'd thought all that, there was nothing I *could* say, because he had already walked to his truck and he wouldn't have heard me.

I did step out onto the porch, though, and Sam was right. It was a little bit different.

I was a little bit different.

Malaika had said, when we'd talked about how she had fallen for Darryl, that there had been something about him, just something, and every time he'd come around she had noticed it more. She had liked it more.

Sam put his things in the back of his truck, lifted Bandit up onto the seat of the cab, and got in himself, as I had seen him do countless times. And as he always did, he raised his hand in a brief wave goodbye as he backed out.

I waved back.

The night was a clear one, the wind blowing sharp from the bay. It was cold on the porch, and I hugged myself tighter, but I stayed and watched the red taillights of Sam's truck roll up the long driveway, and in that one moment I knew, beyond all doubt, why I hadn't cared much when Tyler had gone.

⁂

Malaika had noticed that I was distracted at work the next morning, but she put it down to the aftereffects of our board meeting. "It was a beautiful thing, seeing Sharon shut down," she said. Sinking into the chair on the opposite side of my desk in my office, she swiveled to look out the window. "What on earth is Sam doing now?"

I'd been acutely aware of exactly what Sam had been doing since I had arrived. I'd tried not to be. I'd reminded myself I was probably just on the rebound, and that it was never a good or professional thing to get mixed up with men in the workplace, and that Sam had never done anything anyway to make me think he was interested back, but it still hadn't kept me from noticing what he was doing and where he was, so I could answer Malaika with no hesitation, "He's building a platform for Willie to use when he starts on the chimney."

The stonemason and his mate were on their last day of foundation work, two days ahead of schedule, and given that this was the last month they could work outside before it got too cold for their mortar to set, they were wasting no time moving on to the great central chimney. "A wee bit of scaffolding," Willie had told Sam, "would be just the thing." What he was getting was more than a wee bit, but Sam never did things by halves.

Malaika, watching Sam's surefooted steps along the roof's ridge, shook her head. "I don't know how they even do that. I hate heights. But then I guess with Sam it's in his blood." And seeing that I didn't understand, she said, "His father was an ironworker. It's a Mohawk thing, Sam tells me, walking up there in the open on those steel beams. It's tradition."

I had heard about the famous Mohawk ironworkers who'd earned the respectful nickname "skywalkers" by working on the skyscrapers and bridges of New York and other cities. In fact, one of the men who had served as a consultant at my previous museum had been a retired ironworker, and he'd told me that many of them came from a community near Montreal, where I'd been born. I wondered if Sam's family came from there as well.

Malaika didn't know. She said, "I think he comes from Brooklyn."

He could not have heard us talking. It was cooler out that morning and I'd had my window closed, but when I'd seen his head begin to turn I'd looked away abruptly, feigning sudden fascination with the papers on my desk, and that had made Malaika notice them.

She'd asked me, "What's all that?"

"I'm doing research on our painting." I had started with the inventory made by Captain Wilde's wife. A lot of inventories, since they were usually taken to value a person's estate when they died, left out things like people's portraits that would stay within the family and weren't seen as having value to anyone else, but because our inventory had been taken for a special purpose while the homeowners were still alive, they had left nothing out.

My father's portrait, Captain Wilde's wife had noted first among the contents of the parlor, *in a gilded frame. 1 writing desk with leather bottom chair, 4 mahogany chairs, 2 arm chairs, 1 square walnut table, 1 pair andirons with tongs, 1 carpet, 1 bookcase*—the books listed separately on their own page—*3 brass candlesticks*, and last of all, *a painting of the Bellewether at Halifax*.

"And that," I'd told Malaika, "isn't Halifax."

We'd looked toward the painting, leaning up against the far wall of my office out of everybody's way, with quilted padding on the floor beneath its frame. Except the impact of my statement had been lessened by the fact the painting had been turned around, so we were looking at the back of it.

I'd thought I'd left it facing out when I'd carried it up after our meeting, but that morning my thoughts were admittedly muddled while I'd sorted through this new shift in my feelings for Sam, and I couldn't rely on my memory. I'd risen and turned it around again, so I could prove my point.

It was a beautiful painting, not flat in its imagery like some colonial paintings could be. It had life. It showed a half-constructed ship careened upon its side with three men hard at work upon it, framed by tall trees casting shadows on a curve of beach that was, without a doubt, the beach here at Snug Cove.

The broad gilt frame was beautiful as well, and bore a narrow brass plaque with the title of the piece: *The Building of the Bellewether*.

I wasn't an expert on ships, but the ship in the painting did look like the *Bellewether* when I compared it to the other images I had collected—and there were a lot of them. Benjamin Wilde had been captain of several ships over his lifetime, but only one

became part of his legend. Like Drake's *Golden Hind*, Nelson's
Victory, and Charles Darwin's *Beagle*, the *Bellewether*'s name was
forever bound to Captain Wilde's. Her portrait had been painted
and engraved as many times as his had, and historians had written
of the sloop's exploits as though she'd been alive.

"The Fearless *Bellewether*" was actually the title of the article
I reached for first when trying to explain my doubts about the
painting's subject. "Here's the thing," I told Malaika. "I don't
think this shows the building of the *Bellewether* at all. It says here
she was built at Jackson's shipyard, which was here on the North
Shore somewhere, but from all the accounts that I can find it was
a proper shipyard, and that's not what's in this painting."

Thoughtfully Malaika had agreed, "No, that's our cove."

"With just one ship and a few men. Not a shipyard. But here
in this article it says the *Bellewether* had to be overhauled. Listen to
this: 'In autumn of 1759, the brave sloop was attacked by enemy
pirates in the West Indies, the crew and captain were killed, and
she was brought home in a sad state, barely afloat. Instead of giving
up on her, William Wilde had the little privateer brought to the
cove, where she was restored to better than her former condition
and lengthened by fifteen feet.'" Turning again to the painting,
I said, "I think *that's* what this shows. See? She's being repaired,
not built."

"You may be right." She'd side-eyed me as though my theory
was amusing.

"What?"

"You're just determined to get that old Seven Years' War in
there somehow, aren't you?"

I'd smiled. "I have a whole display space planned. You want
to see it?"

We had gone downstairs so I could walk her through the room
below my office, which, when we'd restored the kitchen to its
former size, would still leave space for an exhibit on the early life
of Captain Wilde; his childhood, and his family. And his sister.

And her doomed, beloved French officer—assuming I could find sufficient proof that he'd existed, that the legend of their love affair was true, so Sharon and the board would let me tell the story.

From the floor above, a muffled thud had interrupted us. It had been light, not loud, a little like a footstep, but although we'd stopped and listened, there had been no other sound. Malaika had dismissed it. "Someone walking on the roof," she'd said.

I'd been less sure.

When she had gone and I was left alone again, I'd climbed the stairs back to my office warily. I'd hovered in the doorway for a moment.

My desk had been just as I'd left it, all the papers in their semi-ordered piles, and through the window I'd seen Sam at work just as he'd been all morning, in his jeans and hooded sweatshirt. There'd been sunlight coming in my window, and the branches of the nearly leafless tree that grew beside it sent a lacy web of shadows slanting from the window ledge across the wall behind.

But the painting had been turned again so that its back was facing me, the way it had been earlier.

In the old part of the house, a door had slammed, and then another, and another, and I'd done a thing I almost never did: I swore, beneath my breath. In French, because the first swear words I'd learned in childhood in our house had been in French, and somehow they just always came more naturally. And then, because it struck me that the ghost, from all accounts, also spoke French, I'd kept speaking in that language and addressed him as I'd crossed the room to turn the painting so that it faced out again. "I like it this way, thank you."

It had been a fleeting moment of bravado, nothing more. I wasn't even sure why it had seemed important to me to assert myself against a force I couldn't even see, much less control, and I'd felt foolish and self-conscious as I'd sat behind my desk again, determined not to look up from my papers, and yet equally determined not to be a coward.

For a long and stretching moment there'd been silence in my office.

Then I'd heard a lightly muffled thud, not loud. A little like a footstep.

It had taken me at least a minute before I had summoned up the nerve to look, but I'd already known what I would see. The painting leaned where I had left it, up against the wall. Except its back had, once again, been turned toward me.

❦

At least the painting wasn't heavy. I was grateful for that now as I leapt back in time to let the yellow taxi speed on past while I watched safely from the sidewalk's edge. It was a busy Sunday afternoon, and though I'd found space in a garage up on East Twenty-Fourth Street, I still had a few blocks to walk to my cousin's apartment at Gramercy Park.

To be honest, I didn't mind. Gramercy Park was one of my favorite neighborhoods in New York City. Built in the nineteenth century, it had retained the grandeur and the elegance of that lost age, its brownstones and mansions and trees like an echo of Europe a stone's throw from midtown Manhattan.

At its center was the park itself, a stately green garden enclosed by a fence of high wrought-iron bars that allowed you to see what you couldn't enjoy, since the park was kept private for residents who paid a steep yearly key-rental fee. Even those who gained entry were restricted by the tidy iron posts strung with determined chains that kept people from straying off the neatly graveled paths into the garden borders.

The lowly little sparrows, in a show of class rebellion, took no notice, hopping where they had a mind to, chirping noisily, in company with pigeons who strolled freely in defiance of the militant gray squirrels on patrol, tails up and bristling, who tried to chase them off. One squirrel doing lookout duty from the high branch of a tree that overhung the sidewalk watched me with suspicion, but when I got close it scrabbled down the roughly channeled bark and took off like a shot.

It was quieter here. I could hear the occasional honk of a car horn from farther up Lexington or farther still on Park Avenue South, and a siren passed by in the distance, but in Gramercy Park life moved slowly and gracefully. People walked dogs and pushed strollers. They sauntered.

The towering maidenhair trees in a line down the sidewalk were starting to let go of their golden, fan-like leaves, as were the willow oaks with branches like a lacy web of copper, and every time the breeze picked up it sent a swirling fall of jewel-like color to the ground.

My cousin's building held court like a grand old lady at the east end of the square, its soaring white facade a true baroque revival masterpiece, ornamented with arches and heraldic shields and scrolls, guarded by gargoyles, the entryway protected by two pedestals that held medieval-looking suits of shining armor.

The doorman didn't recognize me even though I'd been here several times before. I wasn't that surprised. We shared a surname, but my cousin Wendy and I moved in different spheres entirely.

Our grandfathers were brothers, born in Amsterdam just after World War I. The next world war had sent them separate ways. My own grandfather, Werner, had escaped the Nazi occupation of his homeland and come over to America. His older brother, Anton, Wendy's grandfather, had stayed behind and worked for the resistance as an art thief, stealing back paintings the Nazis had looted. He'd been good at it. When the war ended he'd had a small room filled with pieces he'd worked to return to their owners, or—as was more often the case, sadly—their rightful heirs. His son Martin, Wendy's dad, had carried on this work, and in the process had discovered that he had an eye and passion for acquiring a collection of his own.

My father hadn't talked about his family so I hadn't known these stories as a child, but I had known my father's cousin Martin.

He had visited us in Toronto a few times, a handsome blond man with a much younger, very smart wife. And though Wendy, their only child, was six years older than me, on those visits we'd always been sent off together to play. She had been a good sport. We had played with my Barbie dolls, or we'd played Clue. And she'd once curled my hair with a curling iron, leaving an impressive accidental burn across my forehead that we'd hidden from the grown-ups. But the things that she had talked about were far outside my own realm of experience. Hers had been a world of riding lessons, tennis, summers in the Hamptons, trips to Paris and Vienna—wealth and privilege at a level I could barely comprehend.

"Can you imagine," I'd said to my father once, "living like that?" Then, too late, I'd remembered those photos of Bridlemere, and I had realized he probably could. That his life had most likely been just like that before he'd followed his conscience to Canada. But the whole realm of the rich still seemed foreign to me.

Wendy's apartment reminded me of the divide in our lives. It was so big it had its own foyer, with mirrors, a chandelier, plaster crown moldings, and old original herringbone parquet wood floors. The table at the center of the foyer held a vase with fresh-cut flowers, and in every direction were doors standing open to various hallways and rooms, so that as I came in I could see through the high-ceilinged living room, past the ornate plaster fireplace, to the bow windows that looked out on Gramercy Park.

Unsurprisingly, I had to sidestep suitcases.

"Are you going or coming?" I asked as we hugged. Wendy's hugs were like her—warm and genuine.

"Going," she told me. "To London, but not until later tonight, so the afternoon's all ours." She looked as pleased by that as she had looked when we had played as children, though in fairness Wendy never aged, not really. Today, in fitted jeans and a white broadcloth shirt, her long blond hair pulled back into a ponytail, she radiated youthfulness. I might have felt resentful but her unpretentious nature made her too completely likeable.

"I love this." She was looking at the narrow crate I'd set down on the floor. "I love the handles. Where did you buy it?"

"Sam made it."

"New man in your life?"

"No. At least, not in that way. He's the contractor restoring our museum building, meaning both of us work for the board of trustees, and that makes us coworkers, so no, our relationship's purely professional. I just broke up with one guy, I don't need to get mixed up with someone else. Not for a while."

"Wow."

"What?"

"Well, I have a friend in the FBI," she said, "and he says whenever a suspect gives really long answers to yes-or-no questions, you know you're not getting the absolute truth." She suppressed a smile, then asked, "Who did you break up with?"

"Tyler."

"Was he the one with you at Niels's funeral? You made the right choice, then. I thought he was kind of a jerk."

"Why was that?"

"Because," she said, "instead of looking after you he spent the whole time trying to convince me he could give me the best rate on my insurance for the gallery. I told him maybe now is not the time, you know, over my cousin's casket, but he didn't quit."

He wouldn't have. "You should have told me."

"Why? I'm a big girl. And you had other things on your mind, that day." Her eyes grew serious. "How are you doing now? How are your parents? How's Rachel?"

She'd brewed coffee. We sat in the kitchen and talked, catching up. And eventually we moved into the small room across from the kitchen, and opened the crate Sam had built for the painting.

This room was where Wendy worked. I could see why. A corner room, its windows faced in two directions, with a tall bow window like the ones that graced the living room, that also overlooked the beauty of the park. The hardwood floors had been left bare, and the furniture was minimal, the dominant piece being a long, solid block of a worktable right at the room's center. And while the walls in all the other rooms were filled with artwork, here there was a single painting hung with care—a path through a forest with shadows and soft morning sunlight on fallen trees, everything quiet and green.

"It's by Shishkin," Wendy told me, when she noticed I was looking at it. "Ivan Shishkin. First auction my dad ever took me to, when I was eight years old, he let me bid on that."

She'd inherited her father's eye and instinct for collecting, with a better head for business that had made her SoHo gallery a notable success. A lot of people looked at Wendy, at her privilege and her pretty face, and underestimated just how smart and competent she was. But in addition to her two degrees, she'd spent a lifetime learning from the experts in the field. She knew her stuff.

On the table she'd spread out a cushioning layer of felt covered by a thin, smooth sheet of polyester film to keep the painting and its frame from being damaged while she was inspecting it. Donning skintight plastic gloves that wouldn't snag on any surfaces, she passed an extra pair to me so I could help her lift the painting free of its padded case and lay it flat and faceup on the table.

I told her, "It's signed in the bottom right corner. 'J. Pigott,' it looks like." I'd searched the name but only found a British politician born two centuries too early to be useful.

Wendy didn't recognize the artist, either. "Let's see what Sebastian says." Taking her phone out, she snapped a quick picture and messaged it off somewhere. "He likes a challenge."

I took her again through the old painting's history—its provenance. How it had been in the Wilde House until being sold off in Arthur Wilde's auction, and how it had then been passed down through the Fishers until reaching Isaac. "But before that," I said, "before the auction, it's all family history. No documentation. It's not listed in the inventory made by Captain Wilde's wife."

"Well, no, it wouldn't be," said Wendy, looking closely at the painted sky. "Whoever painted this most likely wasn't even born when Captain Wilde was alive."

"What?"

"Of course, we'd need to put it under a microscope to be certain," she told me, "but I'm fairly sure this, right here, is cerulean blue, a Victorian pigment. It didn't exist until the 1860s. And if you look at the canvas… Here, this will be easier." Carefully turning the painting, she set it facedown so the back was exposed.

I had studied the back of that painting myself, many times, since the ghost in my office had gone to such trouble to turn it around. I'd been curious, and I had harbored a childish hope there might be something really important to see there—a mark or a label or some other clue that the ghost had been trying to get me to notice. But there had been nothing.

The back of the painting was plain. No one had ever covered it with paper or anything else, so there was only the simple rectangular back of the frame, and within that, the inset wooden stretcher over which the canvas had been fastened and secured. The back of the plain canvas, openly visible, had the patina of age.

But my cousin said, "See how the lines of the canvas are perfectly straight? That's machine made. A handwoven canvas would have more uneven lines."

I frowned, trying to remember when power looms had been invented.

Wendy wasn't sure of the exact date. "But with a machine-woven canvas, you're looking at a painting that's no earlier than the second quarter of the nineteenth century. So once again, Victorian. Although," she said, "it looks as if it's been relined, as if they've glued another piece of canvas to the back of it, to give it more support. That's sometimes done with paintings when they're really old. But this"—she tapped the canvas lightly with her fingers, like a drum—"this looks old, too. And it's a little loose."

She was taking out the tools she'd need to separate the wooden stretcher with its canvas from the outer frame so she could check the edges of the painting, when her phone received a message with a loud, triumphant ping.

"That was fast." Raising her eyebrows, she checked it. "Sebastian says it isn't 'Pigott,' it's 'Pigou.' John Pigou. 'Born in London in 1809, arrived in New York in June 1830,' it says, 'known for his gouache drawings of lively country scenes which were often turned into engravings.' It says his oil paintings are more rare, he didn't do them very often, and they were—oh, here you go: 'They were usually rendered as gifts for his circle of friends, which included'—and it lists a few more artists here, and some of *them* I've heard of—'and the celebrated poet Lawrence Wilde.'" She glanced up from her reading with a look of satisfaction. "So I'd say that's pretty helpful, then, for provenance."

An understatement if I'd ever heard one, and she knew it, too. I said, "You'll have to thank your friend Sebastian for me."

Smiling she said, "That would only encourage him." But she did make a reply to his message, and something about her smile moved me to ask:

"Have I met him?"

"Sebastian? Not through me, you haven't, and you can count yourself lucky. He's one of those good-looking men who knows just how good-looking he is, and he knows that he just has to smile at most women and they lose their minds, and you just want to smack him. He has this whole line of ex-girlfriends who all think he's God's gift, because, I mean, who would find fault with Sebastian St. Croix, right?"

I looked at her. "Wow. That's a really long answer," I said, "to a yes-or-no question."

She grinned. "Brat," she called me, and bent to her work. "Now, let's see what's going on here with this canvas." Lifting the stretcher free of the bigger gilt outer frame, she set it gently on its own on a clean section of the table. "Well, that's really weird. There are two...no, three...there are three layers of canvas here. What's going on with you?" she asked the painting, then turning to me said, "I'm going to take it right off of the stretcher, okay?"

It took time.

She'd been right. There were three separate layers of canvas—the painting itself on the front, and a plain liner right at the back, but the layer we found in between them was what left me speechless for more than a minute.

At last I recovered enough to ask Wendy, "Have you ever...?"

"No," she said. "Never."

There hadn't been any adhesive between the three layers, and now we knew why. Because fastened to that middle layer was a single sheet of paper, with a drawing on it. And that drawing, done in what looked to be graphite—"black lead pencil," as they used to call it—was an almost perfect copy of the painting.

Almost.

In the painting, there were three men working on the *Bellewether*—an older, white-haired man, a younger man, and one aged somewhere in between them, all dressed in the fashion typical of this part of America in the mid-eighteenth century.

But in this drawing, that third man was wearing a soft cap and wooden shoes and a distinctive waistcoat that, in combination, made me think that he might just be an Acadian.

And also in the drawing there were two men not included in the painting.

One, from his skin tone and features, appeared to be black. Tall and finely dressed, he also seemed to be directing what the other men were doing.

The second man wore a sharply cocked black hat pulled low over his eyes, and a coat that stood out from the clothing of the others by its lack of shading, which suggested it was white. The coat's sides were split at knee level, and the corners of its hem turned back and hooked up to allow for freer movement of his legs. And on his legs, incredibly, he wore *mitasses*—distinctive full-length leggings that, from how they fitted, looked to be of the same deerskin as the moccasins he wore upon his feet. I knew this uniform. I'd researched it enough when I was at the Hall-McPhail Museum. Catalogued the pieces of it that we'd had in our collection.

He was not a commonplace French soldier, but a soldier from the Troupes de la Marine.

A tiny chill that went beyond discovery climbed my spine. The ghost had been trying to tell me this, when he'd kept turning my painting around. He'd been trying to get me to look at the back. He had known this was there.

He had known.

Wendy's focus stayed fixed on the art itself. She said, "This might have been a sketch John Pigou made before starting his painting, but I don't know. This doesn't look like the same artist's hand, to me." She didn't try to pry the drawing loose from where it had been mounted, but she did turn its supporting sheet of canvas over, gently.

There was writing on the back.

And as I read the words, the tiny chill I'd felt became a shiver.

The sloop Bellewether, the penciled note read plainly, *being overhauled at Snug Cove in the last years of the French war. Drawn from life,* it said, *by Captain Wilde's sister.*

LYDIA

H ER FINGERS REJOICED AT the feel of the paper. This morning they'd been in the dirt, pulling turnips, and for these
days past they'd been pricked with her mending and wearied
with housework. They'd washed countless apples, pared apples,
cut apples for sauce, done it over and over until they had ached,
and had narrowly missed being scalded today on a potful of boil-
ing chicken. They'd earned the right, she thought, to hold the
portcrayon, as surely as she'd earned the right to steal this hour
for herself.

She might have chosen anything to be her subject, chosen any
corner of the property to sit and draw in solitude, but she'd come
here, to sit upon the fallen log that marked the boundary of the
beach, and draw the men at work upon the *Bellewether*.

They hadn't noticed her. To guard against the cold wind from
the bay she wore her gray wool hooded cape over her plain brown
petticoat and jacket, so there would have been no flash of color to
attract their eyes as she'd approached. There on her log she would
have blended with the hues of the late-autumn woods behind her,
and she'd had the perfect freedom to observe their interactions.

Mr. Ramírez was clearly in charge today. He and Joseph,
bonded by their skills and their experience, worked well with
one another, each man leading in his turn depending on which
task most closely fitted with his expertise. This afternoon, Mr.
Ramírez held the plans, and everybody looked to him.

She'd drawn him first. She'd tried to capture something of
his presence in the thin, dynamic lines before she'd moved on to
French Peter. He'd been easier to render, with his solid form and

simpler clothes. But there'd been nothing simple about drawing Mr. de Sabran.

New York had altered things. It was as if she had been given spectacles with lenses of a new and different color, and in looking through them now she found that everything was changed.

It had begun, she thought, that day at the de Joncourts' when Mr. de Sabran had been upstairs with his sergeant, and Captain Bonneau had sought to charm her in the parlor. That he'd been unsuccessful had amused the eldest daughter of the family—Jeanne, her name in French was, though she'd introduced herself as Jane—who had remarked, "He thinks quite highly of himself, Miss Wilde. You'll wound his pride."

"My pride is unassailable," Captain Bonneau had promised.

"Yes," had been Jane's smooth reply. "It is a failing common to your people."

He had laughed. "I think it shocks Mademoiselle Wilde to hear you offer me such insults."

Lydia had not intended anything to show upon her face, and she'd apologized. "It's only…I assumed you were both French."

"Ah. Yes, we are," Captain Bonneau said, "but my hosts, regretfully, are Huguenots, and Protestant. A different faith."

"A persecuted faith," said Jane. "My father's family fled from France, and lived in London for a time, then Ireland. And now here."

"You want to watch them very carefully," Captain Bonneau remarked to Lydia. He winked. "They will take over and control New York. Already one of them has been made governor."

She had not given much thought to the heritage of Governor DeLancey, even with the war, for it was widely known that he'd been born here in New York, and there were none to doubt his loyalty. But she had always looked upon the French as being all one people, so to be confronted lately with all these divisions into neutral French, Canadian, and Huguenot was something very new.

Captain Bonneau appeared to understand her thoughts, because he said, "A common language does not make a common people, sadly. But it also is a truth the man who is your enemy today may be your friend tomorrow. Mademoiselle de Joncourt, here—her grandfather and mine would have been fighting one another."

Jane de Joncourt nodded. "Very likely."

"And today," the captain said, "we sit here drinking coffee in this parlor, so they would be scandalized. But this, I think, is nicer. We move forward, yes? And so it will be, too, one day, with your side," he told Lydia, "and mine. You are too young, perhaps, to see this now. You cannot have much more than eighteen years…"

"I'm twenty."

"Twenty. Ah. Then you are maybe old enough. And *you*"— he turned to Jane de Joncourt—"may find you are sorry to be rid of me, when I have been exchanged."

"You have been saying that for far too long for me to harbor hope," said Jane.

He'd smiled in quick appreciation of her wit. "But this time it is sure to happen, now the English have Quebec, though how they mean to hold it is a mystery. Come the spring, when the supply ships come," he said, "we'll have it back again. And in the meantime, they will have the winter to endure."

Lydia had asked him, "Are winters in Quebec so very dreadful?"

He had answered with a sidelong glance. "I'd tell you stories, but I fear it would alarm the children."

The young boy whose name she had forgotten spoke up from his chair across the room. "*I'm* not a child." There was no accent to his English, making Lydia suspect that the de Joncourt children, just like Governor DeLancey, had been born here, in New York.

Captain Bonneau, whose English, even with its accent, was impeccable, assured the boy, "The winters in Quebec would frighten grown men as well. Ask the lieutenant, he will tell you. He'll have better stories anyway than mine."

The youngest daughter, gazing at the captain with adoring eyes, spoke up. "Your stories are the very best I've heard."

"You're kind to say so. But Lieutenant de Sabran is of the Troupes de la Marine, he'll have had many more adventures. He was probably," he told them, "raised by Indians."

The boy appeared excited by this prospect, and Bonneau advised, "You ask him, when he comes downstairs."

The boy had watched the stairs and waited with anticipation. He had waited even after Captain Wheelock had arrived, when chairs were shifted round and conversation in the parlor turned to news the English captain had brought with him from the Jerseys and the gossip of events he'd missed in New York while he'd been away.

But when Mr. de Sabran rejoined them, he hadn't looked to be in any mood for conversation. When he'd taken Captain Wheelock to the side and spoken privately, the tension of his stance betrayed a barely contained anger, and his face had stayed grim as he'd taken his seat. Lydia had silently been willing him to turn and see the boy who sat beside him, fairly squirming with impatience. And at last he had.

As always, she was struck by how that single act of smiling, even faintly, so transformed his face, and though the smile was for the boy and not for her, she felt its strong effect. It was an effort to refocus her attention on the captain, and she did not fully manage it. He, too, was watching Mr. de Sabran and the de Joncourt boy.

"He must have sons," he commented, "or brothers, at the least, to have such patience with the child."

It never had occurred to her that Mr. de Sabran might be a father. Have a wife. It gave her a peculiar sort of feeling to imagine it.

That feeling, these past days, had not diminished.

She pushed it aside now and focused on drawing his shoulders.

There was nothing simple about that task, either, because she remembered too well how those shoulders looked, filling the field of her vision, close up. She remembered the stone-solid feel of them under her hands when she'd suddenly found herself swept from the street's edge and into a doorway while Mr. de Sabran, his back to the rioting crowd, made his body a shield for her. Keeping her safe.

Later on, when the mob and its pitiful victim had moved down the street and the danger had gone, she'd been able to reason through what had just happened; to realize the name of the man that the crowd had been calling down curses and shame upon—Spencer—matched that of the man William had mentioned only that morning. The man who'd informed against those involved in the illegal trade. The man William and his merchant friends had decided to make an exhibit of, so none would dare to do likewise. All these things had been clear to her later.

But during those terrible moments, caught up in a whirlwind of panic and fear, her whole world had been tightly reduced to the calm sound of Mr. de Sabran's low voice speaking comfort, the feel of his body pressed warmly on hers, and the sheltering strength of those shoulders.

She could have drawn them now from memory. Could have closed her eyes and called to mind that same confusing swirl of feelings that were nothing she had felt before. When Moses held her close, it had been comfortable. But Moses had been Joseph's friend from childhood, she had known him all her life, and when he'd asked her if she'd marry him it had seemed a continuation of the course that had been set for both their families—she would marry Moses, and his sister Sarah would be Joseph's wife. It had seemed natural.

And Moses had been kind. He had laughed often, and worked hard, and he'd been honest, and she'd liked him.

Those who'd killed him at Oswego had not only stolen one of the strong pillars she had leaned on day to day, they'd also stolen what she might have built together with him in the years to come—a home, and children, and a life she knew would have been good.

But he had never smiled like Mr. de Sabran. He'd never made her feel off-balance just by looking in her eyes. And she had never trembled at his touch.

She'd fought those feelings all she could, while standing in that doorway. She had told herself the trembling was from fear, and nothing else. But it had been an unconvincing explanation, and her heart had not believed it.

Hearts were stubborn things, and often inconvenient.

Hers had traitorously softened when she'd seen the streaks of mud and filth across the back of his white coat, mute witness to the brutal blows he'd taken while protecting her. He'd done his best to clean it but the telling tracks remained, and she could faintly see them even now as she sketched the shape of the coat.

She was shading the lining when Violet's voice said at her shoulder, "You've made him too tall."

The pencil skipped across the paper before Lydia regained control. "You startled me."

"I wasn't trying to be quiet." Violet held up one fold of her heavy skirts in evidence. "You need to pay more attention." She sat on the same log. "And Mr. Ramírez is not that tall."

Lydia studied her drawing and privately disagreed, but she knew Mr. Ramírez had done or said something of late that had made Violet angry—she'd seen the way Violet's jaw set when he passed and how Violet avoided his eyes—and not wanting to fan those flames Lydia only said, "I'm out of practice."

"You could make your living drawing, if you needed to. My mother said so."

"I suspect she only said it to be kind."

That drew a smile from Violet. "Mama never wasted time pretending kindness. Every word she spoke, she meant."

And Lydia, remembering, smiled, too. "I miss your mother."

"So do I. Though I suppose His Highness ought to count his blessings she's not here. She would have slipped some poison in his food by now."

Lydia realized how thoughtless she'd been to leave Violet with Mr. de Brassart alone. "Did he bother you?"

"He only has to be breathing to bother me."

"I'm sorry. I didn't think. I should have stayed with you."

Violet, although she was younger than Lydia, sent her a look that had lived lifetimes longer. "It isn't your business," she said, "to look after me. I can look after myself."

The bay was beginning to freeze at its edges. The ice lay in thin clinging sheets on and over the rocks at the edge of the shoreline, veined with solid threads of white against the half-transparent surface, like the web of unseen spiders weaving frost.

Thoughts of Silas rose darkly in Lydia's mind and she pushed them aside. "Did your mother really try to poison Uncle Reuben?"

"If she did, she didn't get the dose right." Violet looked to where the men were working. For a minute she was silent, then she said, "The Lord took her too soon, that's what I tell Him every Sunday, but I feel her with me sometimes. Like He lets her come back down awhile and be with me. Do you ever feel your mother?"

Lydia's pencil stilled. "Yes," she said, quietly. "Sometimes I do."

Later that evening, when supper was finished, she took up her mending and curled herself into her mother's old chair with its leather seat slung in the low X-shaped frame like a welcoming lap. She could almost imagine her mother's arms holding her, here in this room with the warmth of the fire and the light of the candles, the wind rising hard at the glass of the window.

The men were still sitting around the long table in cross conversations, her brother and Mr. Ramírez discussing the length of the *Bellewether*'s deck, while her father and Mr. de Brassart debated the merits of some play by Shakespeare, and Mr. de Sabran sat back and observed.

All the voices ran into and over each other and blended like billowy waves folding into the sea, and she struggled to stay on the surface while all of those waves with the troubles they carried went by. "Feel them passing?" her mother asked, rocking her gently.

Except they weren't passing. They bore her relentlessly down like great weights on her shoulders until she was sinking.

And then in place of her mother's arms she felt the strong ones of Mr. de Sabran, protecting her as they had done in New York, and it suddenly wasn't so terrible, drowning. She held him and drifted down into the dark.

JEAN-PHILIPPE

THEY HAD FORGOTTEN HER.

He'd had to rise and come into this room before he could believe it. In the faint light of the fading embers of the fire he could make out her sleeping figure in the chair close by the window, where she'd sat when they had finished with their evening meal.

She'd been there when her brother had excused himself and gone up to his room. She'd been there when her father and de Brassart had retreated to the parlor to—according to de Brassart—find some passage in a book. And she'd been there when Ramírez had removed himself as well to talk to Violet in the kitchen.

Jean-Philippe, at supper's end, had stayed exactly where he was. He'd sat in silence, searching all the corners of his memory for a time when he'd last felt so deep a peace. It was unwise. No good would come of it. A belly full of homely food, a warm fire burning on the hearth, a woman he could share it with—such things were past his reach, just like the swirls of smoke in battle that lured soldiers to pursue them, wasting musket fire on phantoms that weren't real.

And yet he'd sat and let that feeling settle in his mind, so he could carry it away with him when he had gone. An extra piece of armor.

Until she'd begun to dream, and stir, and since he had not wished for her to wake and find him sitting watching her, he'd risen very quietly and gone to his own chamber. That had been over two hours ago.

He knew the nightly rhythm of the household. Lying in his bed, he'd listened. First Ramírez, bidding Violet a good night, had gone upstairs. De Brassart, not long after, had come in and, having fussed for several minutes in his preparations, finally settled and began to snore. Next Violet, finished with her work, had run with lighter footsteps up the narrow back stairs. For the pattern to play out in perfect order, the next person to ascend should have been Lydia.

Except she hadn't.

He'd heard Monsieur Wilde's familiar firm and heavy footsteps climb the stairs, and then the house sank into slumber as though everything was in its place.

And Jean-Philippe had realized they'd forgotten her.

He didn't know how that was even possible. If she were his, he'd never overlook her; never fail to notice everything she did. If she were his...

He killed the thought before it had a chance to fully form. They were divided by a war. Soon he'd be back on its front lines and she would carry on her life here and the world would turn as if they'd never met. That was reality, as was the fact the room was growing cold. This was no place for her to spend the night.

He touched her shoulder. Shook it lightly. Said her name. She did not wake. And then, after considering his options, he reached down and gently lifted her and carried her upstairs.

Had he been able to stop time, he might have stopped it then. The weight of her within his arms, the warmth of her against his chest, the softness of her breath against his shirt—these were sensations that he wanted to remember. He climbed slowly, set his feet with care, and told himself it was because he did not wish to rouse the household, but he knew that was untrue, just as he knew he'd have to rouse at least one person.

Taking her into her room would risk her reputation and his own. He'd have to wake her father.

Monsieur Wilde, to his relief, slept lightly. Jean-Philippe had barely knocked upon his chamber door before it opened. Moonlight slanted through the window just behind and made the older man a silhouette in shadow while illuminating Lydia, and Jean-Philippe searched through the English words he'd learned to find the right ones to explain. "She sleeps," he said, "downstairs." And so there could be no misunderstanding, added, "In the chair."

The pause that followed made him wonder if he'd been mistaken in his phrasing, but at last Monsieur Wilde nodded and stepped out and motioned Jean-Philippe to follow him across the landing to the other bedchamber. The moonlight here, though not as strong, was still enough to show him where to lay her on the bed. But as he lowered her, she wrapped her arms around his neck and clung to him more closely. Forced to bend, he did not mind the time it took to set her down and cautiously extract himself from her possessive hold, but when he drew the blankets over her and straightened he was glad he could not see her father's face, and that they neither of them knew the other's thoughts.

✑

Next morning after breakfast, Monsieur Wilde addressed him briefly, indicating that de Brassart should translate the words.

"It truly is a most peculiar language," said de Brassart, as they watched the older man walk off toward the barn. "He talks of being 'in' your debt when clearly what he means to say is that he has a debt to you, and even then there is no way to know if he is speaking in the sense of obligation or of money." He was prying, seeking details.

Jean-Philippe did not enlighten him. He'd understood the sentiment enough, as he had understood Monsieur Wilde's short nod, one man to another. And if Lydia—who earlier had merely said good morning in her normal way—had not been told about last night's events, then no one else had any need to know.

De Brassart waited for an explanation. When none came, he shrugged and turned his collar up against the wind that shook a swirling fall of leaves loose from the trees. "What's that they're building, there?"

"A hog pen."

"But they keep no hogs."

"A neighbor's bringing two this morning." It was satisfying knowing that his growing understanding of the language and his daily conversations with Pierre not only made him less dependent on de Brassart, but at times better informed.

"Ah. More payment, is it?"

"Probably." These past weeks they'd seen evidence of how important Monsieur Wilde's skills were to this community, as several people brought their payments for the carpentry he'd done for them this year.

De Brassart said, "It's a provincial way of doing things."

"It's practical. He lays a floor for somebody, or puts up shelves, or hangs a door, and in return they bring him winter wheat, or ewes, or hogs. A fair exchange."

"But if they simply gave him money, he could buy the things he needs."

"He needs hogs," said Jean-Philippe, and raised one shoulder in an echo of de Brassart's shrug. "This way is easier."

De Brassart showed no interest in continuing the argument. He coughed, and watched the mist of his breath briskly dance away. "I don't know how you stand this weather."

Jean-Philippe, who thought the day was fine, glanced upward at the sun that had now broken through the clouds, but didn't offer a reply. De Brassart was determined to be out of sorts today, having been "driven" from the house—as he described it—by the women making candles in the kitchen. While the pungent scent of tallow rendering took Jean-Philippe back to his childhood, it was clear de Brassart didn't share that same nostalgia, leaving Jean-Philippe to wonder how and where he had been raised, that he had so little connection to the things of common life.

And if he didn't like the smell of candle making, he'd find even less to like about the smell of hogs.

The cart that carried them arrived just before midday. Joseph had gone down with Ramírez to the ship already and Pierre had stayed at home so it was left to Jean-Philippe and Monsieur Wilde to load the stubborn animals into their pen, while the young, round-faced man who'd brought them leaned against the top rail of the fence and offered his advice before remembering he'd brought them something else besides.

The conversation was too quick for Jean-Philippe to follow but he caught the words "from Henry" and he knew that Monsieur Wilde's nephew Henry kept the post office at Millbank, so it was no surprise to see the letter and the newspaper.

He *was* surprised though when Monsieur Wilde handed him the letter, still unopened. "It's for you."

It was from Captain Wheelock, and enclosed a second letter in his sister's careful handwriting. She was a careful woman. She'd have known her letter to him would be read by others, so she told him only that their mother had arrived before the battle and the two of them were safe, and that the hospital itself, although now occupied by English troops, was still allowed to tend the wounded officers and men of their own side. Their cattle and their wheat had all been seized, she wrote, so how long they'd be able to subsist she did not know, but she put everything in God's hands and hoped he would do the same, and sent her love. *Our mother will not tell you*, she had written him in closing, *but she lights a candle every day for Angélique, so if you find forgiveness in your heart, I pray it one day guides you home.*

He read the letter quietly a second time and folded it deliberately before he turned again to Captain Wheelock's. While the captain spoke in flawless French, it seemed he either could not write it or preferred to dictate, for this letter had been written not in Wheelock's hand but one more flowing and without the same precision.

Sir, I have this day received from General Amherst letters carried from Quebec, and am enclosing one addressed to you. I also write to send you news...

It was a longer letter than the one from Athanase. He was still finishing it when de Brassart clapped him on the shoulder, interrupting.

"The best news!" De Brassart's smile was broad. "Look, Monsieur Wilde just showed me here in this *New York Gazette*, the second page. It says that General Amherst gives his orders for those prisoners who are of your militia or your Troupes de la Marine to come immediately to New York to join those of our regiments preparing now to go to Albany to be exchanged. It's a cartel!" He said the word in joyous tones. "And if they send our men, that means we'll be exchanged as well, so finally—"

"No," said Jean-Philippe. "We won't." He handed Wheelock's letter over, as the proof. "We won't be part of the exchange."

De Brassart frowned down at the letter. "What's this?"

"Cartels must exchange officer for officer, and rank for rank. They have room," he explained, "for four lieutenants only. And those places have been filled."

"No." With a firm shake of his head, refusing to accept the truth, de Brassart said, "Impossible." He turned away and took a step and then turned back and threw the letter to the ground, together with the newspaper, and stomped them with his foot. "It is an outrage! I will write the captain. I will protest!"

"You'll control your temper," Jean-Philippe advised him coldly, "before you upset Mademoiselle Wilde."

He was well aware Monsieur Wilde and the neighbor stood just steps from them beside the hog pen, looking on with wariness, but right now he concerned himself with nobody but Lydia. She'd come out by the kitchen door as he'd been handing Wheelock's letter to de Brassart, and he'd seen her start across the clearing, carrying a bucket.

But she'd stopped dead when de Brassart had begun to yell.

"Control yourself," said Jean-Philippe, more low.

De Brassart was in no mood to be reasonable. "You're not my superior. You're not even my equal. Don't you ever give me orders." In contempt, he spat and headed for the house, marching past Lydia, who held her ground as he went by.

The newspaper and letter had been trampled into muddy soil. Before the wind could shake them loose and scatter them against the fence posts, Jean-Philippe bent silently and picked them up. He straightened, still in silence.

Then to Monsieur Wilde he said, slowly in English, "I am sorry. He is…" Words escaped him, although there were many he might wish to use in his own language.

Monsieur Wilde suggested one in English. "Angry."

"Angry, yes."

She'd reached them now, her bucket, full of kitchen peelings for the hogs, still gripped within her hands. She asked her father something and he answered her and although it was difficult for Jean-Philippe to follow what was said, he heard the word "exchanged" and realized that, not knowing French, she and her father would not know he and de Brassart were not part of this cartel.

It would be hard for them to learn the truth, he thought.

She looked at him, and he could see her eyes were guarded. "I am sorry," he told her directly, "we are not exchanged."

Her eyebrows drew together faintly. "*Not* exchanged?"

He was not sure if "yes" or "no" was proper in this instance, so he simply said it over. "Not exchanged."

"Oh."

As he watched, incredibly, her eyes grew slightly happier. He held that knowledge even when she'd looked away.

And in that moment, when the wind rose up and struck him sharply, it seemed only half as cold as it had seemed before.

CHARLEY

I COULDN'T FEEL MY FINGERS. An hour ago the sun had been warm
and my coat felt so stifling I'd taken it off, but the blue sky,
crisscrossed with the thin trails of jet planes, was being overtaken
by a solid bank of cloud that rolled in stealthily from the north-
west. It raised a chilling wind that crept up on me, softly; wrapped
around me. By the time I felt the cold it had already penetrated
deeply and was hard to chase away again.

"Here." Sam, coming up beside me, put a cup of takeout
coffee in my hand, to match the one he carried.

"Thanks. You shouldn't spend your money, though," I told
him, even as I wrapped my hands around the warmth. "We have
a coffee maker in the kitchen."

"It makes something. But I wouldn't call it coffee." He'd been
taking down the scaffolding. The roof and outside walls were
finished, all the windows had been re-installed, and Willie had
the chimney done down to the shingles, so starting on Monday
the work would move indoors. He asked me, "How's he doing?"

He meant Santa Claus, who sat not far away from us, in an old
sleigh that Frank had borrowed from one of his farmer friends.
We didn't have the reindeer to go with it, but the children who
had lined up for a turn to have their picture taken didn't seem
to mind. And Santa—Gianni's uncle Tony, who looked the part
perfectly, down to his naturally bushy white beard—was giving his
performance everything he had. "He's doing great. He's already
said he'll come back next year. Except next year, when all the
restoration work is done, I think we'll do it by the fireplace in the
kitchen. Where it's warm."

"I kind of like the sleigh." He was better dressed than I was for the cold, a long-sleeved layer underneath his flannel work shirt, and his gloves tucked in his tool belt. "It's a good fundraiser."

I couldn't take the credit. "It was Harvey who suggested it."

"You've got him on your side, I think."

"I'm learning how to manage him. He likes to be the center of attention. I'm just finding ways to channel that."

"Like having him do that TV thing."

"Exactly." I was starting to feel warmer now, not only from the coffee but because his body blocked the wind. "He loves wearing that Revolutionary War costume, and he's better connected around here than I am, so it was a win-win. We've already had people calling to offer donations because of that interview."

We'd also put up lists—in Gianni's deli, Lara's store, and in the library—of items we were trying to acquire, and the response had been encouraging. The Sisters of Liberty might have refused us their grant of support, but the community seemed ready to step up and do their part.

"And," I told Sam, "I finally heard back from that museum in New Jersey, saying I could come pick up the Spanish chair."

"It took him long enough."

"It was his assistant who called, actually. I don't think the director himself really wanted to loan us the chair. I think he just got tired of me calling to ask. He knew I wasn't going to give up."

"Nothing wrong with knowing what you want," said Sam, "and waiting for it."

It was tempting to read something more into that comment, but I forced myself to take it at face value. Nothing in his voice had changed, or his expression, and he wasn't even looking at me. He was watching Uncle Tony Claus, who at that moment by coincidence was saying nearly the same thing to the two wide-eyed children on his knees.

"Keep wishing hard, kids, and be patient, and you'll get good things on Christmas morning." Sage advice he followed with some light extortion. "And if you want *really* good things, make sure you leave me cookies."

I smiled, and glanced at Sam as the photographer snapped one last picture of the kids before they were released to run around the clearing, getting messy in their Sunday best. "Long Island Santa."

"Hey," he told me. "We have our priorities." We watched the next kids have their turn. "When are you going to get the chair?"

"Well, ideally I'd have liked to go tomorrow, get it done before the weather changes, only my car's not big enough. I'd have to borrow Dave's van, and he needs it tomorrow to go to an auction."

Sam raised his coffee cup, his eyes still on the kids, one shoulder lifting in a careless shrug. "Good thing you know a guy who's got a truck."

༒

"Look at you!" Gianni grinned approvingly as I came through the living room. Rachel had been having trouble sleeping. She was still in her pajamas, hair unwashed, but Gianni had her settled on the sofa for a day of watching movies on TV.

"She's going out with Sam," said Rachel.

"I am not," I told them, "going out with Sam. He's taking me to pick up something in his truck."

"He's taking her," said Rachel, "to New Jersey."

Gianni asked, "Where in New Jersey?"

She told him, and he whistled. "That'll take you a couple of hours."

"I know," I said. "That's why we're leaving now." I used the microwave door as a mirror while fixing my loose earring. I didn't think I looked particularly fancy. Sure, I'd maybe taken more care with my hair this morning, and I'd worn a nicer sweater. And I'd put on makeup.

"Here he is," said Rachel, as we heard the truck's door slam. I had my shoes on by the time he reached the side door.

He'd brought Bandit, who wagged once at me and made a beeline for the sofa, where he curled between Gianni and Rachel, right at home.

I checked my pockets. Rachel held her hand up with my cell phone in it. Cleared her throat.

"Oh. Right. Thanks. Bye."

"Have fun, guys." Gianni winked. Ignoring him, I stepped onto the porch and locked the door and turned to Sam.

He said, "Nice sweater."

"Thanks." I hadn't blushed since high school.

"Got a coat?"

"I'm fine."

"How's Rachel doing?"

"She's been better. It's good she'll have Bandit today."

He walked around with me to open the passenger door of the truck. "Her boyfriend seems to look after her okay."

"He's not her boyfriend. At least, that's what she keeps telling me."

"He acts like her boyfriend. You in? Watch the coffee, there. Yours is the one with the sticker." He closed my door and came around to get behind the wheel. "The traffic looks good so I'm thinking we just take the Belt to Verrazano and across that way. Okay with you?"

"Okay with me."

It was a good day for a drive. I liked this season of the year, when fall changed into winter.

The trees had grown more bare now and the colors of their leaves were lost, the smudge of branches on the hillside faded to a quiet mix of brown and gray and burnt sienna, marked in places by the skeletal white outline of a sycamore. I watched the trees, Sam watched the road, I drank my coffee.

Given my awareness of the man beside me, I'd have thought the silence in this closed space would feel awkward, but it didn't. It felt comfortable. There was just something peaceful about him that put me at ease.

There was just something. Malaika had used those same words when she'd talked about falling for Darryl. *Sometimes the right man,* she'd said, *just sneaks up on you.*

I was still pondering this when the traffic on the Belt Parkway slowed, then crawled and stopped and crawled again to show we'd hit construction or an accident. Sam steered us off at the next exit and began to navigate a grid of unfamiliar streets without a map or GPS. I was impressed.

He said, "Don't worry, I grew up here. I know where I'm going."

"Oh. So this is Brooklyn?"

"Yeah." His sideways glance was curious.

I said, "Malaika mentioned it."

"Just randomly?"

"She also said your father was an ironworker."

"Yeah, he was. My dad was a connector. That's one of the guys who climbs up on the beams, you know—bolts them together. He died when I was ten."

"I'm sorry."

"That's okay," he said. "I don't mind talking. Keeps him close."

It turned out both Sam's grandfathers were ironworkers also, but from two different communities—one up by Montreal, the other just west of Niagara Falls. Historically, as Sam explained, the Mohawk territories in Quebec had been more closely allied to the French than British, while the opposite was true for Mohawks in the province we now called Ontario. "I got a bit of every-thing," he told me. "Mohawk, English, French, Oneida, Scottish, Catholic, Protestant—you name it. Keeps life interesting."

His mother's parents were both residential school survivors. "My mom's dad had this big scar, here, from being beaten. Wouldn't ever talk about it."

I'd known nothing about residential schools until a royal commission in Canada held public hearings that brought many hard stories into the light, how for over a hundred years many Indigenous children had been taken from their own families and put into boarding schools where the objective was, as the founder of one such school in Pennsylvania put it, to "kill the Indian" in the child. Their clothes were taken from them, and their hair was cut; they were forbidden to speak their own language, often even separated from their siblings at the same schools; forced to labor for their "teachers," and subjected to abuse both physical and sexual that left them, if not dead, forever traumatized. From watching the survivors talk I knew their scars were carried on the inside too and passed down through the generations.

"So when he came back from the Korean War, he traded in his helmet for a hardhat and took Grandma down to Buffalo, off reservation, so their kids wouldn't ever have to go to residential school. That's where my mom and dad met—Buffalo. He brought her back here. *His* mom ran a boardinghouse for ironworkers. Used to be a lot of Mohawks living here in Brooklyn."

"And so you were born here?"

"Yeah. My mom," he told me. "She's a nurse. She got a job here at the hospital, and Dad tried not to travel too much with his work, and his mom helped look after us. My sister and me."

"Is she older or younger, your sister?"

"Younger. She's moved back up to my mom's home community. So did my mom's parents, when they retired. And Pete and my mom live in Rochester."

"Who's Pete?"

He smiled. "My stepdad."

I thought back and tried to keep everyone organized. "The one who hangs the new doors for your grandmother?"

"He used to. Yeah." He turned a corner, brought us back out onto the Belt Parkway with the Verrazano-Narrows Bridge in view. "My dad's mom didn't like Pete to begin with. Didn't like him taking my dad's place. But he's a hard guy not to like. He kind of grew on her."

Sam's stepfather, a carpenter, had met Sam's mom when he had needed stitches in his hand and she was on shift at the hospital. They'd married two years later. As a teenager, Sam worked construction with Pete in the summers, and got interested in that, and earned his university degree in architecture before he decided he liked building structures better than designing them. And so he'd gotten certified as a construction manager and started his own business.

"Why in Millbank?"

"I don't know." He gave it thought. "I guess it feels right. Of the places I feel I belong, Millbank's the one that fits me best."

I wondered what that felt like, feeling you fit perfectly somewhere.

"Besides," he said, "Malaika keeps on finding projects for me."

We were on the bridge, now. Its high towers and suspension cables made me dizzy if I looked up, but the view was something else.

It was a shame to leave it and cross onto Staten Island, but we made good time from there. We stopped for lunch near Princeton and arrived at the museum in New Jersey right on time, although I had the strong impression the director would have been a whole lot happier if we'd been late, or better yet, not come at all.

He was a tall and well-dressed man who looked like someone who still carried proper handkerchiefs. And used them.

His assistant, on the other hand, was just as she had sounded on the phone—young, nice, and ready to be helpful. She had the Spanish chair set out and waiting for us in the entry hall.

It was a gorgeous piece. I'd also seen these called Campeche chairs, but I'd never seen one of this age before. Viewed from the side, its mahogany frame had been shaped like a smooth, rounded X that supported a long piece of dark-brown tooled leather to form both the back and the seat, like an early recliner. The leather with age had acquired a lovely patina, and most of the brass tacks that held it in place seemed to still be there. Both the chair's arms were intact, curved, and graceful, and worn at their edges from use, and the crest above the leather at the chair back had been carved to make a darkly gleaming seashell.

I could see why the director here had not been keen to part with it, not even as a loan.

Which made me wonder why he seemed so quick to help us wrap and load it in Sam's truck. All I could think was that it must be us, and not the chair, he couldn't wait to see the back of. Gingerly he shook Sam's hand, then mine, and turned without so much as a goodbye. He'd nearly made it back to the front door of his museum building when his young assistant told us, "Don't mind him. He might seem grumpy, but he's actually relieved."

I saw him stop, and start to turn again toward us, and his eyes revealed a blend of disbelief and resignation.

His assistant, smiling, friendly, remained unaware. "He was a little worried," she confided, "that you'd ask him for the sword."

❧

It was like setting up for the best kind of show-and-tell. I'd laid everything out on the dining room table so all the trustees could see clearly.

"So, let's start with this," I said, meaning the drawing, now protected and supported in its storage box. My cousin had authenticated it and given it a valuation that, together with the painting's, had made Isaac Fisher very happy. "It says right here, clear as day, that this was by Benjamin's sister—by Lydia Wilde—when the *Bellewether* was being overhauled in the last year of the Seven Years' War. And it's a documented fact that the *Bellewether* was indeed overhauled, after a pirate attack in the fall of 1759. So that all fits. Now this"—I showed them, holding up an open reference book with brightly colored illustrations—"is the uniform the man here in this drawing's wearing. See? Same leggings, everything. Which makes him from the Troupes de la Marine, a French Canadian. An officer. And *this*"—I held the button up, the one

I'd found on-site—"would be consistent with the buttons that his uniform would have."

I paused and looked around to make sure everyone was following. They were, though Sharon wore a frown.

Her disapproval energized me. "So," I said, "I think we can agree that a French officer was living here at the same time the legend says he was. And so was Lydia."

I let that sink in, waited for the nodding heads, before I carried on.

I'd kept the sword in the long wooden storage box that the director from New Jersey had produced it in. He'd really loved it, and I knew that it had wounded him to have to show me, let alone to give in to my logical persuasion that it properly belonged in our collection, not his own. But to his credit, he had kept it in immaculate condition. When I opened the box now to show my trustees, the silver of the hilt gleamed in the room's light and I heard the gasps. It satisfied me knowing the effect was what I'd hoped it would be.

"Wow," Tracy said.

Harvey leaned in closer, looking at the words inscribed along the blade. "That's French, right?"

With a nod, I gave him the translation: "'Draw me not without cause; sheathe me not without honor.' Now, that's a pretty common motto for those times. It shows up on a lot of swords, both French and Spanish, but bear with me, because this one has a name." With gloved hands, carefully, I turned the sword so they could read it. "See there? 'De Sabran.' Now, in the inventory made by Captain Wilde's wife, she wrote... Frank, can you just read the third to the last listing there, on page fourteen?"

He cleared his throat dramatically. "'My brother-in-law's sword, with silver hilt, marked *de Sabran*.'"

I said, "The first time that I read that, I assumed she meant the maker's mark. But look, the maker's mark is here, in this cartouche." I showed them. "So then de Sabran would likely be the name of the sword's owner."

Sharon interjected, "Likely. But not definitely."

"Joseph Wilde," I said, "was Captain Wilde's older brother. So, to Captain Wilde's wife, he'd have been her brother-in-law, right? And he's the one the legend says killed Lydia's French officer."

Eve followed Sharon's lead, though her voice lacked the same belligerence. "Well?"

I took a breath. And played my ace.

"This note," I said, and set it down, "came with the sword when it was sold at auction in the 1800s."

Signed by Lawrence Wilde, the poet—and the grandson of our Captain Benjamin—the note read: *This belonged to Joseph Wilde, who took it from the officer imprisoned at Snug Cove.*

Everybody read the note by turn, and Frank said, "I'll be damned."

When Sharon looked about to argue, Harvey shut her down. "You said when she found proof, then we'd discuss it," he reminded her. "And I'd say that's pretty convincing proof." Looking across at Malaika, he asked, "Can we have a new vote on it?"

"Sure. Make a motion."

He made it with confidence. "I move we broaden our mandate to add in the story of Lydia Wilde and the French guy."

"I second," said Don.

With a faint smile, Malaika asked who was in favor, and only two hands stayed down—Sharon's and Eve's.

"Motion passed."

Frank leaned over and patted my shoulder and winked. "Merry Christmas," he said.

⤳

It was never going to be an easy holiday, this first year without Niels.

I knew that going in, but I still tried. I did the things we'd always done. I went and bought a Christmas tree and strung the lights and decorated. I switched my car radio to the all-Christmas-carols station, watched the TV specials and the movies that we always watched, and tried, if not to find the feeling for myself, to conjure it for Rachel.

She was having a hard time and sinking deeper into sadness; sleeping poorly, eating worse, and crying when I wasn't supposed to see. If Gianni had been there it might have helped, but he and Mrs. Bonetti had gone down to Florida to gather with their family at her sister's house. "Away from all this snow that's coming," Mrs. Bonetti had said with feeling when she'd dropped off a tin of her chocolate mostaccioli cookies. "You can take those with you when you go spend Christmas with your parents in Toronto. And next year, I'll make you some nice braciole for your Christmas dinner."

Their house next door looked lonely with the lights off when I came home in the evenings. And I noticed, driving down the shore road, that there were no Christmas lights at Bridlemere. My grandmother must also have been gone, or else not in the mood for celebration.

At the Wilde House, though, Malaika made us all draw names and do a Secret Santa gift exchange. "Nothing expensive," she had warned. "And Willie, put your name in there. And you, too, Sam. You're family."

I had hoped I might draw Sam's name, but I drew Rosina's, which was fine. I bought a pair of earrings for her, in the pink and yellow tones she liked. And while I didn't know for certain, I suspected it was Lara who drew my name, because my gift was a scarf that looked an awful lot like those from the last shipment I had helped her to unpack the week before, at her boutique. But when we'd given all our gifts and I went back upstairs to work, I found a narrow gift bag on my desk, the tag marked *Charley* in a sure and slanting hand that looked familiar.

Opening the door between my office and the old part of the house, I told Sam, "Hey."

He turned from where he'd gone back to his own work on the paneling.

I held the gift bag up. "What's this?"

"Looks like a present."

"I already got my Secret Santa gift."

He shrugged and told me, "Santa does what Santa does."

The wine bottle inside the bag had an expensive label. "Santa shouldn't have," I said. "But thank you."

"Guess he thought you needed it."

I really liked his smile. I hadn't realized how much I'd come to rely on it—on him—until he, too, was gone; until he'd packed his truck and driven up to spend the holidays in Rochester, with his mother and stepfather. He'd stopped to pick up Bandit at our house before he left, and when I'd walked out on the porch with him he'd hugged me. Quick and casual, but it took all my self-control and concentration not to hug him back too hard or hold him longer than I should, when all I really wanted was to lean on him and tell him all my troubles.

I could do that with my parents, I thought.

I was looking forward to our time up in Toronto, lapsing back into the less demanding role of daughter, being able to pass off at least a piece of my responsibility to someone else. My mom would cut my sandwiches and talk with me while we washed dishes and my dad would have me help him with a jigsaw puzzle, and at nights I'd sleep in my old room. It would be restful. I might even get to read a book.

And then a big low-pressure system started moving over the Atlantic, with the promise of becoming a nor'easter. And my phone rang.

"No," my mother said, "it's just not worth the risk. They're saying that it's going to be bad, and we don't want you driving in that."

"So we'll fly."

But I had known she wouldn't let that happen, either. Even if we could get tickets at a price we could afford, and even if the planes were flying, they would worry. And the last thing my dad needed, with his healing heart, was worry.

"We can send the gifts," she promised. "We can Skype."

"Not if the power's out." I heard the gloomy tone in my own voice and knew that it would make her feel bad, so I forced myself to sound more cheerful. "But you're right. It's fine."

It isn't really Christmas anyway, I felt like adding.

As it was, the forecasted nor'easter didn't even come at Christmas. Tracking slowly up the coast it kept the weather just as miserable as Rachel's mood, and finally slammed ashore on New Year's Day. It struck with vengeance. I could feel the house shake under the relentless gusts of wind that rattled glass and shrieked at every window, blotting out the world behind a blinding swirl of snow so thick I thought we might be buried.

We lost our electricity, and when the worst had passed and I could venture out to check the damage, I saw why.

Two trees had been knocked down in the backyard. It was a miracle they'd fallen in the way they did, and not toward the house, but one had taken down the power lines. The other one had landed squarely on my brother's shed and now the whole yard was a mess of branches, broken shingles, shattered siding, and scattered debris encased in ice and hardened snow that came up to my knees.

I didn't cry. Not then. I took one look at Rachel's face when I came in, and knew I had to hold myself together so she wouldn't fall apart. I tried to focus on the positive. "Your father never liked that shed," I said. "At least now we can get a new one."

She tried to smile. I saw her make the effort. But it was too much. She turned and went upstairs and went into her room and got in bed and pulled the blankets up and stayed there.

After spending all the next day on the phone in fruitless calls to our insurance company, I was strongly tempted to go join her. But instead, I took the wine that Sam had given me, and found myself a glass and, sitting at the kitchen table, hitched my chair close to my brother's.

"See?" I told him as I filled my glass. "Look how much fun

you're missing. You should be here." Unexpectedly, my eyes filled. "You should be here," I repeated, but the words this time came quietly and hurt my throat. I took a drink.

The bottle was half-empty by the time I fell asleep.

❦

I woke up the next morning to a sky that promised sunshine, and a digital alarm clock that was blinking to announce we once again had electricity, which seemed enough encouragement to get up, pull on jeans and an old sweatshirt, and go down to brew a very badly needed cup of coffee.

I was standing at the sink to fill the kettle, looking out the kitchen window, when I saw the dog bounce past, a joyful, flop-eared burst of movement in the drifted snow.

I put the kettle down. Turned off the tap.

Outside, the snow was deep enough to work itself between my boot tops and my jeans as I walked down the slope of our backyard. I felt it soaking through my socks. I didn't mind.

Sam straightened, having gathered up a load of splintered siding. "Morning."

He'd been working for a while already, I could tell. He'd cleared a section maybe six feet square, and worn a deep track through the snow from walking back and forth to where he'd parked his truck. It had a snowplow on the front. He'd cleared the driveway.

Bandit deftly changed course and began to bound toward me, long ears sailing up with every stride.

Sam said, "It's going to take a few loads, but I'll get some guys down here with chainsaws and we'll get this cleared for you."

Thank you, I wanted to say, and *I'm glad that you're back*, and *I missed you*. But I had a lump firmly wedged in my throat and the sun felt too bright in my eyes. It was making me blink. I just nodded.

He moved past me, taking the armful of siding to throw with the rest in the back of his truck. By the time he returned I was crouched in the snow, petting Bandit a little too fiercely. I'd found my voice.

"Thank you," I said.

"Anytime. Hey, come and tell me what these are, though." Guiding me cautiously through the debris, he stopped me at what would have been the shed door, pointing up to the one shelf that hadn't been smashed. "Those look like they're something."

I looked at the three olive-drab canvas bags. They were dusted with snow, but unharmed. "Yes," I told him. "They are."

When we brought them inside the house, Rachel came down from her room. "What's all that?"

"All that," I said, "is your grandfather's kayak." I opened the top of one canvas bag so she could see the wood pieces inside. "It's a folding kayak. German made. When I was little, Grandpa used to take me out in it a lot, but then it started leaking, and an oar broke, so it all got put away."

She frowned. She seemed to find it natural that Sam was in our living room, with Bandit. Bending down to scratch the beagle's ears, she asked, "So how did we get it?"

"Your dad was going to fix it."

Rachel stared down at the bags so long I wondered whether I'd made a mistake in bringing them inside—if maybe they were too much a reminder of the things my brother's death had left unfinished. But at last she asked Sam, "If I wanted to do that, to fix it myself, could you help me? Show me how to use the tools?"

I warned them, "There are no instructions. My dad lost them."

Sam looked from my face to Rachel's and studied the bags on the floor. "That's no problem," he said. "We can figure it out."

LYDIA

T HE DAYS GREW SHORTER. Darkness fell late in the afternoon and when she went around to light the candles it was common to find Joseph with his pencil and his plans spread on the table in the keeping room, adjusting the dimensions of their work upon the *Bellewether* in answer to some new request from William.

"For a man who owns four ships, he doesn't know a thing about how they're constructed," Joseph told her. "What he asks for is impossible, unless I alter this as well." He pointed to a section of the latest drawing. "And I can't do that, unless…" He paused, and took the pencil up again and drew a fresh line as he sought a new solution to the problem.

He was good at that. He always had been. "Joseph doesn't see a wall," their mother used to say, "only the ways to get around it."

He drew the candle closer to inspect the change he'd made. "It will take time. We'll need more timber."

"William doesn't seem to worry how much time you'll take."

"Just how much money it will cost him." When he grinned, he did it with such ease she caught her breath.

She had forgotten what he looked like when he did that. She might have forgiven William many of his failings, for the part he'd played in helping Joseph heal. But she had not yet forgiven William altogether.

Word had reached them from New York that several of the merchants there had been indicted for their part in stirring up the riot in the streets against George Spencer. She'd been half afraid that William would be one of them, and then she had been angry with herself for hoping he was not, and then she'd been resigned to the reality that William, with his powerful connections and his gift of personality, knew how to dance around the rules of justice.

For her family's sake, she hoped his luck held out. He and his friends might have shamed and frightened Mr. Spencer, and reportedly they'd even had him thrown in jail for debt, but as long as a reward purse stood to tempt would-be informers there were bound to be some who would take the risk.

She knew that Silas would.

"Be careful, William," was the last thing she had told her brother when she'd left New York, because whatever else he was, he was her brother, and the thought of Silas living near him left her mind uneasy.

She was growing equally concerned about Mr. de Brassart. His burst of temper was behind him, but it seemed to her that, just as Joseph's health and sociability improved each day, Mr. de Brassart's worsened. He offered his apologies. "It is the cold, you understand. My home in France is in Bordeaux, a city in the south, where it is not so inhospitable. Your winters here for me are an affliction."

It did not help that the first days of December were the coldest ones in recent memory.

Violet, coming from her milking, held her hands up to show Lydia how red they were from even that small time outdoors. "His Majesty," she said, "should be rejoicing he's not with that group of prisoners they're taking back to Canada. They're going to lose their hands and feet to frostbite."

But Mr. de Brassart did not seem to find that any consolation. He was eating well enough—perhaps too well, as he began to thicken at his waist—but in between meals he no longer sat and read or joined their conversations, only kept within his chamber, often sleeping.

"I suspect," Mr. Ramírez said one afternoon, "he is down-hearted after being left behind. A man deprived of freedom may survive as long as he has hope, but when that hope is taken from him…" There he stopped, and glanced at Violet, who along with Lydia was salting up the pork.

It was a tedious but necessary task, since meat when fresh would spoil too soon were it not dried or salted, and they had a house of men to feed throughout the winter. First the pork was cut in pieces, cleaned, and washed in brine, then laid in rows and rubbed with salt and layered in a covered tub and left three days, then turned into a second tub and rubbed again with salt and left a week to sit. When that was done, they'd pack it into salt-lined casks and strain the brine through coarse cloth over it and store it in the cellar with the stone jars full of applesauce and pumpkin and the other fruits and vegetables they'd worked hard to preserve, but every step must be done carefully and with a mind to cleanliness to keep the meat from rotting at its core.

Violet didn't lose the rhythm of her movements but she raised her head and told Mr. Ramírez, "When this war is ended he'll be free. So there's his hope. And there are plenty who'd trade places with him just to taste it. Even you, I think, if you tried stepping off this property."

His smile was slight. "No, you are right. I cannot even take you to Cross Harbor, to your church, for fear I'd find myself in jail."

Lydia said, "We would never let that happen."

The weight of knowledge in his eyes seemed to indulge her innocence. "You're very kind. But there have been men of my country, men of Spain, whose ships were carried here as prizes in the last war, and if there were any on those ships whose skin was dark, like mine, the English had them sold as slaves. It did not matter then if they were free, and had the papers that could prove it, or had friends—kind friends—to stand up at their sides and say that this was wrong. The laws could not protect them and the English sold them anyway. So thank you, no, I will stay here." And then, as if he felt the mood had grown too somber, he put in, "Although that is no hardship, I assure you. I am better fed here than I can remember. And I have a ship to build, to keep me busy."

❦

Mr. de Sabran, too, appeared to have no trouble finding tasks to occupy his time.

When work on the *Bellewether* slowed in December because of the storms and the ice, he helped her father take apart the cider press and store it in the shed. Together with her father and French Peter he cut timber in the woods and hauled it back to lie and season to be ready in the spring. He helped in butchering the hogs. He helped chop firewood.

It didn't seem to bother Joseph, seeing Mr. de Sabran take up an axe and swing it with both hands.

But it was different on the day Mr. de Sabran asked her father for the hatchet.

She was standing at the kitchen window when he did it, and she saw him pass the large axe to her father by its handle; saw her father pause, and nod, and fetch another item from the shed. She didn't see exactly what it was until Mr. de Sabran walked away, toward the woods. And then she saw it in his hand.

A hatchet had killed Moses. She had not been meant to know that. Mr. Fisher and her father had discussed the details privately, but they had left the parlor door ajar and she'd been in the kitchen and she'd heard enough of what was said to know what happened.

It was just a common tool, she told herself. She'd seen her father use one since, and never found it troubling. And it helped that Mr. de Sabran, while technically their enemy and French, was not a stranger. Not a man she feared would ever do her harm.

She stood a long time at the window, held there by the simple weight of that one truth: he'd never do her harm.

She was still there when he came back into the clearing, carrying a hickory sapling taller than himself, and straight. He laid it flat across an angle of the kitchen garden fence, not far away, and took the hatchet from where he had tucked it in his belt, and in a practiced manner sheared the rough bark from the sapling, squared it off, and split it carefully and evenly along its length.

It took some time. He didn't seem to notice she was watching him. But when he finished with whatever he was doing, took the two slim lengths of hickory wood in hand and headed for the shed, both he and she at nearly the same moment noticed Joseph, standing very still beside the barn.

Her father, too, stepped from the shed. Like her, he must have held his breath.

She did not know how much Mr. de Sabran knew about her brother and Oswego and the things he would have seen there, but clearly he knew something of it, because while he'd been about to put the hatchet back into his belt, he turned it neatly now within his hand and walking the last few steps to her father, held it out for him to take. And with the tall, straight pieces of the sapling he passed on into the shed, and Joseph, after a long moment, carried on toward the house.

He came in by the kitchen door and stamped his boots to shake the snow off, bringing in a freezing blast of winter air that made the fire dance. Lydia had moved to stir the panful of potatoes she had set to roast, relieved to find they hadn't burnt to blackened crisps.

She turned, expecting she would have to cheer him, but he only sniffed the air and told her, "That smells good." And went upstairs.

∽

She doubted they would ever become friendly, Joseph and Mr. de Sabran. They were too watchful of each other, too on guard against each other's movements. But at least they could share the same room without hostility. And Joseph was the first to guess what Mr. de Sabran was making.

"Snowshoes," Joseph said. "It has to be. That's why he asked for the hide, when we slaughtered the steer."

They had wondered about that. Her father, refusing the offer of payment, had gifted the hide to him, not asking what he intended to do with it. Mr. de Sabran had scraped the hide, soaked it with ashes and taken the hair off, and nailed it to dry on the wall of the shed, but he hadn't done anything further to tan it. And then he had cut it in long narrow strips, which had baffled them all.

Now she followed his progress with interest. She'd seen snowshoes worn, but she'd never seen anyone make them.

He wound the hide strips tightly into a ball, left them outdoors to freeze in the snow, and then thawed them and wound them again, which she reasoned would make them less likely to stretch. With that done, he took both lengths of hickory wood, soaked them and steamed them and, one by one, bent them around into oval shapes, binding the back joints and adding a single crossbar for stability.

Finally, with patience and strength, he wove the leather strips by hand into an intricate, taut web that filled the inside of each frame, leaving a half-circle hole at the crossbar, the purpose of which became clear when, after January brought a snow that drifted to their knees, he showed them how the snowshoes worked. Her father tried first, with his feet loosely bound to the snowshoes by leather thongs so that the toes of his boots could dip down through the holes when he walked while the long shoes stayed virtually level.

Mr. de Sabran smiled encouragement. "Good. Very good." He tapped the back part of the snowshoe. "This rests always down." And then the front part. "This rests up. No falling."

Violet did it easily, and earned another smile. Mr. Ramírez watched her proudly but declined to try himself. So next the shoes were passed to Lydia.

She found it an odd feeling to sink partway in the snow and yet be buoyed by it, and finding it exhilarating she forgot to mind her steps and did what he'd said not to do. The front part of the snowshoe dropped and caught the snow and as she stumbled, pitching forward, Mr. de Sabran reached out and took her hand to steady her. It had the opposite effect.

The feelings that had started in New York, instead of fading with the dull routine of every day, had deepened. She thought of him as often by his first name as his last, having heard it twice—the first time when his letters had been read out in the orchard, and more recently when he had introduced himself to Captain Bonneau at the home of the de Joncourts: Jean-Philippe. A nice name. She imagined herself saying it, and hearing him say "Lydia." She watched his hands too much, and waited for his smile too often, and the feelings were uncomfortable and thrilling all at once; unwanted and—when he came close to her—confusing.

When the ice that bound the waters of the bay began to break, and February's frozen days gave way to March, a time for breaking ground and digging stones and pruning back the dead wood from the apple trees, she couldn't help but have the sense that something in herself was thawing also. Starting over. Starting new.

And then in mid-March suddenly the wind changed to the eastward, blowing in a violent snowstorm that was unexpected so late in the season. It lasted all day Sunday and continued into Monday and on Tuesday they had word from William.

Benjamin was home.

꙳

The snow had melted from the upper field but still the ground was soft and wet and she was forced to step with care to keep from sliding into puddles. The mare, some distance off, lifted her head and looked, but from some instinct seemed to know that Lydia, now walking up the path along the orchard wall, had not come here for her. She'd come for Benjamin.

He'd been too quiet after dinner. While she'd cleared the table he'd said he was going for some air, and when he hadn't yet returned an hour later she had guessed where he would be. This was the place he'd always gone when seeking solitude, where he could stand and watch the ships.

His homecoming had been a festive time of food and talk. He'd brought them gifts—sugar and wine and molasses, and for

Lydia and Violet, caps and sleeve ruffles of lace as finely fashioned
as a spider's web. "Captain del Rio insists Spanish lace is the best
in the world, and I've learned not to argue with Captain del Rio."
The captain, having business to detain him in the islands, had
sent them his apologies that he and *El Montero*'s crew had not
delivered Benjamin themselves, instead arranging passage home
for him aboard a New York privateer. "And we shall send Mr.
Ramírez home, in our turn," had been Benjamin's assurance, "on
the *Bellewether*, when she is fit to sail."

Mr. Ramírez had thanked Benjamin, and no more had been
said of it, but Lydia had thought he seemed dispirited.

And strangely, it had seemed to her that Benjamin as well had
grown more thoughtful as the meal progressed. She didn't know
what troubled him, but they'd been too close growing up for her
to leave him now without a confidante.

He turned, as had the mare, and watched her walk the last steps
up to join him before smiling, very slightly, as he looked away
again across the deep blue of the Sound, the sun above the farther
shore exposing a dull patchwork of brown fields and greening
meadows and the darker lines of trees, while in the foreground a
brave scattering of billowed sails and tiny ships moved busily about.

She'd stood in nearly this same spot to watch him sailing out
on *El Montero*. That had been barely six months ago, but he
seemed older.

He'd always stood with confidence but now he held himself
with true authority, head up and shoulders braced.

"You've changed," she told him.

"Have I?"

"Yes."

"I would suspect that's part of growing up," he said. The smile
tightened briefly, and then faded. "Am I better now, or worse?"

"I've not decided. Either way, you're still my brother." She
had come to stand directly at his side now. "How was William,
when you left him?"

"He was well." He paused. "He thinks you're angry with him. Are you?"

"Yes."

"But you'll forgive him."

"Possibly." She saw no point in skirting round the obvious. "What did you think of Monte Cristi?"

"I enjoyed it. There's not much to see besides the harbor, but that's always lively." With his focus on the sails he told her, "William isn't wrong, you know. About the British."

"We are British."

"Not to them, we're not. To them, we'll always be colonials, and never equals. Their ships can sail freely where they wish, and carry what they wish, and trade at any port that strikes their fancy, but let one of our ships dare to try the same and we are suddenly a danger to their profits. No, the Flour Act is a hard and unfair law, and if we do not stand against it there'll be harder laws to come."

"You sound like William."

He looked down at her. "I've seen things these past months that I could never have imagined." For a moment he appeared to be considering the wisdom of describing what he'd seen, but in the end he simply told her, "I know what the British are, and what they're capable of doing. And I know exactly what they think of us."

The wind blew cold along the bluffs and chased a bank of clouds across the sun so that a shadow fell across the shoreline opposite—a long, dark line that settled on the forests and the fields like an impassable divide.

He told her, "William's made me captain of the *Bellewether*."

She knew how much it meant to him, and yet the word "congratulations" had a hollow feeling on her tongue.

"When she's rebuilt and ready, we will find a crew and take her out. My first command."

"Does Father know?"

"Not yet."

"Where will you sail?"

"That is for William to decide."

The clouds were moving swiftly and the shadow on the farther shore had faded.

In a quiet voice, she said, "He promised me she'd never sail to Monte Cristi."

"Yes, I know."

"And?"

"And you have my word as well. The *Bellewether* will never enter Monte Cristi harbor." He was looking in her eyes, and she could tell he meant it.

"Thank you."

Reaching out he hugged her close against his side. "I'm not so changed," he said, but in a low, abstracted tone that made her wonder whether he was trying to convince her, or himself.

JEAN-PHILIPPE

F OR YEARS THE SPRING had meant the start of the campaigning
season. It should have left him at a loss, as April softened into
May, to have no men to train, no orders, no objective, but he'd
found new outlets for his restless energy.

There was the ship, of course, although the work on that
progressed in stages broken by some new instruction from the
elder brother in New York, whose interference at first frustrated
Ramírez then amused him.

"He is doing it on purpose," said the Spaniard to him one day
as they worked to caulk the seams between the hull's new planks,
a tedious chore that involved driving strands of tarred hemp into
place with a mallet and sharp-edged iron.

"Doing what?" asked Jean-Philippe.

"Delaying the repairs." They were working side by side and
speaking French but still Ramírez glanced behind to make sure
Joseph Wilde was out of earshot. "He's no fool, the brother. If he
lets the ship be launched too soon, the English will impress her
for their service, do you see? To carry troops up to their camp."

The British had been mustering their troops for some weeks
past, and Captain Wheelock was in Massachusetts now, apparently, attending to the business of recruiting there. He'd sent a
letter from a town called Worcester, to explain what he had done
in seeking justice for La Réjouie.

*Your sergeant's case was brought before a Regimental Court
Martial, and I regret to say the charges were dismissed against the
private soldier and the corporal who attacked him, but I've written*

General Amherst, giving my opinion that the charges, as a capital offense, are great and serious enough to warrant civil jurisdiction, and I hope to see the case tried in another court. Meantime, I did succeed in seeing all your other men included in the late exchange of prisoners and assure you Captain Bonneau, who went with them, gave his word he'd see them safely up to Montreal.

With luck, they would be rested and re-armed by now and ready to retake the city of Quebec.

It would be half a month or more before the British could assemble all their regiments at Albany, equip them, send them north, and see them properly encamped. If William Wilde preferred to keep this ship from being used to aid that effort, Jean-Philippe was not about to argue.

He set another twisted strand of caulking in the seam that he was working on and with his mallet drove it home. Ramírez did the same, except his caulking iron stuck between the planks and as he wrenched it out he lost his balance. In a reflex action Jean-Philippe reached out and grabbed Ramírez by his shirt, and though he felt the fabric tear within his grasp the older man was saved from falling.

"Thank you." Straightening, Ramírez set his clothes to rights and, noticing the torn seam at his shoulder, drew his waistcoat up to cover it, but not before the shirt had gaped enough that Jean-Philippe could see the scar.

No, not a scar. A brand made by a heated iron, for although it was slashed across, the letter *R* was still as clear to read as if it had been printed. He could feel Ramírez watching him, and he knew why.

He met the Spaniard's eyes. "If you are worried that I'll tell, I won't."

Ramírez looked behind them once again, and this time Jean-Philippe knew he was looking to see who might be a witness, and because he also knew no man who bore a brand like that had cause to trust another's promise, he showed his own trust by turning back to his work.

"The year my father's mother died," he said, "my grandfather brought home a slave, a girl he bought from a ship's captain who had come from the West Indies. He had other slaves already. Panis. You know what this is? Pani?"

The Spaniard nodded. "Indians."

"Yes. He had Pani slaves to work his farm, but none to keep his house. So he bought Angélique." He could not say her name without emotion, but he knew that she deserved the honor of him saying it aloud. "Like you, she had the brand of her first owner on her shoulder. She was close to Violet's age, then. I was six years old. She told me stories. Sang to me. I loved her very much." He held the iron to the hemp and struck it hard and deep into the seam. "My grandfather, he always told her, when he died, she'd have her freedom. We all heard him say this, many times. He made my father promise." It was harder than he'd thought it would be, telling this, but he had started now and felt the need to finish. "I was fifteen when he died. I was already a cadet, and on campaign. I came home three months afterward. And Angélique was gone. My father sold her." He could feel the force of that betrayal even now, and swung the mallet to give vent to it. "He sold her to a man who one week later beat her. Killed her. Said it was an accident. The judge believed him." With a shrug that couldn't quite contain his anger, he said, "That was the last time I've seen my home. I don't like slavery. And I keep my word." He faced Ramírez, and repeated, "I won't tell."

The Spaniard studied him a minute longer, gave a silent nod, and took his own tools up and they went on with what they had been doing, side by side, and nothing more was said.

❦

When work stalled upon the ship, there was the farm. May was the time of plowing, planting, mending fences, carting dung and spreading it, and setting fire to the dead leaves and the briars. In the field, a calf was born. A pair of wild doves built their nest beside the barn, their bright eyes always watching him to see he did not step too near the soft brown fledglings hidden on the ground, nearly invisible. And then the fledglings took to flight and at the month's end all the apple orchard came in bloom, a mass of white and pink that filled the air with fragrance.

He'd forgotten, having lived so long with fighting and with death, how life looked when it was beginning over. Beautiful.

Pierre was philosophical. "You see, Marine," he said, "it's how life is. One thing will end, another will begin." His wife had lately had another child, a little girl, and while it could not have removed the pain of his lost son, he seemed happier.

Today he'd come to help them wash the sheep. The weather, after days of rain, was finally warm enough and promised to hold clear, and the broad creek at the pasture's edge was running full and fast. It was a job that took four men and needed doing several days before the shearing, so the sheep could dry in sunlight. Benjamin and Monsieur Wilde were working as a team to scrub the sheep with soft, brown soap before they passed them to Pierre and Jean-Philippe, who stood thigh deep in the cold water, making sure each sheep was well-rinsed in the current that would carry all the dirt and oil away.

"Sheep," Pierre remarked, "are stubborn animals." He set the one he held upon the shore and watched it scamper up the bank. "They seldom walk in a straight path. Like us, they always try to look behind."

Jean-Philippe set his sheep down and squeezed the water from its thick fleece with his forearms before straightening to stretch his shoulders. His sheep wandered two steps up the bank then stood, feet planted, bleating loudly.

Pierre grinned. "You see? In this, too, they're like us." He waded out and took the sheep and turned it so its head was pointed to the others in the pasture, and the sheep stopped bleating and began to walk. "The trick in life," Pierre told Jean-Philippe, "is not to look behind so long you miss where you are being led."

ॐ

That evening after supper, Monsieur Wilde brought out the cider and the cribbage board.

It had become their habit through the winter months, begun when Jean-Philippe had seen the narrow wooden gaming board set on the corner bookshelf and in studying the holes and pegs had drawn his host's attention. It was not a game he'd played before, but given it used cards it did not take him long to learn it, and he'd come to find it an agreeable diversion.

In honesty, had he not liked the game he would have played it for no other reason than his host enjoyed it, and he'd come to like the company of Monsieur Wilde.

The parlor, with its blue walls, was a cool and peaceful place this evening. Other than the two of them—the cribbage board set on the little table in between their high-backed chairs before the unlit hearth—there was only Ramírez at the writing desk, and Lydia ensconced within her corner by the window, with the small board on her lap to hold her drawing paper. Joseph, after working on the ship all day, had gone upstairs. Violet had gone out to do the milking. And de Brassart, having spent another week in bed with some vague illness, was now up and out of doors and standing underneath the rowan tree engaged in what appeared to be some new debate with Benjamin.

As Jean-Philippe was dealt his cards he briefly watched the two men through the window, not because he cared what they were arguing about, but because doing so allowed him an excuse to turn his head in that direction and observe her without seeming to observe her.

She was drawing him. In profile, it would seem, because her pencil stilled the minute he began to turn, then moved again as he looked back toward the game. He hid his smile, and tried to look appropriately dignified.

He viewed his cards and sorted them. The great frustration of this game was that its play relied on simple chance as much as strategy.

The value of a hand relied not only on what cards you kept, but which ones you selected to discard, and all would turn upon the one card, yet unseen, that would be turned at random from the waiting deck. He frowned, sorting his cards again, considering.

Monsieur Wilde made a comment Jean-Philippe did not completely catch, and then Ramírez answered and both men were smiling when Ramírez translated: "He said he would have thought a soldier would be more decisive, so I said you're not a soldier, you're an officer."

Jean-Philippe smiled too, before remembering that it would spoil his profile for her drawing. He selected his two cards and set them down, and when the older man spoke next the words were easier to understand.

"If you ask me," Monsieur Wilde told him, "you were born to be a farmer."

He wasn't often taken by surprise. The comment was a simple one and offered with sincerity and so he answered, "Thank you." But the impact that he felt was unexpected.

It was the phrasing of the words, in perfect counterpoint to those his uncle once spoke with such confidence. *This one will never settle… He was born to be a soldier.* And yet what if that had, after all, been nothing more than chance—one card selected, and another left unplayed?

What if his uncle had not been a soldier, but a merchant, or a miller? It was interesting to think what course his own life might have taken then; how each card dealt a man could change the outcome of the game.

The turn was his. He played his four, and wished he'd kept his ace, and somehow scored six points in spite of it. He dealt the next hand in his turn, and moved his pegs around the board, and drank his cider, liking the companionship. When Violet came back from the barn, Ramírez went to help her, leaving only him and Monsieur Wilde and Lydia within the quiet parlor, and he liked that even better. Liked the comfort and contentedness of sitting with them in that room, with evening coming on.

The words he'd built his life upon seemed small and distant in his mind: *This one will never settle.*

And he wondered, for the first time, if his uncle had been wrong.

⟳

The best way to deal with a man like de Brassart, he knew, was to give him no time to come up with a lie.

So that night as he sat on the edge of his bed he asked, straight out, "What did you arrange with him?"

All innocence. "What do you mean?"

"With Benjamin." He didn't offer details of his own, because to watch de Brassart thinking back to what might have been seen or overheard was more revealing.

He could see the choices being weighed—mislead, deny, or tell the truth. De Brassart's mouth thinned to a line of resignation. So, the truth.

"His brother has provided him a flag and papers giving him authority to carry a French prisoner to be exchanged." As wary as a miser being asked to share his wealth, he said, "One prisoner. Not two."

"I see."

A man with more discretion might have left the matter there. De Brassart said, "Now that the English soldiers have gone to their camp, and there's less danger that the ship will be impressed, they will be working hard to get it finished, and his orders are to sail the ship, as soon as it is ready, to the port of Cap-François, at Saint-Domingue."

"I see."

"My brother lives at Saint-Domingue. I should imagine that's why they decided I should be the one to go."

Jean-Philippe privately thought it more likely that William Wilde, after they'd met in New York, would have known well enough what reply he would make to an offer that skirted the bounds of legality. William might be driven by his own self-interest and ambition, but he was intelligent. It came as no surprise to learn his trade was like his nature—neither good nor bad but falling in the gray and shifting space between. Remembering what Captain Wheelock had told the de Joncourt boy about how people here bought flags of truce for their illicit trade with France in the West Indies, Jean-Philippe could not help wondering just how much Lydia knew of her brothers' business ventures.

From the way she had behaved toward her brother in New York, he guessed she knew as much as he did, maybe more. And she did not approve.

He lay back on his bed and laced his hands behind his head. "Does Captain Wheelock know?"

"I don't need his permission. By the terms of our parole, to leave this place I only need permission from a governor, and I'm assured a governor has signed my papers. Anyway, I don't recall your thinking that the captain was owed any information other than what was required."

There was logic to that reasoning.

De Brassart said, "I promised nothing else except that I would neither serve against the English king nor any of his allies until after I have been exchanged." He said that with defiance and then waited, as if expecting Jean-Philippe to argue. "Well?"

He shrugged. "I wish you luck."

"What's that supposed to mean?"

"Exactly that. I've met the brother in New York. I'll lay you odds the papers and the flag of truce were purchased and not given. And I promise you the English are aware of this, so if you think they'll let the ship sail unmolested into a French port, then you're delusional."

That seemed to wound de Brassart's pride. "At least I'm doing what I can to get back in this war."

"Yes, you'll be right on the front lines, in Saint-Domingue."

Rolling, he turned his back, feeling the daggers that filled the long silence.

De Brassart lay down. "I will be on French soil. Not forgetting my place, or what country I serve." Seeking to drive the blade home, he went on, "Not pretending that people who hate me could ever accept me as anything else but their enemy."

Over their heads the old beams of the house sighed and settled and Jean-Philippe tried not to think of how close and how far he was, just at that moment, from all that he might have been.

He heard the creak of a mattress and knew that de Brassart had turned his back also, dismissively. And in the darkness, the cultured French voice held a frozen disdain. "I don't think I'm the one who's delusional."

CHARLEY

I T'S NOT YOUR FAULT," said Sharon, in a tone that meant the
opposite. "You're not from here. But anyone who's local
could have told you it's impossible."

She didn't come right out and call me "idiot," although it was
implied, and from the coughs and shifting looks around the table
I could tell this was a hill I wouldn't want to die on. But I took it
one more step and asked her, "Why?"

"Because Millbank's main business is weddings. Every venue
here is booked up months, and sometimes years, ahead of time.
There simply isn't anywhere *to* hold a dance."

I looked across the table. "Harvey? What about the Privateer
Club?"

"Sorry, but we're taking bookings now for next November,
and if anybody cancels, there's a waiting list, so I can't help. I wish
I could." He said that like he meant it, and from Sharon's tightened mouth I knew she still hadn't forgiven him for switching
sides. She wasn't a forgiving sort of woman.

Diplomatically, Malaika said, "It's not a bad idea, but—"

Don interrupted. "What about the barn?"

But Eve reminded him the barn roof leaked. "And we don't
have the budget to replace it. Even if we did, it would just cancel
out whatever profit we'd be making in return. So there's no point."

There was a momentary silence in our meeting room.

"I'd rather rip my liver out," Frank told me, "than agree with
Sharon, but she's right. There's no way we can have a dance this
year."

❧

"It *was* a good idea, though," I said to Sam and Willie as I watched them working in my favorite room of the old house—the big upstairs bedchamber I could walk into like Narnia, from my own office.

Willie had been called away last month to do emergency repairs on an old church upstate, but he was back today and picking up where he'd left off. His usual assistant was home sick, so Lara's eldest son was helping. Just like Sam, the big Scotsman seemed to enjoy teaching others the tricks of his trade. With the boy's help he had opened up the fireplace and they'd both had their heads up the old flue, inspecting the parged lining. Now he turned and said, "I'd dance with you."

"Thank you."

"Mind you, I can't dance like I used to. Not with my old mason's back." When Sam glanced at him sideways, Willie told him, "It's a true affliction, mason's back. The price we pay for spending all those hours crouched in people's cellars. Ruins the lower muscles."

Lara's son asked, "So how do you make it better?"

"Drink a lot." He grinned, and then appearing to remember that the boy was barely in his teens, he said, "And swimming. Swimming's best."

"Oh."

"Well," I said, "it looks like neither of us will be dancing for a while."

"A shame. I do a decent tango."

Lara, coming through the doorway from my office, lightly said, "I'd pay to see that."

Willie's smile grew broader as it always did when she was near. "You, my love, could have the show for free."

She said, "I might just take you up on that. But right now, it's your big strong arms I need. I have a box of books, a big one, in my trunk. A gift from Dave for Charley."

Sam tapped one last nail into the piece of trim he'd been

refitting on the paneled wall, and set his hammer down. "I'll go," he said to Willie. "Save your back." And taking Lara's keys, he headed down the front stairs.

Lara smoothed her son's hair. "You're all scruffy."

"He's a mason in the making, this lad," Willie told her. "Watch this. Tell your mum what you've just learned, now. How big should a flue be, compared to the fireplace opening?"

"Seven to ten percent."

"And why is that?"

"Because if it's too small, then the smoke comes back into the room."

"Right. And if it's too big? What then?"

"You get a lazy fire."

Willie looked proudly at Lara. "See there? I'd hire him."

"I may take you up on that, too."

Sam came back up the stairs with the box in his arms. "You weren't kidding," he told Lara, handing back her keys. "These things are heavy."

I had him bring them through into my office, and his shoulder brushed the floor lamp. Set it rocking. "You should move that thing," he said. "There's room behind your desk."

I couldn't tell him that the ghost refused to let me plug anything in there, but I could say with full honesty, "That outlet isn't useable."

I should have known Sam would see that as something to fix. With the box of books safely set down, he selected a screwdriver. Knelt by the plug.

I said, "Shouldn't you turn off the breaker, first?"

"I'm just going to look."

I couldn't bear to. I pretended interest in the books that Dave had sent, instead: *The Works of the Most Reverend Dr. John Tillotson*, printed at London in 1743 and containing *two hundred and fifty-four sermons and discourses on several subjects*. It was a beautiful set, bound in full calf with gilt and raised bands on the spines. Twelve volumes, marked with numbers on the sides. I counted all of them, hoping in silence the ghost wouldn't mess with Sam.

"Look at this," Sam said.

I sighed. "What?"

"This wiring. A good thing you didn't plug anything in here," he told me.

I felt the hair lift on the back of my neck as I turned.

"If you'd left something plugged into *that* mess," he said, very sure, "you'd have burned the whole place down."

❧

Childhood fears and childhood wishes never lost their power. At the moment you were certain they'd been set aside, they rose up unexpectedly and took you over just as strongly as they had before, as though reminding you that no one ever truly left the past behind.

I wasn't sure which held me strongest, fears or wishes, but I felt them both as I approached the redbrick posts that framed the iron gates of Bridlemere.

I'd actually begun this long walk in my mind two days ago, when I'd been in my office and Malaika came in with the morning's mail. There'd been a card from somebody donating fifteen dollars to our artifact appeal, a little padded package that had held an old clay pipe—one of the items on our list—and a slim envelope, addressed to me. I'd smiled at the pipe. "Dance or not," I had said to Malaika, "we're doing okay with our fundraising."

"Yes, we are."

Then I had opened the envelope.

It held a check, with *For the Wilde House Fund* marked on the memo line. I'd looked at the amount, and at the signature. I'd had to sit.

Malaika had asked, "What?"

I'd shown her. She'd sat, too. She'd told me, "That's enough to take us past our goal."

"I know."

"That's more than we asked from the Sisters of Liberty."

I knew that, too. What I didn't know was, "Why?"

Malaika, watching me, had said what both of us were thinking. "I guess you'll just have to ask her."

I'd known she was right. I'd known it, just as I'd been well aware a huge donation like the one my grandmother had made deserved a formal thank-you. But it was one thing to know it, and another altogether to work up the courage to approach these gates.

In childhood dreams I'd knocked and they had opened and my grandmother had met me with a hug of welcome, taking me inside as though this place had always been my home.

Today, the gates were firmly locked. A gardener was working just beyond them in the flower beds that edged the path. It might have been a woman or a man, I couldn't tell, but they wore overalls, a denim shirt, and one of those Australian hats whose brims could be snapped up to make them look more stylish. The gardener's hat brim was left down, forgoing style for common practicality.

I'd parked the car beside the road, because I'd felt it would be harder, if I was on foot, to run away. I'd set out walking with my head up, showing confidence, but now that I'd come right up to the gates, with every window of that mansion staring down at me like disapproving eyes, I lost my nerve.

I took the thank-you note I'd written from my pocket, and prepared to pass it through the black iron bars. "Excuse me," I said to the gardener, "could you give this to Mrs. Van Hoek, please? It's from the museum."

There. That sounded formal enough, in control, and polite.

Except when the gardener straightened and faced me, she wasn't a gardener.

My grandmother's eyes met mine with the same cool reserve they'd held that day at the Privateer Club. My hands shook a little, the way they'd done then, but I held the card steady so it became almost a dare to see if she would cross the small distance between us and take it.

She did.

I said, "That was a generous donation you made to us. Thank you." And then, in the hope I would look like a dignified grown-up, I turned away.

"Charlotte."

Her voice was melodic. A likeable voice. When I turned back and met her eyes this time, I realized my father's eyes looked like that when he was on unfamiliar ground, worried he'd make a mistake.

She said, "I was about to have lunch." She reached over to touch a post, and the gates started to part. "Would you like to come in?"

~

Her favorite room appeared to be the one I found most beautiful—an elegant conservatory, ringed with windows, filled with light. It opened to a terrace with a view across the gardens and the lawn down to the bay. The room was done in white and green and lilac, rich with texture, and my chair beneath its cushions was an Art Deco revival of the style of Spanish chair we'd just retrieved for our museum. We had lunch here, chicken sandwiches and tiny sweet tomatoes tossed with olive oil and herbs, brought by a woman who was either a devoted servant or a nurse, I couldn't tell. She gave my grandmother a pep talk on the benefits of protein before leaving us alone.

I had expected explanations from my grandmother. Instead she asked a thousand questions, everything from whether we'd had pets when I was young to where we'd lived and where we'd traveled, and inevitably everything came back to, "And your father, what did he do? What did Theo say?" and "What did Theo think of that?"

It wasn't that I didn't understand. I couldn't keep from thinking of my father, either. Everywhere I looked I'd think: my father used to climb those stairs, watch sunsets through that window, cross that hallway. Even so, her desperation to have word of him was touching and infuriating all at once, and finally I just had to set my teacup down and say, straight out, "I need to ask you why."

She turned her head away, and watched the shadows lengthen on the lawn. "It was a different time."

"He was—he is—your son."

"I had two sons." She said it quietly. "My handsome boys. They were a handful, let me tell you, and I was the only woman in the family, all those years. Even the dogs were male." Her smile was faint. "I didn't mind. I had my boys. And then," she said, "I didn't." In the pause that followed she turned back to me. "When they sent Jack home in that body bag from Vietnam, I was so angry, Charley. May I call you Charley? That's what Sam said you prefer, but... I was angry. I just wanted to go over there myself and take a gun and shoot whoever killed him. Burn that country to the ground. The whole place. Burn it all. I couldn't understand why anybody wouldn't feel the same. But Theo," she began, then stopped. Another pause. "He couldn't kill things. Ever since he was a little boy. If he went fishing, he would take the fish right off the hook and put it back."

"He's still like that. He never kills a spider, he just traps it in a glass and takes it outside."

"Yes, that's Theo. And he told us. When his draft card came, he stood right there and told us that he couldn't do it, couldn't kill someone. He told us that he thought the war was wrong. And I told *him* he was a coward."

I could see the sadness touch her face when she remembered that. I asked her, "Did you mean it?"

"I don't know. I think I did, yes. But I didn't understand, back then." She looked away again. "I watched a documentary a while ago, on Vietnam. They interviewed some men who, like your father, went to Canada. I heard them say how hard it was to leave their loved ones, leave their country, and I knew for Theo we had made it so much harder."

"You disowned him."

"No. We threatened to. We never did. He'll still inherit everything. But we didn't give him support when he needed us."

"We managed fine." Two hours ago my tone would have been more defensive. Now it sought to reassure. "I never felt deprived."

"You're very sweet." She studied me. "I wish I'd met your brother, too. He sounded like a nice young man."

"He was."

"He phoned here once, and left a message saying that your father was in surgery. He thought I'd want to know. It was a shock, you understand. I should have called him back immediately, but I thought I'd take a few days, pull myself together. Only..."

"Only Niels," I finished for her, "didn't have a few days left to wait. Is that why you weren't at the funeral?"

"Who would have wanted me there?" she asked. "Nobody. I would have been a distraction. Besides, I felt so dreadfully ashamed. He was my only grandson, and I'd never even taken time to stop and say hello. I knew what people would be saying. What they'd have a right to say."

"You came to see me at the luncheon, though." Now I knew why. But I still wondered, "Why did you leave?"

"Because while I was waiting to speak to you, two women at the next table were talking, as women will do, about how your face looked when I came in the room, and one commented I was most likely the last person you would have wanted to see."

I wasn't sure I understood. "You left because you didn't want them gossiping?"

"I left because I realized they were right."

There was the sadness, pushed down deep behind her elegant facade. I didn't see her, at that moment, as a woman of authority and influence. I saw her as a lonely woman, sitting in a big house, on her own. And while I never liked to lie, I reasoned this was for a good cause.

"They were wrong," I said. "I'd actually been hoping you would come that day, so we could meet."

The sadness vanished briefly as she smiled. "You know, your father, when he said something that wasn't true, would do that same exact thing."

"What thing?"

She smiled, but didn't answer. Her tea must have grown as cold as mine had, but she sipped it. "As I said, you're very sweet." Setting her cup down, my grandmother settled back into her chair, looking thoughtful. "Sam tells me you're thinking of having a dance."

❧

The last time there had been a ball at Bridlemere, my father was in high school, Elvis Presley was a newlywed, and NASA had just publicly announced the crew of the first manned Apollo mission. So when we started planning one for the first Saturday in June, it caused a stir in Millbank. Before we'd even posted an announcement, word of mouth took over. People started calling the museum, and within a few days every ticket had been sold.

"You'll need a dress," said Lara. She'd just added a new section in a corner of her boutique, selling vintage clothing, and she had the perfect piece in mind. "It's from the 1960s," she said, smoothing down the layers of pale-yellow silk that floated from a bodice set with delicate pearl beads and tiny rhinestones. When my grandmother had seen it, she'd produced a rhinestone necklace that lay lightly on my collarbone, and small earrings to match.

"When I was your age," she told me, "everyone wore rhinestones. I had diamonds, but I liked these better. There. Now, if you do your hair just simply, put it up like this," she said, and showed me. In the mirror I could see the happy concentration on her face as she combed back my hair, and it reminded me of what she'd missed—what we'd both missed—for all these years.

The lost time we were making up for. With an expert twist she slipped a final hairpin in to hold the updo. "There. Just like Grace Kelly." She was smiling when her eyes met mine in our reflection. "Perfect for the ballroom. You'll look right at home."

The long ballroom at Bridlemere, impressive in the daylight, became dazzling after dark. It had a grand, palatial feel—white marble floors, a soaring ceiling, chandeliers with sparkling strings of crystals. There were mirrored walls, and tall french doors in pairs that had been opened to the evening air, allowing guests to move outside and stroll along the terrace and the gardens, and the whole effect—the white and gold and glittering of guests and light—was beautiful.

Frank had expressed his doubts about it being a black-tie affair. "I'll have to shave," had been his main complaint. But he looked right at home himself in a tuxedo. "It's a great invention," he admitted. "You rent it, you wear it, you take it back. And if I don't spill a beer on it, they give me ten percent off." He looked around the crowded room. "Besides, it's a great leveler. You put a group of guys in penguin suits, it's hard to tell the farmers from the millionaires."

He had a point. Men stood straighter when they were in formal wear, and it wasn't always easy telling who was who.

Except the man now coming in, more than an hour late, from the main entry hall. Even through the swirl of people I knew him immediately from the way he walked. A short way in, he stopped to talk to Darryl and Malaika, and Frank said, "I see Sam finally made it," and excused himself and made his way across the busy floor to join them.

I would have followed if a big man hadn't stepped in front of me and started chatting as though we'd already met and he felt very certain I'd remember him. I didn't, not until he looked toward the silent auction table while he was explaining something, and I glimpsed the dark edge of his neck tattoo, and then I recognized him as the man who'd come up after our first ghost hunt in the woods at Halloween, to thank me. "So I made you something for the auction," he concluded. "Want to come and see?"

He'd built a wooden model of the *Bellewether*, to scale, complete with rigging, sails, and miniature cannon. It had already attracted several bids.

I said, "It's gorgeous."

"Thanks." He was showing me some of the smaller, meticulous details—the hatches that opened on hinges, and the real glass windows in the captain's cabin—when he glanced past my shoulder. "Hey, Sam."

"What's up, Tiny?" He greeted me, too, before leaning in to look more closely at the model ship. "Very cool. How many hours did that take you?"

The two men were discussing the materials, mechanics, and tools needed to build such a faithful model when my grandmother came by, a little flushed and sipping ice water but looking otherwise unruffled for a woman in her eighties who'd just spent the best part of the past hour on the dance floor. "It's lovely, isn't it?" she said, of the *Bellewether* model. "I was admiring it earlier. He used to make beautiful yachts, too—real ones— before his father sold the shipyard. I suppose he has to put all that creativity somewhere."

I put my local knowledge to the test. "Before his father sold the shipyard? At Cross Harbor? So then he's a—"

"Fisher, yes," she said. "He's Isaac's nephew."

"Everybody really is related here, aren't they?"

"Oh, yes. You have to be careful what you say to whom, in Millbank." She'd been watching the couples whirl by us, but now she sent a pointed look toward a short, round woman standing near the mirrored wall. "And be especially careful, my dear, what you say to *her*."

"Who is she?"

"Carol Speck." I'd heard the name before, but couldn't place it until she continued, "She's one of our Sisters of Liberty. This year's vice president." Then I remembered Sam saying he thought the reason we hadn't got funding was because of Carol Speck. He'd told me she was friends with Sharon.

I studied Sam's bent head, as nonchalantly as I could.

My grandmother went on, "When I had shingles last spring, she was only too happy to take over running the meetings, and move them to the Privateer Club. Out of my hands. I should really have said something then, but I didn't. I just felt so ill and so tired, and so much was happening, what with your father in the hospital and your brother dying and…well, I just didn't feel up to doing very much of anything."

I glanced toward the anteroom where the refreshments and the bar had been set up, with Tracy's Veronica in charge of catering, and Gianni helping serve the food and drinks, and Rachel keeping close to him. I hadn't thought she'd come—she was still working to reconcile with my grandmother, and was too anxious to feel comfortable in such a large crowd, but Gianni had asked her and she'd said she'd give it a try, for him.

I said, "It's called situational depression. I think we're all working through it, on some level."

"That may be. Anyhow, watch what you say around Carol. With people like that, you just say what you need to, and keep the rest private."

Advice I could take, I thought. "I'm good at hiding things."

I heard the smile in my grandmother's voice as she followed my gaze to Sam's shoulders. "Not everything."

Then, as I blushed, the musicians changed tunes and she said to the man Sam called Tiny: "George, come dance this waltz with me. And Sam, get Charley out there. She's been wasting that dress all night."

Sam, left alone with me, held out his hand. "It's a nice dress."

It seemed I'd been waiting so long to be close to him, to have him hold me, that I didn't know how to process these feelings. They came in a rush, tumbling over each other, confusing and breathtaking. I couldn't speak. Didn't want to, afraid I might spoil it.

He smelled nice. He danced well. He held my hand lightly, his other hand warm at the small of my back. He felt solid and perfect and just so incredibly *right*.

My eyes closed. Sam folded my hand in his strong one and brought it against his chest, holding it there as he lowered his head so his jaw rested right at my temple. And for all the rest of that song and the one that came after, I drifted contentedly, letting him lead.

LYDIA

S HE COULDN'T REMEMBER THE last time her father had danced.

"William's wedding," was Benjamin's guess.

"Surely not," Sarah said. They were standing with Lydia off to the side in the barn, near the table her father had roughly built only that morning, to hold food and drink for the guests that had come. "Surely there's been occasion to dance since then."

But they could think of none. Now they had several occasions to celebrate, all come at once.

First, the shearing was over with. That in itself would have been cause enough. And then one sunny morning a boat had arrived full of workers from Joseph's old shipyard, to say word had reached them the *Bellewether* was being overhauled and they had come to help where they were able. They'd worked by day, and slept in hammocks belowdecks at night, and now the ship was masted, rigged, and crewed, and ready to set sail upon the midnight tide.

And that, too, would have been enough cause for this evening's revelry, the whole crew having brought their wives and children to farewell them.

But earlier today, at dinner, Joseph had announced that he'd been offered—and was taking—a position at the shipyard. He had been advanced the wages to allow him to start work upon a small house on the land he'd purchased years ago, and which had long been waiting for that purpose, between Millbank and Cross Harbor. And when work on that was done, no later than September, he and Sarah would be married.

Sarah radiated happiness tonight, her blond hair twisted into curls and held with silver pins, her blue gown adding to the fanciful array of color making their swept barn a match for any ballroom in New York. The men who would be sailing on the *Bellewether* that night were in their ordinary clothes, but Mr. Fisher and her father wore their Sunday best, as did her cousin Henry and his eldest son, who'd ridden up together for the gathering.

The women's gowns and petticoats, in silks and printed cotton, swirled in ever-shifting patterns with the music of each dance. Not having time or fabric for a new gown, Lydia had settled for her yellow one, but she had trimmed the shift she wore beneath it with soft lace that lay around the neckline in a ruffle and cascaded loosely from beneath the sleeves. She'd stitched new ribbon bows onto her slippers and her elbow cuffs, and used a matching ribbon for her hair, which she'd arranged the way she'd worn it since the day Mr. de Sabran had first smiled at her and told her it looked nice.

He wasn't dancing. He was standing to the side, a dashing figure in his uniform. Remembering the way it had affected her last August when she'd seen his white coat in her kitchen—everything she feared and hated most, wrapped in one garment she could barely stand to touch—it seemed remarkable that yesterday, by her own choice, she'd beaten it and brushed it, using fuller's earth and vinegar and lemon juice to sponge away the stains remaining from the riot in New York, until the coat was left as white and clean as when it had been made.

The symbolism of the gesture seemed not to be lost on him. He'd thanked her very quietly and she could plainly see that he was moved.

Tonight, it pleased her that his spotless coat made him—Canadian or not—appear more gentlemanly than Mr. de Brassart, though she had the sense he wasn't much at ease in social settings and would rather have been anywhere than with so many people.

There were moments in the evening when she sympathized with how he felt; when the people and the music and the movement made her feel a little dizzy. But she counted it a fair exchange to see her father dancing.

For a big man, he stepped lightly and with style. His partner this song was French Peter's wife, Mrs. Boudreau, a pretty woman with a fetching laugh that rang out frequently. Her husband had surprised them all by asking for a fiddle, and then playing it with such skill Mr. Fisher, his own fiddle raised, decided they should play together. Both the fiddles were now chasing one another up and down the tunes in lively harmony.

Returning with more cider for the table, Joseph asked, "Is Father still dancing?"

"It's your fault," said Lydia. "You've made him happy."

Benjamin tried hard to look offended. "I thought *I* was the one who'd made him happy."

"By leaving?" asked Joseph. "You may have a point." His dry voice and the teasing light deep in his eyes were both things she had missed and thought lost, and to see them now made her heart swell even more.

The music had changed and their father, his face flushed and smiling, came over to fetch them. "Come, stop holding up the wall. We need more couples."

Joseph obligingly took Sarah's hand, but Benjamin said, "I'm afraid I can't. There are a few things I still need to do before we sail." He looked behind him but there were no men nearby except the two French officers.

Mr. de Brassart, hands raised, said, "I thank you, no. I have a knee that has never been right since Chouaguen, and tonight it is not letting me dance."

Mr. de Sabran's gaze slid between Mr. de Brassart and Joseph, then came back to rest on her own face. She could not tell what he was thinking, but clearly he'd understood their conversation because he stepped forward and silently offered his hand.

"There," her father said. "There is your partner now, Lydia. Well done, sir."

Bravely done, she amended, for Mr. de Sabran must surely have felt, as she did, all the watching eyes turned on them—some of them curious, some disapproving, some hostile. But as they took up their positions on the floor, the men in a line on one side and the women on the other, Mr. Fisher made the choice of dance and called it out: "In two groups of four couples, if you please. The 'À la Mode de France.'"

French Peter set his fiddle to his shoulder and she saw him smiling broadly at her as Mr. de Sabran took her left hand in his right one, turning her to face the top of the room, and that smile calmed her nervousness, making her realize she cared not what anyone else thought. They weren't the first couple, which was a good thing because although the dance had a French name it soon became obvious Mr. de Sabran had never encountered it. When he missed a step the first time, falling back into the wrong place, he was frowning. When he missed a second step, she smiled to show him that it didn't matter, and he shrugged and smiled back at her, the smile that tilted to one side and carved the handsome lines into his cheeks. And by the time he'd missed the third step, all the other couples and a few within the crowd around them started calling out instructions to assist him, and he took it in good humor, and he laughed.

It was a wondrous thing to hear him laugh. It had a strange effect upon her, and when all the partners had come round to their right places and the music stopped and she was standing facing him, she could not think what she should do next.

Holding out his hand to her again he said, "We take the air, yes?"

"Yes," she said, because air sounded just the thing she needed.

Outside, the night was soft and fresh. There was a half-moon shining brightly in a field of stars, a glowing ring of light surrounding it, and it had made a trail across the bay that showed in places through the darker screen of trees.

They walked in silence, and she breathed the mingled scents of wildflowers sleeping in the shadows, and the salt air of the sea.

He had not let go of her hand. She did not want him to. They did not leave the clearing but at length they reached its edge, where rustling branches stretched above them and the light and noise and music of the barn seemed far away. One heart-shaped leaf fell from a nearby tree and landed on his shoulder and unthinkingly she lifted her free hand to brush it off before it marked the white coat she had worked so hard and long to clean.

She felt him looking down at her, and glancing up self-consciously she started to explain. And lost the words.

And then he bent his head and kissed her.

Everything around her seemed to stop, and still, and cease to matter. She could not have said how long it lasted. Not long, probably. It was a gentle kiss but at the same time fierce and sure and full of all the pent-up feelings she herself had fought these past months, and now she knew he had felt them just as she had, and had fought them, too. It was a great release to give up fighting. Give up everything, and float in the sensation.

But of course it had to end.

He drew his head back slowly, and they stood there a long moment in the shadows, saying nothing. Saying everything.

He seemed to be about to speak when suddenly the spell was broken by the sound of running footsteps.

Sarah, bearing down on them. "Oh, Lydia! Come quick!" Her face was pale with worry. "Joseph's going to kill him!"

❦

She thought he'd gotten rid of the gun.

When Mother had first found the pistol in Joseph's belongings brought down from Oswego, she'd worried. A long gun, for hunting or even protecting the farm, that was one thing, she'd said—but a pistol was made for the purpose of violence.

He'd argued he needed it by him at night to feel safe, and they'd all understood, but at length Mother's quiet persuasion had settled the matter. Or so they had thought.

Because here he was holding that same pistol leveled on Mr. de Brassart.

His hand was not shaking as it often did when he grew agitated, and Lydia didn't know if that was good or bad. He didn't turn his head as she came into the kitchen, but she could tell he was aware.

He said, "Tell them to go."

He meant Mr. Ramírez and Violet, who stood at the room's farther end, by the buttery. Mr. Ramírez had Violet behind him, and stood in watchful readiness, as though prepared to intervene yet trying not to make things worse.

Like Mr. de Sabran, who'd wanted to come in the house but had agreed instead to stay outside the kitchen doorway in the shadows at her back. She felt the tension of his silent presence, and could only hope that Joseph didn't.

Joseph said, "I don't want them to see."

Mr. de Brassart looked to Lydia. He seemed to have been trying to come out of his own bedchamber before the pistol had been drawn to stop him where he stood. His face showed fear, and arrogance. "He's crazy. I did nothing."

In the hearth a log gave way and splintered, falling with a sudden crash of sparks, and Joseph flinched.

She said, "Mr. Ramírez, will you please take Violet upstairs? Thank you." Gently, she told Joseph, "Let me have the gun."

"Where's Sarah?"

"I don't know." Which wasn't entirely true. She'd sent Sarah for Father. "She's not here, though. Give me the gun, Joseph."

Mr. de Brassart said, "Listen to her. You don't like me? Fine, I am leaving, I told you. See here, all my things. I am ready to leave."

The pistol didn't waver.

The French officer repeated, "I did nothing."

"You were there."

She'd seen him lose his hold on what was real before—slip backward into some remembered moment that consumed him in its pain. She knew the danger. "Joseph."

"He injured his leg at Chouaguen. That's what he said tonight. You heard."

"Yes, but I—"

"Chouaguen," Joseph said, "is what the French call Oswego." His eyes on de Brassart's, he said in a low, anguished tone, "You were there."

She heard voices and movement outside, but they'd be too late. His grip on the pistol was tightening. So without thinking, she moved.

The helplessness of that one moment lived with her long afterward—her senses flooded painfully at every side, the sudden stench of gunsmoke and the blast of sound, the stinging in her shoulder where it had struck Joseph's arm away, the panic of not knowing if she'd managed it in time.

She had.

Mr. de Brassart straightened slowly from where he had crouched within the doorway of his chamber. Looked at Joseph, who'd regained his balance after Lydia had lunged and was now standing close beside the hearth. And then looked past them.

Lydia turned, too.

Her father leaned against the open kitchen door, his breathing heavy as though he'd been running. Benjamin stood next to him, with others scattered in the dark behind. She looked for Mr. de Sabran and was concerned she did not see him, until realizing that he'd reacted faster than them all and was now standing close behind her, like a guard.

"It's all right," she assured them. "No one's harmed."

Mr. de Brassart said, once again, "Crazy." Then added, to Benjamin, "I tried to tell him, if he kills me, then you can't sail where you need to, but—"

"Quiet," said Benjamin.

Lydia felt a new pain in that silence—the small, certain twist of the knife of betrayal. A pain she was learning to recognize, lately. And learning to bear.

But she thought of the people now watching and listening. Thought about Joseph, and what would be best for him. Thought of her family, and its reputation. And clearing her throat, said to Benjamin, "Would you take Mr. de Brassart's things down to the *Bellewether* for him, please? I trust you have his papers safe on board already."

Benjamin said, "Yes." He tried to meet her eyes, and she allowed him to, but only briefly.

Then she laid her hand on Joseph's and said, "Let me have this, now."

This time he handed her the pistol, without protest, and she thanked him for it, stepping to the side as Sarah, pushing forward from the gathered crowd outside the doorway, crossed to stand next to Joseph.

The moment of danger had passed now, and everyone knew it.

She wanted to move, but she couldn't stop trembling. She wanted to turn to the strong man behind her for comfort, but she couldn't do that with everyone here. Not with what had just happened.

His hand touched her back, very gently—a gesture that nobody else in the room could see. Then he moved past her and stood near the door, near her father, and then other people came into the room and in all the confusion she looked once again for him. But he was gone.

JEAN-PHILIPPE

H E FOUND HER FATHER in the barn.

The ship had sailed. De Brassart and Ramírez had been on it, and the guests who'd come to see them off had piled into their small boats and their wagons and departed, leaving Monsieur Wilde, his nephew Henry, and his nephew's son to clean up afterward. Pierre was there as well, although he'd sent his wife and children home to bed.

"Well now, Marine," he said when he caught sight of Jean-Philippe. "How goes your night?" He asked the question dryly, as though trying to make light of what had happened.

Jean-Philippe took slow steps forward, stopping where he'd danced with her. He pushed the hollow echoes of the music from his mind. "I need to speak with him."

"With Monsieur Wilde?" Pierre looked, too, toward the big man trying now to stack the pieces of a disassembled table into some shape that was orderly, as though that work, that order was of great importance. "I think maybe now is not the time."

"There is no other time," said Jean-Philippe. "Will you translate for me?"

Pierre frowned and assessed him as though searching for a sense of what was coming. "You don't need my English. Yours is good enough."

"It's late. I'm tired. And it's important."

The Acadian considered this, then with a nod agreed.

Monsieur Wilde turned at their approach.

Jean-Philippe motioned for Pierre to step between them. "Tell him he's been very kind to me. I never will forget this."

Pierre looked at him in silence.

"Tell him."

When Pierre was finished speaking, Monsieur Wilde frowned also. "It has been my pleasure."

Jean-Philippe said, "His nephew brought a letter for me when he came today. I have been ordered to join Captain Wheelock in New York, but I must have an escort for my travel. I would like to pay his nephew to accompany me."

This was duly translated, and Henry Ryder glanced up apprehensively. "I do not think I could."

"I will." The nephew's son stood not far off, a boy of fifteen or sixteen. "I will take him."

Jean-Philippe did not catch the exchange between Monsieur Wilde and his nephew that came afterward, it was too swift and spoken low, but he heard Monsieur Wilde say, "a gentleman."

And that appeared to settle things.

But Monsieur Wilde had seemed to bear this news like one more burden. He'd seemed sad, and it took all of Jean-Philippe's resolve to thank him, bow respectfully, and walk away.

He never should have kissed her. It had complicated things beyond all measure. It had been the hand of Providence that brought the interruption, or he might have gone a step too far and told her how he felt. And there would never have been any coming back from that.

Outside the barn, Pierre caught up with him. "What are you doing?"

"What I must."

Pierre reached out and took his arm to stop him walking. Pulled him round until they faced each other and could talk. "What does it really say, your letter?"

He stayed silent. Did not tell Pierre the letter, from Madame de Joncourt in New York, said only that his sergeant had improved a very little, and was resting well.

"You cannot leave her," said Pierre.

That broke the wall. "It is because of her I cannot stay."

"That makes no sense."

He exhaled, hard. "What future can I give her? None. I'm not the kind of man she needs. And this is not the time," he said. "When I'm exchanged, I have to go. So better I go now, than make it worse. I can wait in New York."

"New York is not where you belong." Pierre seemed sure of that. "You think this war will last forever? I can tell you it will not. You think the king in France, who sits in comfort, cares enough to save Quebec? I tell you, from experience, my friend, no help will come. If life has taught me one thing only, it is never to look back. Be happy where you are. Grow roots where you are standing. If you have the ones you love, then you have everything." His eyes were sure. "You love her."

Jean-Philippe did not—would not—deny it.

Pierre sighed. "You're like the sheep, Marine, so stupid. Always you look back at where you've come from, what you've been, what you believe you are, and so you do not see the path you should be taking."

"I'm a soldier. I don't get to choose my path." He'd meant for that to stop the argument.

It didn't. "You're a soldier, so you follow, yes? Then follow this." Pierre's hard finger jabbed him in the chest, above his heart. "God gave you this. He set it like a light within you, so that you could see it well and know the way to go. You follow *this*, Marine. Don't look behind."

And with a rough slap on the arm meant to encourage him, Pierre walked back to finish helping with the cleanup in the barn.

❧

It was not light when they rode out. Monsieur Wilde fetched the mare for him and saddled her himself and said his nephew would provide a better mount when they reached Millbank, and return the mare to them again.

There was not much to carry. Just the haversack and pack that held the things he long had taken where he traveled, camp to camp. Things that were practical, not permanent. He'd left behind the wooden locking box that Monsieur Wilde had made him, all those months ago, to keep his few possessions safe beneath his bed. It, too, was practical, and he would have been happy to have kept it, but it was not built for traveling, and he knew it was not the kind of thing a man like him was meant to keep.

But Monsieur Wilde refused to let him leave with empty hands. He brought the cribbage board, and cards, and pegs, and motioned Jean-Philippe should add them to his pack. He had insisted. "It's my gift," he'd said, a little roughly. "So you won't forget us."

Jean-Philippe could have assured the older man he never would forget them, that it was impossible, but words were hard to find just then, so in their place he gave Monsieur Wilde what remained of his tobacco and said simply, "Thank you."

Turning, he prepared to mount the horse and Monsieur Wilde stopped him with, "Lydia. She'll want to say goodbye. Wait, I will get her."

"No." She was asleep, and must remain so until after he was gone, or it would be too difficult. He found the tight edge of a smile to smooth the word as he told Monsieur Wilde again, more quietly, "No."

He swung into the saddle, took the reins, and turned the horse's head toward the path that led into the woods. The path that life had set him on.

And out of the advice Pierre had given him, he took one piece and followed it: he did not look behind.

CHARLEY

RACHEL FILLED HER WATER bottle at the kitchen sink and set it down. "So she just left?"

Malaika, sorting paint chips at the table with my grandmother, looked up. "It was Sharon. She had things to say. *Then* she left."

I cut in with, "I thought I was telling the story."

Malaika said, "You're leaving out all the good parts."

"She does that," said Rachel. She looked so much better, I thought. Her hair was cut and styled, and she was standing taller. Brighter. So I let the minor insult pass.

"What part did I leave out?" I asked Malaika.

"Eve."

"Oh." She was right. I backtracked. "Well, we've had some extra items donated, some duplicates. They're mostly smaller artifacts, so I had the idea we could make some outreach kits, you know, to loan out to the schools so they could use them in their classrooms. And that means learning the curriculum and how those kits could fit with it, so I asked Eve, because she'd been a teacher, whether she would like to take the lead on that, and be our outreach supervisor."

"Smart," said Rachel.

With a nod Malaika told her, "Yes, it was. So Eve was flattered, and said yes, and—"

Rachel guessed, "And that's when Sharon lost it."

"More or less," I said.

Malaika put in dryly, "It was definitely more. But all *that* did was get Rosina—little, sweet Rosina—mad enough to make a motion that we offer Charley an extension on her contract."

Rachel grinned. "It passed, I hope?"

"It did. The only vote against was Sharon's, and that hardly matters anyway, now that she's quit the board. She's left an opening," Malaika told my grandmother.

"Don't look at me, dear. I've got better things to do these days than sit in meetings." Pulling out a paint chip from the ones fanned across the table she said, "That one, I think. It's the closest."

She was right. We'd had a specialist come out to analyze the layers of the Wilde House walls and test the colors, and Sam knew a guy who knew a guy who made authentic reproduction paint, and he'd made us sample chips we could compare to the originals, from room to room.

"I like that blue one," Rachel said.

My grandmother smiled. "That's my favorite, too."

They had been getting along better with each visit, although I still had my doubts about what they'd planned for this morning, and those doubts grew stronger when I heard the footsteps on the porch.

"Here's your boyfriend," my grandmother said.

Rachel's eyes rolled. "He isn't my boyfriend."

I told her, "He acts like your boyfriend."

She said, "You can talk."

"What is that supposed to mean?" But she'd already gone past to open the door.

Gianni breezed into the kitchen like a blast of cheerful sex appeal, with perfect hair, an easy smile, and a fluorescent life jacket held swinging in one hand. Hot pink. "It's not for you," he said, when Rachel raised her eyebrows. "It's for your great-grandma."

"Are you *sure*," I asked my grandmother, "you want to do this?"

"Certainly."

"We'll keep her safe," said Rachel. "I've been out in it already, and it doesn't leak."

Malaika reassured me it had passed Darryl's inspection. "He knows boats. If he says this one floats, then you can trust his word."

Agreeing, Gianni added, "Rachel did a real good job."

"I know she did." I'd watched her. Watched the care she took. I'd been impressed. I'd told her, joking, "Maybe this can be your new career."

She'd answered, seriously, "I know. Sam said if I wanted to, I could apprentice with him. Learn to be a carpenter."

I'd left it there and hadn't pushed her further, but I'd noticed lately she'd been reading articles online about apprenticing. And watching her be interested in anything was wonderful.

She told me not to worry now, and then she told my grandmother, "I'll go help Gianni get the kayak on the car, Elisabeth. Just wait here for a minute."

As she went outside, Malaika's phone rang and she left us, too, to step out on the porch and take the call.

Across the kitchen table, my grandmother's eyes met mine. "If I know Sharon Sullivan," she said, "she didn't walk out of that meeting without saying something hurtful."

I still had the scorch marks, but I lied. "It wasn't bad."

My grandmother just looked at me. By now, I knew what that look meant.

"What is it that I do?" I asked her. "What's my tell?"

"If I let you know that, I'll never know when you're not telling the truth, will I?" After a brief smile, she asked me straight out, "What did Sharon say?"

I shared the least of the insults. "Just, in essence, that I don't belong here."

"Well, what does she know? Her family only moved here in the seventies. Your family's lived on this same shoreline for eight generations. You remember that, my dear. You're not just a Van Hoek, you're a Boudreau, like me. Our ancestors came here with nothing, not even a chicken to put in their pot. Or a pot, for that matter," she said. "But they dug in, they worked hard, they put down roots, little by little. Held on to each other. Possessions and land, anybody can take those away from you—they knew this, being Acadians. But family…" Her voice dropped off wistfully. "If you have your family, you have everything."

I knew who she was thinking of, specifically. I knew she thought about my father every day.

Gently, I said to her, "Why don't you write him a letter, and tell him that?"

I watched her think it through. "Maybe I will."

And then Rachel was back. "Ready?"

"Don't dump my grandmother into the bay," was my final request.

"If they do," said my grandmother, "I've got my life jacket."

Rachel reached over and lightly touched Niels's chair as she was leaving. "Bye, Dad. See you later."

Left alone at the table, still wrapped in the love and the friendship and warmth that had been in that room, I looked over at Niels's chair, too, and I smiled. "Yes, I know," I said. "Better, right?"

No answer came, but the side door swung open. Malaika leaned in. "Get your shoes," she said.

"Why? Where are we going?"

"Road trip."

"Where?"

"You'll see."

"I hate surprises."

With a smile she promised me, "You'll like this one."

⤮

The carriage house stood at the edge of the road, framed by trees and the green of a park at one side, with the millpond behind, and beyond that, the steep, mounded rise of the bluffs. It was built as a simple block, two stories high, its bottom level dominated by the twin arched double doors of old white-painted wood that hung a little crooked on their rustic iron hinges. Next to them a square window and quaint, glass-paned entry door made it look more like a welcoming home, as did the shingle-sided upper story with its larger, white-framed windows underneath a sloping roof. Someone had painted it a rich barn red that stood out warmly next to the old stone of its foundations.

"This is *it*," Malaika said, as we pulled in and parked. "This is the one."

"The one what?"

She looked satisfied. "The perfect Sam house." Seeing that I looked confused, she explained: "You get to know what kind of place your client's looking for. The things they like, the things they don't. When Sam first came to live here, I sat down with him and we went over everything he wanted and I found a house that fit all that. And what did he do? Fixed it up and flipped it. Not his perfect house, that's what he said." She imitated Sam's voice: "'It's just not my perfect house, Mal.'"

We got out. She carried on. "So I said, fine, I'm up to this. Let's find the man his perfect house. But every single one—it's fix and flip, that's what he does with them. I ask him what he's missing, what he's looking for, and he just says, 'I'll know it when I see it.' Like that's helpful."

She did such a good job imitating Sam I couldn't help but smile. "But isn't it to your advantage, profit-wise, to have him keep on buying homes and flipping them?"

"My profits aren't the point. Now it's the challenge. It's like hunting a damn unicorn. And, baby," she addressed the house directly, "I have got you now."

It *was* unique. I'd seen some carriage houses, but I'd never seen one done like this, or in this kind of setting. "Can I look around?"

She opened the front door and told me, "Be my guest."

The door hung slightly crooked on its hinges. Sam could fix that, though. Or even hang a different door, in keeping with his grandmother's insistence that it never hurt to walk through new doors now and then, to see where you end up.

I felt that promise of discovery as I stepped across the threshold. And besides, I didn't want to just be standing there outside when Sam drove up. I didn't want to be that girl you danced with once in high school who decided on her own that you were dating and kept getting in the way.

We'd danced. And it had altered everything for me, but Sam was…Sam. A steady, certain presence in my life who worked close by me in the daytime and some evenings turned up at the house, helped Rachel with the kayak, hung a shelf here, fixed a baseboard there, and sometimes stayed for popcorn and a movie.

He liked science-fiction thrillers. But not horror. Rachel tried to show him the same movie she'd been watching on the morning after Gianni took her out to see the ghost light in the woods— the old haunted-house thriller that gave me the creeps. Sam had tapped out after twenty minutes. "Nope," he'd said.

Rachel had used the same argument she'd used with me. "But the ghost isn't trying to hurt anybody, he's trying to right an old wrong. He just wants them to listen."

But Sam had held firm. Handing her the remote, he'd said, "Find me a movie where something blows up."

She'd obliged him, and while we were watching he'd stretched his arm out on the back of the sofa and I'd leaned into it and we had stayed like that the next two hours, comfortable.

But if someone had strapped me to a lie detector and asked, "Are you dating him?" I wouldn't have known what to answer.

By the time I heard his truck pull up outside, I was upstairs inside the carriage house. The walls were old, the windows were uninsulated, so I caught most of Malaika's sales pitch as she told him all the features of the property and showed him how the carriage bay was perfect for his workshop. And I felt a little tug within me, wanting him to buy it, and yet wishing that he wouldn't, because every step I took across the floorboards made me feel more strongly this house wanted to be *mine*.

It wasn't something I could put in words, it was just that—a feeling. Folding slowly over me the way a blanket wraps you in its warmth, it drew me deeper into it as I moved through the big room at the back.

It had no furniture, but it would be a bedroom. Where the ordinary window looked out now, across the shaded grass that rolled toward the millpond, with the deep-green trees along the moraine ridge stretched out against the cloud-flecked sky, there I would put the huge round window Sam had taken from Malaika's shed, and it would be a perfect fit.

I was half lost in daydreams when I felt the nudge of Bandit's nose.

I heard Sam's work boots on the stairs, and turned to find him looking at me.

"Come and see," I told him. "Look at this."

He came across, and stood beside me.

"Can you just imagine waking up to *this*," I asked him, "every day?"

He looked, and didn't speak at first. And then he told me, "Yeah."

And then he kissed me.

Everything just stopped. And then it spun, and when he slowly raised his head I felt like everything was different. Better. Just as when we'd danced, I felt that sense of total rightness. Of belonging. As though I had been away for a long time, and had just found my way back home.

"Sam?"

His forehead lowered till it rested warm on mine.

"Do that again," I said, and with a smile, he did.

Malaika was outside and waiting when we came downstairs. She didn't comment on the fact that we were holding hands, or that it must have been completely obvious what we'd been up to.

But she looked a little smug. She asked Sam, "Well? Did I deliver? Does this one have everything you're looking for?"

Indulgently, he let her score the point. He turned my hand in his and interlaced our fingers. And said, "Yeah. I think it does."

⸙

I was ridiculously happy when I stopped by the museum Sunday morning to pick up my work boots. Sam had told me if I wanted to be upstairs in the carriage house, I'd have to wear my proper footgear because he'd found loose nails on the floors.

I'd only meant to grab my boots and go, but as I bent to pick the boots up from the floor beside my desk my office door swung shut. And when I went to open it, the doorknob wouldn't turn.

I tried the door that led into the old part of the house, but it, too, wouldn't budge.

"Okay," I said, in French. "Joke over. Let me out."

I'd become used to him, by now. I knew deep down he wouldn't hurt me. But the feeling, being held there in my office, was uncomfortable.

"I mean it. Let me out."

I tried the doors again. No luck. Reached for my cell phone, and discovered I had left it in the car.

I sighed. And sat down at my desk. Because there really wasn't anything else I could do.

I waited.

Half an hour, maybe more, had passed before I figured maybe he'd get bored if I ignored him, so I started doing work. Against my wall I saw the box of books that Dave had bought at auction. All the sermons of the Reverend Tillotson, twelve volumes, that still needed to be properly accessioned. So I hauled the box across and started dealing with them, one by one.

And while I worked, I talked to him, because it made me feel a little braver.

But he didn't let me leave the room.

I closed the cover of a book and set it to the side. "You really are the most infuriating man, you know? If you have something that you want to tell me, maybe try just telling me, instead of doing all this hocus-pocus stuff."

He must have heard me, because when I looked down at the

book I had just closed, it had reopened to the first page of a sermon with the title printed crisply in italics: *The patience of God*.

"Fine," I said. "I'll be patient."

I finished with all twelve books, noting their details and carefully writing the number in pencil to enter them in our collection. I cleaned out the drawers of my desk. I was closing the last one when, all of a sudden, the door leading into the old house swung quietly open.

I picked up my work boots again, told him, "Thank you," and would have slipped into the big upstairs bedchamber I always thought of as Lydia Wilde's. Except I could hear footsteps now, climbing the stairs at the front of the house, from the entrance.

Light footsteps, not heavy.

I stood there half-frozen and watched as a woman appeared in the bedchamber doorway. An elderly woman. And to my relief, not a ghost.

"I am sorry," she said, in a lovely, French-accented voice. "I did knock, but your front door was already open. I hope I don't trouble you?"

I found my voice and said, "No, not at all."

"I can see you're not ready for visitors, but I have only this day left before I go home, and I hoped—" With a smile she paused, starting again as though wanting to place the words in a more logical order. "For me it's a pilgrimage, you understand, every time I am here in America. I like to pay my respects. But the young lady tells me they no longer have it, they've loaned it to you. So I wonder, if it's not a great inconvenience," she asked, "may I please see the sword of Lieutenant de Sabran?"

LYDIA

HER FATHER WAS BUILDING a coffin.

She watched him at work, his head bent, his hands sure. She'd watched him countless times like this, but now she saw the concentrated effort he was making to shave every piece of roughness from the wood, to keep it smooth. She knew the cost of such an effort.

The dew-wet grass had bent where she had walked across it, and her feet had made so little sound he had not heard her, so she stood a moment longer in the open doorway of the shed, while he was unaware.

Last night had aged him. He looked weary. And she did not want to cause him more distress, but in the end she cleared her throat and wished her father a good morning, and she told him. "Violet's gone."

His hands stayed steady in their movements. "Is she?"

"Yes. On the *Bellewether*, it seems, with Mr. Ramírez. She left a note."

"That's thoughtful of her."

She looked more closely at his face. "You knew."

He raised one shoulder in what might have been a shrug, and her suspicion became certainty.

"You knew Mr. Ramírez was her father."

"Not at first," he told her. "Phyllis never would say who the father was, you understand, but for my part I reckoned it was one of Reuben's Spanish Negroes. He had four, at one time, on his farm at Newtown. Bought off prize ships at New York, with the misfortune to first fall into my brother's hands, and then be taken up in the conspiracy."

She'd been a baby in the year that madness gripped New York, but growing up she'd heard the tale in pieces—how a fire at Fort George had led to claims the black men in that city meant to start a riot, setting off a chain of baseless accusations, mass arrests, and trials that were mockeries of justice. She had heard about the hangings, and the burnings at the stake.

Her father did not tell those details now, but only called the memory of it to her mind.

"It got so terrible," he told her, "that the governor of Massachusetts wrote our own, and told him he must stop it, for he saw that it was taking on the tone of their own witch trials."

"But they didn't stop it."

"No. Like many fires, it choked to death on its own ashes. But it was an evil time, and good men died unnecessary deaths because of it."

He shaved another careful curl of wood from one end of the coffin. "I had hoped," he said, "that Violet's father might be one of those who had survived. Two of my brother's Spanish Negroes were not killed. One was deported. And the other disappeared. Took passage on a ship, most likely, for there were then sympathetic captains in the harbor, privateers, who for a price would take a Spanish Negro to a port at Hispaniola, where he might in time meet with the son of someone he'd once sailed with." He was speaking in an offhand way, his focus on his work. "And later, if he chanced to trade with Daniel, he might learn the woman he'd once loved had come to live with us, here at the cove. And he might learn he had a daughter."

Lydia was quiet for a moment. "Did he know you knew?"

"It was not something we discussed. But clearly it had been arranged with Benjamin, and he will see they get to *El Montero*."

He said nothing of what other things had been arranged with Benjamin. He did not mention William or his trade to the West

Indies, or the flag of truce that Benjamin now carried on the *Bellewether*, and Lydia could not help wondering whether her father had long known the truth about her brothers' business, also.

Standing there, she only said, "I hope it will go well for Violet. I hope she'll be free." A darker thought intruded. "But," she asked him, "what of Uncle Reuben?"

"I have money. I can pay him."

But she knew, as he did, that it had never been about the money, with her uncle. "Will he hunt her?"

"Even Reuben," he informed her, "will not hunt a corpse." He finished with the coffin lid and set it in its place, and then she understood.

"You mean to tell him she is dead?"

"I mean to tell all who will listen that she drowned early this morning, and I found her. If they want a pretty story, I will say that when Ramírez left, she lost the will to carry on. It is not so implausible, considering her mother threatened once to do the same."

She thought of this, and with a nod conceded it might work.

"I'll go and do the milking, then. Just let me put the tea on first, for you and Mr. de Sabran."

He straightened. "Lydia."

She had begun to turn away but now she stopped, and looked at him.

He told her, "Violet's not the only one who's left us."

❧

She'd learned the way to deal with loss. She knew that, like a clinging vine, if given space it would wind over everything, blot out the color and the light and leave her there in darkness. So she did not give it space. She filled each moment of her waking day with work—an easy thing, with Violet gone. And in the night she fell into a sleep too deep for dreams.

The dreams still tried to come. They crept in quietly and

pressed for entry, promising the quick flash of a smile, and warm oblivion. But she withstood them, and kept hold of her emotions.

Till the day that Silas came.

He came at midday, on the mare. The morning had been warm and he had used the mare so harshly she was foaming sweat, her eyes rolled partly white in indignation.

Lydia came forward, took hold of the reins, and lost her temper. "What's the matter with you? Off. Get off her now."

He raised his eyebrows. "And good day to you, too, Cousin." Dropping indolently from the saddle he watched Lydia begin to tend the mare. "I don't believe I've seen you angry since our childhood. It becomes you."

She could tell that he was hoping for a heated answer, and she did not give him satisfaction. "I'll fetch Father."

He'd been clearing out the well. His clothes were streaked with dirt and dust. He nodded. "Silas." Not a greeting of affection.

"Uncle Zeb." He looked around expectantly. "Where's Joseph? Is he well? We heard a most distressing story, although I was certain it could not be true. As I told everyone, my cousin could not kill a man." He made it sound a failing, rather than a virtue.

Lydia had walked the mare to soothe her and had taken off the saddle and now with a rag began to rub and raise the hair along the horse's legs, where blood cooled faster.

"Joseph's fine," her father said. "You've come for payment."

"Yes. My father has your letter and accepts the sum you've offered. With a penalty of course, for such an early and untimely loss of property."

She watched her father bite his tongue. He said, "I'll get your money."

He was gone for a few minutes, in the house, and Silas broke the brittle silence. "I hear Benjamin's made captain of the *Bellewether*."

It was a probing comment, not a question, and she did not choose to rise to it. "You seem to hear a lot of things."

"I do. I hear that a French officer came lately from this cove to take up lodgings at the house of the de Joncourt family." He smiled faintly, seeing the effect of that remark. "But only one, though. So I wonder, since we sent you two French officers, what happened to the other?"

She said nothing. She was grateful when her father reappeared, a calfskin purse of money in his hand.

"Here. You don't want to waste the daylight."

"You would send me back to Millbank now, on foot, and without dinner?" Silas raised his eyebrows higher. "This is hardly hospitality. Or do you worry I might learn the secret of whose body you have truly buried up there on the hill?"

A weighted silence hung between them.

"Fine." Her father shattered it, decisively. "You wish to see who's buried there? Come and see. I'll get my shovel."

As he stormed toward the shed, he said, "Let's hope you have the stomach for it, though, because a body drowned is not a pretty sight, and being buried rarely does improve it."

Silas made no move to follow, and her father stopped.

"Well? Are you coming?"

Silas, caught within the web of his own cowardice, said, "No."

Her father calmed, and walked back down to stand in front of Silas. "No." He did not say it mockingly, but in full understanding of the limitations of her cousin's nature. "Go home, boy. Tell my brother our account is settled. It is done. Go home."

She was not sure it was a wise thing, sending Silas off this way, but it felt good to watch him trudging down the road to Millbank, through the darkness of the trees.

Her father seemed to stand a little straighter, having shaken off the yoke he'd carried on his shoulders for so many years. She asked him, "What would you have done, if he had gone to see the coffin opened?"

"I'd have laid him in it," said her father.

And with that, he went to finish clearing out the well.

❧

August was a month of storms. And Henry brought bad news.

They sat together in the parlor—she and Henry, Joseph, Sarah, and her father—and the blue walls seemed to run with mournful shadows as the rain chased down the window glass. They drank a toast, respectfully, to Governor DeLancey. To his memory.

"It's an unexpected death," said Henry, "though of course he was a good age."

Her father reminded them dryly, "He is—he was—younger than me."

"But the new acting governor's older, so he may be much better able to deal with the merchants," was Henry's opinion. "They have been complaining of late that they cannot find crews for their ships, since the sailors are moving to other ports where they're less likely to find themselves pressed into service in our Royal Navy. I'm told that not even the market boats these days are safe from the press."

Her father was of the opinion that it would get worse before it would get better. They'd all seen the newspaper Henry had brought, with the list "Flags of Truce, taken by Men of War and Privateers, and carried into Jamaica."

The *Bellewether*, Lydia noticed, had not been among them.

"But tell us some good news," said Sarah. She sat with her arm slipped through Joseph's, their wedding not many weeks off now, their house nearly finished. "It cannot be all sad and gloomy. There must be some good."

Henry thought for a moment, then ventured, "They say General Amherst will march soon against Montreal. And you know that Quebec is secure, of course, after the French tried and failed to retake it. So finally it looks as though all of the victories will be on our side."

She fell silent, and nobody noticed. Nor did they see how it affected her when Henry added, "In fact, there is a ship now in the harbor at New York that's carried upward of a hundred of our own men, several officers included, just released by their French captors and sent down to be exchanged, and surely having them back in the fight will be an asset."

"What rank?" she asked him.

Henry turned. "I beg your pardon?"

"What rank are the officers to be exchanged?"

"I've no idea. All ranks, I'd imagine." Henry smiled. "Is it important?"

"No," she said. "I don't suppose it is."

But she could not stop thinking of that ship in New York harbor, waiting now to take French prisoners—French officers—back home in an exchange.

She thought of when they'd first arrived. When *he* had first arrived. And she remembered how impatient she had been to have him gone.

So now he would be going. Now, perhaps, he was already gone. And she could find no joy in it. No joy in it at all.

✎

That evening, when she went to do the milking, she stood quietly alone and for a long time at the center of the barn. There was no music. Nothing left to mark the place where they had danced.

And yet she stood there and remembered how it felt when he had held her hands and missed the steps and laughed. When loyalties and uniforms and war had seemed like things of no significance, and they had been a woman and a man and nothing more.

She heard the barn door creaking open and she went on standing there and did not move, because she suddenly became aware that she'd begun to cry. The tears slid hotly down her cheeks and would not stop, so she stayed still and held her head up and hoped whoever it was would go, and leave her with some dignity.

A harness thudded on the wall as someone hung it on its peg. The door began to creak again, then stopped.

French Peter said, "You think he left because he did not care."

She didn't move. She didn't speak. She felt sure she would fall to pieces if she tried.

He said, "He thought he could not offer you a future. Not a future that was good for you. He thought that you deserved a better man."

French Peter paused, and when he spoke again his voice held sympathy. "He did not leave because he did not care," he said. "He left because he loved you."

JEAN-PHILIPPE

T HIS IS AN INFURIATING game." Captain Bonneau surveyed the cards he had been dealt, while Jeanne de Joncourt took her seat within the family's parlor.

"Then you're well-suited to it," she remarked. She looked at Jean-Philippe. "How is your sergeant?"

"Sleeping." *Dying* was the truest answer. After all these years he knew the signs. But there was nothing to be gained by being truthful in this instance, and La Réjouie for his part seemed content to drift and doze without confronting the reality.

He thought that Jeanne de Joncourt knew. At least, he thought it probable, because these past two days she had been watching Jean-Philippe with an expression of shared sympathy.

Bonneau said, "Truly, too much of this game depends on changes in the play I can't control." He spoke with feeling that came more from life than the cards. He'd been here for two months already, having brought his prisoners to New York in the first days of July, only to have to wait a month for Captain Wheelock to arrive from Massachusetts to begin arranging the exchange, and that, in turn, had brought him more frustration.

Still, Bonneau was an experienced negotiator—levelheaded, flawlessly polite, and firm in his demands. And he'd decided he was bringing Jean-Philippe back with him, this time. He'd told Wheelock, "Monsieur le Marquis reminds you that to settle the mistake made in your last exchange, you still owe him a captain, twenty-two Canadians, and two lieutenants of the Troupes de la Marine. And there is one of them." He'd pointed with his glass at Jean-Philippe.

Wheelock had said, if it were up to him, he would allow it. "But the general is reluctant to exchange the Troupes de la Marine."

"Because he doesn't trust them, yes? You are too highly capable," Bonneau had said to Jean-Philippe. "You make the English nervous. But"—he'd turned again to Wheelock—"this is why it would be better to exchange this man, and get him off your soil."

To watch the back-and-forth between the two men could be entertaining.

Jeanne de Joncourt often joined them, though her own attention rarely strayed from Captain Wheelock. It was very obvious to Jean-Philippe the two of them were smitten with each other, and he envied them.

He envied Captain Wheelock, too, for being able to come call upon the family of the woman he was courting, and be greeted as a friend.

Today, the captain looked preoccupied when he arrived.

Bonneau informed him, "As you see, I'm forced to play the very irritating game of cribbage, so if you must tear me from it, I will not complain."

But Captain Wheelock was first drawn aside by Jeanne de Joncourt, to a quiet corner of the parlor, where they bent their heads and talked in private.

Bonneau glanced at them and smiled. "Such comfort," he told Jean-Philippe, "is not allowed for you nor me. A shame, but there it is. Some men get wives while others get the battlefield." He pointed to the cards and asked, "Now, which will you discard?"

Wheelock came across and said to Jean-Philippe, "Lieutenant, may I see you for a moment? On your own."

The room he chose was plain, but private. Wheelock closed the door and took a seat and motioned Jean-Philippe to sit as well, and for a moment they sat looking at each other, as they had the first day they'd met, at the Wildes' house on Long Island.

"Last summer," Wheelock said, "when I was first sent down here, one of my superiors suggested rather strongly I should try persuading prisoners to change sides, and come fight for us." His tone of voice told how he'd felt about that order.

Jean-Philippe asked, "And how did you answer your superior?"

"I told him a worse instrument than myself could hardly be found for the purpose. Had any of the prisoners applied to me to change sides, I might then have helped, but I could hardly promise to be active in persuading people to do what I'd disapprove of in myself." His mouth turned downward at the corners. "That said, I find myself right now, Lieutenant, in a singular position."

Jean-Philippe had learned to wait for men to state their meaning clearly.

Captain Wheelock took his time.

"You are like myself, I think," he said. "A man who values honor." Rising from his chair, he moved to stand beside the window. "I have been led round the world for these twenty years past by a passion for doing what seems to me right. I've followed this passion to the detriment of my fortune and I believe to the hindrance of my promotion, yet it endures," he explained, "and obliges me sometimes to go beyond prudence, and even politeness."

It was a curious speech. Jean-Philippe tried to reason where it might be leading.

"Forgive me," Captain Wheelock said, "for I know what I'm going to ask is well beyond politeness, and you're not obliged to answer, but when you were on Long Island, did you enter into any understanding with Miss Wilde?"

He felt his features turn to stone. He did not answer.

Captain Wheelock said again, "Forgive me. I ask this because she has written a letter." He drew it out now from his pocket. "A personal letter. To you."

"You have opened it."

"We are at war."

Jean-Philippe held his hand out. He opened the letter. "It's written in English."

"Yes, but I had my—that is, I had Miss de Joncourt translate it. Below the original. There."

He read her words, turned into French for him. And for a moment he felt he had ceased to breathe.

Wheelock was talking. "The thing is, I've just had a letter myself today, from General Amherst. Your Marquis de Vaudreuil has signed a surrender at Montreal."

Jean-Philippe's head came up. "What?"

"Montreal has been taken. Vaudreuil has surrendered. Your colony's no longer French, it is British. Your Troupes de la Marine will soon be disbanded, no doubt," Wheelock told him, "and you'll be exchanged with the rest of the prisoners, and sent to France."

Jean-Philippe frowned. "To France?"

"Yes." The captain's eyes held a faint bitterness. "I have my orders. No prisoners are to be sent back to Canada now. Not even those who have farms there, and family there—children, and elderly parents, and wives. Doesn't matter. The men who are here go to France. No exceptions."

"But this is—"

"Unjust?" Wheelock offered. "Yes. Wrong? Absolutely. But those are my orders. They're very clear. Only those men who took oaths of allegiance to King George before word of Montreal's fall reached New York are permitted to travel to Canada, as British subjects." He stopped then, and looked very steadily at Jean-Philippe. "Do you understand?"

"I serve my own king."

"That's your choice," said Wheelock. "An honorable choice. And I'm sure, once in France, you can make a new life, and I'll wish you the best of it."

Jean-Philippe looked down again at the letter he held. Read her words for a third time.

The captain said, "But, if you have entered an understanding with Miss Wilde, and wish to uphold that, there's honor in that, too, Lieutenant." He smiled with the eyes of a man who had finally found love himself, and knew its worth in a changeable world. "There will be an express on the road as we speak, bringing news to New York of the Marquis de Vaudreuil's surrender, and once that arrives, I can't help you."

He looked down at the papers in his hands. *Some men get wives while others get the battlefield*, Bonneau had said. *Now, which will you discard?*

And in the end, for Jean-Philippe, it was an easy choice to make.

❦

There was a woman in the water.

He had seen her when he'd come around the headland. He was walking, relishing the freedom of the forest and the road that was his own to walk alone now, if he wanted to. The sun was high and falling warm across the bright September sky and he was thinking it would soon be time to gather corn and start the harvest in the orchard, when the wind had blown the branches at his shoulder and they'd parted on a view down to the water of the bay.

And he had seen her, standing in her yellow gown, some little distance from the shore.

Now every time the trees grew thin, he looked for her, and felt a growing sense of peace.

Her head was turned halfway to him as though she somehow sensed that he was near. She'd gathered up her skirts above the waterline. She stood more still and for a longer time than any woman he could call to memory, as though she were fixed in place by some force yet invisible, within that clear blue water.

By the fifth time he caught sight of her, he knew that he was nearly home.

And had you asked, she'd written him, *my answer then and always would be yes. For I will not believe there is no future for us. I cannot believe it, when my heart wants nothing more than to be yours. This war*

will end, and all the things that now divide us will be gone, and I will set
my hopes upon that day and wait for your return.

And she had signed it with, *Your Lydia.*

His Lydia. His, now.

He had not far to go. Already he could see the lighter greens
that marked the clearing's edge, and he could hear the steady
swing of Monsieur Wilde's axe.

Except as he stepped from the path into the clearing, he discovered his mistake. Because it wasn't Monsieur Wilde. It was Joseph.

Face-to-face they stood, and nothing moved.

Or so it seemed.

Then Joseph's hand tightened its grip upon the axe. And Jean-
Philippe reached, very slowly, for his sword.

He drew it, just as slowly, cautiously, until the silver caught the
sun along the etched words that reminded him to never draw that
blade without good cause.

And then he turned the hilt away from him, and bowed his
head, and with the blade flat in his hand he held it out, and offered
it to Joseph.

CHARLEY

B ut no, it did not happen in the way you say." My elegant French visitor was smiling at the thought.

We were sitting on the bottom two steps of the dog-leg staircase in the downstairs entry hall, the front door of the old house standing open to the softness of the cooling afternoon.

She'd seen the sword. And I'd brought out the drawing, done supposedly by Lydia, that showed the men at work upon the *Bellewether*, and I'd just finished telling her the story of the officer and Lydia, as I'd heard it from Frank.

"He did not die," she told me. "I don't know where *that* began, but it's a fairy tale. They lived a long and happy life together, Lydia and Jean-Philippe."

That was his name, I'd learned: Lieutenant Jean-Philippe de Sabran de la Noye.

"La Noye," she told me, "was the *seigneurie*, you understand. The family farm estate along the St. Charles River, near the city of Quebec. It's still there, you can go and visit. They have weddings there now. Wine tastings. It stayed within the family many years, but now it's school teachers who own it. A young couple. Very nice. After the Seven Years' War, many of the buildings there were burned and left in ruins by the British, but when Jean-Philippe and Lydia moved up to take it over, they built everything back as it was. You know, the big stone house, the barns. The whole estate is beautiful. I have a drawing of that house by Lydia, as well."

I blinked, and held our drawing up to her. "So this was done by Lydia? You've seen more drawings by her?"

"Oh, yes. Yes, her style is very recognizable, when you have seen enough of her work," she assured me. "And particularly in the portraits."

"Portraits?" I was happy I was sitting down, because I felt my knees begin to buckle. "Whose portraits?"

"Oh, everyone. Her children, Jean-Philippe, his sister, and I think her brothers. Many people. She was really very talented."

"I don't suppose," I said, "that I could pay to have some copies made of those?"

She smiled again, and gave my arm a pat. "I'll send the real ones to you. You should have them. One I gave last Christmas to my nephew's son, because he always loved it since he was a little boy, but all the others, and the hat, I think that you should have them."

I was starting to feel light-headed. "The hat?"

She laughed. "I'll send it to you. Every family needs its own historian, someone to guard the stories, yes? Or else they will be lost. But now I'm eighty-six," she said, "and have no children of my own, so someone else must guard the pieces I have gathered." She looked up, toward the newly restored ceiling and the beautifully replastered walls, and told me, "This is nice. It's very good, what you have done here, with this house. The love of Lydia and Jean-Philippe, this is where it began, so it is right that what remains of them returns here."

❧

"Eighty-six," said Rachel. "Wow."

I looked around from where I sat, beside Sam on my brother's porch, and asked her, "Really? That's your takeaway from everything I just got finished telling you?"

"Of course. The woman's eighty-six and French and still flies over every year from Paris. *That's* the life I want."

I admitted she had made it look pretty fabulous. "But I don't think I'll look that good at eighty-six."

"Sure you will," Rachel said. "Sam loves to keep old things looking like new."

"Ha-ha."

Sam stretched his legs out, feet propped on the porch railing, and said, "It's true."

"Partly true," I corrected him, as Rachel left us alone. He was proving my point, moving one foot just slightly to test how far the railing wobbled. I said, "You like fixing things. Broken things."

I hadn't meant for the tone to creep into my voice, but it did, and he heard it. "Hey."

"No, it's okay. It's just…"

"What?"

"Well," I said, "it's what you do, I know. Just like the houses. You fix things. And people. And beagles." I couldn't help smiling a little because he was pushing his boot on the railing again, nonchalantly. "I guess I'm messed up enough that I'll stay interesting."

"You think I'm with you because you need fixing?" He looked at me, serious. "Charley, I'm with you because when I came down that staircase last summer and saw you, it messed *me* up. I haven't been the same since. Okay?"

He had the best eyes. "Okay."

"Now, come here."

And of course that was when the porch railing decided to fall off entirely, right to the gravel. Of course I looked up and saw my parents' car pulling in at the front, unannounced, unexpected.

Sam grinned. Held my face in his hands. Held my gaze. "Breathe," he told me. And kissed me.

And that, as it turned out, made everything right.

POSTERN

S OME HOUSES SEEM TO want to hold their secrets. The Wilde House seemed to have decided that the time had come to let them go.

One morning Willie, working on the massive kitchen hearth, pulled out a flintlock pistol, in four pieces, from a hollow in the stones. "There'll be a story goes with *that*, I'm sure," he said, and Lara's youngest boys had started coming up with story possibilities.

"I bet it was a bank robber."

"I bet it was a rogue assassin."

"Rogue assassin?"

"Yeah. He had a job to do here in the house, and when he finished he broke up the gun so nobody could trace it to him."

Willie looked at me and winked. "That's how it starts," he told me.

I'd decided that I liked the story of the French soldier and Lydia much better now I knew they both survived and had a happy-ever-after ending.

And when the box from France arrived, it felt like Christmas morning.

It came wrapped up like a sculpture, thickly padded, but when all the packing layers had been peeled away they left a simple deal-box, three feet long by two by one and made of pine, with old forged hinges neatly inset so they would be more secure, and iron loops that once had held a lock.

There was a note to say the box itself had been made here for Jean-Philippe when he'd arrived, so he would have a place to keep his things, and that he'd liked it so much he had kept it all his life, and it had been passed down the family as a relic of their ancestor's captivity.

And in the box, she'd sent the promised treasures.

A cocked tricorn hat of black wool felt with trim that had once been bright gilt. A square of faded yellow silk, much treasured from the look of it. And under those, shielded between sheets of acid-free cardboard, protected by Mylar, she'd sent us the drawings by Lydia Wilde.

I'd hoped there might be a self-portrait. There wasn't.

But there were the drawings she'd done of her husband, and they were worth all of the rest. I could see why she'd fallen in love with him. Not just his looks, but the warmth of his eyes and the way that he seemed to be smiling privately, only for her.

There were two drawings of a much older man, kind-eyed and heavy-jawed, who had been labeled as Zebulon Wilde. And labeled or not, there was no way I could miss Benjamin—I'd seen enough of his portraits in oils to be able to know him as soon as I saw his face. Benjamin Wilde as a teenager was my particular favorite, because of the flow of his hair and the glint in his eye that seemed ready to take on the world.

There was also a young man resembling Benjamin but with more serious eyes, and I'd guessed his identity even before I had read the name: Joseph. The brother who'd taken the blame for a murder that never occurred. We could fix that.

I had plans to have quality copies made of these Wilde portraits; to frame them and hang them throughout the house, telling the stories of those who had lived here and helping them come back to life for our visitors.

So it was almost a mystical moment when, out of the bundle of drawings, I lifted the portraits of Phyllis and Violet.

Two drawings of each of them, beautifully rendered—rare representations of African American women of Benjamin Wilde's time.

And then, at the bottom, below several drawings of children, was Patience Wilde. Lydia's mother. Her eyes seemed to follow me, smiling, no matter which angle I viewed her from.

"Maybe," I said to Sam, later that afternoon, "Lydia looked like her mother."

He agreed it was possible. "Where am I putting this chair?"

We were starting to furnish the keeping room, now that the walls had been paneled and plastered and painted the soft gray-green color they had been in Benjamin's day.

Sam was holding the Spanish chair, carefully, waiting for me to direct him.

I said, "By the fireplace, right there. It's a nice, cozy spot for it."

He set it down.

As we stood watching, the chair began moving of its own accord. Sliding over the planks of the floor on a perfect diagonal, it came to a stop by the large window right at the front of the room, before pivoting slightly to rest at an angle.

I looked at Sam and he looked back at me. I'd expected him to look incredulous, even alarmed, but he didn't. In fact, he appeared to be taking it all in stride.

"Well," he said, "I guess that's where she wants it."

"Where who wants it?"

"You know. Our resident ghost."

"He's a man."

Sam said, "Nah, she's a woman. I've seen her."

"You've *seen* her? When?"

"Couple of times. Just her shape, not her face, but she's clearly a woman." When he looked at my face, he asked, "What?"

It was such a relief to be able to tell him the things that had happened to me in this house, without worrying whether he'd think I was crazy. I couldn't help adding, "But you're awfully calm about this, for a guy who can't watch scary movies."

He shrugged. "She's not trying to hurt anyone. She's a comfortable ghost, if you know what I mean."

It was not a bad word for her: comfortable. Really, the things she had done were designed to protect me, to show me my way in the dark, help me find things, remind me I ought to be patient. Unless…

"Oh," I said.

"What?"

"Sam, I think I know who she is." All the pieces began to connect, and the final one fell into place with the sermon. The one in the Tillotson book in my office: *The patience of God*. Not advice, but a name.

Her name.

"I think it's Patience Wilde." Setting the record straight. Righting old wrongs. Bringing all of her family together.

The wind gently rattled the window glass next to the Spanish chair, and the old house seemed to settle around us at last with a human-like sigh of contentment.

And all down the path to the cove and the bay, and across the bright waters of Long Island Sound, every whisper fell silent.

The Wildes had come home.

THE END

About the Characters

Nearly all my novels have their roots in some small episode of history, but it isn't often that the history is my own.

Having been born into a family of amateur genealogists, I've always known that one branch of my ancestors, the Halletts, had settled on Long Island in the mid-seventeenth century, at Hallett's Cove, eventually establishing themselves at Hellgate and at Newtown, where during the Seven Years' War they had taken in French officers on their parole of honor.

But it wasn't until I read Thomas M. Truxes's absorbing history book *Defying Empire: Trading with the Enemy in Colonial New York* (New Haven and London: Yale University Press, 2008), that I gained a full appreciation for the intrigue of the times.

As always with my novels, I've mixed characters who really lived with ones that I've invented. And when writing real-life characters, I've tried wherever possible to use their own words as I found them in my research documents, and use those sources to establish dates and times of things that happened.

George Spencer, for example, and his treatment by the mob in New York City, is recorded down to the route and time of day, and I've changed none of it, choosing to weave my fictional characters into the tapestry of what actually happened.

The Wilde family is fictional, a blending of my own ancestors with their Long Island neighbors, the Lawrences, whose real-life privateering schooner, *Tartar*, in combination with the New York sloop *Harlequin*, inspired my fictional *Bellewether*.

Another of the Hallett's neighbors, an Acadian refugee known as French John, has echoes in my character Pierre Boudreau.

Big-Headed Tom—whose last name was Stephenson—was a real-life character I stumbled across by chance while reading old issues of *The Caledonian Mercury* newspaper, which, on January 13, 1762, published a lengthy extract of a letter from an officer on board the *Pembroke* (a ship captained at the time, coincidentally, by John Wheelock, younger brother of Captain Anthony Wheelock) relating "the character and adventures of a very strange fellow… commonly known by the name of Big-headed Tom," with details of Tom's piracy and hatred of the Spanish.

Captain del Rio will not be a complete stranger to my readers, as his equally fictional father played a prominent role in my earlier novel *A Desperate Fortune*. And his first mate, Juan Ramírez, although fictional as well, is nonetheless inspired by all the Spanish mariners caught up in the disgraceful so-called Slave Conspiracy and trials that took so many lives so needlessly in New York City in 1741.

Every now and then, while reading for research, I come across voices of good people—quiet ones, usually—swept to the corners of history, forgotten and overlooked, when they deserve to be heard and remembered. Before I had finished the first of his letters, I knew Captain Anthony Wheelock had one of those voices.

Born and raised in the parish of Westminster, London, England, he seems to have inherited his "strong passion for doing what seems to me right" from his father, Bryan Wheelock, a clerk of the Board of Trade in London, who was once briefly dismissed from that position in retaliation for testifying honestly when questioned by the House of Lords about some secret letters he had seen. Bryan Wheelock, thanks to family connections, had also traveled with Anthony Ashley Cooper, the third Earl of Shaftesbury, a highly respected and influential philosopher who believed that all men had an inner moral sense of right and wrong, that "the love of doing good" was "of itself, a good and right inclination," and that "Prejudice is a mist, which in our journey through the world often dims the brightest and obscures the best of all the good and glorious objects that meet us on our way."

Bryan spent the last year of the earl's life with him in Naples, Italy, and was with him when he died there. It's my belief that Bryan chose to name his firstborn son in memory of the earl, since up to then there'd never been an Anthony within the Wheelock family.

Anthony Wheelock, born December 31, 1716, followed a different path from his father. In the 1740s the records show him as a captain of marines on board various ships, eventually in command of his own Company, but by the summer of 1759 he was in America, a self-described "late Captain of the 27th Inniskilling Regiment of Foot," being sent by General Amherst to New York to be in charge of the French prisoners.

His letters to Amherst reveal him as a man of great compassion and integrity, speaking up often in defense of others' rights. When Amherst failed to pay the mandated provision money to the colonists housing and feeding the prisoners, Wheelock objected to the hardships it would cause. Amherst relented, and paid. Wheelock also argued on behalf of the Canadian prisoners who, in his view, should have been allowed to return to their homes and families after the war, instead of being forced to go to France. It clearly bothered him.

In the early 1770s he served as the crown agent for the British colony of East Florida, and eventually returned home to London, where he died in 1781, leaving everything to his son Jeffrey, and his "dear wife Jane"—the former Jane, or Jeanne, de Joncourt, whom he'd met and lost his heart to while he had been working in New York.

They married in 1761, a year after the events of this novel, and finding the entry of that marriage in the registers of the French Church of Saint-Esprit at New York was, for me, a happy discovery.

Jane's late father, Peter de Joncourt, a merchant and tavern keeper, had served for years as an "Interpreter of the French language" by commission from the Lieutenant Governor of New

York, so I passed this duty on to Jane, particularly since Wheelock in his letters often wrote of needing somebody to help him write in French.

And since the de Joncourts had also taken care of the captured French commander Baron Dieskau a few years earlier, when he'd been brought to New York gravely wounded, I decided they would be good hosts for my own wounded sergeant in this novel.

The sergeant is a composite of two real-life men, one whose name I've not yet learned. The unnamed soldier who was robbed and beaten on the road to Hempstead was the subject of a letter Captain Wheelock wrote to General Amherst. Wheelock was dismayed the man had not received the justice he felt such a crime deserved. In spite of my searches, I've since found no further references to this man, just as I could find no information on another man I came across—a sergeant of the Troupes de la Marine whose death was noted in the registers of the French Church of Saint-Esprit at New York as: *Jacques le Roy, dit La Réjouie, prisoner of war.*

So I decided to combine them.

A word about La Réjouie: in French North America, men joining the army were given nicknames, or "dit" names (pronounced "dee," for the French word that, in this sense, means *called*). These "dit" names could refer to anything from the place a person came from, as with Depoitiers (of Poitiers) and Lavallee (the valley), to a physical descriptor like Le Grand (the large) or La Jeunesse (the young), or to an aspect of their character, like Belhumeur (good-natured) or La Pensée (the thoughtful one).

Captain Louis de Preissac de Bonneau was very real, with a dashing personality that leaps easily out of his letters and seems to have made him a favorite of the ladies. When he was taken prisoner the first time, in 1758, one officer in Quebec wrote to his commander, "My wife will weep for her friend Bonneau." He was well known in New York, and I've kept his movements and activities there as true and accurate as possible.

When Fort Niagara fell to the British in August 1759, several

French soldiers and officers remained unaccounted for. One of these, according to the records, was named "La Noye." And Wheelock, writing to Amherst about the Canadian officers, noted, "La Noue a Lieutenant has a settlement in Canada..."

That was all my imagination needed to create my fictional character of Jean-Philippe de Sabran de la Noye, whose career was pieced together from the histories of several real-life Canadian officers in the Troupes de la Marine. I gave him an imagined *seigneurie* on the bank of the St. Charles River, not far from the very real General Hospital, which still stands, and where a poignant monument commemorates those who died there in the Seven Years' War, watched over by the tomb of Montcalm.

There is no town of Millbank on the north shore of Long Island, but after you've read this book, the real village of Roslyn may have a familiar feel. The Wilde farm occupies land not dissimilar to Garvies Point Museum and Preserve, although I've taken the liberty of placing a fictional house there that has a lot in common with the Raynham Hall Museum, found in Oyster Bay. And there's a strong resemblance between the real-life Mosquito Cove, near Sea Cliff, and this book's Snug Cove—a name I borrowed from the cove of the same name on Campobello Island, where another of my ancestors, Colonel Christopher Hatch, owned two houses and a wharf.

That same ancestor—a United Empire Loyalist who left New York for Canada in the wake of the Revolutionary War—brought with him at least one slave: Violet Tucker.

I have no record of her being granted freedom. While the British abolished the slave trade in 1807, slavery itself continued until the Slavery Abolition Act came into effect in 1834 for the greater part of the Empire, and for the whole of it in 1843.

Violet married Rueben Alexander in 1792, when she was thirty-seven, and together they raised a family of several children, and when the 1851 census was taken she was still alive, at the age of ninety-six.

But a *Pictorial History of St. Andrews*, drawn and written by Frances Wren in 1937, claimed that Violet "could remember as a little girl in Africa when the slave ship came and took her away."

That always stayed with me.

The character of Violet in this book is in her memory.

Phyllis is also based on a woman who actually lived. Sometimes, in my research, I find people I just feel are reaching out to me. They take hold of my heart, somehow, and I just can't forget them.

In my reading for this book, I came across this entry in the Minutes of the Coroner's Proceedings for New York:

Sunday, October 22d, 1758:

Having received information that one Louder, a taylor in this city had starved his wench so that she died I made enquiry about the same but could make nothing more of it than what is contained in the following disposition—viz:

    Susanna Roome wife of Cornelius Roome of the said city feltmaker being sworn according to law deposeth & saith that about five weeks past a Negro wench named Phillis was committed to the jail of this city on suspicion of poisoning her master one Lowder a taylor who lives in the house with the deponent that James Mills the jailor and undersheriff came & desired the said Lowder to take her away she being taken sick and discharged from thence, that her said master Lowder then confined her in a small room in the garret having a chain round one of her arms made fast to the partition of the aforesaid room that he gave her suppon [a sort of cornmeal mush] to eat that the deponent was informed by the girl the meal was full of worms and the wench could not eat it that the deponent then gave her tea and other things to nourish her at two severall times that when her master discovered it he was very angry that he then made the room close so that the deponent could not farther help her that she called for drink from ten a

clock one morning till three a clock in the afternoon, that she was
confined in the aforesaid room almost all the time from her coming
out of jail till ffryday Saturday and Sunday last that she believes
the said wench had suppon enough to suffice nature.

Sworn the 22d of October 1758 before me
John Burnet Coroner.

That entry brought tears to my eyes and made me angry. It still does. And while I agree with the wonderful historical novelist Beverly Jenkins that there can be no happy endings in slavery, I wanted to honor and recognize Phyllis the best way I knew how to, in this novel.

Angélique, while entirely fictional, represents the many people, both black and Indigenous, who were held as slaves in French and English Canada, and about whom I was never taught at school.

In the *Final Report of the Truth and Reconciliation Commission of Canada*, entered into the public domain in 2015, the commissioners state:

"The reconciliation process is not easy. It asks those who have been harmed to revisit painful memories, and those who have harmed others—either directly or indirectly—to be accountable for past wrongs."

It's an ongoing process, for all of us. But as a writer, I also feel strongly that, as the commissioners promise, "The arts help to restore human dignity and identity in the face of injustice."

And that's what I've tried to do.

Reading Group Guide

1. Patience is only partly right when she tells William he's spelled the name of his ship wrong. *Bellewether* is, in fact, the original Middle English spelling of the word *bellwether*. Apart from its literal meaning—a sheep that wears a bell to lead the flock—the term can also apply to a predictor or harbinger of something. When asked about the meaning of the book's title, the author said, "In the book, the ghost is a literal bellewether, leading Charley toward the truth, while the divisions forming between Britain and her colonists, and among the colonists themselves, are a bellewether of the coming revolution." What bellewethers have you experienced in your own life? Did you know they were harbingers at the time? Or only when you looked back after a significant event?

2. The legend of Lydia, her French officer, and the ghost that haunts the Wilde House grounds turns out to be wrong in several respects. Did you see the twists coming? Were there any stories passed down in your own family that turned out, in the end, to be not entirely true?

3. Did you guess who the ghost was? Do you believe in ghosts? Have you ever encountered a ghost in your own life?

4. Charley and Lydia are both struggling to hold their families together through difficult times. Who is the person in your family who holds everyone together through difficult times? Have you ever had to play that role?

5. Both the past and present storylines feature multiple genera-tions interacting. Do you like this in stories? Do you have difficult or colorful characters in your family? What is the best thing about your own family dynamics?

6. Did you relate more to the historical story line or to the story line in the present day? Why?

7. The use of two viewpoints in the past—Lydia's and Jean-Philippe's—means that sometimes we see the same scene from two different perspectives. Have you ever talked to someone about an event from the past and found that they saw the event completely different from how you did?

8. Charley's feelings for Sam, like Lydia's for Jean-Philippe, develop over time. Have you ever been in a relationship or friendship that had a slow build like this? What was it like at the beginning? What is it like now?

9. Tyler uses charm to get his own way, and Jean-Philippe tells us de Brassart is "a man who used his charm the way another man might use his sword, and with as deadly an effect." Is there anyone in your life who is charming in this way? How do you deal with them?

10. Even though the Seven Years' War was arguably the first true world war—drawing in every great European power, with battles on five continents—relatively few novels are set in this period. Did you know much about this war, before you read *Bellewether*? What was the most interesting thing you learned? If you could go back and visit any historical period, which one would you visit?

11. Was it a surprise to you to learn that Canada had slavery?

Had you ever heard about the trials and burnings in New York in 1741? Why do you think this history isn't widely taught in schools? Do you know about other events or historical truths that aren't taught widely?

12. The system of parole of honor worked well enough in the eighteenth century, but it would still have had its difficulties for those involved. What would have been the most difficult part for you, as either a prisoner or a host?

13. Is Lydia and Jean-Philippe's romance the only example in the book of love and greater understanding overcoming prejudice and intolerance? Can you think of any others? Do you feel this has a particular resonance for our modern lives?

A NOTE OF THANKS

I owe a debt of gratitude to Harriet Gerard Clark, Executive Director of Raynham Hall Museum in Oyster Bay, New York, for allowing me to tag along with her to bring me up to speed on what had changed (and what had stayed the same) since I worked as a curator.

I could not have written Juan, Phyllis, or Violet without the expert guidance of Beverly Jenkins, just as I could not have written Sam without the generous help of John Moses. I'm beyond grateful to them both, and to Jesse Thistle and Shiloh Walker for casting a critical eye over Sam's scenes. Please note that their help should not be seen as an endorsement, and if any mistakes remain, after their efforts, it's entirely my own fault.

Thanks to Sarah Callejo for correcting my Spanish and refining the voices of Captain del Rio and Juan, and to Jean Alix and Danièle Coulombe of Le Château Frontenac in Québec City, for going above and beyond to assist me in researching scenes that, although they didn't, in the end, make it into this book, may well find their way into a future one.

Thanks also to Rob Hutchinson, honorary contractor in charge of my fictional Wilde House restoration project, and to Bobby Watt—whom I first met nearly thirty years ago when I was a young museum assistant and he was the mason in charge of our building's restoration—for taking time, as he did then, to answer all my questions. My stonemason character, Willie McKinney, is named for Bobby's father.

I'm indebted to Francine Strober Cassano of the North Bellmore Public Library, for cheerfully venturing out in all weather to help with my research.

To my mother, who from the very first has been my most demanding editor, and to Laurie Grassi and Nita Pronovost of Simon & Schuster Canada, and Deb Werksman of Sourcebooks, my thanks for their hard work in drawing the best from both me and the story.

Thank you to Marty Karlow, Gretchen Stelter, Patricia Esposito, and Heather Hall for being exceptional copy editors.

To those who gave me help whose names I didn't think to ask, and those who helped but whom I have forgotten to acknowledge here, please know I'm in your debt.

This book took longer to write than intended, and I'd like to say a special thank-you to my publishers—Simon & Schuster in Canada, and Sourcebooks in the USA—and to everyone who works there, from Kevin Hanson and Dominique Raccah on down the line, through all the many people and departments without whom my books would never see the light of day, for giving me their understanding and support and, above all, the gift of time, to write the book the way it wanted to be written.

To my wonderful agents, Felicity Blunt and Shawna McCarthy, my thanks for their loyalty, love, and belief, and for carrying me through a difficult time.

And to all the librarians, booksellers, bloggers, and readers who give my books life—thank you so much for waiting. I'm glad I can finally share *Bellewether* with you. I hope you enjoy it.

ABOUT THE AUTHOR

New York Times and *USA Today* bestselling author and RITA award winner Susanna Kearsley was a museum curator before she took the plunge and became a full-time author. The past and its bearing on the present is a familiar theme in her books. She is known for her meticulous research and exotic settings from Russia to Italy to Cornwall—and now Long Island—which not only entertain her readers but give her a great reason to travel.

Her lush writing has drawn comparisons to Mary Stewart, Daphne du Maurier, and Diana Gabaldon. She won the coveted Romance Writers of America RITA Award for *The Firebird*, and hit the bestseller lists in the United States with *The Winter Sea* and *The Rose Garden*, both RITA finalists and winners of RT Reviewers' Choice Awards. Her popular and critically acclaimed books, available in translation in more than twenty countries, have also won National Readers' Choice Awards, the Catherine Cookson Fiction Prize, and finaled for the UK's Romantic Novel of the Year Award. She lives in Canada, by the shores of Lake Ontario.